国家双高"铁道机车专业群"系列　多语种教材
——铁道车辆技术专业

Air Conditioning System for the Passenger Train
客车空调装置
（中英文对照版）

主　编　王　洋　李晓科　尚　宇
副主编　郭晓斌　李建华　王明辉
主　审　于文涛

西南交通大学出版社
·成　都·

图书在版编目（CIP）数据

客车空调装置：汉文、英文／王洋，李晓科，尚宇主编. -- 成都：西南交通大学出版社，2024.1
ISBN 978-7-5643-9686-2

Ⅰ. ①客⋯ Ⅱ. ①王⋯ ②李⋯ ③尚⋯ Ⅲ. ①旅客列车 - 空气调节设备 Ⅳ. ①U271.038

中国国家版本馆 CIP 数据核字（2024）第 020957 号

Air Conditioning System for the Passenger Train
客车空调装置
（中英文对照版）

主　编　　王　洋　李晓科　尚　宇

责任编辑	张文越
封面设计	何东琳设计工作室
出版发行	西南交通大学出版社
	（四川省成都市金牛区二环路北一段 111 号
	西南交通大学创新大厦 21 楼）
邮政编码	610031
营销部电话	028-87600564　028-87600533
网址	http://www.xnjdcbs.com
印刷	郫县犀浦印刷厂
成品尺寸	185 mm×260 mm
印张	19.75
插页	2
字数	524 千
版次	2024 年 1 月第 1 版
印次	2024 年 1 月第 1 次
定价	59.00 元
书号	ISBN 978-7-5643-9686-2

课件咨询电话：028-81435775
图书如有印装质量问题　本社负责退换
版权所有　盗版必究　举报电话：028-87600562

前言

随着中国铁路技术的快速发展和国际交流的日益频繁,"一带一路"沿线国家对中国铁路技术的需求量大大增加,如亚吉铁路、中老铁路、中泰铁路等。随着中国铁路标准走向全世界,与其配套的技术培训需求也日益增加。客车空调装置的维护检修是铁道车辆运用维修中的一项重要工作。在此背景下,为满足国内外学员对客车空调装置学习的需求,我们从技术需求和中英文教学需要等实际情况出发,编写此书。

本书的编写坚持理论与实作相结合、机械结构与电气控制为一体的原则,从热工基础知识出发,详细讲解制冷原理;以主流的25T客车为载体,全面讲述其制冷系统、客车采暖与通风系统的相关设备的结构与原理,并剖析其空调电气控制系统;引入现场检修作业流程,理论联系实际,学以致用,解决现场实际问题。本书旨在的扎实学生基础知识,使学生掌握客车空调的结构、工作原理及控制过程;培养学生维护与检修客车空调的技术能力及职业素养;使学生能够满足铁道车辆运用与维修的工作要求。

本书内容的构建是以职业资格标准为依据,根据车辆电工在检修运用生产中的典型工作任务来设置本书的教学项目。本书包含中国铁路文化模块,讲述中国铁路从无到有、从弱到强,从自用到造福全人类的发展进程,将人文素养和职业道德的培养融入教材中,在学习技术的同时,让学生了解中国铁路的发展历史,培养学生的爱国情操、独立自主的拼搏精神和崇高的职业道德。

本书由郑州铁路职业技术学院王洋、郑州轻工业大学李晓科和郑州铁路职业技术学院尚宇担任主编，由郑州铁路职业技术学院于文涛教授主审。参加本书编写工作的有：郑州轻工业大学李晓科编写项目一和项目二的中文和英文部分；郑州铁路职业技术学院王洋编写项目三、项目四和项目六的中文部分；中国铁路郑州局集团有限公司李建华编写项目五任务一和任务二的中文部分；郑州铁路装备制造有限公司王明辉编写项目五任务三的中文部分。郑州铁路职业技术学院尚宇编写项目三和项目四的英文部分，郑州铁路职业技术学院郭晓斌编写项目五和项目六的英文部分。

本书具有双语教学、校企合作特色，编者力求满足国内外学员和教师的需求，但由于编者水平有限，书中不足之处在所难免，恳请读者提出宝贵意见。

编　者

2023 年 10 月

Preface

With the rapid development of China's railway technology and the increase of international exchanges, under China's "the Belt and Road" initiative, the demand for China's railway technology from countries along the line has increased significantly, such as the Addis Ababa-Djibouti Railway, China-Laos Railway, China-Thailand Railway, etc. With the development of Chinese railway standards around the world, the demand for supporting technical training has also been greatly increased. The maintenance and repair of passenger car air conditioning device is an important work in the operation and maintenance of railway vehicles. In this context, in order to meet the needs of domestic and foreign students for the study of passenger car air conditioning devices, we have prepared this book based on technical needs of the actual situation and teaching needs in Chinese and English.

The compilation of this book adheres to the principle of combining theory with practice, integrating mechanical structure and electrical control, and explains the refrigeration principle in detail from the basic knowledge of thermal engineering; Taking the mainstream 25T passenger car as the carrier, the structure and principle of the relevant equipment of its refrigeration system, passenger car heating and ventilation system are comprehensively described, and its air conditioning electrical control system is analyzed; This book introduces the on-site maintenance operation process, and integrates theory with practice, applies what is learned to solve the actual problems on site; It consolidates students' basic knowledge, so that students can master the structure, working principle and control process of passenger car air conditioning; It cultivates the technical ability and professional quality of students to maintain and repair passenger car air conditioners; It also enables students to meet the working requirements of railway vehicle operation and maintenance.

This book was jointly developed by colleges and enterprises. The personnel involved in the preparation include Li Jianhua, the chief technician of China Railway Zhengzhou Group Co., Ltd., the technical expert of the whole railway, and the technical personnel of Zhengzhou Railway Equipment Manufacturing Co., Ltd. The construction of the content is based on the professional qualification standards, and the teaching items of this book are set according to the typical work tasks of vehicle electricians in the maintenance, operation and production. This book contains the module of Chinese railway culture, which tells the development process of Chinese railway from scratch, from weak to strong, from self-use to benefit the whole mankind. It integrates the cultivation of humanistic quality and professional ethics into the teaching materials, and cultivates students' noble patriotism, independent fighting spirit and noble professional ethics while learning technology.

This book is edited by Wang Yang from Zhengzhou Railway Vocational and Technical College, Li Xiaoke from Zhengzhou University of Light Industry and Shang Yu from Zhengzhou Railway Vocational and Technical College, and reviewed by Professor Yu Wentao from Zhengzhou Railway Vocational and Technical College. Participants in the preparation of this book are as follows: Li Xiaoke of Zhengzhou University of Light Industry wrote the Chinese and English parts of Project 1 and Project 2; Wang Yang from Zhengzhou Railway Vocational and Technical College wrote the Chinese part of Project 3, Project 4 and Project 6; Li Jianhua of China Railway Zhengzhou Group Co., Ltd. wrote the Chinese part of Task 1 and Task 2 of Project 5; Wang Minghui of Zhengzhou Railway Equipment Manufacturing Co., Ltd. wrote the Chinese part of Task 3 of the Project 5. Shang Yu from Zhengzhou Railway Vocational and Technical College wrote the English part of Project 3 and Project 4, Guo Xiaobin from Zhengzhou Railway Vocational and Technical College wrote the English part of Project 5 and Project 6.

This book has the characteristics of bilingual teaching and school-enterprise cooperation. The editors strive to meet the needs of students and teachers at home and abroad. However, due to the limited level of the editor, the inadequacies in the book are unavoidable. We sincerely invite readers to put forward valuable suggestions.

Editor
October, 2023

CONTENTS

Project 1　Basic Knowledge of Thermodynamics ··············001

　The History of Railway Development in China 1: China's First
　Self-built Railway ··············001
　Task 1　Basic Gas Parameters and Ideal Gas State Equation ··············003
　Task 2　Thermodynamic Law and Its Application in Refrigeration ··············021
　Task 3　Heat Transfer Modes ··············026

Project 2　Wet Air ··············031

　The History of Railway Development in China 2: The First
　Electrified Railway in China ··············031
　Task 1　Status Parameters of Wet Air ··············033
　Task 2　Cognition and Application of Psychrometric　Map of Wet Air ··············039

Project 3　Refrigeration Principle ··············046

　The History of Railway Development in China 3: "Chengdu—Kunming Spirit"
　Shines Brightly ··············046
　Task 1　Principle of Vapor Compression Refrigeration ··············049
　Task 2　Other Refrigeration Methods ··············053
　Task 3　Refrigerant and Compressor Lubricating Oil ··············058

Project 4　Air Conditioning and Refrigeration System of Passenger Cars ······ 070

　　The History of Railway Development in China 4: China's High-speed
　　Railway Benefiting Mankind ··· 070
　　Task 1　Refrigeration Compressor ·· 073
　　Task 2　Heat Exchanger ·· 088
　　Task 3　Automatic Control Device of Refrigeration Device ············ 096
　　Task 4　Auxiliary Equipment of Refrigeration Device ··················· 105
　　Task 5　Leak Detection and Air Tightness Test of　Refrigeration Device ······ 111

Project 5　Air Conditioning and Refrigeration System of Passenger Cars ······ 120

　　The History of Railway Development in China 5: The Achievements of
　　China-Africa Friendship ··· 120
　　Task 1　Electric Heating Device ··· 122
　　Task 2　Ventilation System ··· 127
　　Task 3　Structure and Maintenance of Ventilation System of
　　　　　　25T Passenger Car ·· 136

Project 6　Electrical Control System of 25T Passenger Car Air Conditioner ···· 145

　　The History of Railway Development in China 6: The Ties between
　　Chinese and Lao people ··· 145
　　Task 1　Main Circuit and Power Supply Line Conversion Control of
　　　　　　Air Conditioner ·· 147
　　Task 2　Test Mode and Automatic Mode Control of Air Conditioning ··········· 159
　　Task 3　Operation and Fault Information Acquisition of Air Conditioner ······ 167

References ··· 171

目 录

项目一 热力学基础 ······172

　中国铁路发展史1　中国第一条自建铁路······172
　任务一　气体基本参数及理想气体状态方程······174
　任务二　热力学定律及其在制冷中的应用······187
　任务三　热量传递的方式······191

项目二 湿空气 ······195

　中国铁路发展史2　中国第一条电气化铁路······195
　任务一　湿空气的状态参数······196
　任务二　湿空气的焓湿图认知及应用······201

项目三 制冷原理 ······207

　中国铁路发展史3　"成昆精神"熠熠生辉······207
　任务一　蒸气压缩式制冷原理······209
　任务二　其他制冷方法······212
　任务三　制冷剂与压缩机润滑油······216

项目四 客车空调制冷系统 ······224

　中国铁路发展史4　中国高铁造福人类······224
　任务一　制冷压缩机······226
　任务二　换热器······239
　任务三　制冷装置的自动控制器件······244
　任务四　制冷装置的辅助设备······251
　任务五　制冷装置的检漏及气密性试验······256

项目五　客车空调采暖及通风系统 263

　　中国铁路发展史 5　中非友谊的结晶 263
　　任务一　电热采暖装置 264
　　任务二　通风系统 268
　　任务三　25T 型客车通风系统结构与检修 275

项目六　25T 客车空调电气控制系统 282

　　中国铁路发展史 6　中老民心的纽带 282
　　任务一　空调主电路及供电线路转换控制 283
　　任务二　空调试验模式和自动模式控制 293
　　任务三　空调的运行及故障信息获取 300

参考文献 304

附　录 305

　　Appendix 305
　　附图 1　25T 型硬卧客车空调电气原理图 306

Project 1
Basic Knowledge of Thermodynamics

【 Chinese Railway Culture 】

The History of Railway Development in China 1: China's First Self-built Railway

Beijing—Zhangjiakou Railway is the first railway in China that is designed, built and put into operation by Chinese people without using foreign funds and personnel. The Beijing—Zhangjiakou Railway was built under the direction of Zhan Tianyou. It was started in September 1905 and completed in 1909, with a total length of about 200 kilometers. It connects Fengtai District of Beijing and Zhangjiakou of Hebei Province through Badaling, Juyongguan, Shacheng, Xuanhua and other places.

Figure 1-0-1　Construction Site of Beijing—Zhangjiakou Railway

In 1905, Zhan Tianyou presided over the proposal to build the Chinese railway, namely the Beijing—Zhanghai Railway. After four years of acceptance, Zhan Tianyou started the construction of the Chinese railway. On September 4, 1905, the construction of the railway

Zhangjiakou Railway is "separated by steep mountains, with the largest number of stone works, and over 7658 feet height of bridges. The work is ever harder than elsewhere." In particular, "Juyongguan and Badaling, with mountains and steep rocks, are the most difficult to examine the roads that have been built in various provinces. That is to say, the books of Taixi also regard thees projects as extremely difficult". "From Nankou to Badaling, the height is 1969.2 feet apart, and every 43.76 feet must be raised by 1.094 feet." After the news of China's self-run Beijing-Zhangjiakou Railway came out, foreigners ironically said that the Chinese engineer who built the railway was probably not born.

Zhan Tianyou personally led the engineering team to survey and determine the route. Due to the limited funding of the Qing government and the time constraints, Zhan Tianyou selected from the three routes surveyed from Xizhimen to Zhangjiakou via Shahe, Nankou, Juyongguan, Badaling, Huailai, Jiming Post and Xuanhua. The most difficult section of the Beijing—Zhangjiakou Railway was from Nankou to Badaling, which was not only dangerous, but also steep. On the first day of track laying, a coupler chain of an engineering vehicle was broken, causing a derailment accident. This has become evidence that Chinese people can't build railways by themselves, and all kinds of slanders have come in one after another. Zhan Tianyou came up with a solution: add the automatic hook invented by American Jenny to each carriage to combine it into a solid whole to ensure the safety when climbing. He also used the "reverse line" principle to build a "zigzag" line to reduce the climbing slope, and used the two ends to pull cars to cross.

Four tunnels including Juyongguan, Wuguitou, Shifo Temple and Badaling were opened, of which the longest Badaling tunnel is 1092 m. At that time, it was only possible to rely on the hands of workers to dig the middle of the tunnel at both ends of the tunnel at the same time. Meanwhile, the vertical shaft method was used to dig the tunnel. Two vertical shafts were dug in the middle of the tunnel, which could be dug in the opposite direction respectively, increasing the working face, and relying on manpower to build the first long tunnel in the history of Chinese road construction.

The Beijing—Zhangjiakou Railway was officially started on September 4, 1905, and the opening ceremony was held in Nankou on October 2, 1909. It took only four years. The construction period of the Beijing—Zhangjiakou Railway was two years ahead of schedule. According to the original budget, the cost for the construction of Beijing—Zhangjiakou Railway and the purchase of locomotives and vehicles was 7.29 million taels of silver, but only about 7 million taels were actually used.

The Beijing—Zhangjiakou Railway is the first railway trunk line designed and constructed by the Chinese people. It is an honor for the Chinese people and the Chinese engineering and technical circles, and also a victory in the anti-imperialist struggle of the Chinese people in the modern history of China. Although the construction of the

Beijing—Zhangjiakou Railway by the Chinese themselves was a bitter victory under the special historical background at that time, Zhan Tianyou and the Beijing—Zhangjiakou Railway, as well as the national spirit contained therein, have become the eternal pride of the Chinese people.

【Project Description】

Thermodynamics mainly studies the thermal properties of substances from the point of view of energy conversion, which indicates the macroscopic laws that energy is converted from one form to another. The working process of air conditioning and refrigeration equipment is the conversion process of thermal energy and mechanical energy. The mutual conversion between thermal energy and mechanical energy is realized through the cycle state change process of working medium in the thermal equipment. The first and second laws of thermodynamics are the basic laws that must be followed for the conversion of thermal energy and mechanical energy.

【Project Objectives】

1. Knowledge objectives

(1) Master the basic parameter definition of gas.
(2) Understand the content and expression of the ideal gas equation of state.
(3) Master the first and second laws of thermodynamics.
(4) Master the three ways of heat transfer.

2. Capability objectives

Be able to use the basic knowledge of thermodynamics to understand and analyze the refrigeration process.

3. Quality objectives

(1) Cultivate the ability of reasoning, logic and abstract thinking.
(2) Cultivate teamwork ability.

Task 1 Basic Gas Parameters and Ideal Gas State Equation

【Task Objective】

(1) Master the definition of basic gas parameters.

(2) Understand the equation of state of ideal gas and be able to calculate practical problems.

【Knowledge Reserve】

1. Introduction to Thermal System

The medium for energy conversion is called working medium. For example, in the steam power plant of thermal power plant, the medium materials that convert heat energy into mechanical energy, water and steam, are the working medium; For another example, in the refrigeration device, the refrigerant absorbs heat from the cold storage or other space, and after the compressor is compressed and pressurized for temperature rise, the refrigerant releases heat to the external environment in the condenser, which converts mechanical energy into heat energy. The refrigerant is also the working medium.

The requirements for working medium are: ① expansibility; ② liquidity; ③ heat capacity; ④ stability and safety; ⑤ friendly to the environment; ⑥ cheap and easy to obtain in large quantities. The characteristics of energy conversion of different working fluids are different, some of which are very different.

When people study the mutual transformation and transmission of various forms of energy, for the convenience of analysis, they often separate the parts or the whole that are connected with each other as the research object. This artificially separated object for thermodynamic research is called thermodynamic system, which is called thermodynamic system or system for short. The part outside the system is called the outside world. The most common example of the outside world is the natural environment that is closely related to the energy conversion or transmission of the system. The interface between the system and the outside world is called the boundary. The thermodynamic system interacts with the outside world through the boundary.

According to different analysis objects, common thermodynamic systems have the following two classification methods.

1) According to whether there is material exchange between the system and the outside

(1) The closed system.

The thermodynamic system without material exchange with the outside world is called the closed system. Because the quality of the working medium in the closed system is fixed, it is also called a quality control system. The energy exchange between the system and the outside world is only in the form of volume change work and heat. As shown in Figure 1-1-1, the outside world does volume change work on the piston, and the piston moves from position 1 to position 2. If the system boundary can exchange heat with the outside world, the system absorbs heat from the outside world.

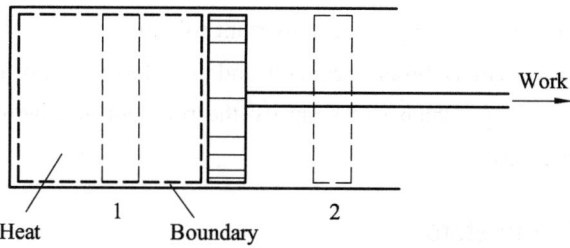

Figure 1-1-1 Schematic diagram of a closed system

(2) Open system.

The thermodynamic system with material exchange with the outside world is called the open system. Generally, the open system has a relatively fixed space, so it is also called a volume control system. The main feature of this type of thermodynamic system is that the working medium is flowing in the analyzed system, as shown in Figure 1-1-2. Most equipments and devices in the project are of open systems.

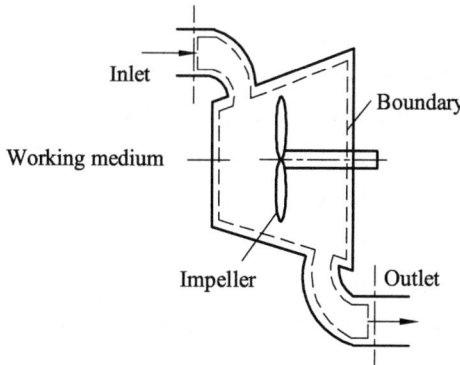

Figure 1-1-2 Schematic diagram of an opening system

2) According to whether there is energy exchange between the system and the outside at the boundary

(1) Isolated system.

This kind of thermodynamic system has neither energy exchange nor material exchange with the outside world at the interface.

(2) Thermal insulation system.

This kind of thermodynamic system has no heat exchange with the outside at the interface, but can exchange active energy and material.

(3) Non-isolated system.

The characteristic of this kind of system is that there is energy or material exchange between the system and the outside world at the interface.

Isolated system and adiabatic system are special cases in thermodynamics. Most of the actual thermodynamic systems are in the state of non-isolated system. However, because these two special thermodynamic systems play an important role in the study of thermodynamics, the actual thermodynamic system is often idealized and transformed into an isolated system or adiabatic system for analysis, which can simplify the problem and better grasp the essential characteristics of the problem.

2. Gas State Parameters

The macroscopic physical state of a thermodynamic system at a certain moment is called the state of the system. Some macroscopic physical quantities used to describe the state of the system are called state parameters. The state parameters commonly used in engineering thermodynamics include temperature (T), pressure (p), specific volume (v), heat (Q), specific enthalpy (h) and specific entropy (s). Among them, temperature, pressure and specific volume are the most common parameters. They can be measured directly or indirectly with the help of instruments, so they are often called basic state parameters.

1) Temperature

Temperature is a physical parameter used to indicate the degree of heat and cold of an object. The hotter people feel, the higher the temperatureis; The colder people feel, the lower the temperatureis. However, it is unscientific to use human subjective feelings to represent temperature, because it is not conducive to quantitatively representing the temperature of an object, and sometimes leads to some wrong conclusions. For example, in winter, when you touch the wood and iron blocks with your hand that put together in the open air, you will feel that the iron block is colder than the wood. According to the above statement, the temperature of the iron block should be lower than that of the wood. But in fact, as long as you measure them with instruments, you will find that their temperatures are the same.

According to the theory of gas molecular motion, the temperature of a gas is a measure of the average kinetic energy of the thermal motion of a large number of molecules that make up the gas. The higher the gas temperature is, the more intense the irregular thermal motion of molecules is, and the greater the average kinetic energy of molecules is.

Temperature is also the basis for judging whether there is heat transfer between the working medium and the outside or between two objects. Heat is always transferred from the side with high temperature to the side with low temperature. If two systems with different degrees of heat and cold are contacted with each other, heat transfer will occur between them. Under the condition that they are not affected by the outside world, after a long enough time, they will reach a common degree of cold and heat without heat exchange. This situation is called heat balance, that is, the temperature of the two is equal.

In order to measure temperature, it is necessary to have a numerical representation of temperature, that is, to establish a temperature scale. Any thermometer is made according to a certain temperature scale. There are three commonly used temperature scales in the world.

(1) Celsius temperature scale.

In daily life, the temperature of human body is 37 °C and the temperature is 20 °C. The Celsius temperature scale is used, that is, the Celsius temperature, which is expressed by the symbol t, and the unit of measurement is Celsius, which is expressed as °C.

In 1742, the Swedish astronomer A. Celsius (1701—1744) formulated the hundredth scale method. He divided the freezing point and boiling point of water into 100 temperature intervals. In order to avoid negative values when measuring the low temperature below the freezing point, he set the boiling point of water as zero and the freezing point as 100 °C. Later, he accepted the suggestion of his colleague and reversed the scale. This is the Celsius scale used now.

(2) Thermodynamic temperature scale.

The thermodynamic temperature scale based on the second law of thermodynamics is a temperature scale independent of the properties of the material to be measured. The temperature determined by this temperature scale is called thermodynamic temperature, also known as absolute temperature, which is expressed as T, and the unit of measurement is Kelvin, or K for short.

After 1954, it was internationally prescribed to select the three-phase point of pure water (the state point of solid, liquid and gas three-phase equilibrium coexistence of pure water) as the standard temperature point, and the value of temperature under this state was 273.15 K. In 1960, the International Conference on Metrology adopted a resolution stipulating that the Celsius temperature is obtained by moving the zero point of the thermodynamic temperature, that is, the conversion relationship between the absolute temperature and the Celsius temperature is:

$$t = T - 273.15 \quad (°C) \tag{1-1}$$

(3) Fahrenheit temperature scale.

The Fahrenheit temperature scale is a commonly used temperature scale in some European and American countries. The freezing point temperature of pure water is set at 32 °F, and the boiling point temperature of water at standard atmospheric pressure is set at 212 °F. The middle part is divided into 180 equal parts. Each equal part represents 1 °F, which is the Fahrenheit temperature scale. It is represented by the symbol t_F, and the unit is °F.

The conversion relationship between Fahrenheit temperature and Celsius temperature is:

$$t = \frac{5}{9}(t_F - 32) \quad (°C) \tag{1-2}$$

In the state parameters of the working medium, temperature usually refers to the absolute temperature of the working medium.

2) Pressure

Pressure refers to the force acting on the unit area in the vertical direction, which is also called pressure in physics, and is represented by the symbol p, namely:

$$p = \frac{F}{A} \tag{1-3}$$

In the formula, F - vertical force (N);

A – area (m^2).

For the gas working medium in the container, the pressure is the macroscopic statistical result of the frequent impact of a large number of gas molecules on the container wall when they move irregularly, that is, the gas pressure is the statistical average of the collision force between a large number of molecules and the container wall. As shown in Figure 1-1-3, the water in the kettle can be atomized and sprayed out after the external air is pressed into the kettle and pressurized.

Figure 1-1-3 A pressure kettle spraying water

In the international system of units, the unit of pressure is Pa, that is, 1 Pa=1 N/m^2. In engineering, because the unit Pa is too small, kPa and MPa are usually used as pressure units. The relationship between them is:

$$1 \text{ MPa} = 10^3 \text{ kPa} = 10^6 \text{ Pa}$$

Units of bar and atm (standard atmospheric pressure) were also used as pressure units, and atm is the abbreviation of atmosphere, which refers to standard atmospheric pressure. However, with the promotion of international standardization, these two pressure units have been canceled. The relationship between them and the international standard pressure units is:

$$1 \text{ bar} = 0.1 \text{ MPa}$$
$$1 \text{ atm} = 1.013 \times 10^5 \text{ Pa}$$

Our living environment is in the atmosphere, which means there is atmospheric pressure around us. The atmospheric pressure on the unit area of the earth's surface is called atmospheric pressure or atmospheric pressure, which is expressed by the symbol p_b. The atmospheric pressure at different locations on the earth is different. The atmospheric pressure at sea level with temperature of 0 °C and latitude of 45° is called standard atmospheric pressure. Generally, atmospheric pressure is inversely proportional to altitude.

The actual pressure of working medium such as air on the vessel wall is called absolute pressure, which is expressed by the symbol p. The reading of the pressure in the container is usually completed with a pressure gauge. The pressure gauges used in the project are measured in a specific environment (such as in the atmosphere). The common ones are U-shaped tube pressure gauge (see Figure 1-1-4) and capsule pressure gauge. The measured pressure values are the relative values under the atmospheric pressure p_b, not the absolute pressure of the gas in the system. There are two situations:

In the first case, as shown in Figure 1-1-4 (a), the absolute pressure p in the container is higher than the atmospheric pressure p_b, and the reading indicated by the pressure gauge is called the gauge pressure, which is expressed in p_e, namely:

$$p = p_b + p_e \qquad (1\text{-}4)$$

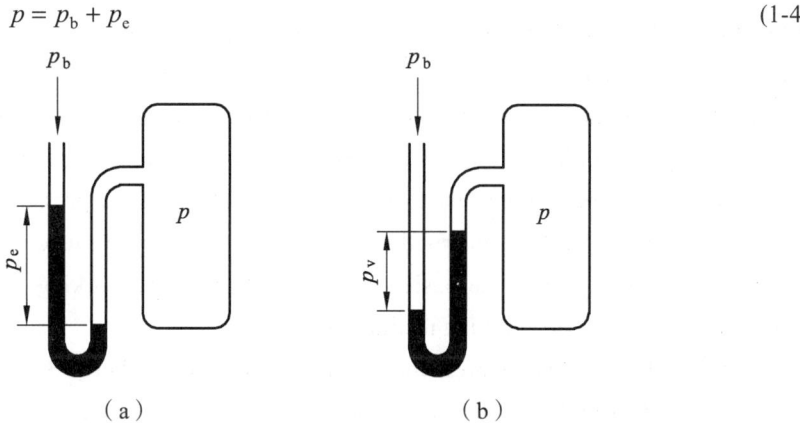

Figure 1-1-4 Schematic diagram of U-type pressure gauge

In the second case, as shown in Figure 1-1-4 (b), at this time, the absolute pressure p in the container is lower than the atmospheric pressure p_b, and the reading indicated by the pressure gauge is called vacuum degree, which is expressed in p_v, namely:

$$p = p_b - p_v \qquad (1\text{-}5)$$

It can be seen that when the absolute pressure is greater than the atmospheric pressure, the gauge pressure is positive; When the absolute pressure is less than the gauge pressure, the gauge pressure is negative, which is referred to as a vacuum. As shown in Figure 1-1-5, the area on the right side of the dial is positive pressure; The area where the pointer is on the left side of the dial is negative pressure; When the pointer points to 0, it means that the absolute pressure is equal to the atmospheric pressure. When the pointer is in the left area of the dial, the lower the absolute pressureis, the higher the vacuumis; On the contrary, the closer the absolute phase pressure is to the atmospheric pressureis, the lower the vacuumis.

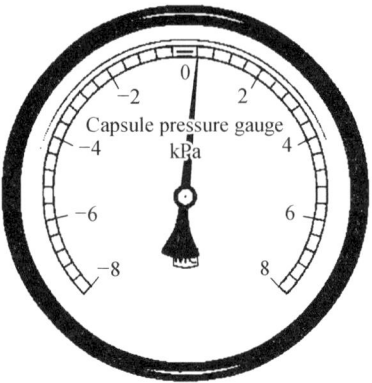

Figure 1-1-5   A capsule pressure gauge

The atmospheric pressure varies with the time and place of measurement, and can be measured by atmospheric pressure gauge. In engineering calculation, if the pressure of the measured working medium is much higher than the atmospheric pressure, the atmospheric pressure can be regarded as a constant, usually approximately 0.1 MPa. If the pressure of the measured working medium is low, it must be calculated according to the specific value of local atmospheric pressure. Therefore, even if the absolute pressure is constant, the gauge pressure and vacuum will also change due to the change of atmospheric pressure. Only the absolute pressure can truly reflect the thermodynamic state of the working medium, which is the state parameter. Pressure, one of the basic state parameters of the working medium, refers to the "absolute pressure" of the working medium or system.

Example 1-1: The gauge pressure p_e of the steam in the boiler is 3.1 MPa, and the vacuum pressure of 94,643 Pa is maintained in the condenser of the steam turbine. If the local actual atmospheric pressure p_b at that time is 101,974 Pa, calculate the absolute pressure in the steam boiler and condenser. If the atmospheric pressure changes to 97,975 Pa, what are the readings of the pressure gauges of the steam boiler and condenser?

Solution: (1) According to the meaning of the question, the local atmospheric pressure at that time was:

$$p_b = 101,974 \text{ Pa}$$

The absolute pressure in the boiler is:

$$p_{steam} = p_b + p_e = (101,974 + 3.1 \times 10^6) \text{ Pa} = 3.202 \times 10^6 \text{ Pa} = 3.202 \text{ MPa}$$

The vacuum degree in the condenser is:

$$p_v = 94,643 \text{ Pa}$$

The absolute pressure in the condenser is:

$$p_{coagulation} = p_b - p_v = (101,974 - 94,643) \text{ Pa} = 7,331 \text{ Pa}$$

(2) When the atmospheric pressure is 97,975 Pa

$$p_b = 97,975 \text{ Pa}$$

The reading of the pressure gauge in the boiler is:

$$p_e = p_{steam} - p_b = (3.1 \times 10^6 - 97,975) \text{ Pa} = 3.104 \times 10^6 \text{ Pa} = 3.104 \text{ MPa}$$

The reading of the pressure gauge in the condenser is:

$$p_v = p_b - p_{coagulation} = (97,975 - 7,331) \text{ Pa} = 90,644 \text{ Pa}$$

3) Specific volume and density

Specific volume refers to the volume occupied by the working medium per unit mass. It is expressed by the symbol v, and the unit is m³/kg in the international system of units. If the volume occupied by the working medium with a mass of m (kg) is V (m³), the specific volume of the working medium is:

$$v = \frac{V}{m} \tag{1-6}$$

The mass of working fluid per unit volume is called density, which is indicated by the symbol ρ is expressed in kg/m³. Obviously, the density of working medium ρ and specific volume V are reciprocal to each other, i.e

$$\rho = \frac{m}{V} = \frac{1}{V} \tag{1-7}$$

Both specific volume and density are physical quantities that describe the degree of molecular aggregation and density of the working medium in a certain state, and can be used as state parameters of the working medium.

4) Work and heat

In the refrigeration equipment, the energy transfer between the working medium and the outside world is realized through work and heat transfer. Therefore, work and heat are the measures of energy transfer and important physical quantities.

(1) Work.

Work is a way for the system to exchange energy with the outside world. In mechanics, the energy transferred between objects through the action of force is called work, and it is defined that work is equal to the product of force F and the displacement x of the object in the direction of force action, namely

$$W = Fx$$

If the object produces a small displacement dx in the direction x of the force under the force F, the work done by the force is:

$$\delta W = F\mathrm{d}x$$

If the object is displaced from x_1 to x_2 in the direction of force F, the work done by force F is:

$$W = \int_{x_1}^{x_2} F\mathrm{d}x$$

In the international system of units, the unit of work is J (joule) or kJ (kilojoule), and the unit of unit work is J/kg or kJ/kg. The process of converting heat into mechanical energy is realized by the volume expansion of the working medium. The work done by the working medium during volume expansion is called expansion work, which is a basic work of thermodynamics.

As shown in Figure 1-1-6, assuming that there is working medium with mass m in the cylinder, its pressure is p, and the piston area is A, the force acting on the piston by the working medium is pA. Suppose that the piston moves a small distance dx to the right under the effect of the working medium pressure. Because the volume expansion of the working medium is very small in this process, its pressure is almost constant. If this process is a balance process, the work done by the working medium to the piston is:

$$\delta W = pA\mathrm{d}x = p\mathrm{d}V \tag{1-8}$$

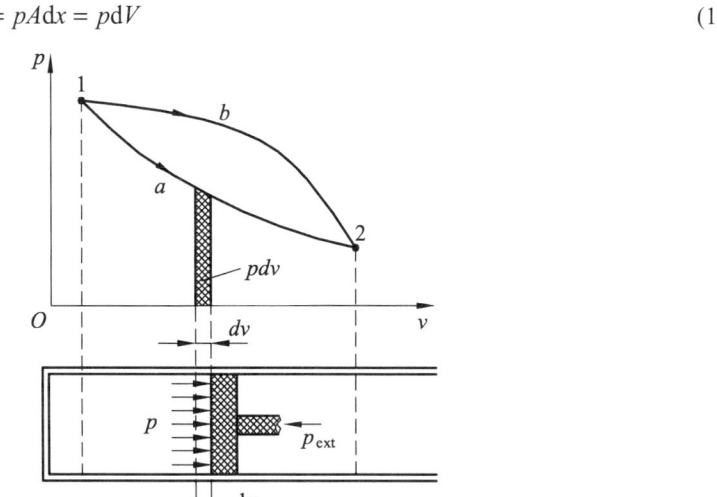

Figure 1-1-6 Indicator diagram

If the piston moves from position 1 to position 2 and the process is balanced, the expansion work done by the working medium is:

$$W = \int_1^2 p\,dV \tag{1-9}$$

The expansion work done by unit mass working medium is called unit expansion work, expressed in w. It can be obtained from Formula (1-8) and Formula (1-9)

$$\Delta w = p\,dv \tag{1-10}$$

$$w = \int_1^2 p\,dv = \int_{v_1}^{v_2} p\,dv \tag{1-11}$$

In the formula, p - absolute pressure of working medium (Pa);
  V_1 - initial specific volume of working medium (m³/kg);
  V_2 - final specific volume of working medium (m³/kg).

The total work done for the working medium with a mass of m (kg) is:

$$W = mw = \int_{v_1}^{v_2} p\,dV \tag{1-12}$$

In the formula, p - absolute pressure of working medium (Pa);
  v_1 - initial volume of working medium (m³);
  v_2 - final state volume of working medium (m³).

The above derivation assumes that the thermodynamic process is reversible, and the formula obtained is also the formula for calculating the expansion work of the reversible process. In addition to the initial state and final state of the working medium, it is also necessary to know the change law between the pressure and specific volume of the working medium in the process of state change. As shown in Figure 1-1-6, the expansion work of curve a and curve b from position 1 to position 2 is different. It can be seen that the expansion work depends not only on the initial and final states of the working medium, but also on the process, so the work is a process quantity rather than a state quantity.

A reversible process can be represented by a curve on the p-v diagram with pressure p as the ordinate and specific volume v as the abscissa, as shown in curve a in Figure 1-1-6. According to the principle of calculus, the value of integration $\int_1^2 p\,dv$, that is, the size of unit expansion work $w_{1\text{-}2}$, can be expressed by the area under the process curve, so the p-v diagram is also called the indicator diagram.

Although the expansion work is derived from the expansion process, it is also applicable to the compression process. According to Formula (1-11) and Formula (1-12), when the working medium expands, $dv > 0$, $w > 0$, the expansion work is positive work, indicating that the working medium does work to the outside world; When the working medium is compressed, $dv < 0$, $w < 0$, the compression work is negative work, indicating that the outside world does work on the working medium; When the volume of the working medium is constant (constant volume process), $dv = 0$, $w = 0$, and the volume work is equal to zero.

(2) Heat.

In thermodynamics, the energy transferred between the thermal system and the outside world by temperature difference is called heat, which is expressed in Q, and the unit is the same as the unit of work, which is J or W. Heat transferred by unit mass working medium, expressed in q, in J/kg or kJ/kg. When systems with different temperatures are in contact with the outside world, the party with higher temperature always transfers part of the heat to the party with lower temperature. From the microscopic point of view, this energy transfer is completed by molecular collision or thermal radiation at the mutual contact.

Like work, heat is the energy transferred by the thermal system in the process of interacting with the outside world. Heat energy and heat are two different concepts. Heat energy refers to the energy of the molecular thermal movement inside the working medium, which is stored inside the working medium; Heat is the part of heat energy that is transferred between the system and the outside world. Like work, it is a measure of energy transfer and only meaningful in the process of energy transfer.

The heat depends on the initial and final state and the process of state change. It is a process function, not a state parameter. In a given state, we can say how much heat the system has, but not how much heat or work the system has.

Engineering thermodynamics stipulates that when the working medium absorbs heat from the outside, the heat is positive; When the working medium releases heat to the outside, the heat is negative.

5) Enthalpy and entropy

(1) Enthalpy.

Enthalpy is a complex thermodynamic state parameter, which represents all the total energy in the system, expressed by H. It is the sum of internal energy and pressure potential energy. When the working medium is in a certain state (pressure P, volume V, temperature T), the enthalpy value represents the total energy of the working medium.

For the open system (that is, a thermodynamic system with both energy exchange and material exchange with the outside world), when the working medium flows into (or out of) the system, not only the internal energy of the working medium is brought into (or out of) the system, but also the driving work it obtains is brought into (or out of) the system. That is to say, for the open system, when the working medium flows into (or out of) the system, its internal energy and driving work always appear at the same time. For example, when heating and cooling air, it is often necessary to determine how much heat the air absorbs or releases. For the convenience of calculation, the sum of internal energy and pushing work of working medium is defined as enthalpy. The enthalpy of 1 kg working medium is called specific enthalpy, sometimes referred to as enthalpy, expressed by the symbol$h$, in J/kg or kJ/kg.

Enthalpy is only a state parameter that is related to the state and independent of the process. In calculation, enthalpy is usually obtained by looking up the table. In the air conditioning and refrigeration cycle, only the magnitude, positive and negative of the enthalpy difference before and after the change of the working medium are calculated, and it has nothing to do with the absolute value of enthalpy.

(2) Entropy.

Entropy is a derived thermodynamic state parameter that represents the degree of heat exchange with the outside world when the working medium state changes. That is, the energy transferred by the system and the outside in the process of heat and work state change. They have some common characteristics. In the process of work, the pressure difference is the power of work, and the change of state parameter specific volume (v) is the measure of whether work is done. Similarly, in the process of heat transfer, temperature difference is the power of heat transfer, and there is also a parameter whose change is the scale to measure whether or not heat transfer. This parameter is defined as entropy, expressed by the symbol S, and the unit is J/(kg/K). When the refrigerant is heated, the entropy increases. On the contrary, when the heat is emitted from the refrigerant, the entropy decreases. As long as the refrigerant does not absorb or release heat, the entropy value remains unchanged.

6) Specific heat

The amount of heat needed to be absorbed (or released) when the temperature of an object increases (or decreases) by 1 K (or 1 °C) is called heat capacity. When a certain amount of material absorbs or releases heat, its temperature change depends on the nature, quantity and process of the working medium.

The heat needed to be absorbed (or released) by increasing (or decreasing) the unit mass temperature by 1 K (or 1 °C) is called the specific heat of the substance (mass specific heat), expressed in c, in J/(kg·K) or kJ/(kg·K).

3. Equilibrium Process and Reversible Process

1) Equilibrium process

The change process of a system from one state to another is called thermal process, or process for short. State change means that the original equilibrium state of the system is destroyed. The thermal process in the actual thermal equipment is caused by the imbalance of temperature, pressure and specific volume in the system, so the intermediate state of the thermal process is unbalanced.

In order to facilitate the analysis and research of the actual thermal process, it is assumed that every state experienced by the system in the thermal process is infinitely close to the equilibrium state. This process is called quasi-equilibrium process, also called quasi-static process. It can be represented by continuous solid lines on the state parameter coordinate diagram. The non-equilibrium process cannot be represented on the state parameter coordinate diagram because it has no definite state parameters.

2) Reversible process

If the system completes a thermal process from the initial state to the final state, and then reversely returns to the initial state from the final state along the original path, the system and the outside world participating in the change will also return to the original state without leaving any change, then this process is called a reversible process. Theoretically speaking, the reversible process is a mechanical movement process when the system and the outside world maintain force balance (no pressure difference) without friction; The heat transfer process when the system is in thermal balance with the outside world (without temperature difference). But there is no heat transfer and mechanical movement without temperature difference and pressure difference, so reversible process can be understood as heat transfer process under infinitesimal temperature difference and mechanical movement under infinitesimal pressure difference. In fact, all actual thermodynamic processes are irreversible, that is, the inverse process is impossible to achieve. However, there is no energy loss in the reversible process, which is theoretically the most effective process of heat to work. Therefore, it is the direction of the actual process.

Reversible process is an ideal process, which is the goal of all thermal equipment working process. The concept of reversible process provides great convenience for thermodynamic analysis. Using this concept, the complex actual thermodynamic process can be approximately simplified into a reversible process for study, and then corrected. Therefore, the study of reversible process is of great significance in theory.

4. Equation of Ideal Gas State

When studying the properties of gases, it is easy to find the changes of gas state parameters. For example, if the rubber ball and inflated tire are exposed to the sun in summer, the pressure, volume and temperature of the gas in the rubber ball and tire will change; When the compressed table tennis ball is soaked in hot water, the air temperature in the ball increases, making the volume increase, and the ball tends to bulge; When oxygen is put into the steel tank, the pressure, volume and temperature of oxygen will also change. Most of the similar phenomena encountered in nature and engineering are that the pressure, volume and temperature of gas change at the same time. Only two quantities change, and the other does not change. For a certain mass of gas, if these three quantities do not change, we say that the gas is in a certain state. If these three quantities or any two quantities change at the same time, we say that the state of the gas has changed. So when the gas state changes, are the changes of these three quantities arbitrary or are they interrelated and follow certain rules?

1) Ideal gas

In the thermodynamic properties of working fluids, the relationship between pressure, specific volume and temperature is of particular importance. For real gases, this relationship is generally complex. However, through a large number of experiments, it is found that when the density is small, that is, the specific volume is large, the basic state parameters of gaseous substances in equilibrium will approximately maintain a simple relationship. Therefore, people put forward the ideal gas model: the average distance between gas molecules is quite large, and the molecular volume is negligible compared with the total volume of gas; There is no force between molecules; The collision between molecules and the collision between molecules and the container wall are elastic collisions.

Ideal gas is an imaginary gas abstracted by science. Although it does not exist in nature, the introduction of the concept of ideal gas still has great practical value. Experiments show that when the pressure and temperature of the gas are not too high and too low, the force between the gas molecules and the volume of the molecule itself can be ignored, and the nature of the gas is close to the ideal gas, and the gas can be treated as an ideal gas.

For example, at normal temperature, as long as the pressure does not exceed 5 MPa, the commonly used gases such as O_2, N_2, H_2, CO and the gas mixture mainly composed of these gases can be treated as ideal gases without great error. In addition, a small amount of water vapor contained in the atmosphere or gas can also be treated as an ideal gas due to its low partial pressure and large specific volume.

2) Equation of ideal gas state

Through a large number of experiments, it is found that there is a certain functional relationship between the temperature, pressure and specific volume of the ideal gas in the equilibrium state. This is what the Boyle-Maliot law, Gay-Lusac law and Charlie's law in physics express. These three laws can be comprehensively expressed as

$$pv = R_g T \tag{1-13}$$

Formula (1-13) is called the ideal gas equation of state. It was first derived by Clabolon in 1834, so it is also called Clabolon equation. For an ideal gas with a mass of m (kg), the equation of state is in the form of

$$pV = mR_g T \tag{1-14}$$

In the formula, p - absolute pressure of gas (Pa);

v - specific volume of gas (m³/kg);

V - volume of gas with mass of m (m³);

T - thermodynamic temperature of gas (K);

R_g - gas constant [J/(kg · K)].

R_g is called gas constant, which has nothing to do with the state of the gas, but has something to do with the type of gas. For the same gas, the gas constant is certain.

In the international system of units, the amount of substance is in mol (mole). The mass of 1mol of substance is called molar mass, expressed in M, in kg/mol. The mass value of 1mol substance is the same as the relative molecular mass of gas. For example, the molar masses of oxygen, nitrogen and air are 32.00×10^{-3} kg/mol, 28.2×10^{-3} kg/mol and 28.96×10^{-3} kg/mol respectively. The volume of 1mol of substance is called molar volume, expressed in V_m, $V_m = Mv$.

For ideal gas, it can be obtained from formula (1-13)

$$pV_m = MR_g T$$

If $R = MR_g$, then

$$pV_m = RT \tag{1-15}$$

According to Avogadro's law, under the same temperature and pressure, the molar volume V_m of all gases is equal. It can be seen from formula (1-8) that the R of all gases is equal, and its value is independent of the specific state of the gas. R is called molar gas constant, and its value can be determined by the parameters of the gas in any state. For example, under the standard state ($p_0 = 101,325$ Pa, $T_0 = 273.15$ K), the volume of 1mol of any gas is 22.41,410 m³, which can be obtained by substituting into formula (1-15).

$$R = \frac{p_0 V_{m0}}{T_0} = \frac{101,325 \times 22.41,410}{273.15 \times 1,000} = 8.313 [\text{J}/(\text{kg} \cdot \text{K})]$$

With the molar gas constant, as long as the molar mass (or relative molecular mass) of the gas is known, the gas constant R_g of any gas is

$$R_g = \frac{R}{M} \tag{1-16}$$

Using the molar gas constant, the equation of state (1-14) of an ideal gas with a mass of m (kg) can also be written as

$$pV = nRT \tag{1-17}$$

In the formula, $n = m/M$, n is the amount of substance.

It should be noted that when the ideal gas state equation is applied to the actual gas, there will be some deviation, because the basic assumption of ideal gas is not true in the actual gas. For example, the volume of 1mol acetylene measured in the experiment is 24.1 dm³ at 20 °C and 101 kPa, while the volume is 0.114 dm³ at 842 kPa at 20 °C, which is very different because it is not an ideal gas.

Generally speaking, gases with low boiling points are closer to ideal gases at higher temperatures and lower pressures. For example, the boiling point of oxygen is − 183 °C, and the boiling point of hydrogen is − 253 °C. The difference between their molar volume and ideal value at normal temperature and pressure is only about 0.1%, while the boiling point of sulfur dioxide is − 10 °C. The difference between their molar volume and ideal value at normal temperature and pressure is 2.4%. Applying a certain amount of gas in equilibrium, its state is measured by P, V and T. The equation expressing the relationship between these quantities is called the equation of state of gas. Different gases have different equations of state. But the equation of real gas is usually very complex, while the equation of state of ideal gas has a very simple form.

Although it is impossible to have a completely ideal gas, many actual gases, especially those that are not easy to liquefy and sublimate (such as helium, hydrogen, oxygen, nitrogen, etc.), are the most close to the ideal gas in all gases because of their small size, small interaction force, and the most difficult to liquefy). At normal temperature and pressure, their properties have been very close to the ideal gas.

The temperature and pressure range of various gases in line with the ideal gas equation of state are different. There are the following rules:

(1) The more difficult the gas liquefies, that is, the lower the boiling point of the gas (such as H_2, He, Ar, etc.) is, the wider the temperature and pressure range of the ideal gas equation of state is, which can be applied at lower temperatures and higher pressures.

(2) The range of temperature and pressure of liquefied gases, i.e. gases with higher boiling points (such as CO_2, NH_3, SO_2, etc.) that conform to the equation of state of ideal gases is narrow, and even at higher temperature and very low pressure, there is obvious deviation from the ideal behavior.

In addition, sometimes it is only necessary to roughly estimate some data. Using this equation will make the calculation much easier.

Example 1-2: An oxygen cylinder placed indoors for a long time has a capacity of 25 L. The gauge pressure of the oxygen in the cylinder indicated by the pressure gauge is 5 bar, the room temperature is 20 °C, and the atmospheric pressure is 1,105 Pa. Try to find the quality of the oxygen in the cylinder.

Solution: According to the meaning of the question, the thermodynamic parameters of oxygen in the bottle are

$$p = (5+1) \text{ bar} = 6 \text{ bar} = 6 \; 105 \text{ Pa}$$
$$T = (20+273) \text{ K} = 293 \text{ K}$$
$$V = 25 \; L = 0.025 \text{ m}^3$$

Molar mass of oxygen $M = 32.00 \times 10^3$ kg/mol

Example 1-3: A container with a volume of 4 m³ is filled with air with $p = 9.81 \times 10^4$ Pa, $t = 20$ °C. The vacuum degree of the container after extraction is $p_V = 93{,}310$ Pa, and the local atmospheric pressure at that time is $p_b = 98{,}055.48$ Pa. If the temperature before and after air extraction remains unchanged, try to find:

(1) What is the absolute pressure of air in the container after air extraction?

(2) What is the mass of air in the container after air extraction?

(3) How many kilograms of air is pumped?

Solution: 1 and 2 respectively represent the state before and after air extraction.

(1) Absolute pressure of air in the container after extraction

$$p_2 = p_b - p_V = (98{,}055.48 - 93{,}310) \text{ Pa} = 4{,}745.48 \text{ Pa}$$

(2) According to the title, the thermodynamic parameters in the container after air extraction are

$$p_2 = 4{,}745.48 \text{ Pa}$$
$$T_2 = (20 + 273) \text{ K} = 293 \text{ K}$$
$$V_2 = 4 \text{ m}^3$$

Molar mass of air: $M = 28.96 \times 10^{-3}$ kg/mol

Gas constant of air: $R_g = \dfrac{R}{M} = \dfrac{8.314}{28.96 \times 10^{-3}} = 287$ J/(kg·K)

The mass of air in the container after extraction is

$$m_2 = \dfrac{p_2 V}{R_g T} = \dfrac{4{,}745.48 \times 4}{287 \times 293} = 0.226 \text{ kg}$$

(3) The air quality in the container before air extraction is

$$m_1 = \dfrac{p_1 V}{R_g T} = \dfrac{9.81 \times 10^4 \times 4}{287 \times 293} = 4.67 \text{ kg}$$

The quality of the extracted air is

$$\Delta m = m_1 - m_2 = 4.67 - 0.226 = 4.44 \text{ kg}$$

Task 2 Thermodynamic Law and Its Application in Refrigeration

【Task Objective】

Master the first and second laws of thermodynamics.

【Knowledge Reserve】

1. Stored Energy of Thermal System

The energy stored in the thermal system is called the stored energy of the thermal system. The stored energy of the thermal system involved in engineering thermodynamics mainly includes two types: one is the internal energy that depends on the state of the system itself; The other is the macroscopic kinetic energy related to the macroscopic motion velocity of the system and the macroscopic potential energy related to the position of the system in the gravity field.

1) Internal energy

The energy of the microscopic particles that make up matter is called the internal energy of matter. When chemical changes and nuclear reactions are not involved, the internal energy is the sum of the kinetic energy of the thermal motion of molecules and the potential energy due to the interaction between molecules, that is, the so-called thermal energy Known from physics, the size of the kinetic energy of gas molecules mainly depends on the temperature of the gas, and the size of the potential energy is mainly related to the specific volume of the gas.

In engineering thermodynamics, the internal energy of working medium with mass is expressed in U, in J or kJ; The internal energy per unit mass (i.e. 1 kg) of working medium is called specific internal energy, expressed in M, in J/kg or kJ/kg.

The specific internal energy of a gas working medium only depends on the thermodynamic temperature and specific volume of the working medium, that is, it depends on the thermodynamic state of the working medium. It is a state parameter, so it can be expressed as

$$u = f(T, v)$$

Because the motion of matter is eternal, it is impossible to have such a state: all the motion inside the working medium stops and the internal energy is zero, so the size of the internal energy is relative. In the calculation of engineering thermodynamics, it is often encountered that the working medium changes from one state to another. What needs to be calculated is the change of internal energy, not the absolute value of internal energy. Therefore, the reference state for calculating the internal energy can be considered as selected, for example, the internal energy of the gas is zero at 0 K or 0 °C.

2) Macro kinetic energy and macro potential energy

In addition to internal energy, the thermodynamic system also has macroscopic kinetic energy due to its macroscopic motion velocity and macroscopic potential energy due to its position in the gravity field, which are expressed in E_k and E_p, respectively, in J or kJ.

If the motion speed of the system with mass m is c_f, the macroscopic kinetic energy of the system is

$$E_k = \frac{1}{2}mc_f^2$$

If the height of the mass center of the system with mass *m* in the external reference coordinate system of the system is z, then the macroscopic potential energy of the system is

$$E_p = mgz$$

2. Thermodynamic Process

Under the influence of environment, the process of system changing from one equilibrium state to another is called thermodynamic process. In the actual process, a series of states experienced by the system are generally unbalanced. If the states experienced are infinitely close to the equilibrium state and there is no friction, it is a reversible process. The reversible process is the limit that the actual process can approach.

Generally, thermodynamic processes are classified as follows:

(1) Isothermal process: the process in which the temperature of the initial and final states of the system is the same as the ambient temperature, and the ambient temperature is constant. The system temperature is not necessarily constant during the change process.

(2) Isobaric process: the process in which the initial and final pressure of the system is equal to the ambient pressure, and the ambient pressure is a constant value. The pressure of the system is not necessarily constant during the change process.

(3) Isovolumetric process: the process in which the volume of the initial and final states of the system is equal, namely $\Delta V = 0$。

(4) Adiabatic process: the system is separated from the environment by an adiabatic wall. At this time, the process in the system is called adiabatic process.

(5) Cyclic process: the process that the system returns to its original state after a series of changes.

3. Thermodynamic Law

Thermodynamic law is the law that describes the thermal law in physics, mainly including the first law of thermodynamics, the second law of thermodynamics, the third law of thermodynamics and the zero law of thermodynamics. The first law of thermodynamics is the law of conservation of energy. The second law of thermodynamics has many expressions, also known as the principle of entropy increase. The law of thermodynamics is the basis of thermodynamics.

1) First law of thermodynamics

The first law of thermodynamics is the law of conservation of energy, also known as the principle of energy immortality. All substances in nature have energy, which has different forms.

Energy cannot be created or destroyed, but can only be transformed from one form to another under certain conditions, and the total energy is conserved in the process of transformation. The essence of the first law of thermodynamics is the law of energy conservation and conversion in the thermodynamic process. It establishes the energy balance relationship in the thermodynamic process and is one of the main bases of the thermodynamic macro analysis method.

The first law of thermodynamics can be expressed as: in the process of mutual conversion between heat energy and other forms of energy, the total amount of energy remains unchanged.

According to the first law of thermodynamics, in order to obtain mechanical energy, we must spend heat or other energy. The attempt to create a machine that can generate power without spending energy is futile. Therefore, the first law of thermodynamics can also be expressed as follows: the first type of perpetual motion machine that can produce work without spending energy is impossible to produce success.

The first law of thermodynamics is the specific application of the law of conservation of energy in the conversion of heat and mechanical energy. It points out that the total amount of heat energy and mechanical energy is constant when they are converted into each other, which is the main basis for thermodynamic macroscopic analysis. It can be expressed as follows: heat and work can be converted into each other. In order to obtain a certain amount of work, a certain amount of heat must be consumed; On the contrary, if a certain amount of work is consumed, a certain amount of heat will be generated.

The first law of thermodynamics is applicable to all thermodynamic systems and processes. Whether it is an open system or a closed system, the first law of thermodynamics can be expressed as

$$\text{Energy entering the system} - \text{Energy leaving the system} = \text{Change in stored energy of the system} \tag{1-18}$$

2) Second law of thermodynamics

The first law of thermodynamics describes the conservation of quantity of thermal energy, mechanical energy and other forms of energy in the process of transmission and conversion. However, experience tells us that not all thermodynamic processes that meet the first law of thermodynamics can be realized. The occurrence of thermodynamic processes has directions, conditions and limits. The second law of thermodynamics reveals this law.

(1) Directionality of spontaneous process.

The so-called spontaneous process is a spontaneous process without any external action. For example, the transfer of heat from a high temperature object to a low temperature object is a spontaneous process, and vice versa.

The process of transforming mechanical energy into heat energy through friction is also a spontaneous process. For example, when a moving car brakes, the kinetic energy of the car becomes heat energy through friction, causing the ground and tires to heat up, and finally escape to the atmospheric environment. On the contrary, if the same amount of heat is added to the tires and the ground, the car cannot run. This shows that mechanical energy can be spontaneously converted into thermal energy, while thermal energy cannot be spontaneously converted into mechanical energy.

Practice has proved that not only the heat transfer, the mutual conversion of heat energy and mechanical energy have directionality, but all spontaneous processes in nature have directionality. For example, water automatically flows from high to low, gas automatically expands from high pressure zone to low pressure zone, current automatically flows from high potential to low potential, mixing process of different gases, combustion process, etc., can only be carried out spontaneously in one direction. If we want to reverse the spontaneous process, we must pay some price, or leave some changes to the outside world. That is to say, the spontaneous process is irreversible.

(2) The expression of the second law of thermodynamics.

The second law of thermodynamics reveals the direction, conditions and limits of all thermal processes in nature. There are many kinds of thermal processes in nature, so there are many ways to express the second law of thermodynamics. Since various statements reveal a common objective law, they are equivalent to each other. Here are two representative statements.

Clausius stated that it is impossible to transfer heat from a low-temperature object to a high-temperature object without causing other changes.

This is the second law of thermodynamics in terms of heat transfer, which was put forward by Clausius in 1850. He pointed out that heat can only be transferred spontaneously from a high-temperature object to a low-temperature object, while the non-spontaneous process is not impossible, but must cost a certain price. For example, the compression-type refrigeration device takes the cost of mechanical energy, that is, the spontaneous process of changing mechanical energy into heat energy as the necessary compensation cost to realize the transfer of heat from a low-temperature object to a high-temperature object.

Kelvin Planck stated that it is impossible to take heat from a single heat source and completely convert it into work without other effects.

This is the second law of thermodynamics expressed from the perspective of heat work conversion. It was put forward by Kelvin in 1851. Planck also published the same statement in 1897. Later, it was called Kelvin-Planck statement. "No other impact" is an indispensable part of this statement. For example, the result of the constant temperature expansion process of an ideal gas is to take heat from a single heat source and turn it all into work. But at the same time, the pressure of the gas decreases and the volume increases, that is, the state of the gas changes, or "has other effects". Therefore, it is not that heat cannot be completely converted into work, but that it can only be realized at the cost of other effects.

Usually, people call the hypothetical heat engine that takes heat from a single heat source and turns it into work completely as the second type of permanent machine. Although it does not violate the first law of thermodynamics and the energy in the conversion process is conserved, it violates the second law of thermodynamics. If this heat engine can be manufactured successfully, it can use the atmosphere and ocean as a single heat source to convert the inexhaustible heat energy in the atmosphere and ocean into work and maintain its permanent rotation, which is obviously impossible. Therefore, the second law of thermodynamics can also be expressed as: the second kind of perpetual motion machine is impossible to produce successfully.

The above two expressions of the second law of thermodynamics reflect the directionality of the thermal process from different angles, and are in essence unified and equivalent.

4. Application of Thermodynamic Law in Refrigeration

Artificial refrigeration is to use special refrigeration equipment to consume a certain amount of external energy, forcing the heat to be transferred from the cooled object with lower temperature to the environment medium with higher temperature, so as to obtain all kinds of low temperature environment that people need. There are many methods of artificial refrigeration, which can be roughly divided into physical methods and chemical methods, while the vast majority of artificial refrigeration methods belong to physical methods. In the field of general refrigeration technology, the most widely used physical methods include phase change refrigeration, steam compression refrigeration, absorption refrigeration, etc.

In these refrigeration methods, there are not only energy transfer, but also heat-work conversion process. The first law of thermodynamics is the law of conservation of energy, which points out that all substances in nature have energy, and energy can be converted from one form to another, from one object to another, while the total amount of energy remains unchanged in the process of conversion and transfer. The first law of thermodynamics points out the quantitative relationship between energy conversion and transfer. The second law of thermodynamics suggests the conditions for energy conversion. The second law of thermodynamics points out that mechanical work can be completely changed into heat, but heat cannot be completely changed into mechanical work unconditionally, that is, it is impossible to take heat from a single heat source to completely change it into work without causing other changes. It can be seen that the cycle process cannot be completed by using a heat source. The second law also points out that it is impossible to transfer heat from a low temperature object to a high temperature object without causing other changes. Therefore, in order to transfer heat from a low temperature object to a high temperature object, there must be a compensation process. The process of artificial refrigeration is the process of transferring the heat of low temperature objects to high temperature objects with external compensation.

In addition, we also use the zeroth law of thermodynamics to measure the temperature. On the premise that the temperature of the measured object cannot be directly obtained, we use the third object to indirectly reflect the temperature of the measured object through the thermal balance.

Task 3 Heat Transfer Modes

【Task Objective】

Master the three modes of heat transfer.

【Knowledge Reserve】

Heat energy is always transferred spontaneously from a high-temperature object to a low-temperature object, or from the high-temperature part of the same object to the low-temperature part. This heat exchange between objects is called heat transfer for short.

The application of heat transfer can be summarized into two categories: one is to try to enhance heat transfer and realize effective heat transfer, such as heat transfer of indoor heating radiator (as shown in Figure 1-3-1); The other is to try to weaken heat transfer, reduce heat transfer and avoid heat loss. For example, some outer layers of heating pipes are insulated with thermal insulation materials (as shown in Figure 1-3-2).

Figure 1-3-1 A household radiator   Figure 1-3-2 Heating pipes

According to the different heat transfer processes, there are three modes of heat transfer: heat conduction, heat convection and heat radiation.

As shown in Figure 1-3-3, when cooking with a stove fire, heat is transferred from the fire to the pot and then to the hands of people. This process is a heat transfer mode of heat conduction; The process of heating water by fire through the boiler is a heat transfer mode of thermal convection; People can directly feel the heat released by the fire when they are near the fire. This process is the heat transfer mode of thermal radiation.

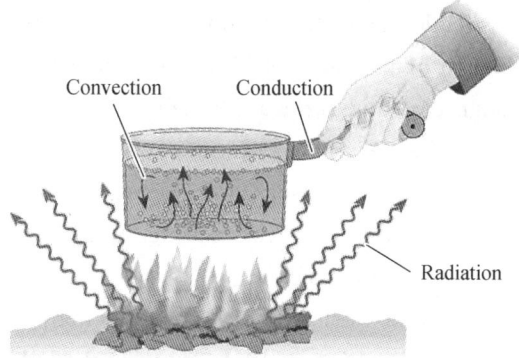

Figure 1-3-3　Three modes of heat transfer

1. Heat Conduction

Heat conduction refers to the process that an object transfers heat energy from the higher part of the same object to the lower part of the same object, or from the higher part of the object in contact to the lower part of the object with the help of the diffusion, collision and lattice vibration of material molecules, atoms and electrons without displacement. Heat conduction can occur in solids and also in static liquid or gas layers.

Thermal conductivity indicates the ability of a material to conduct heat. The greater the thermal conductivity, the better the thermal conductivity. The thermal conductivity is related to the composition, structure, state, temperature and pressure of the material. Generally, the molecular spacing of substances is inversely proportional to the thermal conductivity, so the thermal conductivity of solid substances is the largest, followed by liquid and gas.

For example, chips with high heat output generally need to be equipped with heat sink, and thermal foam is usually required between the heat sink and the chip, as shown in Figure 1-3-4. Thermal conductive foam has a large thermal conductivity and can fully contact with both, so it can ensure good thermal conductivity between the chip and the heat sink.

Figure 1-3-4　The thermal conductive foam and heat sink of a chip

2. Thermal Convection

Thermal convection is a heat transfer phenomenon caused by the relative displacement of various parts of the fluid. While conducting thermal convection, the heat transfer can also depend on the heat conduction of the fluid itself. The heat transfer phenomenon that occurs when the fluid flows through the solid surface is usually called the convective heat transfer process. According to the causes of fluid flow, there are forced convection and natural convection. The heat transfer caused by pressure difference caused by water pump, fan or other reasons and forced flow of fluid through the heat exchange surface is called forced convection heat transfer or forced convection heat transfer.

As shown in Figure 1-3-5, when the household air conditioner is used for refrigeration, the indoor unit takes away the heat of the indoor air to maintain the indoor temperature within a certain range and provide a comfortable environment for people. The indoor air is led by the fan of the indoor unit and forced to flow through the evaporator. The heat is transferred with the evaporator through thermal convection. The evaporator transfers heat evenly in all parts of the evaporator through heat conduction. The refrigerant takes away the heat with the evaporator through thermal convection. Therefore, in general, air conditioning refrigeration is a forced convection heat transfer process.

Figure 1-3-5 Indoor unit of air conditioner

Due to the uneven temperature of each part of the fluid, the heat transfer in the process of movement caused by the density difference is called natural convection heat transfer. Take the radiator as an example. Because the temperature of the radiator is higher than the indoor air, the air close to the surface of the radiator is first heated, so the temperature increases, the density decreases, and floats higher. The air with lower temperature and higher density nearby flows to fill the position left by the rising air, thus triggering the movement of the fluid. The rising air will be further heated if it contacts with the radiator surface in the flow, thus completing the heat exchange over and over again. It can be seen that the heat transfer stimulates the free movement of the fluid, and the free movement makes the heat transfer process continue.

Because the fluid velocity is higher during forced convection heat transfer, the heat transfer process is much stronger than natural convection heat transfer. So air conditioning and cooling usually work in a few minutes, while radiator heating usually takes several hours to work.

Convective heat transfer also includes boiling heat transfer of liquid on solid surface and condensation heat transfer of steam on solid surface. For example, in refrigeration devices, the heat transfer process of refrigerant in evaporator and condenser belongs to convection heat transfer.

3. Thermal Radiation

Thermal radiation is a phenomenon of heat transfer that is realized by the radiation energy in the form of electromagnetic wave emitted by an object into space. When transmitting energy through radiation, there is no need to contact with each other or use intermediate medium. It can be carried out even under high vacuum. Light is also electromagnetic wave. The sun transmits heat energy to the earth through thermal radiation.

Figure 1-3-6 People rely on the sun for heating in winter

All objects in nature radiate energy from the outside, and at the same time, they are constantly absorbing the energy radiated from the surrounding objects. The combined result of absorption and radiation realizes the heat transfer, which is the radiation heat transfer process.

The above three modes of heat transfer can improve the efficiency of heat transfer by increasing the thermal conductivity of solid materials, increasing the flow rate of fluid, and increasing the heat exchange area.

【Task Training】

(1) What are the commonly used temperature scales? What is the relationship between them?

(2) Is the gauge pressure equal to the absolute pressure? If the working medium pressure remains unchanged, can the pressure gauge reading for measuring its pressure change?

(3) What is the definition of specific volume in gas state parameters?

(4) What is the essence of the first law of thermodynamics?

(5) What are two representative expressions of the second law of thermodynamics? How are they expressed?

(6) What are the modes of heat transfer?

Project 2
Wet Air

【 Chinese Railway Culture 】

The History of Railway Development in China 2: The First Electrified Railway in China

Baoji—Chengdu Railway is located in Shaanxi Province, Gansu Province and Sichuan Province. It runs southward from Baoji Station, crosses the Weihe River, climbs 680m through the Qinling Tunnel after a 27 km extension line group, reaches the Qinling Station, then goes down along the Jialing River, passes through Gansu Province, passes through the Daba Mountains, continues southwestward to Guangyuan Station, passes through Jianmen Mountain and enters the Sichuan Basin, and passes through Mianyang and Deyang to Chengdu Station. The total length is 668.198 km. The Baoji—Yangpingguan section is a single-track railway limited by the terrain, and the Yangpingguan—Chengdu section is a double-track railway, which is the first electrified railway in China. Construction started in July 1952, was completed and opened to traffic in July 1956, and was officially put into operation on January 1, 1958. Electrification began in June 1958, and electrification was first realized in China's national railways in 1975.

More than 100,000 road-building troops marched into the Qinling Mountains. They fought hard and fiercely against the natural environment with thousands of cliffs, high waterfalls, and deep valleys. With the lofty ambition of "setting up the Foolish Old Man's ambition to move mountains, and daring to renew the sun and the moon", they were not afraid of sacrifice and overcome difficulties. They opened roads across mountains and built bridges across rivers, rewriting the history of thousand-mile Shu road is not connected with the Qin road.

Figure 2-0-1　Baoji—Chengdu Railway Held the Completion and Opening Ceremony

At 10 a.m. on July 13, 1956, the Baoji—Chengdu Railway held a connection ceremony at the Huangsha River in Huizhou County, Gansu Province. After the red curtain on the triangular connection sign like a tower was removed, the colorful locomotive sounded a long whistle spit out a wisp of white smoke, and pulled the float slowly from south to north to the connection point. More than 200 local people's representatives sitting in the carriage were at the window of the train, and waved away with a smile to the people who applauded and cheered. When the construction entered a tense stage, it used about half of the labor force of China's new railway and four fifths of the mechanical road construction force. The construction of this railway took more than four years, and the connection time was more than 13 months ahead of the date specified in the design documents.

In 1961, Baoji—Chengdu Railway completed the first phase of electrification transformation project, Baoji—Fengzhou section. In July 1975, the electrification transformation of the whole line was completed, becoming the first electrified railway in China. Since then, China's electrified railway has moved from here to the whole country.

As the first railway crossing Qinba Mountains, under the technical conditions at that time, the engineering difficulty was unimaginable, especially the four stations in Qinbei District, with steep mountains and deep cliffs, the famous "Guanyin Mountain Exhibition Line" design and the small station blasted on the cliffs with explosives, which showed the great spiritual strength and extraordinary wisdom and courage of the builders of Baoji-Chengdu Railway to overcome difficulties despite difficulties. Baoji-Chengdu Railway has ignited the fire of electrified railway across the country, nurtured the electrified railway network throughout the country, and promoted China's electrified railway from here to the whole country.

【Project Description】

In the application of air conditioning, no matter in various production workshops, server rooms and other industrial occasions; Or in office, shopping mall, home environment and other civil occasions, the object to be treated is air. Wet air is a mixture of dry air and water vapor. The impact of water vapor in the air on the air cannot be ignored. One of the tasks of air conditioning is to regulate its water vapor content. Therefore, it is necessary to understand the physical properties of wet air. The project mainly discusses the following four issues: ① composition of wet air; ② state parameters of wet air; ③ drawing of psychrometric diagram; ④ the application of psychrometric diagram in practice.

【Project Objectives】

1. Knowledge objectives

(1) Master the meaning of wet air state parameters.

(2) Master the composition of psychrometric diagram of wet air and its application in different occasions.

2. Capability objectives

(1) Be able to correctly apply the wet air state parameters in the field environment.

(2) Be able to correctly use the psychrometric diagram of wet air for analysis according to different situations.

3. Quality objectives

(1) Cultivate the ability of logical thinking.

(2) Cultivate teamwork ability.

Task 1 Status Parameters of Wet Air

【Task Objective】

Master the meaning of wet air state parameters.

【Knowledge Reserve】

1. Composition of Wet Air

In air conditioning engineering, we regard air as a mixture of dry air and water vapor.

Generally, the composition of dry air in the atmosphere is basically unchanged. Although in some local areas, the composition of air may be changed due to some factors (such as the reduction of oxygen and the increase of carbon dioxide content due to human respiration), this change has little impact on the thermal characteristics of dry air. In this way, when studying the physical properties of air, dry air can be considered as a whole for analysis and discussion.

Table 2-1-1　Main Components of Air

Main Components	Molecular Weight	Mass Fraction (%)
Nitrogen	28.016	78.084
Oxygen	32.000	20.946
Argon	39.944	0.934
Carbon dioxide	44.010	0.033

Relatively speaking, the content of water vapor in wet air is very small. It comes from the evaporation of water on the surface of the earth's oceans, rivers and lakes, the metabolism of various organisms, and the evaporation of water during production. In wet air, the proportion of water vapor is not fixed, and often changes with the changes of altitude, longitude and latitude, season, climate, surrounding environment and other conditions. Although the content of water vapor in wet air is small, its change has a great impact on people. For example, in the south, the air is relatively wet, so wet clothes are not easy to dry, and people will feel that the surrounding environment is always wet and uncomfortable. However, in Lanzhou, Beijing and other areas in the north, due to the dry air, the body feels more comfortable at the same temperature. The amount of water vapor in the air is not only important for people's daily life, but also for industrial production. For example, in the textile workshop, when the relative humidity is low, the yarn becomes thicker and brittle, and is prone to flying and broken ends. However, the air is too wet to work, and the yarn will bind, making it difficult to process.

Therefore, from the perspective of air conditioning, the humidity of the air is a matter of great concern to us, which is also the main reason for the special division of water vapor.

2. State Parameters of Wet Air

The physical properties of wet air are determined by its composition and state. The state of wet air can usually be measured and described by parameters such as pressure, temperature, relative humidity, moisture content and enthalpy. These parameters are called the state parameters of wet air.

In thermodynamics, dry air at normal temperature and pressure can be regarded as an ideal gas. The so-called ideal gas is to assume that the gas molecules are some elastic particles that do not occupy space, and there is no force between the molecules. Because the pressure and temperature involved in air conditioning engineering can be regarded as belonging to this category, dry air in air conditioning engineering can also be regarded as ideal gas. In addition, the water vapor in the wet air can also be regarded as an ideal gas due to its small content, overheated state, small pressure and large specific volume. In this way, the relationship between water vapor state parameters can also be expressed by the ideal gas state equation.

1) Pressure

(1) Atmospheric pressure.

The pressure of gas (i.e. intensity of pressure) refers to the force of gas on unit area. In the International System of Units (SI), the unit of pressure is Pa, 1 Pa=1 N/m². The atmospheric pressure on the unit area of the earth's surface is called atmospheric pressure or atmospheric pressure. Atmospheric pressure varies with altitude. At the same time, the atmospheric pressure also varies in different seasons in the same region. Figure 2-1-1 shows the relationship between atmospheric pressure and altitude. At the same altitude, the atmospheric pressure also changes in different seasons and different weather conditions. Generally, the atmospheric pressure acting on the sea level at 0 °C and 45° north latitude is taken as a standard atmospheric pressure (atm), and its value is 1 atm = 101,325 Pa.

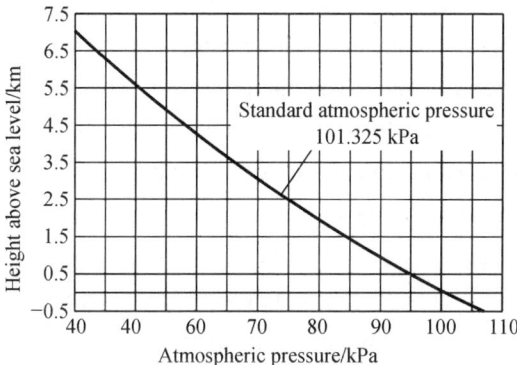

Figure 2-1-1   Relationship between atmospheric pressure and altitude

In the air conditioning system, the air pressure is usually measured by a pressure gauge. The pressure indicated by the pressure gauge is the difference between the absolute pressure of the measured air and the local atmospheric pressure, which is called the working pressure (or gauge pressure). The relationship between the working pressure and the absolute pressure is:

$$\text{Absolute pressure (of air)} = \text{local atmospheric pressure} + \text{working pressure (gauge pressure)}$$

Unless otherwise specified, air pressure refers to absolute pressure. Since the atmospheric pressure is not a fixed value, the error correction caused by different local atmospheric pressure should be considered in design and operation. The working pressure does not represent the true size of the air pressure. Only the absolute pressure is a basic state parameter of the air.

(2) Water vapor partial pressure and saturated water vapor partial pressure.

The partial pressure of water vapor in wet air refers to the pressure when water vapor in wet air occupies the volume of wet air and has the same temperature as wet air. The water vapor partial pressure reflects the water vapor content in the wet air. The higher the water vapor content, the greater the partial pressure; At a certain temperature, there is a limit to the amount of water vapor that can be contained in a certain amount of air. The higher the temperature of wet air, the greater the maximum water vapor allowed. When the content of water vapor in the air exceeds the maximum allowable value, the excess water vapor will be separated out in the form of water droplets, which is the condensation phenomenon. At this time, the water vapor reaches the saturated state, and the corresponding wet air is called saturated wet air. It can be seen that the water vapor content in the unsaturated air does not reach the maximum allowable value, and it also has the ability to absorb water vapor. The atmosphere around us is usually unsaturated air.

2) Moisture content and relative humidity

Moisture content can accurately represent the amount of water vapor actually contained in the air. In air conditioning, the change of moisture content is often used to indicate the degree of air humidification or dehumidification. The mass of water vapor coexisting with 1kg dry air in wet air is called moisture content, which is represented by the symbol d.

From the concept of moisture content, its size only indicates the amount of water vapor in the air, but not the degree of humidity in the air. How can we judge the humidity of the air? When the atmospheric pressure is constant, the temperature is constant, and the water vapor partial pressure of the air increases, the moisture content also increases, and the humidity degree of the air increases. Therefore, the proximity of the partial pressure of water vapor in the wet air to the partial pressure of saturated water vapor at the same temperature reflects the humidity of the air. The ratio of water vapor partial pressure of air to that of saturated air at the same temperature is called relative humidity, represented by the symbol φ and the value is usually in the form of a percentage.

3) Specific enthalpy

Specific enthalpy is used to calculate the heat absorbed or released when heating or cooling wet air under constant pressure. The specific enthalpy of wet air is not a single-value function of temperature, but depends on temperature and moisture content. As the temperature rises, the enthalpy value can increase or decrease, which also depends on the change of moisture content. Therefore, if the moisture content decreases when the temperature rises, the comprehensive result may be that the enthalpy of wet air may not necessarily increase.

4) Dry- and wet-bulb temperature and dew point temperature

Air temperature can be divided into dry-bulb temperature, wet-bulb temperature and dew point temperature according to the formation process and use of air temperature.

(1) Dry-bulb temperature.

The dry-bulb temperature refers to the value read on the dry-bulb thermometer exposed to the air and not directly exposed to the sun, expressed in t. It is the temperature measured by the thermometer in the ordinary air, that is, the temperature we often say in the general weather forecast. The dry-bulb thermometer temperature is the temperature measured by the thermometer when it is freely exposed to the air, and it should avoid the interference of radiation and moisture.

(2) Wet-bulb temperature.

Wet-bulb temperature is also called thermodynamic wet-bulb temperature. Wet-bulb temperature is a means to calibrate the relative humidity of air. The head of the wet-bulb thermometer is wrapped with wet gauze soaked in water at the end. When the air flows through the end of the wet-bulb thermometer, the moisture on the wet gauze evaporates and absorbs the heat of vaporization, making the temperature of the wet-bulb thermometer drop. The temperature difference between the wet air and the wet gauze increases, and the wet air transfers heat to the wet gauze. When the heat carried away by vaporization is in balance with the heat transferred in, the reading on the wet-bulb thermometer is the wet-bulb temperature t_w of the wet air. The greater the saturation difference of the surrounding air, the stronger the evaporation on the wet-bulb thermometer, and the lower its humidity. The relative humidity of the air can be determined according to the difference between the dry and wet bulb temperatures.

The wet- and dry-bulb thermometer contains two ordinary thermometers, as shown in Figure 2-1-2. The temperature measurement package of one thermometer is directly in contact with wet air, and the measured temperature is called dry-bulb temperature; The temperature measurement package of the other thermometer is wrapped with wet gauze to keep wet, and the measured temperature is called wet bulb temperature. The lower the relative humidity of the air, the lower the wet-bulb temperature is than the dry-bulb temperature. If the air is saturated, the water on the gauze will not evaporate because the air cannot accept more steam. At this time, the wet-bulb temperature and dry-bulb temperature are the same. Therefore, there is a certain functional relationship between the difference of dry-wet bulb temperature and relative humidity, as shown in Figure 2-1-3.

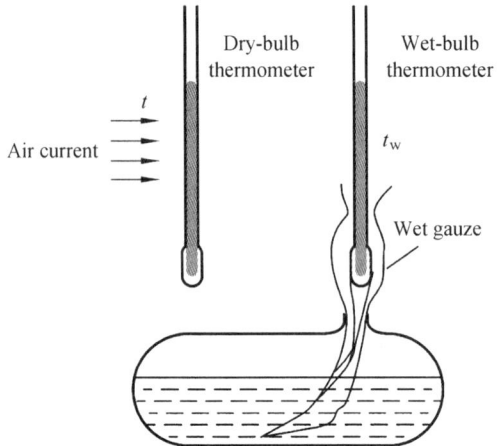

Figure 2-1-2 Wet- and dry-bulb thermometer

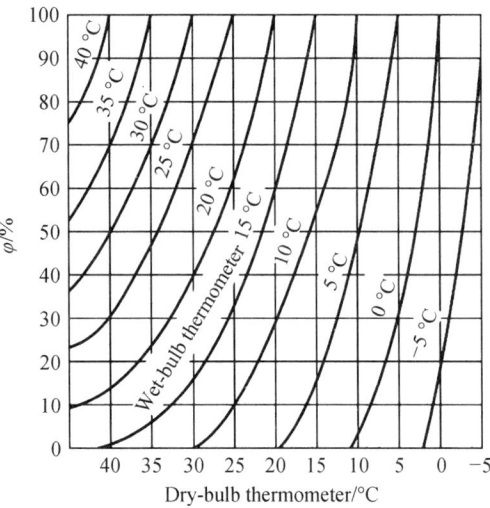

Figure 2-1-3 Relationship between dry and wet bulb temperature and relative humidity

(3) Dew point temperature.

Dew point temperature refers to the temperature of the air when it is cooled to saturation under the condition that the water vapor content and pressure do not change, expressed in t_L. In image, the temperature when the water vapor in the air turns into dew is called dew point temperature. When the water vapor in the air has reached saturation, the air temperature is the same as the dew point temperature; When the water vapor is not saturated, the air temperature must be higher than the dew point temperature. So the difference between dew point and temperature can indicate the degree of water vapor saturation in the air. The moisture content corresponding to the dew point temperature is the saturated moisture content, when $\varphi = 100\%$, the intersection of the isotherm and the 100% relative humidity line is the dew point temperature.

Dew point temperature can often be seen on the glass window in winter or on the water pipe in summer. This phenomenon can be explained by the formation of dew point temperature. The dehumidification process in air conditioning engineering is usually carried out by using the condensation law.

According to the discussion of dew point temperature and wet bulb temperature, the relationship between dry bulb temperature, wet bulb temperature and dew point temperature is as follows:

① For unsaturated air:

Dew point temperature < wet bulb temperature < dry bulb temperature

② For saturated air:

Dew point temperature = wet bulb temperature = dry bulb temperature

Task 2　Cognition and Application of Psychrometric Map of Wet Air

【Task Objectives】

(1) Understand the composition and function of psychrometric diagram of wet air.
(2) Master the application of psychrometric chart of wet air in different occasions.

【Knowledge Reserve】

1. Composition of Psychrometric Diagram

In engineering calculation, it is cumbersome to determine the air state and parameters by formula calculation and table lookup method, and the analysis of the air state change process also lacks intuitive perceptual understanding. Therefore, in order to facilitate engineering application, the relationship between various parameters under a certain atmospheric pressure is usually made into a line diagram for calculation. According to the different coordinate systems, there are many kinds of line diagrams, and the commonly used one in China is the enthalpy and humidity diagram, which is abbreviated as h-d diagram.

With specific enthalpy h as the ordinate and moisture content d as the abscissa, it represents the relationship between various parameters of wet air when atmospheric pressure B is constant. It includes isoenthalpy line, isotherm, iso-relative humidity line, water vapor partial pressure line, heat and humidity ratio line, etc.

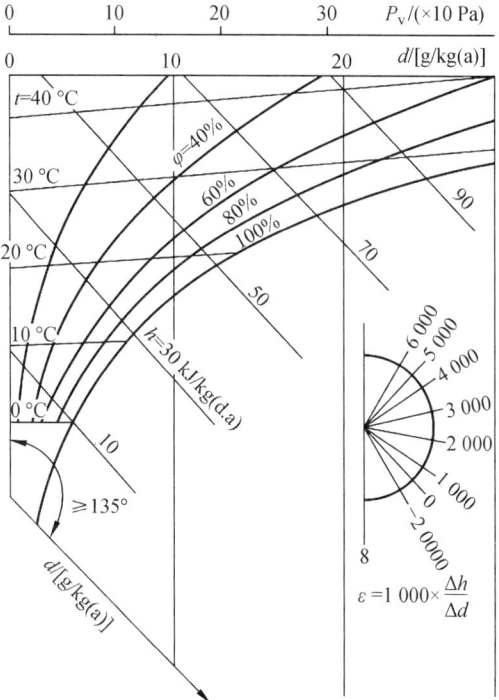

Figure 2-2-1 The enthalpy diagram of wet air

The h-d diagram takes two independent parameters h and d as the coordinate axis, and the other independent state parameter B as the fixed value. In order to make various parameters clearly reflected on the coordinate diagram, the angle between the two coordinate axes is 135°, as shown in Figure 2-2-1. In the diagram, d is the abscissa, h is the ordinate, and the lines parallel to the h axis are the isoenthalpy lines, and the lines parallel to the d axis are the iso-humidity lines. In addition, the following lines are also drawn on the diagram.

1) Isotherm

The isotherm is drawn according to the formula $h=(1.01+1.84d)t+2500d$. When $t=\text{constant}(t)$, the isotherm is a linear equation. Where $1.01t$ is the intercept and $(2500+1.84t)$ is the slope. When the temperature is taken as a certain value, the isotherm can be drawn on the h-d diagram according to the principle that a straight line can be drawn through two points.

The drawing process of isotherm is briefly described below.

(1) Draw the isotherm of $t=0$ °C. When $t=0$ °C, take any $d_1=0$ and $d_2=d_x$, then $h_1=0$ and $h_2=2500d$ can be calculated. From (0, 0) and ($2500d_x$, d_x), two state points O and A can be determined on the h-d diagram, then the OA line is the isotherm of $t=0$ °C.

(2) Draw the isotherm with $t=10$ °C. When $t=0$ °C, take $d_1=0$ to calculate $h_1=10.1$, take $d_2=d_x$, $h=(1.01+1.84d)t+2500d_x$, because (10.1, 0) is on the longitudinal axis, you can intercept the OB segment from point O upwards (the intercept is equal to 10.1) to get point B, and

according to $(10.1+2518.4d_x, d_x)$, you can determine the state point C on the h-d diagram, then BC straight line is the isotherm with $t=10$ °C.

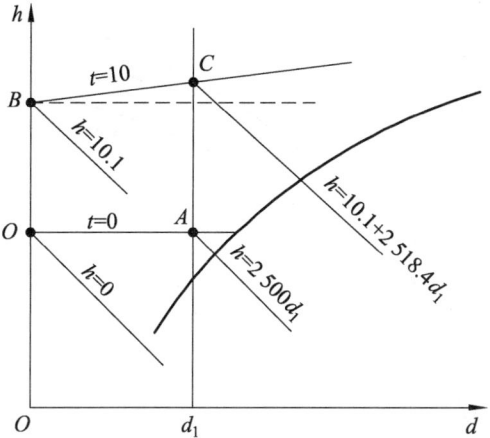

Figure 2-2-2 Drawing of isotherm

When t is taken as a series of constants of 1 °C, 2 °C, 3 °C,..., a cluster of different isotherms can be drawn using the same method above. Because the slope of the isotherm $(2500+1.84t)$ varies slightly with t value, the isotherms are not parallel. However, the value of $1.84t$ is much smaller than 2500, and the change of t value has little effect on the slope of isotherm. Therefore, each isotherm can be approximately regarded as parallel.

2) Isorelative humidity line

Moisture content is the function of atmospheric pressure B, relative humidity φ and the partial pressure of saturated water vapor $p_{v,b}$, that is, $D=F(B,\varphi,p_{v,b})$. Since atmospheric pressure B has been taken as a constant value in the drawing, it is taken as a constant in this formula. The partial pressure of saturated water vapor $p_{v,b}$ is a single-value function of temperature, which can be obtained from the water vapor property table according to the air temperature t. So, in fact, there is: $d=f(\varphi,t)$.

So when φ When taking a series of constants, the iso-relative temperature line can be drawn on the h-d diagram according to the relationship between d and t.

If $\varphi=90\%$, there is $d=622\times0.9p_{v,b}/(b-0.9p_{v,b})$. Take any temperature t, check $p_{v,b}$, and then calculate the moisture content d from the above formula. When t takes different values t_i ($i=1,2,...,n$), $p_{v,bi}$ can be obtained from the water vapor property table, and the corresponding d_i can be calculated. Since each pair of (t_i,d_i) can define a state point on the h-d diagram, and connect n state points, we can get $\varphi=90\%$ iso-relative humidity line. When φ When taking different values and repeating the above process, different iso-relative humidity lines can be made. As shown in Figure 2-2-3, $\varphi=100\%$ is the saturated humidity line, below which is the supersaturated zone and above which is the humid air zone. The water vapor in the wet air zone is in an overheated state.

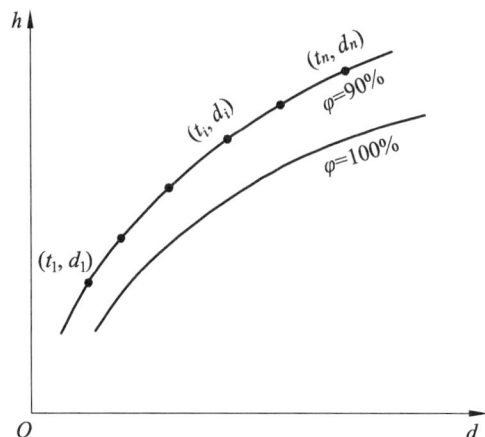

Figure 2-2-3 Drawing of Isorelative Humidity Line

3) Water vapor partial pressure line

From the calculation formula of moisture content $d = 622 p_v /(B - p_v)$, it can be seen that when the atmospheric pressure B is equal to a constant, $p_v = f(d)$, that is, the partial pressure of water vapor p_v and moisture content d are one-to-one correspondence, and a p_v can be determined by one d. Therefore, a horizontal line is set above the d axis to mark the p_v value corresponding to d.

4) Heat and humidity ratio line

In order to explain the direction and characteristics of air state change, the ratio of enthalpy difference and moisture content difference before and after the change of air state is often used to characterize, and this ratio is called the heat and humidity ratio ε, namely

$$\varepsilon = (h_B - h_A)/(d_B - d_A) = \Delta h / \Delta d$$

From the definition formula of the ratio of heat to humidity, ε is actually the slope of the straight line AB. Because the slope of the line is independent of the starting position, two lines with the same slope must be parallel. Therefore, a cluster of rays is made at the lower right of the h-d diagram (ε Line), for use when analyzing the change process of air state on the diagram.

It should be noted that the above h-d diagram is drawn when the atmospheric pressure B is equal to a fixed value. If the atmospheric pressure is different, the calculated parameters are also different. If the atmospheric pressure B of the same two kinds of wet air. They have the same temperature t and relative humidity φ is different, the moisture content d of the two kinds of wet air is different. As shown in Figure 2-2-4, the calculation formula of moisture content d shows that the moisture content d decreases with the increase of atmospheric pressure B, and vice versa. Therefore, if the atmospheric pressure B changes, the iso-relative humidity line will change accordingly, as shown in Figure 2-2-5. Therefore, in practical application, the h-d diagram conforming to the local atmospheric pressure should be used.

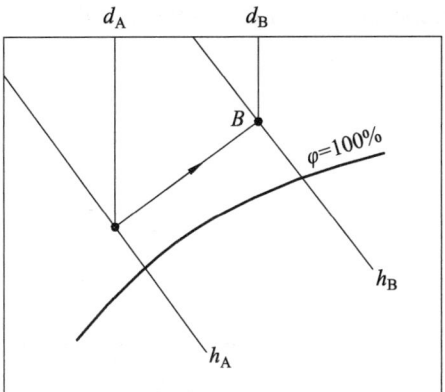

Figure 2-2-4   Relationship between heat and humidity ratio and state change hydrograph

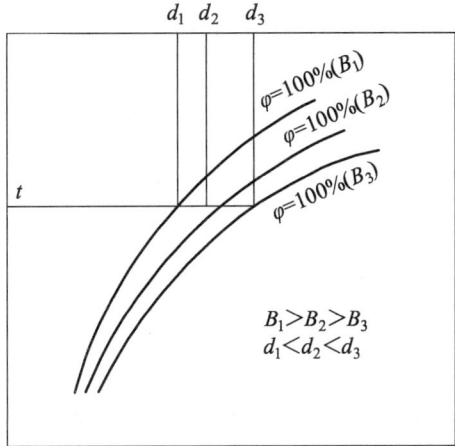

Figure 2-2-5   Effect of atmospheric pressure on relative humidity

2. Application of Psychrometric Diagram

The five independent parameters of wet air include t, d, φ, h and t_s. When the atmospheric pressure B is fixed, the air state can be determined according to any two of them, and the parameters such as t_d, p_v, $p_{v,b}$ and d_b can be found from the h-d diagram.

The air conditioning process includes heating and cooling, humidification and dehumidification. What is the relationship between these air conditioning processes and the enthalpy diagram? The change process of air state can be represented by the h-d diagram, and the direction and characteristics of various change processes can be determined by the ratio of heat and humidity (ε).

Figure 2-2-6 shows several typical processes of air state change. There are six typical air state change processes commonly used in air conditioning: from A to B is the humidifying heating process; from A to C is the humidifying cooling process; from A to D is the isoenthalpy humidifying process; from A to E is the isoenthalpy humidifying process; from A to F is the isothermal humidifying process; and from A to G is the humidifying cooling process.

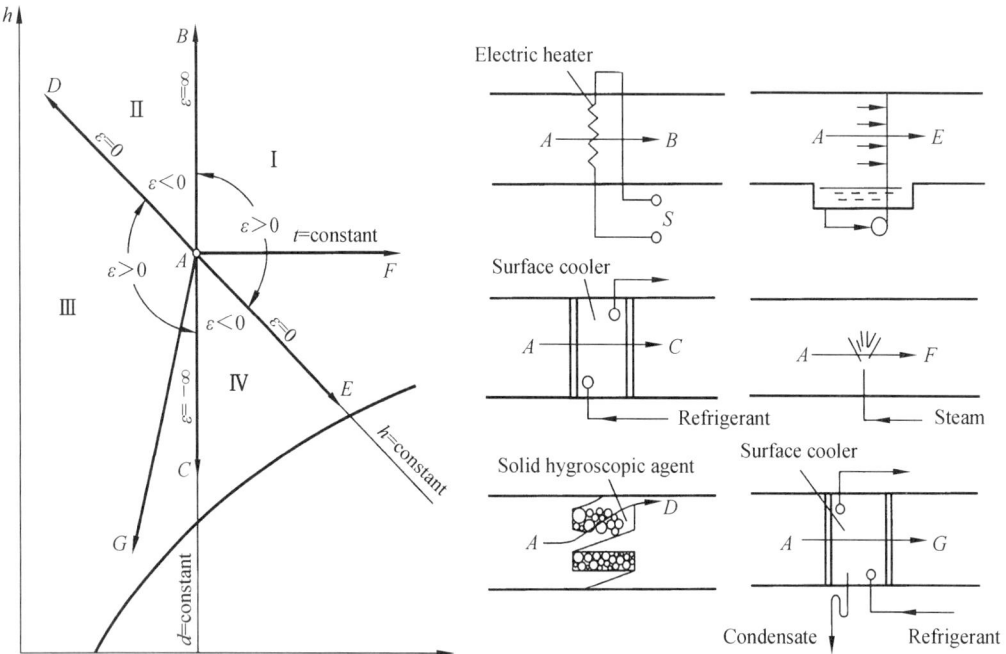

Figure 2-2-6   Several typical air state change processes

1) Isothermal (or dry) heating process

If a surface type air heater, such as an electric heater, is used to heat the air, it gains heat and increases temperature when the air passes through the heater, but the moisture content does not change. From point A to point B is the isothermal enthalpy heating process, that is, $h_B > h_A$, $d_B = d_A$, so

Hygrothermal ratio $\varepsilon = (h_C - h_A)/(d_C - d_A) = (h_C - h_A)/0 = +\infty$

2) Isothermal (or dry) cooling process

If the surface cooler is used to treat the air, and its surface temperature is higher than the air dew point temperature, the air will be cooled with constant moisture content, and its specific enthalpy value will inevitably decrease. Point A to point C is the process of isothermal enthalpy reduction, that is, $h_C < h_A$, $d_C = d_A$, so

Hygrothermal ratio $\varepsilon = (h_C - h_A)/(d_C - d_A) = (h_C - h_A)/0 = -\infty$

3) Isoenthalpy dehumidification process

When air is treated with solid hygroscopic agent, such as silica gel, the water vapor is absorbed, the moisture content of the air is reduced, and the air loses its latent heat to obtain the vaporization heat released when the water vapor condenses, which increases the temperature and slightly reduces the liquid heat carried away by the condensate. From point A to point D, it can be approximately regarded as the process of isoenthalpy dehumidification and temperature rise, that is, $h_D = h_A$, $d_D < d_A$, so

Hygrothermal ratio $\varepsilon = (h_D - h_A)/(d_D - d_A) = 0/(d_D - d_A) = 0$

4) Isoenthalpy humidification process

When circulating water is sprayed into the spray chamber to treat the air in the adiabatic environment, the water absorbs the heat of the air and evaporates into water vapor. The air loses sensible heat, the temperature decreases, and the water vapor enters the air, which increases the moisture content and the latent heat. From point A to point E, it can be approximately regarded as the isoenthalpy humidification process, that is, $h_E = h_A$, $d_E > d_A$, so

Hygrothermal ratio $\varepsilon = (h_E - h_A)/(d_E - d_A) = 0/(d_E - d_A) = 0$

5) Isothermal humidification process

By spraying steam into the air, the specific enthalpy and moisture content of the air are increased. In this case, the added value of specific enthalpy is the total heat of added water vapor. Point A to point F are isothermal humidification processes, and the hygrothermal ratio ε The value is a constant.

6) Dehumidifying cooling (or cooling and drying) process

If the surface cooler is used to treat the air, when the surface temperature of the cooler is lower than the dew point temperature of the air, the water vapor in the air will condense into water, and point A to point G is the dehumidification cooling process, or the cooling and drying process, that is, $h_G < h_A$, $d_G < d_A$, so

Hygrothermal ratio $\varepsilon = (h_G - h_A)/(d_G / d_A) > 0$

【Task Training】

(1) What is the difference between the partial pressure of water vapor in wet air and the partial pressure of saturated water vapor?

(2) What is the difference and relationship between relative humidity and moisture content?

(3) What is the physical meaning of the ratio of heat to humidity?

(4) It is known that the temperature of wet air in a certain state is 30 °C, the relative humidity is 50%, and the local atmospheric pressure is 101,325 Pa. Try to calculate the density, moisture content, water vapor partial pressure and dew point temperature of wet air in this state.

Project 3
Refrigeration Principle

【 Chinese Railway Culture 】

The History of Railway Development in China 3: "Chengdu—Kunming Spirit" Shines Brightly

1. Chengdu—Kunming Railway

The Chengdu—Kunming Railway, which was completed and opened to traffic on July 1,1970, starts from Chengdu, Sichuan Province in the north and ends at Kunming, Yunnan Province in the south, with a total length of nearly 1100 km. It has created 18 of the highest railways in China and 13 of the highest in the world. It has been called by the United Nations as "one of the three wonders that symbolize the conquest of nature in the twentieth century".

Figure 3-0-1　Chengdu—Kunming Railway

Chengdu—Kunming Railway is a Class I passenger and freight railway connecting Sichuan Province and Yunnan Province in China; The line is north-south, one of the trunk railways in southwest China, and one of the three horizontal and five vertical trunk railways in China. The Chengdu—Kunming Railway starts from Chengdu in the western Sichuan Plain in the north and crosses the Minjiang River and Qingyi River; Through Emei, along the Dadu River, across the Liangshan Mountains Cross the Niuri River ten times and arrive at Xichang; Eight times cross the Anning River and Jinsha River; More than thirty detours through the Longchuan River valley, through the Hengduan Mountains, and to Kunming, the Dianchi Lake in the south. At that time, the Chengdu—Kunming Railway was a very difficult project. The zone along the line was called "railway forbidden zone" by foreign experts, and it was considered impossible to build a railway for a long time. The whole line of Chengdu—Kunming Railway runs through mountains, rivers and valleys with steep terrain, diverse terrain and complex geology. It passes through rugged and steep mountains with towering peaks, dense deep streams, crisscross ravines and rushing water. The area where the line passes is known as "The Open-air Geological Museum".

2. Formation of "Chengkun Spirit"

In 1964, under the influence of the tense international situation, China began to carry out the construction of the third line. In 1966, the Chengdu—Kunming Railway entered the climax of construction, with more than 359,700 construction personnel.

The Chengdu-Kunming Railway is a construction project built with flesh and blood. During the construction period, the number of railway soldiers sacrificed reached more than 2,100 according to the statistics of the Ministry of Military Affairs of China, leaving more than 1,000 monuments and more than 20 martyr cemeteries along the line. In the construction of the Chengdu—Kunming Railway, the builders left behind the "Chengdu—Kunming spirit" of loving the motherland, not afraid of hardship, willing to devote and willing to sacrifice.

3. "Chengkun Spirit" passed down from generation to generation

Chengdu—Kunming Railway is a "heroic road" and "happy road", which is a true portrayal of Happy Sichuan and Happy China. The Chengdu—Kunming Railway, which connects Baoji-Chengdu Railway and Chengdu—Chongqing Railway in the north and Guiyang—Kunming Railway in the south, is an important trunk line in China's railway network. It is of great significance to improve the traffic conditions in the southwest region, close the connection between the southwest frontier and all parts of the country, strengthen the unity between nationalities, and promote the economic development of the southwest region. This road drives the economic development of the areas along the line, and becomes the "poverty relief road", "learning road", "hope road" connecting the Ethic Yi's villages to the outside world, as well as the "lifeline" of transportation development along the line. It goes without saying that the Chengdu—Kunming Railway is a "happy road".

The Chengdu—Kunming Railway has been running for 50 years, from "Hero Road" to "Happy Road", which makes us more aware that the Chengdu—Kunming Railway is not only a railway, but also a spirit. The "Chengkun spirit", which is not afraid of hardship, willing to devate and willing to sacrifice, will be passed down from generation to generation.

【 Project Description 】

Using certain methods to make the temperature of an object or space lower than the temperature of the surrounding medium and maintain it within a certain range, this process is called refrigeration. Air conditioners and refrigerators are typical refrigeration devices. In summer, the temperature outside the passenger car is relatively high. In order to maintain the temperature inside the car lower than the external environment, the residual heat (human body heat, solar radiation heat, equipment heat, etc.) entering the car must be constantly "transported" to the external environment.

The refrigeration device plays the role of heat transfer, and it transfers heat from low temperature environment to high temperature environment. According to the second law of thermodynamics, it is a non-spontaneous process to transfer heat from a low temperature object to a high temperature object, and the system must be compensated for energy. There are usually two methods of energy compensation: work on or heat the working medium. Therefore, according to the different compensation methods, there are steam compression refrigeration, absorption refrigeration and other methods. Because of its compact structure, safe and reliable operation, wide range of refrigeration temperature and cooling capacity, and easy to realize automatic control and regulation, the steam compression refrigerator is currently most widely used in railway refrigeration transportation and air conditioning.

This project mainly studies the principle of steam compression refrigeration, steam compression refrigeration cycle, other refrigeration methods, properties and characteristics of common refrigerants and lubricating oils.

【 Project Objectives 】

1. Knowledge objectives

(1) Master the principle of vapor compression refrigeration and the role of the four major refrigeration components.

(2) Understand the principle of other refrigeration methods, the properties and characteristics of common refrigerants and lubricants.

2. Capability objectives

(1) Be able to analyze the working process of steam compression refrigeration cycle.

(2) Be able to select the appropriate refrigerant according to the site needs.

3. Quality objectives

(1) Enhance the awareness of safe production and standardized operation.

(2) Develop a good habit of scientific maintenance of equipment.

(3) Develop teamwork and good habits.

Task 1 Principle of Vapor Compression Refrigeration

【Task Objective】

(1) Master the working principle of vapor compression refrigeration and the change process of refrigerant in the refrigeration process.

(2) Master the functions of the four major components of the refrigeration system.

【Knowledge Reserve】

1. Vaporization and Condensation

As we all know, the process of changing from liquid to steam is called vaporization. Vaporization is the phenomenon of liquid molecules leaving the liquid surface. According to the severity, vaporization can be divided into evaporation and boiling. The vaporization process on the water surface is called evaporation; The intense vaporization process on the surface and inside of water is called boiling. Both evaporation and boiling are endothermic processes, and the heat absorbed is called latent heat of vaporization.

Evaporation can be carried out at any temperature. The speed of evaporation mainly depends on the temperature, and is also related to the evaporation area and the vapor density on the liquid surface. The higher the temperatureis, the larger the evaporation areais, the smaller the vapor density on the liquid surfaceis, and the faster the evaporation speedis; For the opposite situation, the evaporation speed is the slower. The evaporation rate is different for different liquids.

Under certain pressure, boiling will occur only when the temperature of the liquid reaches a certain value, and the temperature will remain constant throughout the boiling process. The temperature of boiling is called boiling point. The boiling point of a liquid corresponds to the pressure bears to. Usually, the boiling point under a certain pressure is called the saturation temperature under this pressure, and the corresponding pressure is called the saturation pressure.

The saturation pressure of the same substance is in direct proportion to the temperature, that is, the higher the saturation pressure is, the higher the saturation temperature is; On the contrary, the saturation temperature is low. The saturation temperatures of different substances are different even under the same pressure, and some of them vary greatly. For example, under a standard atmospheric pressure, the saturation temperature of water is 100 °C, and the latent heat of vaporization is 2,258 kJ/kg; At two standard atmospheric pressures, the saturation temperature is 120 °C, and the latent heat of vaporization is 2,202.2 kJ/kg. The saturation temperature of R12 at a standard atmospheric pressure is − 29.8 °C, and the latent heat of vaporization is 165.3 kJ/kg; At two standard atmospheric pressures, the saturation temperature is − 12 °C and the latent heat of vaporization is 157.3 kJ/kg. In refrigeration engineering, the vaporization process of refrigerant liquid in the evaporator is actually a boiling process, and the boiling point (saturation temperature) is called the evaporation temperature, and the corresponding pressure (saturation pressure) is called the evaporation pressure.

The process of changing a substance from a gaseous state to a liquid state is called condensation (also called liquefaction). Condensation is the opposite process of vaporization. Under certain pressure, only when the temperature around the steam is lower than its corresponding condensation temperature, can the steam release heat to the surrounding and condense into liquid. The heat released during condensation is called condensation latent heat (also known as liquefaction latent heat), and the condensation latent heat is equal to the vaporization latent heat in numerical value; The temperature also remains constant during condensation. The condensation temperature and condensation pressure of the same substance are also one-to-one, which is same as the corresponding relationship between evaporation temperature and evaporation pressure. For example, under two standard atmospheric pressures, the condensation temperature of R12 gas and the evaporation temperature of R12 liquid are − 12 °C. If the vapor under two standard atmospheric pressures is condensed, as long as there is a medium below its condensation temperature of − 12 °C around, the vapor will emit heat and condense into liquid. If ambient air with a temperature of 35 °C is used as the cooling medium of R12 steam, the condensation temperature of R12 steam must be above 35 °C, and the corresponding condensation pressure must be above 0.9 MPa.

2. Working Principle of Steam Compression Refrigerator

The steam compression refrigeration system is composed of four main parts: compressor, condenser, throttling device and evaporator, which are connected by pipes to form a completely closed system. The refrigerant circulates in a fluid state in this closed refrigeration system. Through phase change, it continuously absorbs heat from the evaporator and releases heat in the condenser, thus achieving the purpose of refrigeration.

Refrigerant in a closed system can repeatedly realize the phase change of refrigerant from liquid to vapor, and then from vapor to liquid by consuming only the compression work of compressor, and transfer the heat at low temperature to high temperature through this phase change, which is the working principle of vapor compression refrigerator.

1) Functions of main components (four major parts) of refrigeration system

(2) Refrigeration compressor.

The refrigeration compressor is the power equipment of the refrigeration cycle. It is usually driven by the motor. In addition to timely extracting the refrigerant flowing through the evaporator and maintaining the low temperature and low pressure, it can also increase its pressure and temperature by compressing the refrigerant, creating conditions for transferring the heat of the refrigerant to the medium of the external environment, that is, the low temperature and low pressure refrigerant vapor is compressed to the high temperature and high pressure state. So that the refrigerant vapor can be condensed with normal temperature air or water as the cooling medium.

(2) Condenser.

The condenser is a heat exchange device. Its function is to use air or water and other cooling media to take away the heat of the high-temperature and high-pressure refrigerant steam of the self-made cold compressor, so that the high-temperature and high-pressure refrigerant steam can be cooled and condensed into high-pressure and normal-temperature refrigerant liquid. The amount of heat emitted by the condenser is directly proportional to the area of the condenser and the temperature difference between the refrigerant vapor temperature and the cooling medium temperature. Therefore, sufficient condenser area and certain heat exchange temperature difference are required to meet the heat dissipation requirements.

(3) Throttling element.

The refrigerant liquid with high pressure and normal temperature cannot be directly sent to the evaporator with low temperature and low pressure. According to the principle of one-to-one correspondence between saturation pressure and saturation temperature, the temperature of refrigerant can be reduced by reducing the pressure of refrigerant liquid. Pass the refrigerant liquid with high pressure and normal temperature through the pressure reducing device (throttling element) to obtain the refrigerant with low temperature and low pressure, and then send it to the evaporator for heat absorption and vaporization. The commonly used throttling elements in steam compression refrigeration system include expansion valve and capillary tube.

(4) Evaporator.

The evaporator is also a heat exchange device. The throttled low temperature and low pressure refrigerant liquid absorbs heat and vaporizes (boils) in the evaporator to change into steam, and absorbs the heat of the cooled medium, so as to reduce the temperature of the cooled medium and achieve the purpose of refrigeration. The amount of heat absorbed by the evaporator is directly proportional to the area of the evaporator and the temperature difference between the evaporation temperature of the refrigerant and the temperature of the cooled medium. Of course, it is also related to the amount of liquid refrigerant in the evaporator. Therefore, to absorb a certain amount of heat, the evaporator needs a matching evaporator area, a certain heat exchange temperature difference, and an appropriate amount of refrigerant for the evaporator.

2) Circulation process of refrigerant in refrigeration system (four major parts)

The working process of refrigerant in four major parts is as follows:

As shown in Figure 3-1-1, the refrigerant liquid with low temperature and low pressure absorbs the heat Q_0 of the cooling medium in the evaporator and vaporizes into low temperature and low pressure steam, which is then sucked in by the compressor; The compressor consumes a certain amount of mechanical work W_0 (generally achieved by electric energy driving the motor) to compress the refrigerant steam at low temperature and low pressure into the refrigerant steam at high temperature and high pressure, and discharge it into the condenser; The refrigerant vapor with high temperature and high pressure is cooled by the ambient medium (air or water) in the condenser, and the refrigerant vapor is condensed into liquid after releasing heat Q_K; The refrigerant liquid with high temperature and high pressure is throttled and depressurized by throttling device (expansion valve or capillary), and the temperature is also reduced. The refrigerant with low temperature and low pressure enters the evaporator; In the evaporator, the refrigerant liquid with low temperature and low pressure absorbs the heat Q_0 of the cooling medium, evaporates into the refrigerant vapor with low temperature and low pressure, and is sucked in by the compressor again, thus circulating again and again.

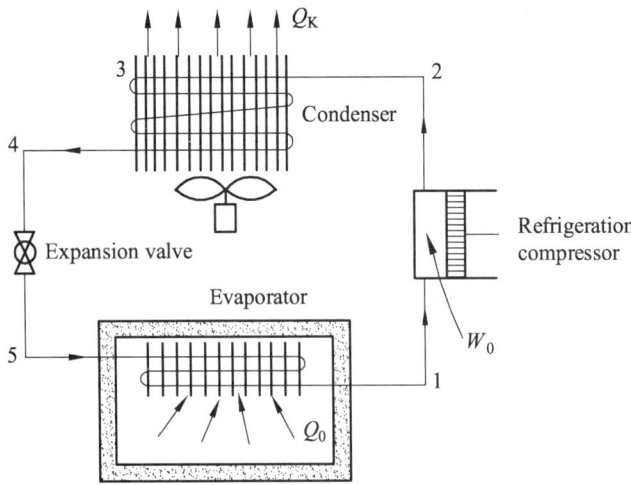

Figure 3-1-1　Working principle of steam compression refrigeration

In this way, the refrigerant in the closed refrigeration system can complete a cycle only through four thermodynamic processes: compression, condensation, throttling and evaporation. In the cycle, the compressor needs to consume a certain amount of work to transfer the heat released by the low-temperature object to the high-temperature environmental medium, so as to achieve the purpose of refrigeration. As long as the compressor operates normally, the refrigerant will continue to circulate in the four major parts, and the continuous cooling effect can be achieved.

Task 2 Other Refrigeration Methods

【Task Objective】

(1) Understand the absorption refrigeration cycle process.

(2) Understand the principle and application of dry ice, liquid ammonia and semiconductor refrigeration methods.

【Knowledge Reserve】

The working process of refrigeration is to use the refrigerator to obtain heat from the cooled medium and transfer it to the high-temperature environment medium. According to the second law of thermodynamics, this process can only be realized by energy compensation. There are two methods of energy compensation: one is to do work; The other is heat transfer. Steam compression refrigeration is a way of doing work. Of course, there are other refrigeration methods besides steam compression refrigeration.

1. Absorption refrigeration

Absorption refrigeration is a refrigeration method powered by heat energy. It also uses refrigerant vaporization and heat absorption to realize refrigeration. Like vapor compression refrigeration, absorption refrigeration uses the physical property that liquid absorbs the latent heat of vaporization during vaporization so as to realize refrigeration. The difference is that vapor compression refrigerator is powered by consuming the mechanical energy of compressor, while absorption refrigerator is powered by heat energy. The absorption refrigerator will obtain better economy when using waste heat as heat source.

1) Principle of absorption refrigerator

The working medium used in the absorption refrigerator is a mixed solution composed of two substances with different boiling points. The substances with low boiling point are refrigerants, and the substances with high boiling point are absorbents, called working pairs. For example, in the ammonia-water absorption refrigerator, ammonia is the refrigerant, water is the absorbent, and the refrigeration temperature range is 1 ~ −45 °C, which can provide a cold source for some process production processes. There are two cycles in the absorption refrigerator (refrigerant cycle and solution cycle). Absorption refrigeration cycle is composed of generator, absorber, condenser, evaporator, solution pump and throttling device.

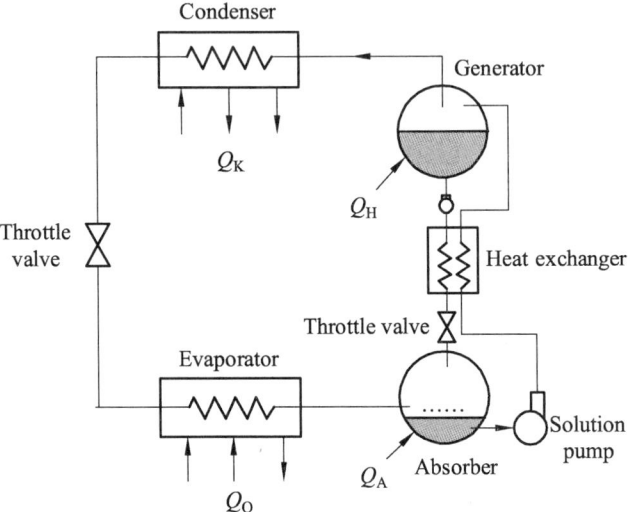

Figure 3-2-1 Absorption refrigeration system

As shown in Figure 3-2-1, in the absorber, the dilute solution from the generator absorbs the refrigerant vapor from the evaporator and becomes a concentrated solution. The heat released during the absorption process is taken away with cooling water. The concentrated solution from the absorber is pressurized by the solution pump and delivered to the generator. In the generator, an external heat source is used to heat the concentrated solution, in which the refrigerant vapor with low boiling point is evaporated, and the concentrated solution becomes a dilute solution. The solution passes through the cycle of absorber → generator → absorber, realizing the transformation of low pressure refrigerant vapor into high pressure refrigerant vapor.

2) Common working pairs of absorption refrigeration cycle

The commonly used working pairs of absorption refrigeration cycle are mainly divided into the following two types according to the different refrigerants.

(1) Working pairs with ammonia as refrigerant.

It mainly includes ammonia water (NH_3-H_2O), ethylamine water ($C_2H_5NH_2$-H_2O), methylamine water (CH_3NH_3-H_2O) and sodium thiocyanate ammonia (NaSCN-NH_3). Using methylamine and ethylamine can reduce the inherent toxicity and explosion of ammonia, while ethylamine is also beneficial for heat pumps because of its low vapor pressure. Sodium thiocyanate has good performance and low cost in solar absorption refrigeration cycle.

(2) Working pairs with methanol and ethanol as refrigerants.

They mainly include methanol-lithium bromide (CH_3OH-LiBr), methanol-zinc bromide (CH_3OH-$ZnBr_2$), methanol-lithium-zinc bromide (CH_3OH-LiBr-$ZnBr_2$), ethanol-lithium-zinc bromide (C_2H_5OH-LiBr-$ZnBr_2$), etc. Methanol has a large heat of vaporization, which can produce low temperature below 0 °C, and has no corrosive effect on metal materials. It is an ideal refrigerant. Using ethanol as a refrigerant, its performance is worse than that of methanol, but its biggest advantage is that the heating temperature of the generator is lower, so it is more suitable for use in solar absorption refrigerators.

In practice, ammonia-water solution and lithium bromide-water solution are usually used.

2. Ice Salt Mixture Refrigeration

The melting temperature of ice is 0 °C. If the physical property that ice melts when absorbing heat is used for refrigeration, only temperature above 0°C can be got. In order to get a lower temperature, the mixture of ice and salt can be used to refrigerate. The salt used is usually table salt, namely sodium chloride (NaCl). If salt and ice are mixed, when the ice-salt mixture melts, two endothermic reactions will occur simultaneously: one is to absorb the melting heat when the ice melts; The other is to absorb the heat of melting when salt is dissolved in water. The combination of these two endothermic reactions makes the melting temperature of ice-salt mixture far lower than 0 °C. In a certain range, the more salt added, the lower the melting temperature of the mixture, but the melting heat also decreases.

Ice salt mixture is widely used as the cold source of refrigerated vehicles on the railway. The refrigerator of the refrigerator car with ice salt mixture is set on the top of the car. When the ice salt mixture melts, the heat absorbed comes from the goods in the vehicle, and the goods get low temperature due to the loss of heat. The temperature in the car is reduced by the natural circulation of air. Refrigerator cars that use ice and salt mixture to refrigerate goods have long been the main means of transportation for railway refrigerated transportation in China. The ice salt mixture refrigeration system has simple equipment and is convenient to use. Under normal servicing conditions, the refrigeration system can be used continuously, safely and reliably. However, due to the limitation of the minimum melting temperature of the ice salt mixture, the refrigerator car can only produce the temperature in the car above − 8 °C, so it is only suitable for cooling the goods during transportation. In addition, the temperature can not be adjusted, and the salt water discharged from the outside of the vehicle corrodes the vehicle structure and rail greatly, which is also the main disadvantage of the refrigerator car.

3. Dry Ice Refrigeration

When the pressure is below 0.518 MPa, the dry ice will produce sublimation after heat absorption, that is, after heat absorption, the dry ice in solid state will directly volatilize into gas carbon dioxide without passing through the liquid state. Due to the low sublimation temperature and large sublimation heat of dry ice, applying the heat absorption process of dry ice sublimation to the refrigeration of refrigerated vehicles can not only obtain a lower temperature in the vehicle, but also obtain a larger refrigeration capacity. There are two forms of dry ice refrigeration for refrigerated vehicles: contact type and non-contact type. Contact dry ice refrigeration refers to the direct contact of sublimated CO_2 gas with goods. When the content of CO_2 in the air in the vehicle exceeds 10%, it is harmful to human body, and the air circulation shall be ensured in the use occasions; When non-contact dry ice refrigeration is used, the CO_2 gas generated by dry ice phase change is directly discharged from the vehicle by the closed dry ice chest.

Figure 3-2-2　Dry ice cooled food

Dry ice is especially suitable for occasions with high requirements for refrigeration and visual effects, such as high-end hotels, as shown in Figure 3-2-2. The refrigerated vehicle with dry ice refrigeration can obtain a temperature of $-20\ ^\circ C$ or even lower. However, the cost of dry ice used for dry ice refrigeration is too high, and the storage and transportation loss of dry ice is large, which limits the use of dry ice refrigeration in refrigerator cars.

4. Liquid ammonia refrigeration

The evaporation temperature of liquid ammonia under one atmospheric pressure is $-33.5\ ^\circ C$. Liquid nitrogen is an inert substance whose characteristics include colorless, tasteless, non-corrosive, non-flammable etc., which can quickly freeze and transport food.

There are two ways to use liquid ammonia refrigeration for railway refrigerated transportation. One is to pre-cool perishable goods with liquid ammonia. The minimum pre-cooling temperature can reach $-80 \sim -100$ °C. The pre-cooling can be carried out on the vehicle when loading or in the cold storage. The cold source in the transportation process is the cold storage capacity of goods and vehicles. The distance that can be transported depends on the initial temperature during pre-cooling, the allowable final temperature of goods, the external air condition, the thermal insulation performance and air tightness of the vehicle body. In fact, this refrigerated vehicle is an insulated vehicle without special cold source. Another method is to set the container containing liquid ammonia inside the vehicle, and use the continuous or periodic evaporation of liquid ammonia to offset the heat transferred from outside the vehicle and the physiological heat of the goods inside the vehicle. Liquid ammonia can be directly injected into the vehicle from the distribution pipe with holes on the top of the vehicle, which is called contact type; Air cooler can also be used to cool the goods in the vehicle. At this time, ammonia does not contact with the goods, which is called non-contact type. When the contact liquid ammonia cooling system is used, it can create an anoxic low temperature transportation condition for fresh fruits and vegetables, so it can reduce the respiratory heat of fruits and vegetables.

The liquid ammonia refrigeration equipment is simple and reliable, but the disadvantage is the high cost of liquid ammonia.

5. Semiconductor refrigeration

Semiconductor refrigeration is a method of directly using electric energy to cool by virtue of thermoelectric effect of semiconductor components, so it is also called thermoelectric refrigeration. Semiconductor refrigeration is realized by semiconductor thermoelectric elements. The most basic semiconductor thermoelectric elements are thermoelectric couples composed of N-type and P-type semiconductor elements in series, as shown in Figure 3-2-3.

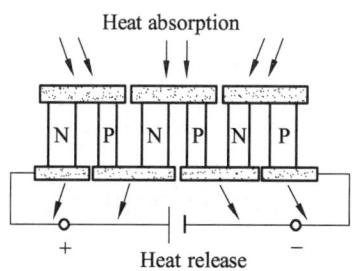

Figure 3-2-3 Semiconductor refrigeration principle

According to the thermoelectric effect, when the DC current flows through the semiconductor thermoelectric element, in addition to generating joule heat, there will be heat absorption at one end of the semiconductor element and heat release at the other end. When the applied electric field makes the electrons in the N-type semiconductor and the holes in the P-type semiconductor move together, in order to supplement the electrons and holes, a large number of electron and hole pairs will be excited near the joint. The kinetic energy and potential energy of these electron and hole pairs are taken from the thermal vibration kinetic energy of the lattice, so there is heat absorption at the joint, which is called the cold end; On the contrary, when the applied electric field is reversed, the electrons in the N-type semiconductor and the holes in the P-type semiconductor move towards the joint, these electrons and holes will recombine near the joint. The kinetic energy and potential energy of the electron and hole pair before recombination will be converted into the thermal vibration kinetic energy of the lattice, so heat will be released at the joint, which is called the hot end. The purpose of refrigeration can be achieved by using the heat absorption phenomenon at the cold end to cool the surrounding medium. If the current direction is opposite, the endothermic end (cold end) will become the exothermic end (hot end), and the exothermic end will become the endothermic end, and the semiconductor refrigeration element will become the heating element.

Due to the limited performance of semiconductor materials, the refrigeration capacity of a pair of thermocouples is generally very small, about several hundred milliwatts to two watts. Therefore, in practical use, several pairs of thermoelectric couples are often connected in series or in parallel to form a refrigeration stack, which can obtain a cooling capacity of several watts to several kilowatts.

Unlike ordinary refrigerators, semiconductor refrigerators have no mechanical moving parts and do not use refrigerants. As long as some semiconductor refrigeration elements are combined, direct cooling can be achieved by using DC power supply, and the cooling capacity and cooling temperature can be easily changed by adjusting the working current. If you change the direction of the current, refrigeration will become heating, so the semiconductor air conditioner is the same as the cooling and heating fan. When the semiconductor cooler works, it has no wear, vibration, noise and refrigerant leakage. It is reliable, easy to maintain and use, and has a long service life. However, due to the limitation of material properties and manufacturing costs, semiconductor refrigeration is only suitable for small refrigeration devices, such as small refrigerators, small air conditioners, small cold sources for instruments and meters.

Task 3　Refrigerant and Compressor Lubricating Oil

【Task Objective】

(1) Master the characteristics and selection of refrigerant.

(2) Master the characteristics of compressor lubricating oil.

【Knowledge Reserve】

1. Refrigerant

Refrigerant is the necessary working medium to complete the refrigeration cycle in the refrigeration system. The thermodynamic state of the refrigerant is constantly changing in the refrigeration cycle. The refrigerator will continuously transfer the heat of the cooling system to the high-temperature heat source by virtue of the thermodynamic state of the refrigerant to complete the refrigeration cycle.

1) Requirements for refrigerant

(1) Thermodynamic requirements.

① The boiling point of the refrigerant should be low, so that lower evaporation temperature can be obtained.

② The critical temperature of the refrigerant should be high and the solidification temperature should be low to ensure that the refrigerant can work safely in a wide temperature range. A gas can be liquefied at a certain temperature and pressure, but when the temperature rises above a certain value, no further increase in pressure can make the gas liquefied. This temperature is called the critical temperature. Refrigerant with high critical temperature can be liquefied at normal temperature, that is, common cooling medium can be used to condense the refrigerant, and the refrigerant can be throttled away from the critical point to reduce the loss and improve the performance of the cycle. The low freezing point can make the refrigeration system safely produce a lower evaporation temperature, so that the refrigerant will not solidify within the operating temperature range.

③ Refrigerant shall have appropriate working pressure. The evaporation pressure is required to be close to or higher than the atmospheric pressure, so as to avoid vacuum in the return air pressure of the refrigerator and increase the chance of air infiltration into the refrigeration system, improve the working efficiency of the refrigerator and reduce the corresponding invalid power consumption. The condensation pressure shall not be too high. Low condensation pressure can reduce the strength requirements for refrigeration machines, equipment and pipelines, and reduce the power consumption of the compressor.

④ The refrigerant is required to have a large latent heat of vaporization and a small specific volume. In this way, the refrigerating capacity per unit volume is large under certain operating conditions. When the required refrigeration capacity is certain, the refrigeration capacity per unit volume is large, the refrigerant circulation capacity can be reduced, and the size of the compressor and system can be reduced, making it easier to install and more economical.

⑤ The adiabatic index of refrigerant is required to be small. The smaller the adiabatic index is, the lower the discharge temperature of the compressor is, and the more beneficial it is to improve the volumetric efficiency and lubrication of the compressor.

(1) Physical and chemical requirements.

① The viscosity and density of the refrigerant should be as small as possible. Low viscosity and density can reduce the flow resistance of refrigerant in the refrigeration system, which is conducive to the circulation of refrigerant and reduce the power consumption of compressor, and can reduce the pipe diameter of the system and reduce the use of metal.

② The thermal conductivity and heat release coefficient of refrigerant shall be as large as possible. To improve the heat transfer efficiency of the heat exchanger and reduce the heat transfer area.

③ Refrigerant has certain water solubility. Refrigerant should be free of moisture, but in fact, a very small amount of moisture is unavoidable in the refrigeration system. If the refrigerant can dissolve a small amount of water, when the evaporation temperature is lower than 0 ℃, the system is not easy to produce "ice jam" and affect the normal operation of the refrigeration device.

④ The refrigerant has good thermochemical stability and is not easy to decompose at high temperature. When refrigerant is mixed with oil and water, it shall not have obvious corrosive effect on metal materials. The swelling effect on the sealing material of the refrigerator should be as small as possible.

(3) Requirements for safety and environment

① Refrigerant is required to be non-flammable and non-explosive within the working temperature range. Flammable and explosive refrigerants should be avoided in general occasions.

② Refrigerant is required to be non-toxic or low toxic and has little impact on biological environment. Because some refrigerants have certain toxicity and danger, it is required that the selected refrigerants should have the characteristics of easy leak detection to ensure the safety of operation. It is required that in case of contact between leaked refrigerant and food, the food will not change color, taste or be contaminated. Refrigerant used for air conditioning shall be harmless to human health and have no irritating smell.

③ Refrigerant shall have good electrical insulation performance. In the sealed compressor system, the motor coil is in direct contact with the refrigerant and lubricating oil. The refrigerant with good electrical insulation can ensure the safe operation of the system.

④ Refrigerant is required to have less impact on the global greenhouse effect and no damage to the ozone layer in the atmosphere.

2) Type and code of refrigerant

(1) Type of refrigerant.

There are many substances that can be used as refrigerants, and their types are as follows:

① Inorganic compounds, such as water, ammonia, carbon dioxide, etc.

② Fluorine, chlorine and bromine derivatives of saturated hydrocarbons, commonly known as Freon, are mainly derivatives of methane and ethane, such as R12, R22, R134a, etc.

③ Saturated hydrocarbons, such as propane, isobutane, etc.

④ Unsaturated hydrocarbons, such as ethylene, propylene, etc.

⑤ Azeotropic mixed refrigerant, such as R502, etc.

⑥ Non-azeotropic mixed refrigerant, such as R407c, etc.

Generally, refrigerants are divided into three categories according to their standard evaporation temperature, namely, high temperature, medium temperature and low temperature refrigerants. The so-called standard evaporation temperature refers to the evaporation temperature under the standard atmospheric pressure, that is, the boiling point.

① High temperature (low pressure) refrigerant. Standard evaporation temperature $t_s > 0\ ^\circ C$, condensation pressure $p_k \leqslant 0.3\ \text{MPa}$. Commonly used high-temperature refrigerants include R123, etc.

② Medium temperature (medium pressure) refrigerant. $0\ ^\circ C > t_s > -60\ ^\circ C$, $0.3\ \text{MPa} < p_c < 2.0\ \text{MPa}$. Commonly used medium-temperature refrigerants include ammonia, R12, R22, R134a, propane, etc.

③ Low temperature (high pressure) refrigerant. $t_s \leqslant -60\ ^\circ C$. Commonly used cryogenic refrigerants include R13, ethylene, R744, etc.

(2) Refrigerant code.

For the convenience of writing, the Chinese national standard GB 7778—2017 specifies the codes of various general refrigerants to replace their chemical name, molecular formula or commercial name. The letter R and a group of numbers or letters after it are specified as the refrigerant code in the standard. The letter R represents refrigerant, and the following numbers or letters are written according to certain rules according to the refrigerant type and molecular formula composition.

① Inorganic compound.

Inorganic compounds used as refrigerants include ammonia, carbon dioxide, water, etc. For such refrigerants, the first digit after the code "R" is 7, and the number after 7 is the integral part of the molecular weight of the substance. For example, the molecular formula of ammonia is NH_3, the integral part of molecular weight is 17, its code is R717, and the codes of carbon dioxide and water are R744 and R718 respectively.

② Halogenated hydrocarbon.

Halogenated hydrocarbon (freon) is the general name of fluorine, chlorine and bromine derivatives of saturated hydrocarbon. At present, methane and ethane derivatives are mainly used as refrigerants. The molecular formula of saturated hydrocarbon is C_mH_{2m+2}. The general formula of Freon is $C_mH_nF_xCl_yBr_z$, and the relationship between its atomic number m, n, x, y, z is: $2m+2=n+x+y+z$.

The code of Freon is "R ×××B ×" express. The first digit after R is $(m-1)$, which is omitted when it is zero; The second digit is $(n+1)$; The third digit is x; The number after B is z. If z is zero, it is omitted with the letter B. For example, the molecular formula of difluorodichloromethane is CF_2Cl_2, and the compound's $m=1$, $n=0$, $x=2$, $z=0$, so the first digit after R $(m-1)=0$, the second digit $(n+1)=1$, the third digit $x=2$, and the number after B $z=0$, so the code of CF_2Cl_2 is R12. The molecular formula of monochloromethane is CHF_2Cl, its $(m-1)=0$, $(n+1)=2$, $x=2$, $z=0$, so the code is R22. The molecular formula of bromotrichloromethane is CF_3Br, $(m-1)=0$, $(n+1)=1$, $x=3$, $z=1$, and the code is R13B1.

③ Hydrocarbons.

Hydrocarbons used as refrigerants include alkanes (such as methane CH_4, ethane C_2H_6, propane C_3H_8) and alkenes (such as ethylene C_2H_4, propylene C_3H_6).

For methane, ethane and propane, the code representation method is the same as Freon. If methane CH_4, $m=1$, $n=4$, $x=0$, $z=0$, then $(m-1)=0$, $(n+1)=5$, $x=0$, $z=0$, the code is R50; Ethane C_2H_6, $(m-1)=1$, $(n+1)=7$, $x=0$, $z=0$, code R170. However, butane is written as R600 instead of following the above rules. In addition, for isomers, add lowercase letters "a", "b" and "c" after the code, such as the code of isobutane is R600a.

For ethylene and propylene, write a "1" after R, and the other numbers are written according to the numbering rules of Freon. If ethylene C_2H_4, $m=2$, $n=4$, $x=0$, $z=0$, then $(m-1)=1$, $(n+1)=5$, $x=0$, $z=0$, the code is R1150. Propylene C_3H_6, $m=3$, $n=6$, $x=0$, $z=0$, then $(m-1)=2$, $(n+1)=7$, $x=0$, $z=0$, code is R1270.

④ Mixed working medium.

The mixed working medium is a mixture of two or more refrigerants dissolved with each other in a certain proportion, which is divided into azeotropic and non-azeotropic working medium.

The nature of azeotropic mixture is the same as that of pure working medium. When evaporating or condensing under constant pressure, the evaporating temperature or condensing temperature remains unchanged, and its gas and liquid phases have the same composition. The number after the azeotropic refrigerant code R is numbered in the order of use. For example, the code of the first named azeotropic refrigerant mixture is R500, and the later named ones are R501, R502,..., and R506 in order.

When the non-azeotropic working medium evaporates or condenses under constant pressure, its evaporation temperature or condensation temperature and the components of gas and liquid phases cannot be kept constant. Because the non-azeotropic working medium will display different thermodynamic properties with different components and mixing ratios, it can meet various refrigeration requirements. The number after the code R of non-azeotropic refrigerant mixture is numbered in the order of use. For example, the code of the first named non-azeotropic refrigerant mixture is R400, and the later ones are indicated by the codes R401,

R402, ⋯ , R407 in order. In order to distinguish refrigerant mixtures with the same components but different proportions (mass fraction), capital letters A, B, C and other suffixes shall be added after the identification number.

3) Properties of common refrigerants

At present, ammonia, freon and mixed refrigerant are widely used in vapor compression refrigeration devices. R22 and R407c are commonly used in passenger car air conditioners.

(1) Ammonia (R717)

Ammonia is an inorganic compound refrigerant. Ammonia has good thermodynamic performance. Its advantages are moderate evaporation pressure and condensation pressure, and large refrigerating capacity per unit volume. The boiling point of ammonia under standard atmospheric pressure is −33.4 °C. When the refrigeration temperature is 5 ~ 30 °C, the evaporation pressure is always greater than the atmospheric pressure, and no vacuum will be formed in the evaporator. When water is used as the cooling medium, the condensation pressure shall not exceed 1.5 MPa.

Ammonia has strong water solubility, and "ice jam" phenomenon will not occur in the system. It is not corrosive to steel, but corrosive to copper and copper alloys (except phosphor bronze) when ammonia contains water. Ammonia is a refrigerant that is slightly soluble in lubricating oil. When there is a lot of lubricating oil in the system, the density of oil is greater than that of ammonia liquid, and it will deposit at the bottom of the liquid reservoir or evaporator and other equipment during the system operation. In order to reduce the oil scale formed by the lubricating oil on the surface of the heat exchanger, the lubricating oil deposited in the system should be discharged regularly, and try to avoid too much lubricating oil entering the system.

The disadvantage of ammonia is that it is toxic, has a strong pungent smell, and can burn and explode. Once ammonia leaks, it will pollute the air and food, and irritate people's eyes and respiratory organs. When ammonia liquid touches the skin, it will form "frostbite". If the volume content of ammonia in the air reaches 0.5% ~ 0.6%, people can be poisoned if they stay in it for half an hour, and explosion can be caused when the volume content of ammonia in the air is 16% ~ 25%. Therefore, it is not easy to use in the air conditioning device of passenger cars. It is mainly used as the working medium of large cold storage, but less used in small refrigeration devices.

(2) Freon

Freon is one of the most widely used refrigerants. It is odorless, not easy to burn, and less toxic. However, Freon containing chlorine atoms can decompose highly toxic phosgene ($COCl_2$) when exposed to open fire; It is highly permeable, easy to leak and difficult to find; Poor heat transfer, high density, high viscosity and poor flow performance; Low adiabatic index and low final compression temperature; The refrigerating capacity per unit volume is small.

Most Freons are soluble in lubricating oil but not in water. In order to avoid the phenomenon of "ice jam", a dryer should be installed in the refrigeration system. When Freon does not contain water, it has no corrosive effect on metals, and has swelling effect on natural rubber and plastics. When freon contains water, it can decompose into hydrogen chloride and hydrogen fluoride, which not only corrodes metal, but also may produce "copper plating phenomenon". Copper plating refers to the phenomenon that when hydrogen chloride contacts the copper surface, copper chloride will be produced under certain conditions. Copper chloride will contact with hot iron surface, and copper and iron ions will replace each other to precipitate copper ions on the iron surface. If copper plating occurs, it will damage the tightness of the suction and exhaust valves of the compressor and change the clearance between the bearing and the journal, which is not conducive to the normal operation of the compressor.

Freon leak detection can be performed with soap water, halogen lamp, etc. Soap water is suitable for system installation and inspection in case of obvious leakage. A small amount of leakage can be checked by halogen lamp. With the increase of leakage, the flame color of halogen lamp changes from light green to dark green to purple. Electronic leak detector can be used for minor leakage, which has high sensitivity.

The main characteristics of several Freons are described below.

① Freon 12 (CCl_2F_2).

R12 is widely used in small- and medium-sized refrigeration devices, such as refrigerators, automobile air conditioners, dehumidifiers, small refrigerators, etc. R12 has a freezing point of -155 °C and a boiling point of -29.8 °C under standard atmospheric pressure. When water or air is used as the cooling medium, the condensation pressure is not more than 1.2 MPa, so it is applicable to the air cooling refrigerator system.

R12 is easily soluble in lubricating oil. It can be dissolved with any proportion of mineral lubricating oil at normal temperature. There will be no stratification in the condenser, and oil scale will not form on the heat transfer surface to affect heat transfer. In order to avoid the excessive content of lubricating oil in the evaporator, which will lead to the increase of evaporation temperature, the reduction of heat transfer coefficient and the reduction of cooling capacity, the non-full liquid evaporator is usually used to make the refrigerant liquid enter from the top of the evaporator and the steam flow out from the bottom, so that the lubricating oil can return to the compressor smoothly with R12. R12 has poor water solubility. In order to avoid "ice jam", the water content of the refrigerant in the system should be strictly controlled to not exceed 0.0025%. Before filling R12, the system must be strictly dried, and a dryer should be installed in the system or on the filling pipe.

R12 is one of the first refrigerants to be banned because of its serious damage to the atmospheric ozone layer.

② Freon 22 ($CHClF_2$).

R22 is mainly used for piston refrigeration compressor, air conditioning refrigeration and lowering temperature. R22 is also commonly used as refrigerant in passenger car air conditioning devices. R22 has a boiling point of -40.8 °C and a freezing point of -160 °C under standard atmospheric pressure. The condensing pressure and unit volume refrigerating capacity at normal temperature are close to ammonia. R22 is colorless, odorless, non-flammable, non-explosive, and safe and reliable to use.

R22 can partially dissolve with lubricating oil. Generally, it can dissolve with refrigerant in the condenser to form a solution, but in the evaporator, due to the low temperature, the lubricating oil can only be partially dissolved in the refrigerant, resulting in layering. The upper layer is mainly composed of lubricating oil and the lower layer is mainly composed of refrigerant. In order to make the lubricating oil return to the compressor smoothly, an oil separator shall be set at the low pressure part of the system. R22 has greater water solubility than R12, but it is still a refrigerant slightly soluble in water. Therefore, the water content of the refrigerant in the system must still be controlled below 0.0025%, and a dryer should be installed in the system.

R22 has a much less destructive effect on the ozone layer than R12, so it is being used as a transitional substitute for some banned refrigerants on some occasions, but will eventually be banned.

③ R407c.

R407c is made by mixing R32 refrigerant, R125 refrigerant and R134a refrigerant in a certain proportion. It is an environmentally friendly refrigerant that does not destroy the ozone layer. At standard atmospheric pressure, its boiling point is $-43.4 \sim 36.1$ °C. That is, the temperature slipped from -36.1 °C to -43.4 °C. However, when applied to air conditioning system, its steam pressure is 10% higher than R22. Under the condition of air conditioning, its refrigerating capacity and coefficient per unit volume are 5% lower than R22; At low temperature, the refrigeration coefficient has little change, but the refrigerating capacity per unit volume is 20% lower.

R407c has very similar characteristics and performance to R22, so it becomes a long-term substitute for R22, and is used in various air conditioning systems and non-centrifugal refrigeration systems. R407c can be used in the original R22 system. Without redesigning the system, only a small number of components of the original system need to be replaced, and the mineral refrigerant oil in the original system can be replaced with lubricating oil that can be miscible with R407c. R407c can be directly filled to realize the environmental protection replacement of the original equipment.

Because R407c is a mixed non-azeotropic working medium, R407c must be filled with liquid in order to ensure that its mixing composition does not change. If the R407c system has refrigerant leakage and the performance of the system has changed significantly, the remaining R407c in the system cannot be recycled, so the remaining R407c in the system must be emptied and refilled with new R407c refrigerant.

R407c has poor heat transfer performance, which directly affects the change of refrigerant. R407c cannot be miscible with mineral lubricating oil, but can be dissolved in polyester synthetic lubricating oil, which has high requirements for drying.

4) On the substitution of freon

The use of freon refrigerant has promoted the rapid development of refrigeration technology. Because of its many advantages, Freon has developed rapidly. At present, R11, R12, R13, R22, R113, R114 are widely used etc.

Freon is the general name of new compounds that are produced by partially or completely replacing hydrogen in saturated hydrocarbons with fluorine, chlorine, bromine, etc. Among them, CFC_S, which do not contain hydrogen, are called chlorofluorocarbons, and are written as CFC_S, which are harmful substances and are restricted and prohibited substances; Hydrogen-containing CFC_S are called hydrochlorinated carbon, written as HCFC, which are low-pollution substances and belong to transitional substances; CFC_S without chlorine are called hydrofluorocarbons, written as HCF, and are pollution-free substances.

The atmosphere on the earth's surface is divided into several layers according to its height, and there is an ozone layer at a height of about 25 km. The ozone layer effectively reduces the radiation damage of solar ultraviolet radiation on the earth's surface. It forms a protective shield for living things and humans on the earth, and is a natural barrier. CFC_S substances have a serious destructive effect on the ozone in the atmosphere and the ozone layer in the upper atmosphere of the earth, and CFC_S has a life span of tens to hundreds of years in the atmosphere, so its destructive effect on the ozone layer is cumulative and persistent. The destruction of the ozone layer increases the ultraviolet radiation intensity of the sun on the earth's surface. CFC_S dispersed in the atmosphere not only has a destructive effect on the ozone layer, but also can stably absorb solar heat, leading to the rise of atmospheric temperature, which is to aggravate the greenhouse effect. It is estimated that ozone is reduced by 1% and ultraviolet radiation is increased by 2%. The increase of ultraviolet radiation will destroy the human immune system, greatly reduce the body's resistance, and increase the number of skin cancer and other diseases; Aggravate the global greenhouse effect, increase the world average temperature, sea level and accelerate desertification; Harm many living things on the earth and destroy the ecological balance. It has been suggested that the reduction of the ozone layer to 1/5 of the original level will be the critical point for the survival of the earth. Therefore, reducing and prohibiting the production and use of CFC_S has become the consensus of the international community.

Since the 1980s, countries around the world, especially the United States, Japan and

Western European countries, have invested a lot of human and financial resources to develop and research alternatives to CFC_S. With regard to the replacement of CFC_S and the reduction of CFC_S damage to the atmospheric ozone layer, the use of CFC_S refrigerants has been banned and the use of HCFC refrigerants or non-azeotropic refrigerant mixtures composed of them has been restricted.

Because HFC substances do not contain chlorine, they have no destructive effect on the atmospheric ozone layer, and the greenhouse effect is relatively small. At present, HFC (hydrofluorocarbon) is widely used as refrigerant, such as HFC134A (R134a) refrigerant and HFC407C (R407c) refrigerant.

2. Compressor Lubricating Oil

Special refrigerant oil is used for compressor lubrication. In the refrigeration system, the refrigerant oil and the refrigerant are mixed together, so there are special requirements for the physical and chemical properties of the refrigerant oil. In the application, the viscosity, freezing point, flash point, water content, paraffin content and chemical stability of the appropriate refrigerant oil are selected to reduce its impact on the operation of the refrigeration system. 18 # refrigerant oil is used in the system using R12 refrigerant, and 25 # refrigerant oil is used in the system using ammonia and R22.

1) Characteristics of refrigerant oil

(1) Viscosity.

The viscosity of the refrigerant oil is used to measure the viscosity of the refrigerant oil. The viscosity is related to the type and temperature of the refrigerant oil. When the temperature rises, the viscosity decreases, and the viscosity is also related to the refrigerant used by the compressor. If R12 and refrigerant oil dissolve each other to dilute the concentration of refrigerant oil, and the viscosity would be too small, then the bearing would not be able to establish the required oil film. But the viscosity cannot be too large. If the viscosity is too large, which would not only produce more foam when the compressor starts, but also increase the resistance, making it difficult to start the compressor. Therefore, the viscosity of lubricating oil should be moderate.

(2) Freezing point and cloud point.

When the temperature of the refrigerant oil decreases, the fluidity becomes worse with the increase of viscosity. When it cools to a certain temperature, the flow stops, and the temperature at this time is called the freezing point of the refrigerant oil.

When the temperature drops to a certain value, paraffin will precipitate from the refrigerant oil, and flocs will appear in the refrigerant oil. At this time, the temperature is called the cloud point of the refrigerant oil. The precipitation of paraffin will not only make the oil turbid, but also block the refrigeration pipeline and affect the function of components, making the refrigeration system unable to work normally.

(3) Flash point.

Heat the refrigerant oil until the generated oil vapor can flash when it contacts with the flame. At this time, the temperature is called the flash point of the refrigerant oil. The flash point of the selected refrigerant oil must be 15 ~ 30 °C higher than the exhaust temperature to avoid combustion and coking of the refrigerant oil.

(4) Breakdown voltage.

The refrigeration lubricating oil used in closed compressors shall have voltage resistance. The breakdown voltage is an indicator of the electrical insulation performance of refrigerant oil and refrigerant. The insulation performance of pure refrigerant oil is good, but when there are impurities such as water and dust in the oil, the insulation performance will be reduced. The breakdown voltage of refrigerant oil is generally required to be above 25 kV. Refrigerant also requires good electrical insulation.

(5) Solubility with refrigerant.

The solubility of refrigerant in lubricating oil can be divided into complete dissolution, slight dissolution and complete dissolution.

When the refrigerant and lubricating oil are completely dissolved, it can create a good condition for the lubrication of the machine parts. It is not easy to form oil film on the heat exchange surface of the condenser and other heat exchangers, and the heat transfer effect is good. However, when the refrigerant and lubricating oil are mutually soluble, the evaporation temperature of the refrigerant will increase, the viscosity of the lubricating oil will decrease, and the foam will increase when the refrigerant boils. The unstable liquid level in the evaporator and the increased oil consumption of the refrigerator during operation will also make it difficult to discharge the oil in the system.

When the refrigerant and lubricating oil are completely insoluble, the evaporation temperature of the refrigeration system is relatively stable. In the refrigeration equipment, the refrigerant and lubricating oil are easily separated, and the oil film is formed on the heat exchange surface of the heat exchanger, which affects the heat exchange.

The advantages and disadvantages of refrigerants slightly soluble in oil are between the two.

2) Deterioration of refrigerant oil

The deterioration of refrigerant oil is usually due to the mixing of water, oxidation reaction, and the mixing of several different brands of refrigerant oil, thus resulting in chemical reaction and sediment formation, and affecting the lubrication of the compressor.

Generally, the quality of refrigerant oil can be judged directly from the appearance color and smell. When the refrigerant oil deteriorates, the color becomes darker, and the oil drops on the white blotting paper. If the central part of the oil drop is not black, it means that the refrigerant oil has not deteriorated, and vice versa. If there is water in the oil, the transparency of the oil will be reduced. If accurate judgment is required, specific equipment is also required for detection.

【Task Training】

(1) Briefly describe the working principle of steam compressor and the basic composition of refrigeration system.

(2) Why should a compressor be used in a refrigerator to increase the pressure of steam?

(3) Briefly describe the working principle of heat pump.

(4) Briefly describe the cycle process of absorption refrigeration.

(5) Briefly describe the characteristics of R22 refrigerant.

(6) What are the thermodynamic requirements for refrigerants?

(7) How to choose the right refrigerant?

(8) What characteristics should be paid attention to when selecting compressor lubricating oil?

Project 4

Air Conditioning and Refrigeration System of Passenger Cars

【 Chinese Railway Culture 】

The History of Railway Development in China 4: China's High-speed Railway Benefiting Mankind

In 1978, Deng Xiaoping visited Japan and took the high-speed train on the Shinkansen Railway. The high-speed railway thus officially entered the view of the Chinese public. In the 1980s, China's railway faced the dilemma of insufficient transportation capacity. The train speed was less than 120 km/h, and the contradiction between passenger and freight transportation increased. The demand for train speed increase was quite urgent. However, limited by the economic, technological and market environment at that time, China's high-speed railway development needed to be carried out in stages.

1. Development history of China's high-speed railway

In the 1990s, China began to tackle and test high-speed railway technology, and took Guangzhou—Shenzhen Railway as the pilot line for quasi-high-speed transformation. On August 28, 1998, Guangzhou—Shenzhen Railway was the first railway in China to reach the high-speed target with a maximum speed of 200 km/h. On August 16, 1999, the construction of Qinhuangdao—Shenyang dedicated passenger line was started, as the first test line of China's high-speed wheel-rail multiple units.

On March 1, 2001, the construction of the Shanghai maglev train demonstration operation line was started, and was completed on December 31, 2002, with a design speed of 430 km/h. It is the first high-speed rail system in China. On August 1, 2008, the Beijing—Tianjin inter-city railway was put into operation, becoming the first high-speed railway with a design speed of 350 km/h. On December 26, 2009, the Wuhan—Guangzhou section of the Beijing—Guangzhou High-speed Railway was put into operation. The maximum operating speed of the train was 350 km/h, which broke the bottleneck of China's railway Spring Festival transport for the first time, and became a symbol of China's official entry into the era of high-speed railway.

On December 28, 2017, the Shijiazhuang—Jinan High-speed Railway was put into operation. So far, the "four horizontal and four vertical" fast track of China's railway has been completed and opened to traffic. On August 30, 2022, China's first sea-crossing high-speed railway, the new Fuzhou—Xiamen Railway, was laid and connected. In 2022, the operating mileage of China's railways will be 155,000 kilometers, including 42,000 kilometers of high-speed railways, ranking first in the world.

2. Development history of EMU in China

Since 2004, China has introduced mature EMUs from Japan, France, Germany and other countries. The representative models are CRH1, CRH2, CRH3, and CRH5, which helped the sixth railway speed increase in 2007.

On February 26, 2008, China launched the research on high-speed EMU trains of 350 km/h and above with independent intellectual property rights. The second generation EMU trains are named CRH380 series, called "Harmony". CRH380A (L) multiple unit is designed and manufactured by Qingdao Sifang Company. CRH380B (L) is developed by Changchun Bus Factory and Tangshan Bus Factory. The continuous operating speed of "Harmony" is 380 km/h, and the actual operating speed is 350 km/h.

Figure 4-1　Fuxing EMU

In 2012, China's standard EMU "Fuxing" officially entered the research and development stage. On June 30,2015, the Chinese standard EMU developed by Sifang and Changke was born. On June 25,2017, the Chinese standard EMU was officially named "Fuxing". At the initial stage of "Fuxing", there were mainly CR400AF and CR400BF, and later CR300 and CR200 series were developed. The operating speed of CR400 series is 350km/h, that of CR300 series is 250 km/h, and that of CR200 series is 160 km/h. Different speed grades of 350 km/h, 250 km/h and 160 km/h, different marshalling forms of 8 short marshalling, 16 long marshalling and 17 super long marshalling, different power traction modes of power concentration and power dispersion, the Chinese standard EMU family has been growing and has formed a series of products.

3. China's high-speed railway benefiting mankind

The opening of the China—Laos Railway is the first time that China's standard EMU has gone abroad. According to the specific situation of Laos, the adaptive design optimization of the EMU is carried out to provide convenient and comfortable travel mode for the Lao people. The China—Thailand Railway is an important project for China and Thailand to jointly build the "the Belt and Road" initiative. This first standard gauge high-speed railway in Thailand uses the Chinese standard EMU technology. For this railway, many Thai people have begun to expect that "from Bangkok to Nakhon Ratchasima, the China—Thailand railway will stop in many places, and will bring great traffic convenience to these places and promote local economic development after opening to traffic."

Relying on the technical system of high-speed railway construction and equipment manufacturing with independent intellectual property rights, China's standard EMU has not only driven into the cold and plateau area, but also achieved the goal of crossing the sea without slowing down, and also contributed to the Chinese plan for the world's high-speed railway, benefiting all mankind.

【 Project Description 】

The refrigeration system of passenger car air conditioning device is composed of compressor, evaporator, condenser, automatic controller and auxiliary equipment. This project mainly studies the structure, working principle, maintenance methods of these equipment, as well as the basic operation methods of cleaning, charging and discharging refrigerant, leak detection and air tightness test of the refrigeration system. Through the study of this project, students will be able to maintain and repair the air conditioning and refrigeration system of passenger cars, clean the refrigeration system, detect the leakage of refrigerant, and test the air tightness, so as to ensure the normal operation of the air conditioning device of passenger cars.

【Project Objectives】

1. Knowledge objectives

(1) Master the structure and working principle of the compressor.

(2) Master the structure and working principle of evaporator and condenser.

(3) Master the structure and working principle of automatic controller and auxiliary equipment.

(4) Master the refrigerant leak detection and air tightness test.

2. Capability objectives

(1) Be able to carry out routine maintenance of compressor, evaporator and condenser.

(2) Be able to deeply understand the role of automatic controller and auxiliary equipment in the refrigeration system.

(3) Capable of cleaning the refrigeration system, refrigerant leak detection and air tightness test.

3. Quality objectives

(1) Use and care for the equipment correctly.

(2) Cultivate the awareness of standardized operation and safe production.

(3) Cultivate team spirit.

Task 1 Refrigeration Compressor

【Task Objective】

(1) Understand the type and structure of refrigeration compressor.

(2) Master the working principle of piston and scroll compressors.

(3) Be able to maintain and repair the compressor.

【Knowledge Reserve】

The refrigeration compressor is the power component of the vapor compression refrigeration device. It converts electrical energy into mechanical energy and compresses the refrigerant vapor. It is the power source to promote the continuous circulation of refrigerant in the refrigeration system. In the air conditioning equipment of railway passenger cars, the compressor mainly adopts the fully closed piston compressor, and some also adopt the scroll compressor and other compressors.

1. Type of Refrigeration Compressor

1) Classification according to working principle

Refrigeration compressors can be divided into volumetric type and speed type according to different working principles.

(1) Volumetric compressor.

Volumetric compressors complete the compression and transmission of gas by changing the working volume. Volumetric compressors mainly include piston type, scroll type, screw type and rolling rotor type (also known as rotary type) compressors. The piston compressor changes the working volume by reciprocating movement of the piston in the cylinder; The scroll compressor changes the working volume through the relative rotation of the two scroll discs to change the crescent shape formed; Screw and rotary compressors change the working volume by rotating the screw or rotor in the cylinder.

Rotary compressors have been widely used in room air conditioners at home and abroad, almost replacing piston compressors. Japan has also begun to use rotary compressors in air conditioning devices of railway passenger cars. Compared with piston compressor, rotary compressor has the advantages of simple structure, small volume, light weight, high volumetric efficiency, stable operation, low noise and vibration, and strong reliability. However, rotary compressor also has some disadvantages, such as high machining accuracy of main parts, high insulation level of motor, large starting torque, etc. With the development of high-tech, these problems have been basically solved, so the rotary compressor is developing rapidly in China.

At present, closed screw compressor and scroll compressor are also used in air conditioning devices of some railway passenger cars at home and abroad. This course mainly discusses the working process, performance and structure of piston compressor and scroll compressor.

(2) Speed compressor.

The speed-type compressor increases the speed of the gas in the high-speed rotating impeller, and then converts the kinetic energy of the gas into pressure energy through the guide, thus completing the task of gas compression and transportation. At present, the commonly used speed-type compressor is centrifugal compressor.

2) Classified by refrigeration capacity

Refrigeration compressors are divided into small, medium and large types according to the refrigeration capacity under standard working conditions.

The refrigeration capacity under standard working conditions is smaller than 58 kW; The refrigeration capacity under standard working conditions is medium in the range of 58 ~ 580 kW; The refrigeration capacity under standard working conditions is larger than 580 kW.

Piston compressors have a long history of development and rich experience in design, manufacturing and operation, and are still widely used and developed in various fields. The continuous progress of refrigeration compressors is also reflected in the diversification of their types. All kinds of compressor types other than piston type, such as scroll type, centrifugal type, screw type, rolling rotor type and scroll type, are being developed effectively and have their own characteristics, which are impressive. This provides more possibilities for technicians engaged in refrigeration engineering to choose the type of refrigeration compressor. In this context, the use range of piston compressor will be affected and gradually reduce, which is more obvious in the range of large cooling capacity. However, in the range of medium and small cooling capacity, piston compressor is still the main type in practice.

With the continuous improvement of the reliability and durability of the compressor itself and the pursuit of compactness and lightweight of the compressor, it is a tendency for the refrigeration compressor to gradually develop from the open type to the closed type. For example, in Japan, more than 90% of the piston compressors with power between 15~22 kW have achieved semi-closed; For ships, vehicles and remote areas that cannot rely on external maintenance, the open compressor for on-site maintenance still has its advantages. For small refrigeration compressors, industry insiders generally call the open piston compressor the first generation, the fully closed piston compressor the second generation, the rotary (sliding vane) compressor the third generation, the scroll compressor the fourth generation, and the annular compressor being developed is the fifth generation of small refrigeration compressor.

2. Piston Compressor

1) Working principle of piston compressor

There are many structural forms of piston refrigeration compressor, but its basic composition (see Figure 4-1-3) usually includes the following parts: the body component composed of the body and various cover plates; The working space with variable volume is composed of cylinders, pistons, suction and exhaust valve plates, etc; Transmission mechanism composed of crankshaft, connecting rod, etc; Lubrication and sealing facilities composed of oil pump, shaft seal, etc. (small compressors have no oil pump, and closed compressors have no shaft seal).

The work of the compressor is to input electric energy into the compressor motor, and the motor shaft drives the compressor crankshaft to rotate. The crankshaft drives the piston through the connecting rod to reciprocate in the cylinder. At the same time, the suction and exhaust valve plates on the top of the cylinder cooperate with the piston to open or close, so that the compressor can complete the compression of refrigerant vapor. Every time the crankshaft rotates, the piston makes a reciprocating motion, and the compressor completes a working cycle.

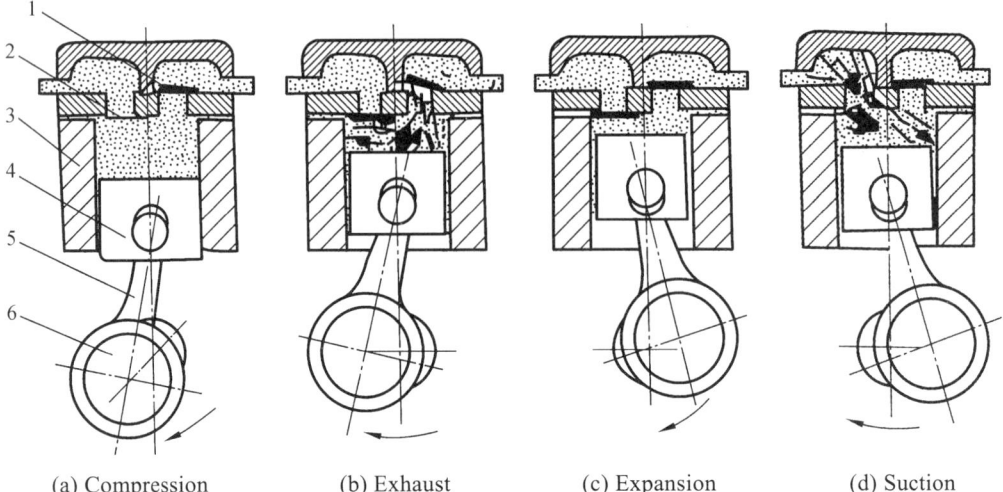

(a) Compression　　　(b) Exhaust　　　(c) Expansion　　　(d) Suction

1—Exhaust valve plate; 2—Suction valve plate; 3—Cylinder; 4—Piston; 5—Connecting rod; 6—Crankshaft.

Figure 4-1-3　Basic composition of piston compressor

2) Classification of piston compressors

(1) Classification according to sealing structure.

From the perspective of sealing structure adopted to prevent refrigerant leakage, refrigeration compressors can be divided into open type, semi-closed type and fully closed type.

① Open compressor.

The power input of the open compressor is carried out through the main shaft extending out of the body. The compressor and motor are separated, and they are connected by the transmission device (coupling, transmission belt or gearbox). In order to prevent the leakage of refrigerant vapor and the infiltration of outside air, the shaft sealing device preventing leakage must be used on the extended part of the main shaft to seal. Because it is impossible for the shaft seal device to achieve absolute reliable sealing, it is difficult to avoid the leakage of refrigerant and the infiltration of outside air from the open refrigeration compressor.

② Closed compressor.

The motor and compressor used for the enclosed compressor are assembled in a body, and share a main shaft, which does not extend out of the body, so there is no need to set shaft seal device, which reduces the possibility of leakage and reduces noise. The use of inhaled low temperature refrigerant to cool the motor is conducive to the miniaturization and lightweight of the machine. However, due to the direct contact between the refrigerant and the motor, the insulation material of the motor is required to be resistant to oil and refrigerant corrosion, and the oil pump of the compressor can work in positive and reverse directions.

③ Semi-enclosed compressor.

The difference between semi-closed compressor and fully closed compressor is that the body and cylinder head of the former can be disassembled if necessary after assembly, and its sealing surface is connected by flange and sealed by gasket; The latter is that the compressor and motor are all installed in a closed enclosure, and the enclosure is welded and cannot be removed, which can greatly reduce the weight of the compressor. However, because the closed compressor is not easy to disassemble and repair, the requirements for the processing, assembly quality, reliability and service life of the machine parts are high. They should be able to guarantee a service life of more than 10 years.

(2) Classification by cylinder arrangement.

Compressors can be divided into horizontal type, vertical type and angle type according to cylinder arrangement, as shown in Figure 4-1-4. The cylinder arrangement of the compressor directly affects the overall dimension and weight.

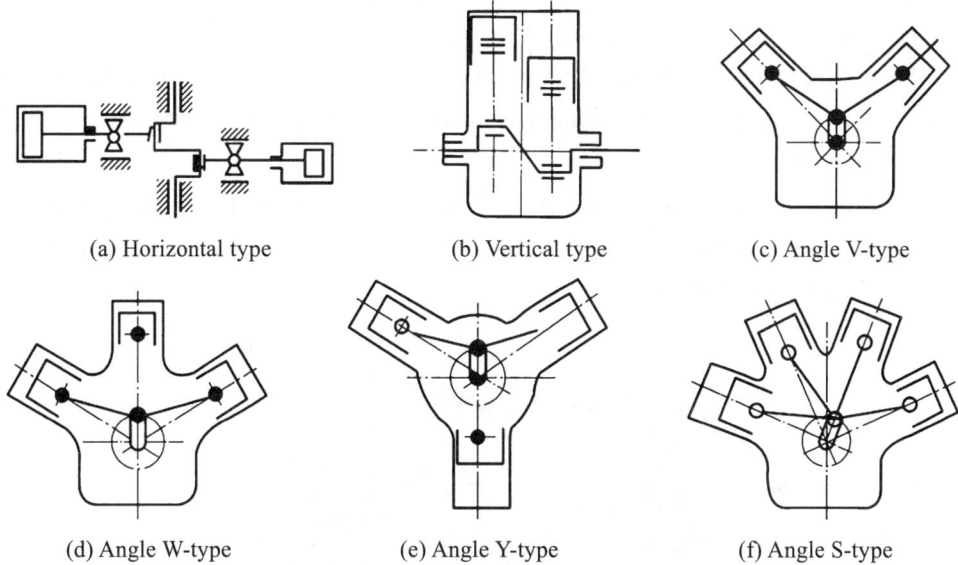

Figure 4-1-4 Compressor cylinder arrangement

① Horizontal compressor.

The cylinder axis of the horizontal compressor is horizontally arranged. This form is more common in large refrigeration compressors, and also used in fully enclosed refrigeration compressors.

② Vertical compressor.

The cylinder axis of vertical compressor is arranged vertically. Considering the compactness of the compressor structure, the smoothness of operation and the size of vibration, the double-cylinder vertical type is the common form.

③ Angle compressor.

The cylinder axis of the angle compressor is arranged at a certain included angle, which can be divided into V-type, W-type, Y-type and S-type (fan type). Angular arrangement can make the compressor have the advantages of compact structure, small volume and floor area, small vibration, stable operation, etc., so it is widely used by modern medium and small high-speed multi-cylinder compressors, and is a typical compressor cylinder arrangement.

3) Structure of piston compressor

In the refrigeration system of the unit-type passenger car air conditioning unit, the main engine is totally enclosed compressor, mainly including 505FH2-H, JH514YZ and JH519YZE made in Japan, and COPELAND made in the United States. The structure of JH514YZ compressor is introduced as an example.

JH514YZ compressor is a totally enclosed compressor produced by Mitsubishi Electric Company of Japan. It is widely used in KLD29 unit air conditioning unit. Its main technical parameters are:

Cylinder diameter: 44.45 mm, Refrigerant: R22, Piston stroke: 24 mm, Refrigeration capacity: 12,767 W (for air conditioning), Number of cylinders: 3, Motor power: 3.75 kW, Speed: 2,880 r/min.

The structure of JH514YZ compressor is shown in Figure 4-1-5. It is mainly composed of casing, body, motor, crankshaft, connecting rod, piston, cylinder, air valve and exhaust muffler. Its working process is as follows:

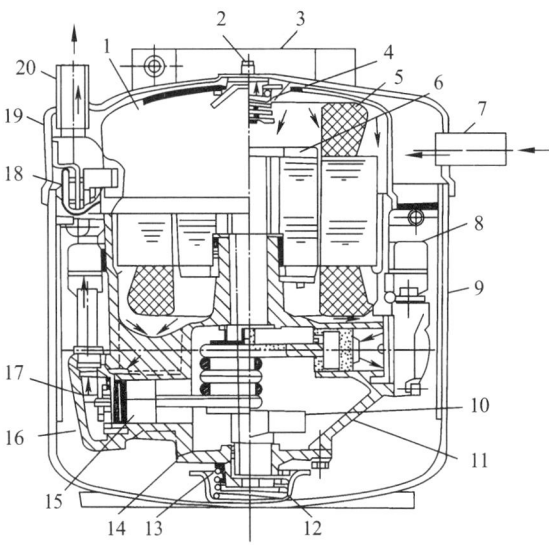

1—Motor shell; 2—Sling; 3—Terminal box; 4—Upper spring; 5—Stator coil; 6—Rotor; 7—Suction pipe;
8—Exhaust muffler; 9—Lower shell; 10—Crankshaft; 11—Crankcase; 12—Lower spring;
13—Lower bearing; 14—Support frame; 15—Piston connecting rod;
16—Cylinder head; 17—High voltage chamber;
18—Transverse spring; 19—Upper shell;
20—Exhaust pipe.

Figure 4-1-5　Structure of JH514YZ Compressor

When the compressor is working, the low-pressure refrigerant vapor with lower temperature enters the casing through the suction pipe and fills the whole casing, which can cool the motor. Then, it would enter the inner cavity of the body through the suction channel on the body inside the motor stator. When the piston moves downward from the top dead center, the low-pressure refrigerant vapor enters the cylinder through the suction hole on the valve plate and opens the suction valve. After being compressed by the cylinder, the refrigerant steam with high temperature and high pressure is discharged into the high-pressure chamber by opening the exhaust valve, and then discharged into the exhaust muffler through the connecting pipe on the cylinder head and the exhaust muffler, and then discharged from the compressor through the exhaust pipe on the exhaust muffler. The exhaust muffler not only plays the role of noise elimination, but also makes the high-pressure gas pressure uniform and stable.

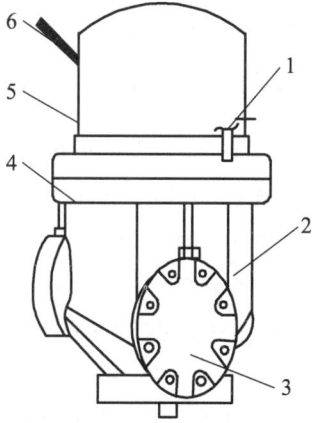

1—Exhaust pipe; 2—Body; 3—Cylinder head; 4—Exhaust noise elimination;
5—Motor shell; 6—Power cord.

Figure 4-1-6　Schematic diagram of movement appearance

The casing of the compressor is made of hot-pressed or cold-pressed steel plates with a thickness of 5 mm, which are stamped into upper and lower parts. After being installed into the core composed of the motor and the compressor, the upper and lower casings are welded together. There are only suction pipes, exhaust pipes and power leads outside the casing. The appearance of the movement is shown in Figure 4-1-6. In order to reduce the vibration of the machine during operation, the movement is supported on the casing by three damping springs, and the casing is connected with the steel skeleton of the unit through the rubber damping device. The upper part of the core is the compressor motor, and the lower part is the compressor body. There are three cylinders in the lower part of the body arranged in a horizontal star-shape, with the center line at an angle of 120°. The annular exhaust muffler is arranged outside the engine body, with three pipes at the lower part connected with three cylinders, and one pipe at the upper part extending out of the engine shell.

The compressor crankshaft is a vertically installed eccentric shaft. The upper end of the shaft is installed with the motor rotor iron core, and the lower eccentric pin is sleeved with three integral connecting rods. The piston is of cylindrical and flat top structure. In order to simplify the structure, the piston has only one piston ring, which is a gas ring. There is an oil groove under the gas ring. The piston structure is shown in Figure 4-1-7.

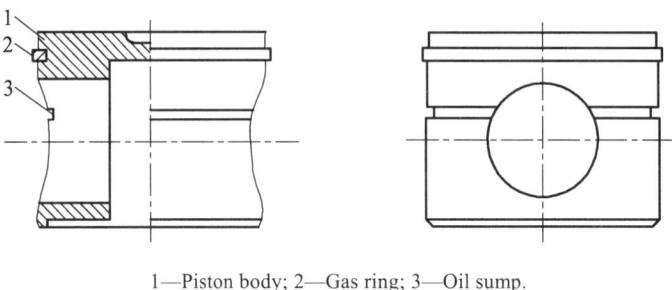

1—Piston body; 2—Gas ring; 3—Oil sump.

Figure 4-1-7　Piston structure diagram

The air valve adopts reed valve. The air valve group is composed of valve plate, suction and exhaust valve plate and exhaust valve lift limit plate, which are riveted together by rivets at the center. The structure of air valve group assembly and valve plate is shown in Fig. 4-1-8 and Fig. 4-1-9. Because the reed valve has good elasticity, the suction and exhaust springs are canceled. During suction, the suction valve plate bends downward, and its lift is limited by the four bosses on the outer circle of the valve plate and the corresponding groove depth on the cylinder wall; When exhausting, the exhaust valve plate bends upward, and its lift is limited by the lift limit plate of the exhaust valve plate.

The muffler structure is shown in Figure 4-1-10. It has three intake pipes under the outside, which are connected with three cylinders respectively. There is an exhaust pipe above, and the upper part of the pipe extends to the outside of the casing. Its interior is divided into upper and lower layers; The upper and lower layers are only connected at the gap around the lower part of the exhaust pipe. The lower part of the exhaust pipe extends to the lower part of the muffler. The high-pressure gas in the three cylinders first enters the lower layer of the muffler through the three intake pipes, and then exits the casing through the exhaust pipe. This not only makes the pressure of high-pressure gas discharged from each cylinder uniform and stable, but also eliminates the noise caused by high-speed gas flow.

JH514YZ-type compressor uses the oil hole on the crankshaft to throw oil to realize lubrication. Two through longitudinal oil holes are opened at the center line of the crankshaft and 3 mm away from the center line. When the crankshaft rotates at high speed, the lubricating oil is sucked up axially and flows to each moving pair under the action of centrifugal force.

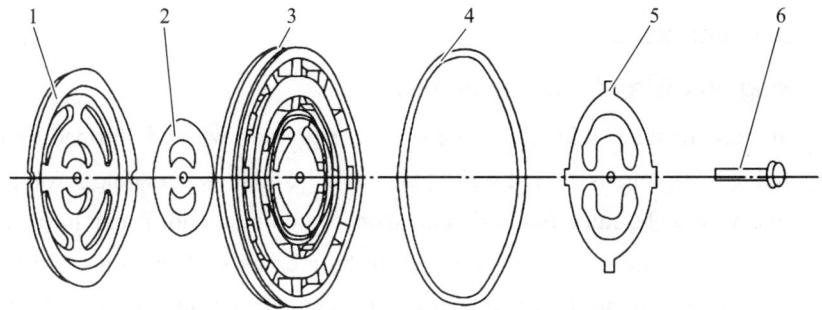

1—Lift limit plate of exhaust valve; 2—Exhaust valve plate; 3—Valve plate;
4—Sealing ring; 5—Suction valve plate; 6—Rivet.

Figure 4-1-8   Air valve group assembly

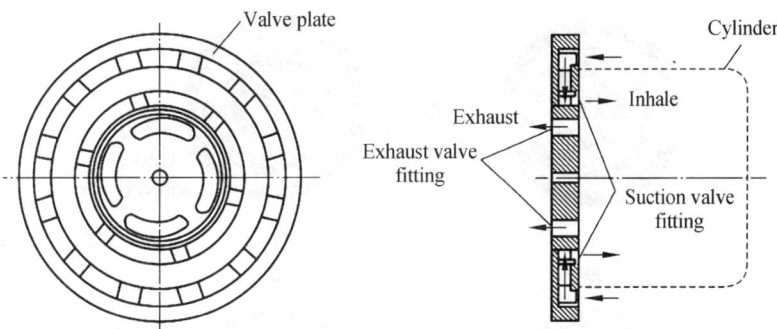

Figure 4-1-9   Valve plate structure

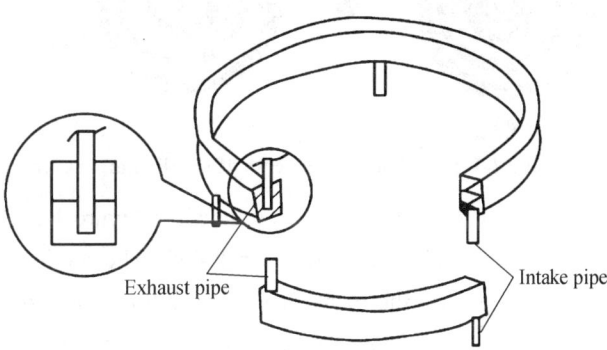

Figure 4-1-10   Exhaust muffler

  The motor of the compressor will sometimes be burnt due to excessive temperature due to excessive load, frequent intermittent operation of the compressor, serious leakage between the cylinder and piston, system pipeline blockage, poor cooling effect and other reasons. Therefore, in order to prevent the motor winding from overheating, a temperature relay is installed in the motor stator winding. When the temperature is too high or the current is too high, the power supply of the motor is cut off and the compressor is forced to stop.

3. Scroll Compressor

1) Working principle of scroll compressor

The scroll compressor is a kind of volumetric compressor, which is formed by two scroll plates staggered by 180°, one is a fixed scroll plate, and the other is a rotating scroll plate. They contact on several straight lines (several points on the cross section) and form a series of crescent volumn. The rotating scroll plate is driven by a crank shaft with a small eccentricity and moves horizontally around the fixed scroll plate. The contact line between the two moves along the scroll surface during operation. The relative position between them is ensured by the cross slip ring installed between the rotating scroll and the fixed parts.

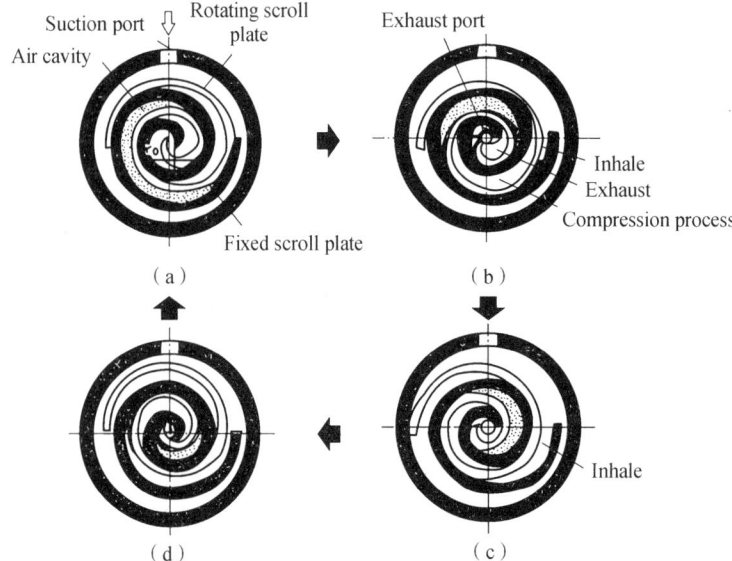

Figure 4-1-11 Working process of scroll compressor

The working process of the scroll compressor is shown in Figure 4-1-11. The solid disk is a fixed scroll disk, and the hollow disk is a rotating scroll disk. The suction port is located at the top of the fixed scroll plate. Because the crank drives the hollow plate to rotate clockwise, the gas is sucked in and sealed in the crescent. As the contact line between the rotating scroll plate and the fixed scroll plate advances towards the center along the scroll surface, the crescent volume gradually shrinks and the gas is continuously compressed, and finally the high-pressure gas is discharged through the axial center hole on the fixed scroll plate. Figure 4-1-11 (a) shows the position when the suction is completed, Figure 4-1-11 (b) shows the suction process, compression process, and exhaust process when the rotating scroll is rotating, and Figure 4-1-11 (c) and (d) show that the suction process and compression process are continuous and simultaneous. In each revolution of the crank shaft, a new suction volume is formed, so the above process is repeated and completed in turn.

2) Structure of scroll compressor

Figure 4-1-12 shows the sectional view of 3.75 kW totally enclosed scroll compressor. The compressor is mainly composed of fixed scroll plate, rotating scroll plate, cross slip ring, crankshaft, bracket, casing, etc. The fixed scroll plate 5 and the motor stator are installed on the inner wall of the casing. The cross slip ring 18 is a ring with two pairs of mutually perpendicular convex keys on the upper and lower sides. The upper convex key is installed in the keyway on the back of the rotary scroll plate 7, and the lower convex key is installed in the keyway of the bracket 10. The function of the cross slip ring is to prevent the tilt and rotation of the rotating scroll plate. A back pressure chamber 8 is set under the rotary scroll plate 7. The back pressure chamber is introduced into the middle pressure air flow through the small hole on the chassis of the rotary scroll plate 7 to automatically inflate, so that the air chamber pressure supports the rotary scroll plate. At the same time, an adjustable axial seal is installed on the top of the rotary scroll plate, so that the rotary scroll plate can move axially, which can compensate for the gradual wear during operation, and can also prevent the overload caused by hydraulic shock or excessive lubricating oil in the compression chamber.

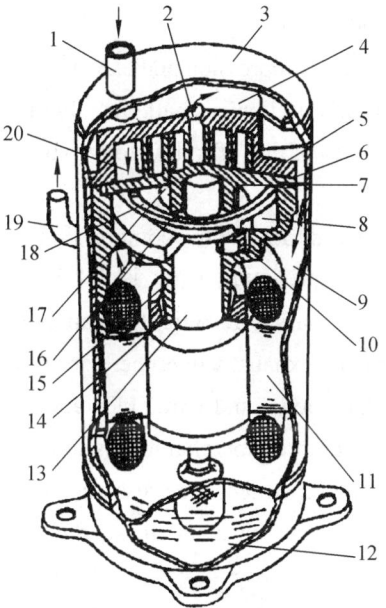

1—Suction pipe; 2—Exhaust port; 3—Sealing shell; 4—Exhaust chamber; 5—Fixed scroll plate; 6—Exhaust channel; 7—Rotating scroll plate; 8—Back pressure chamber; 9—Motor cavity; 10—Support; 11—Motor; 12—Oil; 13—Crankshaft; 14 - Bearing; 15—Sealing; 16—Bearing; 17—Back pressure chamber; 18—Cross slip ring; 19—Exhaust pipe; 20—Suction chamber.

Figure 4-1-12　Profile of totally closed scroll compressor

A rotating seal is installed at the crankshaft pin bearing and the crankshaft passing through the bracket to maintain the air tightness between the back pressure chamber and the casing. The lubricating oil of the bearing is supplied from the bottom of the seal housing through the oil passage on the crankshaft by using the pressure difference between the exhaust pressure and the intermediate pressure, and finally flows from the back pressure chamber to the compression chamber to lubricate the scroll surface, and then is discharged together with the compressed gas to separate the oil in the casing, and then flows to the bottom. Moreover, there is oil flow outside the fixed scroll plate, which supplies oil to the moving part of the scroll plate. The scroll compressor will reverse after it stops running, so a check valve is installed in the suction pipe on the fixed scroll plate.

3) Characteristics of scroll compressor

From the perspective of structure and working principle, scroll compressor has the following characteristics:

(1) High efficiency.

The suction, compression and exhaust processes of the scroll compressor are continuous and one-way, so the harmful overheating of the inhaled gas is small, the pressure difference between the two adjacent chambers is small, as well as the gas leakage. There is no clearance volume, so there is no expansion process that causes the gas transmission coefficient to drop, and the volume efficiency is high, usually more than 95%.

(2) Low vibration, noise and torque.

Because the process of suction, compression and exhaust is continuous at the same time, and the pressure rises slowly, the torque variation is small, the vibration is small, and the noise is small. The torque of scroll type is only 1/10 of that of rolling rotor type and reciprocating type.

(3) Lightweight and reliable.

The ratio of the number of parts forming the compression chamber of the scroll compressor to the number of rolling and reciprocating parts is 1 : 3 : 7, so the volume of the scroll compressor is 40% smaller and the mass is 15% lighter than that of the reciprocating compressor. And because there is no suction and exhaust valve, there are few vulnerable parts, and there is a flexible mechanism with adjustable axial and radial clearance, which allows compression with liquid. Once the pressure in the compression chamber is too high, the end faces of the moving disc and the stationary disc can be separated, the pressure can be released immediately, and the damage caused by liquid hammer can be avoided, so the operation reliability of the scroll compressor is high.

(4) High gas transmission coefficient.

The inner chamber of the casing is an exhaust chamber, which reduces the suction preheating and improves the gas transmission coefficient of the compressor.

(5) Complex manufacturing process.

The machining accuracy of the spiral shape line is very high, and special precision machining equipment must be used, and the sealing requirements are high, and the sealing structure is complex.

4. Compressor Maintenance

1) Preparation before operation

(1) Wear labor protection articles and do a good job of safety protection.

(2) Check that the tooling equipment, iron brush, megger and other tools, tooling and equipment are in good condition, and the instrument measurement verification is not expired.

2) Appearance inspection of compressor housing

(1) Visually inspect the compressor shell, fixing clip and base to ensure that there is no rust, deformation and crack. Remove the dirt on the compressor surface and base. Rust on the shell shall be removed with steel brush and then painted with anti-rust paint and primary paint. The nameplate shall be complete and clear (Figure 4-1-13).

Figure 4-1-13 Compressor

(2) Visually check that the mounting bolts and damping pads are complete, the anti-vibration pads are in good performance, and the aging and damaged ones need to be replaced. Use the special sleeve tool to fasten the bolts to prevent the compressor from being improperly fixed and causing abnormal noise and vibration. After fastening, apply anti-loosening marks.

(3) Visually check the junction box and cover for deformation and damage. Open the compressor junction box and thoroughly clean the dirt inside and outside with a brush.

3) Appearance inspection of compressor plug

(1) Open the compressor power plug (Figure 4-1-14), visually and manually check that the terminal blocks and terminals are well fastened, and replace them with new ones if they are burnt or cracked.

(2) Check whether the cable plug limit device of air conditioning unit compressor is in good condition (see Figure 4-1-15).

Figure 4-1-14　A compressor power plug

Figure 4-1-15　The cable plug limit device

(3) Check whether the three-jaw holder of the air conditioning unit cable plug is intact (see Figure 4-1-16).

Figure 4-1-16　The cable plug three-jaw holder

4) Compressor insulation and sealing inspection

(1) As shown in Figure 4-1-17, use a multimeter to detect whether the U, V and W phase windings are open or short circuited. Use a 500 V megger to detect the insulation resistance of each winding of the compressor, which is not less than 5 MΩ. When the insulation of the

compressor of the passenger train air conditioning unit is less than 5 MΩ, the internal terminals of the compressor shall be derusted and dried, and then measured again. If the insulation is still less than 5 MΩ, replace the compressor. Replace the compressor (including wiring) if the compressor terminal is cracked.

Figure 4-1-17　The cable connector

(2) Check that the appearance of high and low voltage protection devices is good, and there is no protection action in the overall test of the unit. Measure the insulation resistance of the compressor winding to the body, which shall not be less than 5 MΩ.

(3) Check the thermal protection switch of the compressor with a multimeter to ensure there is no open circuit.

(4) Paste the maintenance label inside the terminal box cover and cover the compressor terminal box cover. The incoming and outgoing lines shall be protected with waterproof mastic.

(5) Sealing of wire hole of junction box: use sealant and rubber mud to make a strip clamp between the scattered wires, and then apply sealant or rubber mud on the outside of the wire to press it into a cylindrical shape. Make sure there is no gap between the glue and the wire, then press the cable into the hole, and seal all gaps with glue on the outside of the box, and finally straighten the wire to ensure that the wire hole and the wire are completely sealed.

(6) Apply sealant between the junction box and the compressor housing to ensure that the gap is filled, and smooth the surface with a brush.

(7) After the junction box cover is installed, it must be plugged into the gap between the cover and the box with sealant or rubber mud, and a sealing strip shall be formed by plastering the surface. (See Figure 4-1-18).

5) Arrangement after operation

(1) Paste maintenance marks, and fill in relevant records in one vehicle and one file.

Figure 4-1-18 Sealing treatment for a junction box

(2) Cut off the power supply, count the tools, confirm that they are in good condition and wipe them clean, put them into the tool box, do a good job of equipment maintenance, and leave the post after confirming that the switch is closed, there is no debris around, and no fire source before leaving the post.

Task 2 Heat Exchanger

【Task Objective】

(1) Understand the structure of evaporator and condenser.

(2) Master the main factors affecting the heat exchange of the heat exchanger.

(3) The heat exchanger can be cleaned.

【Knowledge Reserve】

In the air conditioning refrigeration system, in addition to the compressor, there are also heat exchangers (mainly evaporator and condenser), throttling devices, automatic control devices, auxiliary equipment, etc. During air conditioning refrigeration, the evaporator directly cools the indoor air, and the hot air blown by the outdoor unit is the air flow through the condenser. The heat dissipation performance of the heat exchanger has a great impact on the performance of the refrigeration system.

1. Evaporator

In the evaporator, the refrigerant liquid at a certain pressure evaporates (boils) at a lower temperature and turns into steam. The temperature of the refrigerated medium is reduced by using the latent heat of vaporization of the refrigerant to absorb the heat of the refrigerated medium (air or water). Therefore, the evaporator is the equipment that generates and outputs refrigeration capacity in the refrigeration system. The refrigerant in the evaporator changes from liquid to gas to absorb heat; The refrigerant in the condenser changes from gaseous state to liquid state and emits heat.

1) Type of evaporator

Evaporators can be divided into two types according to different refrigeration media: evaporator for refrigerating liquid (water, brine, etc.) and evaporator for refrigerating air.

Evaporators for refrigerating liquid include shell-and-tube horizontal evaporator (refrigerant carrier flows in the tube and refrigerant flows and evaporates in the tube shell), dry evaporator (refrigerant evaporates completely in the evaporator) and immersion evaporator (directly immerse the evaporator in the refrigerant carrier).

There are two types of evaporator for refrigerating air: refrigerating exhaust pipe and direct evaporative air cooler.

The characteristic of the refrigerating tube evaporator is that the air naturally convection outside the tube, the refrigerant vaporizes inside the tube, and the heat transfer coefficient is small. Therefore, it is mostly used in cold storage and refrigerated box.

Direct evaporative air cooler is also called air cooler. It is characterized by refrigerant evaporation in the pipe, forced flow of air outside the pipe under the action of fan, and higher heat transfer coefficient than that of cooling exhaust pipe. It is applicable to various air conditioning units, cold storage and low temperature test boxes. Direct evaporative air coolers are used in the air conditioning system of passenger cars.

The structure of the direct evaporative air refrigerator is shown in Figure 4-2-1. The air refrigerator is also made into a rectangular coil group with a frame outside to form an air channel. The coil tube group is to cover the aluminum fin with pre-punched holes on the copper tube cluster with a laminating machine, and the fin root is provided with crimping to ensure the fin spacing after the installation. Then fill the tube cluster with high-pressure water to expand the base tube, ensure that the aluminum sheet has a good contact with the base tube, reduce the thermal resistance and improve the strength. Since the evaporator is relatively clean when installed in the vehicle, the fin spacing of the air cooler is smaller than that of the condenser. However, in some low-temperature refrigeration equipment, the evaporator is prone to frost due to low evaporation temperature, and its fin spacing should be appropriately increased.

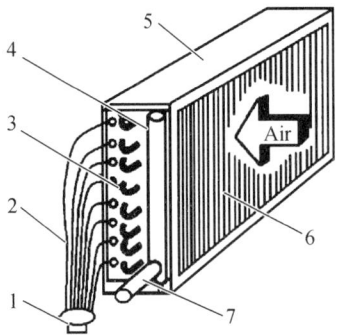

1—Liquid separator; 2—Capillary tube; 3—Snake tube; 4—Manifold;
5—Border; 6—Rib; 7—Return pipe.

Figure 4-2-1　Direct evaporative air cooler

Since whether the refrigerant is evenly distributed to each channel has a great impact on the refrigerating effect of the evaporator, a liquid separator is set at the liquid inlet of the evaporator to make the refrigerant liquid evenly distributed to each coil through the capillary, and at the same time throttle and depressurize. After the vaporized refrigerant vapor converges to the collection pipe, it is sucked in again by the compressor through the return pipe.

2) Factors affecting heat exchange of evaporator

The heat transfer process in the evaporator mainly includes the boiling heat transfer of refrigerant, the convective heat transfer of the refrigerated medium (air or water) and the heat transfer through the metal layer and the dirt layer.

The heat transfer effect of the evaporator is affected by the refrigerant heat transfer coefficient, the heat resistance of dirt on the heat transfer surface and the heat transfer coefficient of the refrigerated medium. The refrigerant liquid in the evaporator is in bubbly boiling state, that is, when boiling, many bubbles are produced on the heat transfer surface. These bubbles gradually increase, detach from the surface and rise in the liquid. The larger the diameter of the bubble, the longer the time from the generation of the bubble to the departure of the heat transfer wall, the less bubbles generated per unit time, and the lower the heat transfer coefficient.

In the structural design of evaporator, the heat transfer coefficient should be improved as much as possible from the aspects of material, wall thickness, fin tube form and structural layout. It should be considered that the steam generated by the refrigerant in the evaporator during boiling can be separated from the heat transfer surface as soon as possible and discharged from the evaporation pipe. In addition to its structure, the refrigerant and the cooled medium have an impact on the heat transfer of the evaporator.

(1) Effect of refrigerant on heat exchange.

① Evaporation temperature of refrigerant. The lower the evaporation (boiling) temperature of the same refrigerantis, the greater the density differenceis (the density difference between vapor and liquid) at saturation temperature; and the greater the surface tension of the liquidis, the larger the diameter of the bubbleis, and the smaller the heat transfer coefficientis. On the contrary, the higher the evaporation temperatureis, the greater the heat transfer coefficientis.

② The wetting ability of the refrigerant. Refrigerant wetting capacity refers to the capacity of the refrigerant to fully contact with the inner wall of the pipeline. If the refrigerant has a strong wetting ability on the heated surface, the bubbles formed during boiling will be small and can quickly separate from the heat transfer surface, and the heat transfer coefficient will be large. If the refrigerant cannot well wet the heat transfer surface, the bubbles formed during boiling will be large and even form a gas film, which will significantly reduce the heat transfer coefficient.

③ Physical properties of refrigerant. It mainly refers to the thermal conductivity, density, viscosity and other factors of the refrigerant. The boiling heat transfer coefficient of refrigerants with high thermal conductivity is large when their thermal resistance in the heat transfer direction is small. The refrigerant liquid with low density and viscosity will produce more bubbles per unit time when boiling, and its convective heat transfer coefficient will be large.

④ The amount of lubricating oil in the refrigerant. The concentration of lubricating oil in the refrigerant has certain influence on the heat transfer coefficient. The experiment shows that when the concentration of oil in the refrigerant is 8%~12%, the heat transfer coefficient is higher than that without oil, but when the oil content is further increased, the heat transfer coefficient will decrease.

(2) Effect of cooled medium on heat exchange.

The refrigerating medium of passenger car air conditioners is usually air. The faster the flow rate of air, whether air-cooled or water-cooled, the greater the heat transfer coefficient. However, over-large coefficient will increase power consumption, and the air flow rate and volume of the passenger car air conditioner into the passenger compartment have specific provisions, so it should be comprehensively considered.

Although the evaporator is usually located inside the unit and is not easily affected by external dust and debris, the heat transfer will also be affected if there is water accumulation or frost on the surface during operation.

2. Condenser

The function of the condenser is to make the refrigerant vapor with high temperature and high pressure from the compressor release heat to the external cooling medium (air or water), cool and condense into the saturated (supercooled) refrigerant liquid with high temperature and high pressure.

In the condenser, the cooling process of refrigerant can be divided into three stages:

cooling from superheated steam to saturated steam; Condensation from saturated vapor to liquid at saturated temperature; If the flow rate of the cooling medium is large or the temperature is low, the saturated liquid can be further cooled to become a supercooled liquid at this pressure.

1) Type of condenser

Condensers are divided into three types according to different cooling media and cooling methods:

(1) Water-cooled condenser: use water as cooling medium.

(2) Air-cooled condenser: uses air as cooling medium, also known as air-cooled condenser.

(3) Evaporative condenser: use a small amount of water and air as the cooling medium, and take away the heat mainly by water evaporation.

Water-cooled and evaporative condensers can obtain lower condensation temperature, but scale is easy to form on the surface of the condenser; The air-cooled condenser has high condensation temperature, large size and large energy consumption. However, in the vehicle air conditioning and refrigeration system, due to the limitations of application conditions, water-cooled or evaporative condensers can not be used, and only air-cooled condensers can be used. Other small refrigerators, such as refrigerators, freezers, automotive air conditioners and civil air conditioners, also use air-cooled condensers due to the limitations of the use environment.

When the air-cooled condenser works, the refrigerant vapor is cooled and condensed (supercooled) in the system pipeline, and the air flows transversely outside the coil under the action of the axial flow fan, thus taking away the heat. Air-cooled condensers are often made of serpentine tubes with fins. The coil is generally made of copper pipes with smaller diameter, and the copper pipe joints are sealed by silver welding. The number of coil rows along the air flow direction is generally 6-8, and the rib is aluminum. In order to make the structure compact, several serpentine tubes are connected in parallel to form a rectangular shape. The fin is sleeved on the tube cluster by a laminating machine, and then pressurized water is filled into the tube to make the tube cluster expand and fully contact with the fin to ensure the heat dissipation effect.

According to the flow of refrigerant in the condenser, there are two types of condensers: up-in and down-out and horizontal in and out. During the operation of the upper inlet and lower outlet condenser, the refrigerant vapor enters each coil from the upper distribution header, and the condensed liquid flows downward along the coil, collects in the header, and then flows into the reservoir. The flow of each coil in this structure is long, and the rear part of the coil is often filled with liquid, which reduces the heat transfer efficiency. Therefore, it is also useful to use the horizontal inlet and outlet structure. The refrigerant basically flows on a horizontal plane during the working process of this condenser, which can realize heat dissipation. Figure 4-2-2 shows the horizontal inlet and outlet condenser.

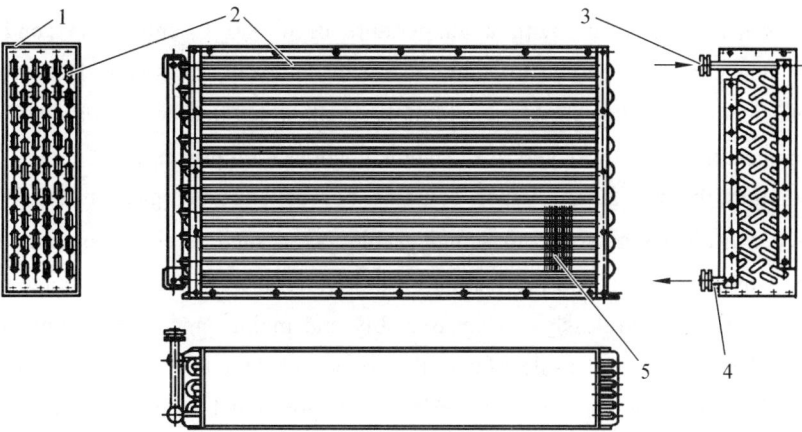

1—Outer frame; 2—Snake tube; 3—Intake pipe; 4—Liquid outlet pipe; 5—Rib.

Figure 4-2-2　The transverse inlet and outlet condenser

In order to expand the capacity of the condenser, the condenser is often designed as two groups working in parallel.

2) Factors affecting heat transfer of condenser

The refrigerant flows in the condenser and dissipates heat through the cooling medium (air or water). In this process, many factors will affect its heat dissipation effect.

For example, the roughness of the inner wall of the condenser and the thickness of the condensate film on the inner wall are not only related to the viscosity of the refrigerant liquid, but also greatly affected by the roughness of the inner wall. When the wall is very rough or there is oxide skin, the flow resistance of the liquid film increases, making the liquid film thicker and the heat transfer coefficient lower. Therefore, the inner surface of the condenser should be kept smooth and clean to obtain large condensation heat transfer coefficient. The following factors also affect the heat transfer of condenser:

(1) Effect of refrigerant on heat exchange.

① The flow rate and direction of refrigerant vapor. The condensation of refrigerant in the condenser is generally film-like. When the refrigerant vapor contacts the condenser wall below the saturation temperature, it condenses into a liquid film, which flows downward under the action of gravity. The liquid film is the thermal resistance of the refrigerant side in the condenser. The thicker the liquid film is, the greater the thermal resistance is and the smaller the heat transfer coefficient is. When the flow direction of refrigerant vapor is consistent with the flow direction of liquid film, the condensation liquid and heat transfer surface (condenser pipeline) are separated quickly, and the heat transfer coefficient increases with the increase of steam flow rate. Therefore, a larger heat transfer coefficient can be obtained by properly increasing the steam flow rate.

② The super-heat of refrigerant vapor. During the working process of the refrigeration system, the superheated steam with a temperature of 40–50 °C enters the condenser. The superheated steam must be cooled to saturated steam before condensation. However, the heat release coefficient of superheated steam cooling is small, so the higher the degree of super-heat, the lower the heat transfer coefficient of the whole condensation process.

③ Whether the refrigerant vapor contains non-condensable gas. In the refrigeration system, there will always be some non-condensable gases, such as air, nitrogen and hydrogen decomposed from refrigerant and lubricating oil at high temperature at the leakage point in the low pressure section or carelessly during assembly and maintenance. These non-condensable gases are attached to the condensate film in the condenser. Due to the high partial pressure of non-condensable gases, the pressure of refrigerant vapor will be reduced, and its saturation temperature will also be correspondingly reduced, The condensation speed of refrigerant vapor is reduced. Therefore, attention should be paid to prevent non-condensable gas such as air from entering the system, and once it enters, it should be discharged in time.

④ Whether the refrigerant contains lubricating oil. If the refrigerant is not miscible with the lubricating oil, the lubricating oil entering the condenser with the refrigerant vapor will form an oil film and deposit on the inner surface of the condenser, reducing the heat transfer coefficient. Generally, refrigerant can be miscible with lubricating oil. When the concentration of lubricating oil is less than 6%–7%, the influence on heat transfer can be ignored. If the limit is exceeded, the heat transfer coefficient will also be reduced.

(2) Effect of cooling medium on heat exchange.

① Flow rate and flow of cooling medium. The heat transfer coefficient increases with the increase of the flow rate and flow volume of the cooling medium. However, if the flow rate is too large, the flow resistance through the condenser will increase, thus increasing the power consumption. In the application of passenger car air conditioning, the technical and economic indicators are comprehensively considered, and the air flow rate is generally 2–4 m/s.

② The cleanliness of the cooling medium of the condenser. After long-term use of the condenser, dust or scale will accumulate on the surface, which will affect the heat transfer effect of the condenser. Therefore, the condenser should be cleaned regularly.

(3) Effect of fins and tubes on heat transfer.

① The efficiency of the fin. Different materials and areas of fins will make their heat transfer capacity different. Aluminum fins are used as fins in passenger car air conditioners to increase the heat transfer area and improve the heat transfer effect.

② Arrangement of rib tubes. The heat transfer capacity of finned tubes varies with their structure and arrangement. For example, the heat transfer capacity of tube bundles is greater than that of bare tubes. The condensers of passenger car air conditioners are connected in parallel with multiple coils.

The current passenger car air conditioners in China adopt the structure of parallel copper coils and aluminum fins. The fin structure has little influence on heat transfer, so the influence of air and refrigerant is mainly considered in application.

3. Heat Exchanger Cleaning

1) Preparation before work

(1) Preparation tools: spray pot, aluminum cleaner, high-pressure washer, aviation plug jacket.

(2) The detergent shall not contact the skin directly, and rubber protective gloves and goggles shall be worn during operation.

(3) Turn on the exhaust fan to maintain good ventilation.

(4) Wrap the aviation plug with sheath to prevent water from entering the wiring and conduit. It is strictly prohibited to land the aviation plug to prevent the pin and socket from being bruised, dirty and blocked.

2) Cleaning operation

Figure 4-2-3　Cleaning operation

(1) Use a spray pot to evenly spray detergent on the surface of the heat exchanger.

(2) After standing for 15 minutes, use a high-pressure washer to clean the evaporator, condenser and other parts of the air conditioning unit.

(3) After washing, use pH test paper to detect the pH value of the residual liquid in the four corners and the central area of the condenser and evaporator fins. The pH value is neutral to ensure that there is no acid or alkaline solution residue.

(4) Place the cleaned air conditioning unit at the assembly station, and place it stably without extrusion of wiring.

(5) Use dry compressed air to remove residual moisture from wiring and aviation plugs.

3) Finishing after work

(1) Cut off the power supply, count the tools, confirm that they are in good condition, wipe them clean, put them into the tool box, maintain the equipment properly, and leave the post after confirming that the switch is closed, there is no debris around, and no fire source before leaving the post.

(2) Fill in relevant records in *One Vehicle, One File*. Be sure that the handwriting is clear, the record is accurate, and there is no omission.

Task 3 Automatic Control Device of Refrigeration Device

【Task Objective】

(1) Master the structure and principle of expansion valve and capillary.

(2) Understand the structure and principle of temperature controller and pressure controller.

【Knowledge Reserve】

Refrigeration automation equipment generally completes the automatic control and protection of the system through controllers, sensors, regulating structures and actuators. The throttling device is an element that controls the liquid supply and throttling and depressurization of the air conditioning refrigeration system. The temperature controller is an element that controls and regulates the indoor temperature. The pressure controller is the pressure protection element of the compressor. The solenoid valve is an automatic valve that controls the on-off of the refrigerant pipeline.

1. Throttling Device

1) Expansion valve

The expansion valve is a valve for throttling, depressurizing and regulating the flow of the air conditioning refrigeration system. It can automatically regulate the flow of refrigerant in the refrigeration system. The following three types are commonly used:

① Thermal expansion valve: control the refrigerant flow by using the superheat at the evaporator outlet.

② Thermoelectric expansion valve: drive the valve rod by the heat generated by electric heating to control the refrigerant flow.

③ Electronic expansion valve: control refrigerant flow through electronic signal.

(1) Thermal expansion valve.

The thermal expansion valve is a throttling and pressure reducing mechanism that can automatically adjust the liquid supply. It uses the super-heat degree of refrigerant steam at the evaporator outlet to regulate the refrigerant flow. Because the expansion valve has the function of automatically regulating the refrigerant flow, the system with expansion valve throttling is usually equipped with a reservoir. The thermal expansion valve was used as the throttling device in the refrigeration system of the split passenger car air conditioning device in the early stage.

The thermal expansion valve can be divided into internal balance type and external balance type according to the pressure detected under the diaphragm. The internal balance type detects the pressure at the inlet of the evaporator, while the external balance type detects the pressure at the outlet of the evaporator.

① Internal balance thermal expansion valve.

The structure of the internal balance thermal expansion valve is shown in Figure 4-3-1. It is mainly composed of thermometer bulb, capillary tube, diaphragm, ejector rod, valve seat, valve needle and regulating mechanism. The expansion valve is installed on the inlet pipe of the evaporator, and the thermometer bulb is wrapped at the outlet of the evaporator. The closed space composed of thermometer bulb, capillary tube and capsule (cavity above the diaphragm) is called temperature sensing system. The temperature sensing system is filled with low boiling point liquid. The system senses the temperature of the refrigerant when it leaves the evaporator. The saturated pressure of the vapor in the temperature sensing system corresponding to the temperature is transmitted to the top of the diaphragm through the capillary tube, making the diaphragm subject to a downward thrust P_1. The lower part of the diaphragm bears two upward forces: one is the refrigerant pressure P_0 after throttling through the valve hole, which is transmitted to the lower part of the diaphragm through the gap between the transmission rod and the valve body; The other is the spring force P_2 under the valve needle, which acts under the diaphragm through the transmission rod. The diaphragm is balanced under these three forces (ignoring gravity), namely

$$P_1 = P_0 + P_2$$

a. When the liquid supply volume of the evaporator is small, the superheat of the refrigerant steam at the evaporator outlet increases, so that the steam temperature in the thermometer bulb increases and the pressure P_1 increases. Due to $P_1 > (P_0 + P_2)$, the diaphragm is bent downward, and the spring under the valve needle is compressed by the transmission rod to move the valve needle downward, the valve hole is opened, and the liquid supply is increased.

b. When the liquid supply volume of the evaporator is large, the superheat of the refrigerant vapor at the evaporator outlet decreases, the pressure P_1 in the temperature sensing system decreases, $P_1 < (P_0 + P_2)$, the valve needle moves up, the valve hole is closed, and the liquid supply volume decreases.

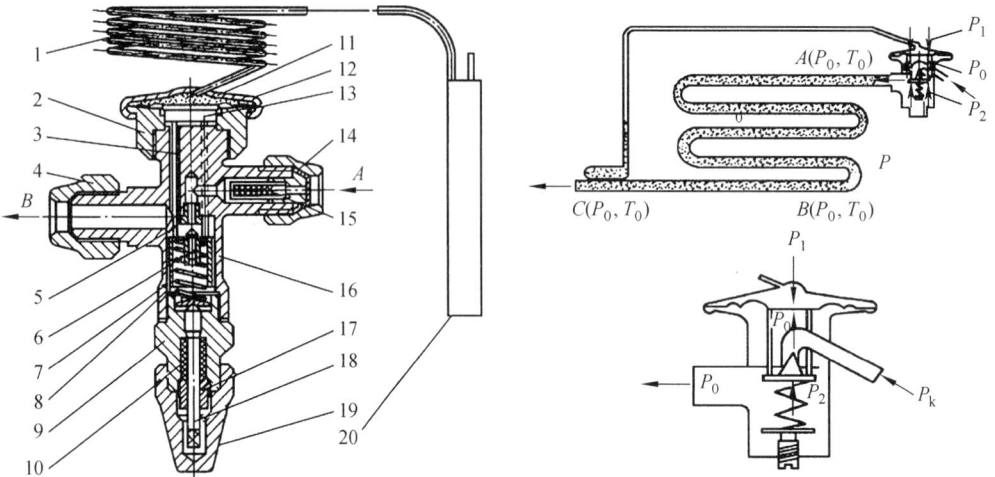

1—Capillary tube; 2—Seal chamber seat; 3—Transmission rod; 4—Pipe outlet lock nut; 5—Seat hole body;
6—Valve needle; 7—Valve needle seat; 8—Spring; 9—Regulating valve; 10—Sealing packing;
11—Sealing cap; 12—Corrugated film; 13—Drive plate; 14—Inlet pipe lock nut;
15—Filter screen; 16—Valve body; 17—Packing gland; 18—Adjusting rod;
19—Nut; 20—Thermometer bulb.

Figure 4-3-1 Internal balance thermal expansion valve

c. When the liquid supply volume of the evaporator is relatively stable, the superheat degree of the refrigerant steam at the evaporator outlet is stable, the pressure P_1 in the temperature sensing system basically does not change, $P_1 = (P_0 + P_2)$, the valve needle does not move, and the liquid supply volume does not change.

In the air conditioning and refrigeration system of passenger cars, the internal balance thermal expansion valve is usually used.

② External balance thermal expansion valve.

The structure of the external balance thermal expansion valve is basically the same as that of the internal balance thermal expansion valve. The difference is that the lower part of the diaphragm of the former is not connected with the refrigerant supplied to the evaporator, but is provided with a cavity, which is connected with the evaporator outlet with a balance pipe. Therefore, the lower part of its diaphragm no longer bears the refrigerant pressure at the evaporator inlet, but the refrigerant pressure at the evaporator outlet. The force on the diaphragm of the externally balanced thermal expansion valve is from the outlet of the evaporator, which can regulate the refrigerant flow more accurately. Therefore, when the evaporator cooling coil is long and the resistance loss is large, especially at low temperature, the external balance thermal expansion valve should be used.

③ Deficiency of thermal expansion valve.

The thermal expansion valve takes the temperature at the outlet of the evaporator as the control signal, and converts this signal into the steam pressure in the thermometer bulb through the thermometer bulb, and then controls the opening of the expansion valve needle to achieve the purpose of feedback regulation. There are some deficiencies in the application of thermal expansion valve:

a. The feedback of the signal has a large lag, which makes the regulated parameters oscillate periodically when the refrigeration device starts and the load changes suddenly.

b. At low evaporation temperature, the superheat increases, the evaporation temperature is unstable, and the efficiency of the refrigeration system decreases.

c. The refrigerant flow regulation range is small. Because of the limited deformation of the membrane, the change range of the valve needle opening is small.

d. Small load variation is allowed.

In order to overcome the above shortcomings, thermoelectric expansion valves and electronic expansion valves have appeared.

(2) Thermoelectric expansion valve.

The thermoelectric expansion valve is to connect a thermistor in series in the circuit of the valve heater. The current in the circuit is related to the resistance value of the thermistor, and the resistance value of the thermistor is related to the refrigerant state of the thermistor. Exposing the thermistor to the refrigerant, when the evaporator outlet is superheated steam, due to the heating effect, the temperature of the thermistor will rise, the resistance value will drop, the current in the circuit will increase, and the voltage on the valve heater will rise, which will open the valve and increase the refrigerant flow. When the refrigerant droplet or wet vapor contacts the thermistor, it will be cooled, the thermistor resistance will rise, and the valve will start to close again. The final result is to stabilize the valve at the opening corresponding to the selected superheat steam state at the evaporator outlet.

In order to achieve good control performance, the thermistor can be replaced according to the superheat required for control. The thermoelectric expansion valve can control the refrigerant flow in a high-precision range, especially suitable for heat pump devices.

(3) Electronic expansion valve.

Electronic expansion valve is a new type of control device for refrigeration system, which uses electronic controller to control the refrigerant flow of refrigeration system and make the refrigeration device in the best operation state. The application of electronic expansion valve overcomes the disadvantages of thermal expansion valve. There are two types of electronic expansion valve: electromagnetic type and electric type. It has the characteristics of fast response and wide range of adaptation.

The composition of the electronic expansion valve is shown in Figure 4-3-2, which consists of detection, control and execution. The motor directly drives the shaft to change the opening of the valve. The valve receives the signal from the controller to act, drives the rotor to rotate, converts its spiral rotary motion into the linear motion of the shaft, and uses the needle valve at the end of the shaft to adjust the size of the orifice opening to adjust the refrigerant flow.

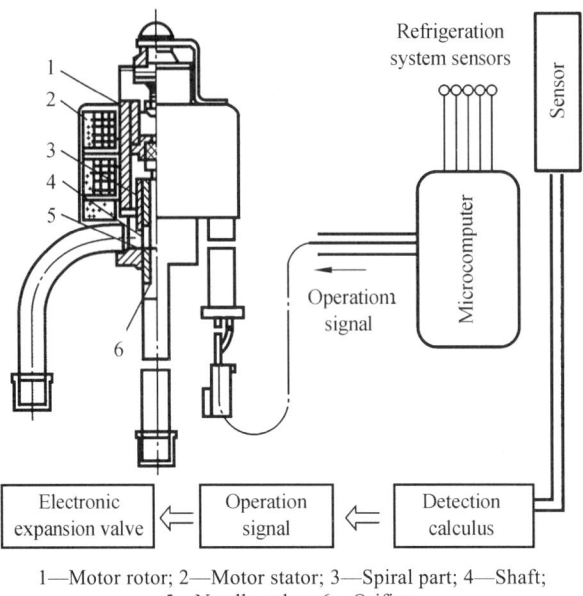

1—Motor rotor; 2—Motor stator; 3—Spiral part; 4—Shaft;
5—Needle valve; 6—Orifice.

Figure 4-3-2   Electronic expansion valve

2) Capillary tube

When the refrigerant fluid flows along the pipe, the pressure drop will occur due to the friction resistance of the pipe. The smaller the pipe diameter and the longer the pipe, the greater the flow resistance and the greater the pressure drop. Taking advantage of this property, in some closed compressors and small refrigeration devices, copper tubes with small inner diameter (0.6 ~ 2.0 mm) and a certain length (0.6 ~ 2.5 m) are used instead of expansion valves as throttling and pressure reducing elements, which are connected between the condenser and evaporator as throttling and pressure reducing elements of refrigeration cycle. This thin and long pipeline is a capillary throttling device.

The capillary throttling device has the advantages of simple structure, low price, no moving parts, no leakage, no inlet and outlet problems of the throttling mechanism, and after the compressor stops, the pressure in the condenser and evaporator can quickly and automatically balance, reducing the load of the motor when starting, which is very suitable for the refrigeration system equipped with a fully closed piston compressor.

However, the main disadvantage of capillary throttling is that its liquid supply cannot be adjusted with the change of working conditions. Because the length and diameter of the capillary are determined according to certain working conditions, if the liquid supply capacity of the capillary can change with working conditions, the diameter of the capillary must change with the working conditions, which is obviously impossible. When the evaporation pressure drops, the wet stroke of the compressor is easily caused by the refrigeration device with capillary throttling; When the evaporation pressure rises, it is easy to cause insufficient liquid supply to the evaporator. Therefore, capillary throttling is suitable for occasions where the evaporation temperature changes in a small range and the load is relatively stable, and the system is usually equipped with a gas-liquid separator to prevent the wet stroke of the compressor without a liquid reservoir.

In addition, the refrigeration device with capillary throttling is very sensitive to the refrigerant charge. Therefore, the refrigerant filling amount should be very accurate, otherwise the normal operation of the refrigeration device will be affected. Capillary tubes can be connected with one or more in parallel. When multiple capillaries are used in parallel, liquid separators should be prepared and carefully adjusted so that the working conditions of these capillaries are roughly the same (can be judged by frost conditions). A filter should be set in front of the capillary to prevent the capillary from being dirty. The liquid supply capacity of the capillary mainly depends on the state (pressure and temperature) of the refrigerant at the inlet of the capillary, as well as the geometric size, length and inner diameter of the capillary.

2. Temperature Controller

Temperature controller, also known as temperature relay, is a circuit switch that controls the room temperature and its fluctuation range. It is often used to control the start and stop of the compressor. The commonly used temperature controllers are of mechanical and electronic types.

1) Mechanical temperature controller

WT-1226 temperature controller is widely used in air conditioning and refrigeration systems, and its operating principle is shown in Figure 4-3-3.

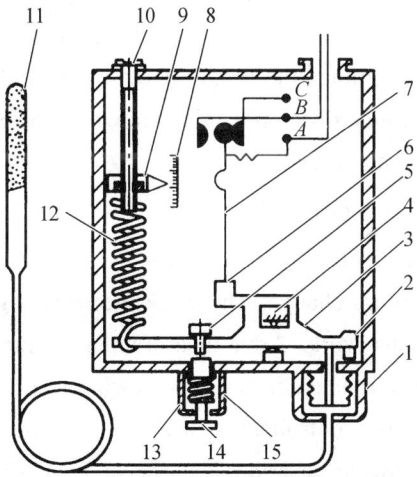

1—Corrugated tube chamber; 2—Stop screw; 3—Lever; 4—Bracket; 5—Screw; 6—Boom; 7—Spring; 8—Master scale; 9—Pointer; 10—Adjusting screw; 11—Thermometer bulb; 12—Main ammunition; 13—Differential spring; 14—Differential knob; 15—Differential device.

Figure 4-3-3   WT-1226 Temperature Controller

WT-1226 temperature controller is a two-position control type, that is, it has two static contacts. The power line is connected with the static contact B and the moving contact A. The moving contact A is connected in series in the coil circuit of the compressor motor contactor. When the moving contact A contacts with the static contact B, and the compressor operates; When the moving contact A is disconnected from the stationary contact B, and the compressor stops running.

The temperature sensing system of the temperature controller is composed of a thermometer bulb, a capillary tube and a bellows chamber. The thermometer bulb is filled with different working fluids (such as ether, acetone, freon, etc.) according to the control temperature range. The thermometer bulb changes the detected room temperature change into the change of the bellows pressure caused by the gas in the bellows chamber (the temperature is proportional to the pressure). The change of bellows pressure causes the lever to rotate around the bracket. When the temperature detected by the thermometer bulb drops to the set value, the jacking torque of the bellows is less than the tension torque of the set value spring, the lever rotates clockwise around the knife edge bracket, the moving contact A and the static contact B are disconnected, and the compressor stops. When the temperature detected by the thermometer bulb rises, the bellows pushes the lever to overcome the tension moment of the fixed value spring and rotates counterclockwise. After turning a certain angle, the lever can continue to rotate only after overcoming the force of the differential spring. When the temperature rises to the setting value plus amplitude difference, the moving contact A and the static contact B are closed again, and the compressor rotates.

Therefore, the tension of the constant value spring (main spring) determines the lower limit of the controlled temperature, namely the setting value, and its value can be adjusted by rotating the adjusting screw to change the tension of the constant value spring. The amplitude difference spring (differential spring) determines the range of the upper and lower limits of the control temperature, namely the amplitude difference (also known as differential value), which can be adjusted by rotating the differential knob.

2) Electronic temperature controller

The electronic temperature controller generally uses the thermistor and other sensitive elements to sense the temperature change. The weak electrical signal formed in the circuit is used as the input signal for its work. After measurement, comparison and amplification, it controls whether the relay acts, thus controlling the closing or opening of the microswitch. At present, electronic temperature controller is used in the bus air conditioning unit air conditioning device. The following describes the use of E5AZ-R3-38 electronic temperature controller commonly used in passenger car air conditioners.

The front structure of E5AZ-R3-38 electronic temperature controller is shown in Figure 4-3-4. The display device and common key functions are as follows:

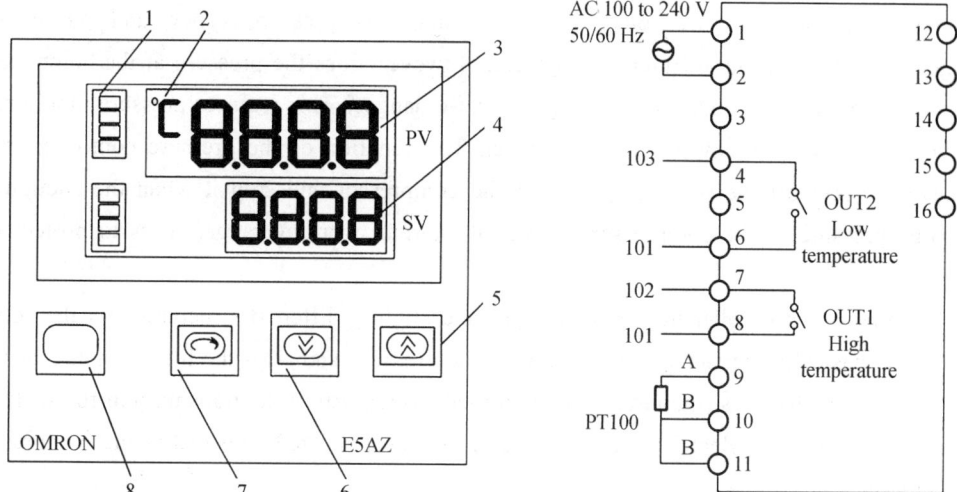

1—Operation display; 2—Temperature unit; 3—Room temperature display, displaying the set bullets; When the temperature controller works abnormally, it displays a fault; 4—Set temperature 1 display, that is, display the low temperature control value set by control output 1; 5—Up key; 6—Down key; 7—Mode key; 8—Menu key.

Figure 4-3-4　E5AZ-R3-38 Electronic Temperature Controller

Press the menu key for more than 3 seconds to enter the initial menu and set the input type of the temperature sensor. Press the up or down key to set the value, which is generally set to 1. Then, by pressing the mode key and cooperating with the up or down key, you can successively set the temperature unit (°C), ON/OFF mode, alarm function of alarm 1—3 (0 is no alarm, 8 is the upper limit of alarm absolute value), initial communication protection, low temperature control output control temperature, low temperature control return difference, high temperature control output control temperature, high temperature control return difference and other parameters.

Press the menu key for more than 1 second to enter the operation menu. Press the menu key and mode key for more than 3 seconds at the same time to enter the protection menu. Press the menu key and mode key simultaneously for more than 1 second to return to the operation menu.

In the temperature controller, a normally open switch of a low-temperature output relay is connected in series in the low-temperature output circuit, which can be controlled by the temperature controller. A normally open switch of a high temperature output relay is connected in series in the high temperature output circuit, which can be controlled by the controller. The PT100 thermometer bulb is connected to the temperature controller through three lines A, B and B, providing real-time temperature data to the temperature controller, which determines the on-off of the low temperature output relay and the high temperature output relay.

3. Pressure Controller

As the power equipment of the air conditioning refrigeration system, the compressor compresses the low-pressure refrigerant vapor into high-pressure vapor, and pushes the refrigerant to cycle in the refrigeration system. However, does the pressure at the compressor outlet meet the requirements? Is it too high to cause danger? This requires pressure monitoring and control device, namely pressure controller. The function of the pressure controller is to automatically cut off the working power of the compressor and stop it when the suction or discharge pressure of the compressor exceeds its normal working range, so as to protect the compressor.

The pressure controller has various forms and slightly different structures, but the action principle is basically the same. After receiving the pressure signal of the high pressure or low pressure part, the bellows (diaphragm) is deformed, which drives the transmission rod or lever mechanism, makes the electric contact connected or disconnected, and makes the compressor work or stop.

Pressure controller includes high pressure controller and low pressure controller, some of which are integrated, and some of which are individually made. The high pressure controller is connected with the exhaust chamber of the compressor to monitor and control the exhaust pressure. If the compressor discharge pressure is too high, the compressor motor will be damaged due to overload operation. Therefore, when the compressor discharge pressure is higher than the normal pressure, the high pressure controller will act to stop the compressor.

The low pressure controller is connected with the suction chamber of the compressor to monitor and control the suction pressure. When the suction pressure of the compressor is too low, on the one hand, it will affect the normal operation of the refrigeration unit, or even waste power due to the failure of refrigeration. On the other hand, the compressor will also damage the motor due to the near-no-load operation of the compressor. Therefore, when the suction pressure of the compressor is lower than the normal value, the low pressure controller will act to stop the compressor.

In the current railway passenger cars, high and low pressure are controlled separately, and the control pressure is not adjustable. The following is a brief introduction to these two pressure controllers.

1) ACB high pressure controller

Figure 4-3-5 shows the ACB high pressure controller. The high pressure pipe joint is connected with the compressor exhaust pipe. In the process of operation, if the exhaust pressure is greater than the specified pressure, the diaphragm will be pushed, and then the ejector rod will be pushed to separate the moving contact from the static contact, thus cutting off the working circuit of the compressor, making the compressor stop working, and protecting the compressor. When the pressure is normal, the moving contact always contacts the static contact under the action of the elastic metal sheet, and the compressor works normally.

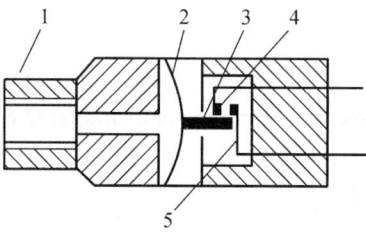

1—High pressure pipe joint; 2—Diaphragm; 3—Ejector pin; 4—Static contact; 5—Moving contact.

Figure 4-3-5　ACB high pressure controller

2) LCB low pressure controller

Figure 4-3-6 shows the schematic diagram of LCB low pressure controller, which works similar to the high pressure controller. When the suction pressure is too low, the diaphragm contracts, and the moving contact separates from the static contact under the action of the elastic metal sheet, cutting off the working circuit of the compressor and protecting the compressor. When the suction pressure of the compressor is normal, the ejector rod pushes the moving contact to connect with the static contact, and the compressor works normally.

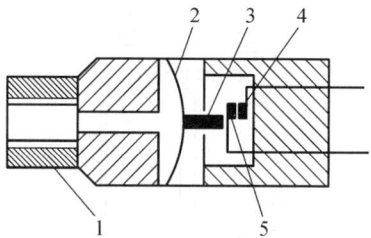

1—Low pressure pipe joint; 2—Diaphragm; 3—Ejector pin; 4—Static contact; 5—Moving contact

Figure 4-3-6　LCB low pressure controller

Task 4　Auxiliary Equipment of Refrigeration Device

【Task Objective】

(1) Master the structure and principle of gas-liquid separator and oil separator.

(2) Understand the structure and principle of heat exchanger, drying filter and reservoir.

【Knowledge Reserve】

In addition to the compressor, heat exchanger and automatic controller, the refrigeration system also needs some other auxiliary equipment to complete the oil separation, gas-liquid separation, refrigerant storage and purification. The state of refrigerant in these auxiliary equipment does not change. They are not necessary for completing the refrigeration cycle. Therefore, in some small refrigerators, some auxiliary equipment is often omitted for the sake of simplifying the equipment. However, in order to improve the working conditions of the refrigerator, ensure the normal operation of the refrigerator and improve the operation economy, these auxiliary equipment are essential in the medium and large refrigeration equipment.

1. Gas-liquid Separator

The gas-liquid separator is used to separate the liquid in the steam at the evaporator outlet, so as to ensure dry compression of the compressor. As the refrigerant flow of the capillary throttling refrigeration device cannot be adjusted automatically, when the load is reduced, the refrigerant in the evaporator may not completely evaporate. If the refrigerant vapor with liquid droplets is inhaled by the refrigeration compressor, it may cause liquid shock and damage the valve plate, piston, connecting rod, etc. Therefore, in order to prevent the compressor from absorbing liquid refrigerant, a gas-liquid separator can be installed on the return pipe of the refrigeration compressor to separate and store the liquid in the refrigerant vapor. The structure of gas-liquid separator is shown in Figure 4-4-1.

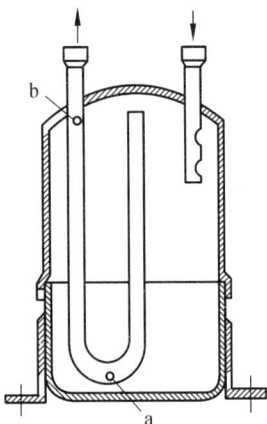

Figure 4-4-1　Structure diagram of a gas-liquid separator

The working principle of the gas-liquid separator is that after the refrigerant vapor from the evaporator enters the separator through the inlet pipe, the liquid droplets are separated and left at the bottom of the container due to the sudden change and deceleration of the air flow, and the gas is sucked in by the compressor through the outlet pipe. A small hole a is opened at the bottom of the U-shaped pipe to enable a certain amount of refrigerant oil to return to the compressor with the suction gas. Hole b is a pressure equalizing hole, which can prevent the liquid in the gas-liquid separator from flowing to the compressor through hole a due to the pressure rise at the evaporator side when the compressor is stopped.

2. Oil Separator

In the air conditioning and refrigeration system, as the power equipment, the compressor needs lubricating oil. Because it can lubricate and dissipate heat for each moving pair and improve the sealing between piston and cylinder. Refrigerant can dissolve with lubricating oil to a certain extent, R12 can completely dissolve, R22 can slightly dissolve, so there is lubricating oil in the exhaust of the compressor. In addition, the lubricating oil in the high temperature part of the compressor is vaporized into oil vapor, which is discharged into the condenser by the compressor together with refrigerant vapor. After cooling, the oil vapor is condensed into liquid and mixed in the refrigerant.

In addition to compressors, lubricating oil in other parts of the refrigeration system has many disadvantages as well as no benefits. When the lubricating oil is brought into the refrigeration system by the compressor exhaust, it will slightly increase the evaporation temperature after it is miscible with the refrigerant liquid, and may also affect the heat transfer performance and cooling capacity. Too much lubricating oil accumulated in the evaporator will reduce the heat transfer surface of the evaporator; If it is accumulated in the pipeline, it may also block the pipeline. When lubricating oil enters the small hole or capillary of the expansion valve, due to the sudden drop of temperature when the refrigerant is throttling, part of the refrigerant oil is stored in the small hole, and its viscosity increases, and may even precipitate paraffin and block the small hole.

In order to improve this adverse situation, a lubricating oil separator (oil separator for short) can be used, which can separate most of the lubricating oil mixed in the refrigerant of the compressor exhaust pipe and automatically return to the compressor. If there is a small amount of lubricating oil in the refrigerant, it can be driven by the refrigerant air flow and returned to the compressor through the suction pipe of the compressor, so as to maintain the oil level in the compressor crankcase and minimize the adverse effect of lubricating oil on the refrigeration process.

The working principle of the oil separator is: the oil separator is installed between the compressor exhaust port and the condenser. Its basic working principle is to use the different specific gravity of liquid oil droplets and refrigerant vapor to make the mixed gas flow through the oil separator with a larger diameter, use the sudden expansion of the passing area to reduce its flow rate, and change its flow direction at the same time or use centrifugal force to make the oil droplets settle and separate. For lubricating oil vapor, the temperature can be reduced by washing or water cooling to make it condense into oil droplets and separate. In some oil separators, filter layers are used to enhance the separation effect.

The commonly used oil separator is used in the ammonia system in three structural forms: washing type, packing type and centrifugal type. Because the refrigeration of ammonia system is rarely used now, the filtered oil separator used for Freon system is mainly introduced. The structure of the filtered oil separator is shown in Figure 4-4-2.

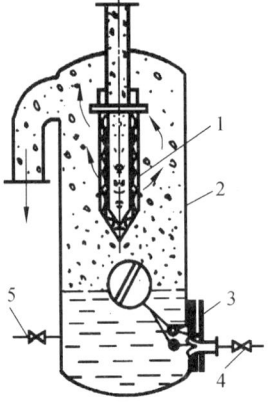

1—Filter screen; 2—Shell; 3—Floating ball valve; 4—Automatic oil return valve; 5—Manual oil return valve.

Figure 4-4-2　Filtered oil separator

　　The shell is welded from seamless steel pipe with upper and lower heads. The top is welded with an air inlet pipe, and the lower part of the air inlet pipe is equipped with a steel wire filter screen. Some separators are equipped with ceramic rings or steel wool. High-pressure steam with oil mist is filtered by the filter screen. A part of the oil mist contacts with the filter screen and is stuck on the filter screen. After accumulating into droplets, it falls to the bottom of the oil separator. On the other hand, the flow rate of high-pressure steam in the exhaust pipe is very high, generally between $10 \sim 25$ m/s. After flowing into the oil separator, because the channel area of the container is more than ten times or even dozens of times larger, the flow rate of the steam after flowing into the oil separator suddenly decreases, and its flow rate generally does not exceed $0.8 \sim 1$ m/s. In addition, the flow direction of the steam when flowing into and out of the oil separator changes, which makes the steam easy to collide with the container wall, and a part of the oil mist sticks to the container wall, gathers and drips to the bottom of the container. At the same time, the lubricating oil is much heavier than the refrigerant vapor. At low flow rate, the oil mist is separated from the vapor under the action of gravity and falls to the bottom of the container. Therefore, most of the lubricating oil in the refrigerant vapor is separated and stored in the container.

　　When the oil level of the lubricating oil stored at the bottom of the container is high enough to float the floating ball, the valve needle connected to the floating ball is opened, and the lubricating oil flows back to the crankcase through the oil delivery pipe connected with the compressor crankcase under high pressure. When the oil level in the container drops, the floating ball also drops, the valve needle closes the valve port, and the oil return ends. It can be seen that when the refrigerator is in continuous normal operation, the oil separator is also continuously separating oil, but the oil return of the oil separator to the crankcase is intermittent. Only when the oil level in the container reaches a certain level can the valve needle be opened by the floating ball to drain the oil.

3. Heat Exchanger

Heat exchanger, also known as "gas-liquid heat exchanger", is a heat exchanger used in Freon refrigeration system. The high temperature refrigerant liquid from the condenser and the low temperature steam from the evaporator exchange heat in it, the liquid gets supercooled, and the steam overheats. This regenerative cycle has three advantages:

(1) For systems using R12, R500, R502 and other refrigerants, the refrigeration coefficient of the refrigerator can be improved through heat recovery.

(2) Make the liquid supercooled to avoid gasification in front of the throttle valve (the liquid gasification in front of the throttle valve will affect the liquid supply of the thermal expansion valve).

(3) Vaporize the liquid droplets contained in the steam (including the dissolved liquid in the oil droplets) to prevent liquid hammer of the compressor.

The structure of heat exchanger is generally in the form of sleeve as shown in Figure 4-4-3. Its shell is made of seamless steel pipes with large diameter and welded with heads at both ends, while the inner tube is composed of ribbed tubes with fins on the outside. Because the heat release coefficient of refrigerant vapor to the wall is smaller than that of liquid, the gas flows along the outer tube on the finned side, while the liquid flows in reverse direction along the inner tube for heat exchange. The installation position of the heat exchanger in the refrigeration system is between the condenser, compressor and evaporator, that is, the liquid from the condenser flows through the inner tube of the heat exchanger and enters the evaporator under the control of the expansion valve after being supercooled again. The steam from the evaporator is introduced into the heat exchanger by the return pipe, which is absorbed by the compressor after overheating.

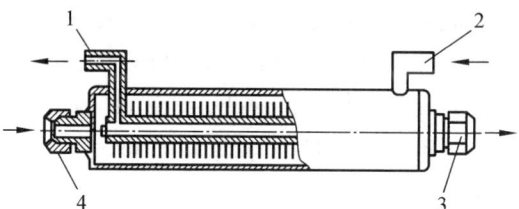

1—Liquid outlet; 2—Liquid inlet; 3—Air outlet; 4—Air inlet.

Figure 4-4-3 Casing type regenerator

The spiral tube heat exchanger is also used in practice. Its structure and working principle are the same as that of the sleeve type. Only the fin tube in the middle is wound into a spiral shape by copper tube to replace it. In the air conditioning device of passenger cars, when the pipeline is long, the infusion pipe and the suction pipe are also wrapped together to replace the heat exchanger.

4. Drying Filter

A drying filter is installed on the infusion pipe before the refrigeration system of the passenger car air conditioning device enters the throttling device, which is the purification equipment of the refrigeration system. Its function is to eliminate the water and impurities (such as metal chips, oxide scale, etc.) in the refrigerant, so as to prevent the water and impurities from causing ice plug and blockage at the expansion valve (capillary) and solenoid valve, as well as entering the compressor to scratch the cylinder and suction and exhaust valve. In addition, it also prevents hydrochloric acid and hydrofluoric acid from corroding metals and emulsifying refrigerant oil due to the long-term dissolution of water in the refrigerant.

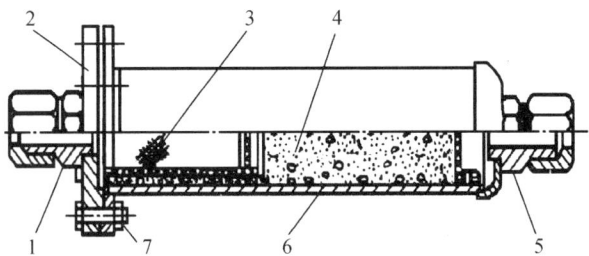

1—Liquid inlet pipe joint; 2—Gland; 3—Filter screen; 4—Desiccant;
5—Outlet pipe joint; 6—Shell; 7—Connecting bolt.

Figure 4-4-4　A Drying filter

The drying filter is mainly composed of shell, filter screen, desiccant, inlet and outlet pipe joints, etc. Its structure is shown in Figure 4-4-4. The shell is made of seamless steel pipe. There are 2 to 3 layers of copper wire mesh with a mesh of 0.1 ~ 0.2 mm in the inlet end. The end covers at both ends are connected with the shell by threads, and then welded by tin welding to prevent leakage. The outer end of the end cap is welded with a pipe joint to connect with the system pipeline. Desiccants are installed between the filter screen and the shell. The commonly used desiccants include silica gel, activated alumina and molecular sieve. Some refrigeration devices will install the dryer and filter separately, such as the split type passenger car air conditioning device refrigeration system. The drying filter used in the unit air conditioning unit is an integral type welded at both ends.

5. Reservoir

The liquid receiver, also known as the liquid receiver, is used to store the refrigerant liquid in the refrigeration cycle to adapt to the change of refrigerant flow when the working conditions change. In addition, when the refrigeration equipment is repaired and the refrigeration system is not working for a long time, all the refrigerant in the system should be collected in the reservoir to avoid leakage and loss.

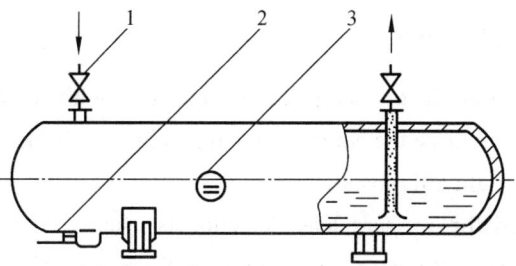

1—Liquid inlet valve; 2—Oil drain outlet; 3—Sight glass.

Figure 4-4-5　The reservoir

There are vertical and horizontal reservoirs, but most of them are horizontal in practical use, and their structure is very simple. Figure 4-4-5 shows horizontal reservoirs. The cylinder of the liquid storage tank is made of steel plate. The inlet and outlet ports are set on the cylinder. The installation position should be lower than the condenser. The volume should be greater than the volume of the refrigerant liquid to be stored. The stored refrigeration dose should not exceed 80% of the volume. For the refrigeration equipment with little load change, such as the refrigeration system of the unit-type air conditioning units, the liquid storage tank can not be used after strictly controlling the cooling dose.

 Leak Detection and Air Tightness Test of Refrigeration Device

【Task Objective】

(1) Master the leak detection and air tightness test methods of the refrigeration device.
(2) Be able to conduct vacuum test.

【Knowledge Reserve】

After the refrigeration equipment and pipeline have gone through idle running, air load test run and system blowdown, connect and seal each equipment and pipeline into a refrigeration system, and then conduct air tightness test on the whole system (referred to as leak detection). Through the air tightness test, the leakage point of the system shall be found and handled in time. The forms of leak detection include pressure leak detection and vacuum leak detection, and the leak point is detected by soapy water or immersion method, halogen leak detection lamp and halogen leak detector. For newly installed refrigeration equipment or overhauled refrigeration equipment, the above methods are generally used for leak detection, especially pressure leak detection. After the leak detection is qualified, the next step can be carried out.

1. Pressure Leak Detection

Pressure leak detection is to charge air or nitrogen with a certain pressure into the refrigeration system to pressurize the equipment and pipeline to check whether the joints, welds, pipes and equipment are tight after installation.

The air source used for pressure leak detection is usually compressed air for ammonia refrigeration unit; Industrial nitrogen is generally used for Freon refrigeration system. Nitrogen has the advantages of low price, no corrosion, no moisture, no combustion and no explosion, and is widely used as the pressure test gas source of Freon refrigeration system. The pressure of compressed nitrogen filled with steel cylinder is as high as 14,710 kPa when it is filled. During use, a pressure reducing valve with a pressure gauge shall be installed at the outlet of the steel cylinder according to the requirements of the operating procedures to control the inflation pressure during leak test.

Due to the different working pressure of different refrigerants in the refrigeration system, the requirements for leak test pressure are different during leak detection. The charging pressure for leak test should be determined according to the refrigerant used in the system. The method of pressure test shall be different according to different compressors.

1) Pressure leak detection of open compressor refrigeration system

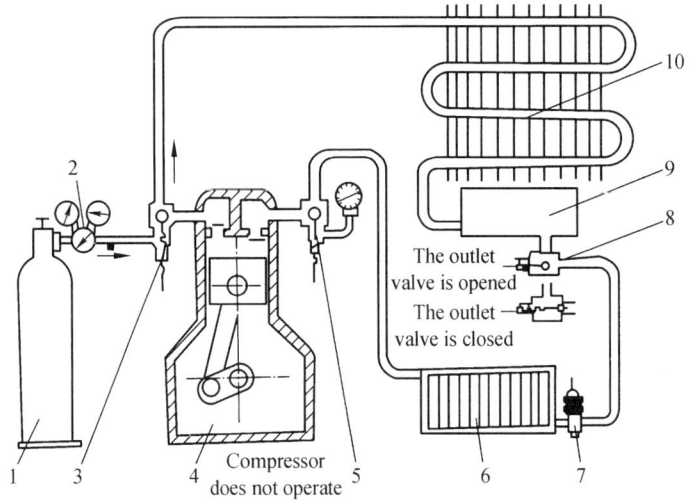

1—Nitrogen cylinder; 2—Pressure reducing valve; 3—Exhaust stop valve; 4—Compressor;
5—Suction stop valve; 6—Evaporator; 7—Expansion valve;
8—Outlet valve; 9—Liquid reservoir; 10—Condenser.

Figure 4-5-1　Pressure leak detection of open compressor refrigeration system

Figure 4-5-1 is the schematic diagram of the pressure leak detection operation of the open compressor refrigeration system.

(1) Close the valves connecting to the atmosphere in the refrigeration system, and open all

other valves (if there are solenoid valves, power them on to open them). Connect the nitrogen cylinder with the taper joint of the "multi-purpose channel" hole of the compressor exhaust stop valve with a copper tube or pressure hose, and turn the valve rod to make the "multi-purpose channel" and the stop valve fully open.

(2) Loosen the valve on the nitrogen cylinder, and the pressure gauge of high-pressure on the cylinder will indicate the pressure value of nitrogen in the cylinder. Slowly turn the valve rod of the pressure reducing valve in a clockwise direction, and the other pressure gauge indicates the pressure after pressure reduction. This pressure increases with the increase of the opening of the pressure reducing valve, until the indicated value of the pressure gauge reaches the value of specified low pressure, stop rotating the valve rod of the pressure reducing valve, and close the outlet valve of the reservoir when there is enough nitrogen in the system. Then open the large pressure reducing valve to raise the high pressure side in front of the liquid outlet valve of the reservoir to the specified value, wait for 10 ~ 20 seconds to stop the inflation, and close the pressure reducing valve and the multi-purpose channel on the compressor exhaust stop valve to maintain the pressure. However, it should be noted that if the exhaust valve plate has serious leakage, the high-pressure side pressure cannot be charged to the specified value. For this purpose, a measuring range of 1.6 can be installed at the multi-purpose channel of the suction stop valve $\times 10^6$ Pa pressure gauge, check the pressure rise at the low pressure side, and timely find the leakage of the exhaust valve plate.

(3) Remove the inflation pipe on the exhaust stop valve, screw the conical plug up and tighten it. Turn the valve rod of the exhaust stop valve clockwise to close the exhaust stop valve to prevent nitrogen from flowing from the high-pressure side to the low-pressure side.

(4) Apply soap solution to the joints and welds. At each coating, carefully observe whether there are bubbles. If there are bubbles, there is leakage. The leakage point shall be marked. If leakage is found at the joint, try to tighten it and conduct leakage detection again. After all leakage detection is completed, make up for leakage.

(5) Leakage repair: When repairing the leakage, the nitrogen in the system shall be completely vented, and the gas filling and leakage detection shall be conducted again after repair welding, joint replacement of gasket or re-expansion of the bell mouth until there is no leakage in the system.

(6) Pressure maintaining: in order to avoid leakage detection of small leakage, when the leakage detection is completed, do not discharge the nitrogen in the system, record the pressure value and maintain the pressure. After 24 ~ 48 h, observe whether the pressure changes. Generally, due to the change of ambient temperature, the pressure drops by $1.0 \times 10^4 \sim 3.0 \times 10^4$ Pa, which is normal. If the pressure drops obviously, find out the cause or recheck it.

(7) Use subsection inspection method to find the leakage point: for the system with many auxiliary valves or equipment, if the pressure drops significantly during the leak detection, but

the reason is not easy to find, the subsection inspection method can be used, that is, close all valves and cut off the interconnectivity between the pipelines. After holding the pressure for 7 ~ 8 h, check the pressure gauge at the high pressure side, unscrew each valve one by one, and observe the reading of the pressure gauge. If the pressure value drops significantly after opening a valve, it indicates that there is probably a leakage point at a section of pipeline after the valve, which should be checked. If necessary, the components of this section can be removed, inflated separately to maintain pressure, and immersed in the pool for leak detection.

Sometimes, the refrigeration system can also be filled with a small amount of Freon vapor, and then filled with nitrogen at the specified pressure, and the leakage can be corrected with a leak correction lamp.

2) Pressure leak detection of refrigeration system of unitary air conditioning unit

Because the refrigeration system of the unitary air conditioning unit generally adopts the totally closed compressor and capillary throttling, there is no valve in the refrigeration system. Therefore, in order to conduct pressure leak detection for the system, first connect a repair valve at the filling port of the compressor, conduct nitrogen filling and pressure maintaining test, and carry out leak detection.

Before filling nitrogen, inject a small amount of refrigerant, and inject dry nitrogen through the repair valve inlet. For R12 refrigeration system, the filling pressure is 10^6 Pa; For R22 refrigeration system, the filling pressure is 1.5×10^6 Pa. After filling, conduct 24 h pressure maintaining test. In the test, the pressure drop in the first 6 hours shall not exceed 2%, and the pressure shall be stable for the remaining 18 hours (except for the influence caused by the change of ambient temperature).

For other household air conditioning refrigeration units, pressure leak detection can also be carried out according to this method.

2. Vacuum Leak Detection

1) Purposes of vacuum leak detection

Vacuum leak detection is generally to release the pressure air or nitrogen in the refrigeration system after the pressure leak detection is qualified, and then conduct vacuum leak detection. The purpose is to:

(1) Further check the sealing performance of the refrigeration system under low pressure, especially under vacuum, to prevent the defect of one-way air leakage of the equipment and pipeline, and to prevent the continuous infiltration of external air.

(2) Evacuate the air or nitrogen in the system through vacuum leak detection. Because air or nitrogen are non-condensable gases at normal temperature, they will occupy a certain volume in the condenser when the system works, reducing the heat transfer area of the condenser,

reducing the heat transfer efficiency, increasing the condensation pressure, and affecting the cooling effect.

(3) The water in the system is removed through vacuum leak detection, and the water is evaporated under low pressure to achieve the purpose of drying.

(4) Prepare for charging refrigerant.

2) Methods of vacuum leak detection

There are mainly two kinds of vacuum leak detection: using a separate vacuum pump or using the compressor of the refrigeration system itself. For large refrigeration systems, in order to save the time of vacuum leak detection, the compressor and vacuum pump can also be used for cross operation, that is, a large amount of air in the system is pumped out by the compressor of the refrigeration system first, and then the residual air is further pumped out by the vacuum pump.

(1) Using the compressor of the system for vacuum pumping

As shown in Figure 4-5-2, the operation steps for vacuum pumping of the refrigeration system of the open compressor are as follows:

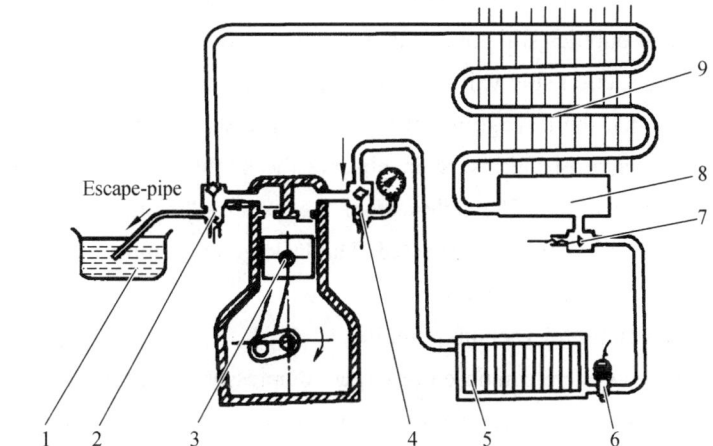

1—Oil cup; 2—Exhaust stop valve; 3—Compressor; 4—Suction stop valve; 5—Evaporator;
6—Expansion valve; 7—Outlet valve; 8—Liquid reservoir; 9—Condenser.

Figure 4-5-2   Vacuum pumping of open compressor refrigeration system

① Close the exhaust stop valve of the compressor, unscrew the plug of "multi-purpose channel", install the taper joint and exhaust pipe, open the suction stop valve less, and install a low-pressure gauge (vacuum pressure gauge) at the bypass hole of the suction stop valve. Turn the flywheel of the compressor by hand or press the power switch to start the compressor, and then turn it on and off, so as to judge whether the compressor turns correctly. Judge whether there is air flow from the exhaust pipe of the compressor. If there is air flow sound, check again. If there is no air flow sound, find out the cause.

② Short circuit the low pressure contact of the pressure controller to keep it normally open, so as to prevent the contact action from affecting the vacuum pumping of the unit during the vacuum pumping process.

③ Start the compressor to extract air until the exhaust pipe can not hear the sound of air jet, open the suction stop valve wide, and immerse the exhaust pipe orifice into the refrigerant oil cup, and observe the gas emission from the pipe orifice.

④ In the process of vacuumizing, if there is no bubble emerging within 5 min, it can be considered that the gas in the system has been basically exhausted and there is no leakage in the system. At this time, you can remove the exhaust pipe, press and hold the "multi-purpose channel" hole interface of the exhaust stop valve with your fingers, or remove the taper joint, screw on the screw plug and pull it tight, reverse the exhaust stop valve rod back enough (close the "multi-purpose channel"), and then stop the machine. Pump, and then the work is basically completed.

⑤ If there are continuous or intermittent bubbles coming out, it means that there is residual gas in the system that has not been pumped out or there is leakage. At this time, it can continue to run for 1 to 2 hours. Through running-in, the leakage caused by the seal friction surface is eliminated. If bubbles still appear, take sectional evacuation to check the tightness of each section. Close the suction stop valve of the compressor first. If there is no bubble within a few minutes, it means that the leakage is not in the compressor; Open the suction valve again, close the liquid outlet valve of the reservoir, observe the bubbles, and then check in sections until the leakage point is found. The tightness of the joint at the suspected position and the possible porosity of the weld shall be inspected. The leakage point must be found and repaired before the vacuum pumping can be continued.

(2) Using vacuum pump for vacuum pumping.

For the refrigeration system composed of larger compressor or semi-closed compressor, it is generally not suitable to use its own compressor for vacuum pumping, but vacuum pump would be used, which can just connect the suction port of the vacuum pump with the "multi-purpose channel" hole of the exhaust stop valve. At the end of vacuum pumping, close the "multi-purpose channel" hole of the exhaust stop valve first, and then stop the vacuum pump.

(3) Using vacuum pump to detect leakage.

A vacuum pump must be used for leak detection of the refrigeration system composed of a totally enclosed compressor. The vacuum pumping operation is shown in Figure 4-5-3.

① Connect the repair valve 5 with the pressure vacuum gauge with the filling pipe of vacuum pump 4 and compressor 1.

② Open the repair valve 5, open the vacuum pump 4, and observe whether the reading of the pressure vacuum gauge moves below the zero scale. If it does not move, it indicates that there is leakage in the system, which should be handled in time.

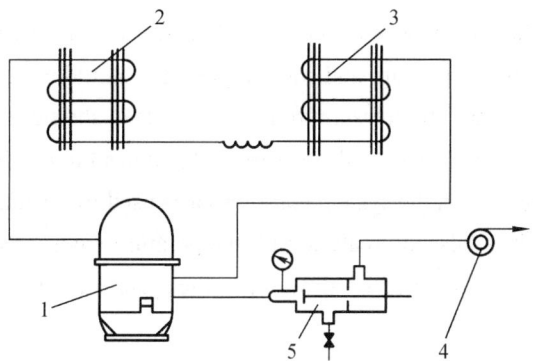

1—Compressor; 2—Condenser; 3—Evaporator; 4—Vacuum pump; 5—Repair valve.

Figure 4-5-3 Installation of a vacuum pump of one totally closed refrigeration system

③ When the pointer of the vacuum pressure gauge reaches or approaches -10^5 Pa, close the repair valve 5, and then stop the operation of vacuum pump 4. The vacuum pumping is completed.

When the refrigeration system vacuums to the specified vacuum degree at one time, it takes a long time, especially when the filling port is at the low pressure side, because of the throttling effect of the capillary, the vacuum degree at the high pressure side is difficult to meet the requirements. At this time, the method of twice vacuumizing can be adopted, that is, after the system is vacuumized for the first time, inject a small amount of refrigerant to make the pressure and vacuum gauge return to zero, and then perform the vacuum pumping again (the pointer of the vacuum pressure gauge points to -10^5 Pa). In this way, a higher vacuum degree can be obtained in a short time. This is because the right amount of R22 gas is filled after the first vacuum pumping, which makes the high-pressure part of the air diluted by R22, and the proportion of air in the remaining gas decreases.

3) Precautions during vacuum leak detection

The requirements for vacuum degree are generally implemented according to the provisions of repair procedures in the factory and depot. For units without clear regulations, multiply the local atmospheric pressure of the day by a factor of 0.96 to determine the degree of vacuum to be pumped. Under this degree of vacuum, maintain the pressure for 18 h. If the degree of vacuum is stable, it is qualified.

(1) During vacuum pumping, the valve cap of each valve shall be screwed tightly to prevent leakage of valve stem packing.

(2) Vacuum leak detection should be completed by vacuum pump as much as possible, especially for the refrigeration system of fully closed or semi-closed compressor, vacuum pump must be used for vacuum leak detection.

(3) In the system pipeline by using vacuum pump for vacuum pumping, it is better to set up a dryer to suck out the moisture and harmful gas in the air of the system during vacuum pumping, and ensure the integrity of the oil in the pump.

When vacuuming the compressor with pressure lubrication, pay attention to its oil pressure. The difference between its oil pressure and suction pressure should not be less than 26.7 kPa. If the system is equipped with oil pressure relay, its contact should be kept normally open temporarily to avoid the action of the oil pressure relay under the condition of lower than the control pressure difference when the system compressor is used for vacuuming.

When vacuuming, it is best to create a high temperature environment around the system, which is conducive to the evaporation of all water in the system and the discharge of the air out of the machine.

3. Vacuum Pumping Test of Passenger Car Air Conditioning System

1) Preparation before work

Push the refrigerant recovery and filling machine into the water flow station of the unit, and prepare to vacuum the refrigeration system.

2) Vacuum pumping of refrigeration system

(1) Release the nitrogen in the pressure maintaining test of the refrigeration system, and connect the high-pressure and low-pressure pipelines of the vacuum pump with the pressure gauge at the same time.

(2) Make sure that the blue high- and low-pressure hoses are connected to the air conditioning refrigeration system and that the high- and low-pressure valves on the control panel are open.

(3) Turn on the vacuum pump power, press the SHIFT/RESET key, and the trigger display will display "PROGRAM VACUUM MINUTES 15.00". 15 min is the default vacuuming time for the device. To change the time, directly press the corresponding numeric key to display the desired time, and then press ENTER. (The set vacuum pumping value of KLD29 air conditioning unit is 30 min, and the set time of KLD40 air conditioning unit is 40 min. Press the corresponding numeric key on the keyboard to display the desired time on the display screen. Then press ENTER).

(4) Press the VACUUM key to start vacuum pumping. At this time, the value on the display will decrease and the remaining time will be displayed.

Note: If "U-HI" appears on the display screen, pressure discharge (refrigerant recovery) must be carried out to reduce the pressure of the air conditioning system before vacuum pumping can continue.

(5) When the set time decreases to 0, the vacuum pump will stop automatically. The display will display "CPL" information. When the high pressure and low pressure of the vacuum pump are expressed to the absolute vacuum of 0 MPa, the vacuum pumping is completed.

(6) When the system is vacuumized to the absolute pressure below 75 kPa, make sure there is no change after 5 min.

Note: The vacuum pump oil must be replaced every 10 hours of cumulative operation of the vacuum pump.

3) Finishing after work

(1) Close the high-pressure and low-pressure valves, and remove the red and green high-pressure and low-pressure hoses connected to the air-conditioning refrigeration system.

(2) Fill in the Vacuum Test Record.

(3) Prepare for refrigerant charging.

【Task Training】

(1) What are the characteristics of scroll compressor?

(2) What are the functions of condenser and evaporator? What types are there? What are the factors affecting its heat transfer?

(3) What types of expansion valves are there? What is the function of thermal expansion valve? Explain the working principle of the thermal expansion valve.

(4) Briefly describe the working principle of ACB and LCB pressure controllers.

(5) What is the function of oil separator? Briefly explain the working principle of the filter oil separator.

(6) Describe the function of vacuum leak detection, and how to conduct vacuum leak detection?

Project 5

Air Conditioning and Refrigeration System of Passenger Cars

【 Chinese Railway Culture 】

The History of Railway Development in China 5: The Achievements of China-Africa Friendship

The Addis Ababa—Djibouti Railway, fully known as Ethiopia—Djibouti Standard Gauge Railway, starts from Seberta Station in Ethiopia in the west and ends at Dolarey Port Station in Djibouti in the east, with a total length of 752.7 km, 45 stations and a design speed of 120 km/h. The Addis Ababa Djibouti Railway is a freight based railway connecting Ethiopia and Djibouti on the African continent, the first electrified railway with standard gauge in East Africa, an early harvest of implementing the "the Belt and Road" initiative, a landmark project of China Africa "three networks and one industrialization" and production capacity cooperation, and the first full industrial chain railway built overseas by Chinese enterprises, known as the "Tanzania Zambia Railway in the new era".

In 2012, the construction of the Addis Ababa—Djibouti Railway began; On October 5, 2016, the Ethiopian section of the Addis Ababa—Djibouti Railway was completed and opened to traffic; On January 10, 2017, the Djibouti section of the Addis Ababa—Djibouti Railway was completed and opened to traffic; On January 1, 2018, the Addis Ababa—Djibouti Railway was put into commercial operation.

The Addis Ababa—Djibouti Railway is the first overseas railway project integrating the whole industrial chain of design standards, investment and financing, equipment and materials,

Figure 5-1 Addis Ababa-Djibouti Railway

construction, supervision and operation management, and is a landmark achievement of the "the Belt and Road" initiative. The Addis Ababa-Djibouti Railway is an extension and development of China Africa historical friendship, a good beginning of China's "the Belt and Road" initiative in Africa business sector, and plays an important role in driving the in-depth economic development of East Africa and even Africa. At the same time, goods from China and other Asian countries can also be transported to Ethiopia and other African countries through the Addis Ababa—Djibouti Railway.

The Addis Ababa—Djibouti Railway is not only a transportation line, but also an economic corridor and a road to prosperity. It has opened a major railway passage to the sea for Ethiopia, the only landlocked country with a population of more than 100 million in the world, and has effectively driven the development of industrialization and urbanization along the railway. It has also demonstrated great value during the epidemic.

【Project Description】

Through the study of this project, students can master the equipment, structure, function and operation principle of the air conditioning heating and ventilation system of passenger cars, and can use the knowledge learned to ensure the daily use and regular maintenance of the heating and ventilation system of 25T passenger cars.

【Project Objectives】

1. Knowledge objectives

(1) Master the principle and maintenance methods of electric heating and heat pump heating.

(2) Master the structure and function of each part of the passenger car ventilation system.

(3) Master the maintenance method of ventilation system of 25T passenger car.

2. Capability objectives

(1) Be able to use the knowledge of passenger train heating and ventilation system for maintenance.

(2) Be able to independently learn the maintenance cycle and items of the ventilation system of 25T passenger cars.

(3) Be able to complete the daily maintenance of the ventilation system of 25T passenger cars.

3. Quality objectives

(1) Cultivate the ability to apply what you learn, think hard and love innovation.

(2) Cultivate the awareness and ability to use and care for equipment flexibly.

(3) Cultivate the awareness and ability of standardized operation and safe production.

(4) Cultivate teamwork spirit.

Task 1 Electric Heating Device

【Task Objective】

(1) Master the structure and principle of electric heating device.

(2) Master the principle of heat pump and understand the difference and relationship between heat pump and refrigeration.

(3) Master the daily maintenance method of electric heater.

【Knowledge Reserve】

In winter, especially in the north, the ambient temperature outside the car is relatively low. In order to ensure the comfort of passengers, the outside fresh air must be preheated before being sent into the car. Preheating means heating in the air conditioning system. The preheated air is blown into the vehicle from each air outlet. For most air-conditioned passenger cars with roof air supply, due to the characteristics of rising hot air and falling cool air, the temperature difference between the upper and lower temperatures in the car is large, and the temperature in the car is very uneven. At the same time, the vehicle body and the external environment are also carrying out heat transfer, and the heat loss in the vehicle is more. Therefore, other heating devices are also installed on the floor surfaces on both sides of the vehicle to compensate for heat loss. Therefore, the heating system of passenger car air conditioning generally consists of two parts, one is the air preheater set in the air duct, and the other is the compensation heater set in the passenger compartment.

At present, domestic mainstream passenger car heating adopts the form of electric preheating and compensation electric heating, such as 25G, 25Z, 25K and 25T passenger cars. Heat pump heating is also used for passenger cars in some areas in the south.

1. Tubular Electric Heating Element

The electric heating device used on air-conditioned passenger cars usually uses tubular electric heating elements (see Figure 5-1-1). By using the thermal effect of current, the current will generate heat through the resistance wire, and the air flowing through it will take away the heat to achieve the heating effect. It has the characteristics of fast heating, uniform temperature, compact structure, convenient control, and not easy to be affected by the external environment.

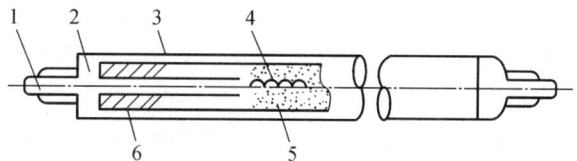

1—Connecting terminal; 2—Insulating mat; 3—Metal sleeve; 4—Electric heating wire;
5—Insulating powder; 6—Sealing material.

Figure 5-1-1 Structure of tubular electric heating element

As shown in Figure 5-1-1, a spiral resistance wire is placed in the metal tube along the axis of the tube, and the gap is evenly filled with crystalline magnesium oxide with good thermal conductivity and electrical insulation. The pipe diameter is reduced by a pipe shrinking machine to increase the density of magnesium oxide powder and improve the thermal conductivity. At the same time, it is also necessary to ensure that the spiral resistance wire in the pipe cannot touch the pipe wall due to the bending or collision of the electric heating element. The outlet of the lead out rod of the resistance wire is sealed with a mixture of barium borate to prevent the water and liquid medium in the air from diving into the magnesium oxide powder and causing poor insulation. Because the resistance wire is buried in a dense oxide medium with high thermal conductivity and does not contact with air, its unit load power can be greatly increased compared with the bare resistance wire, and its service life is also correspondingly improved.

2. Electric Preheater

The electric preheater is a heating device that uses electric heating elements to supplement the heat in the passenger car when heating is needed in winter. The electric preheater adopts the current heating effect. At present, there are two kinds of electric preheaters used in passenger car air conditioners: tubular electric heating element and electric heating plate.

The electric preheater is composed of electric heating elements and frame. When in use, it is electrically interlocked with the ventilator (it must operate at the same time) and electrically interlocked with the refrigerator (it cannot operate at the same time). The electric heating elements are generally divided into two groups, and one of them can work, two groups can work or stop automatically according to the indoor air temperature through the air conditioning temperature controller. The electric preheater is usually installed near the evaporator, and the air supply duct is shared for refrigeration or heating. The air duct connected with the electric preheater shall be made of flame retardant insulation materials.

In order to prevent the surface temperature of the electric preheater from being too high due to poor ventilation, there are two levels of overheating protection:

(1) When the temperature exceeds 70 °C, the relay will trip, cut off the main heating circuit and stop the electric preheater. When the temperature of the electric preheater drops to a certain value, the relay can resume closing and continue heating.

(2) When the temperature exceeds 139 °C, the fuse will blow, cut off the main heating circuit and stop the electric preheater. At this time, the main heating circuit cannot be restored automatically. It is necessary to replace the fuse after manual inspection before the electric preheater can resume heating.

3. Electric Heater

The electric heater is a kind of ground heater, which is electrically interlocked with the refrigeration equipment. Automatic control is realized through temperature controller during operation. The electric heater is mainly composed of electric heater body, electric heating pipe or electric heating plate, fuse protector, wiring board, waterproof box, high-temperature resistant connecting wire and cover plate.

The electric heater body is generally made of steel plate, and the electric heating plate or electric heating tube is the core device. There is no structure of cooling fan, which is similar to household electric heater. Because of its good thermal radiation performance, long service life, small size, light weight, uniform temperature distribution and other advantages, the electric heater for passenger car heating is now mostly electric heating plate. The hot plate is connected to the power supply on the vehicle through the wiring board and connecting wire. Therefore, the wiring board and connecting wire are made of high-temperature resistant materials. Cage spring terminals are used for wiring, and a non-recoverable over-temperature protector is installed on each electric heating plate.

The electric heating plate is mainly composed of heating plate and radiating fin, and its structure is shown in Figure 5-1-2. The terminal post of the electric heating board is sealed with the heat-resistant polytetrafluoroethylene material.

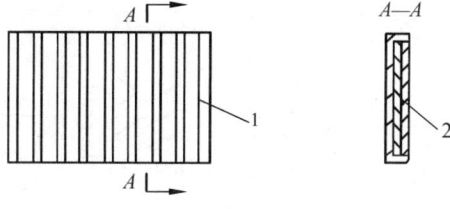

1—Cooling fin; 2—Heating plate.

Figure 5-1-2 Structure of electric heating plate

The electric heater is fixed to the side wall of the car body by M4×30 wooden screws, as shown in Figure 5-1-3. The embedded electric heater is fixed to the side wall of the car body adopting M4×30 wooden screws.

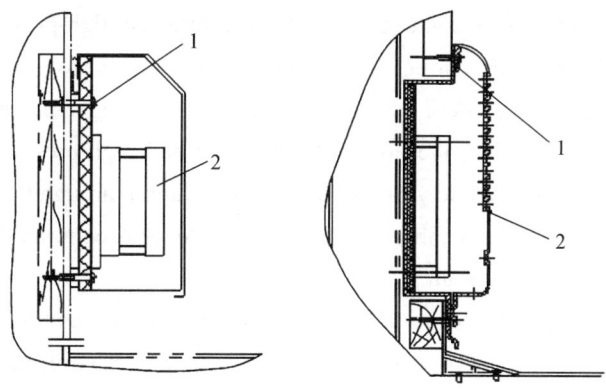

1—Wood screw; 2—Electric heater.

Figure 5-1-3 Electric heater installation profile

4. Principle of Heat Pump

Using a refrigerator to absorb heat from a low temperature environment and release heat in a high temperature environment is much greater than the heat that can be obtained by heating directly using electric energy. This device that "pumps" heat from a low temperature environment into the room is called a heat pump. On the basis of steam compression refrigeration, the heat pump still uses the way of work to make the refrigerant realize heating in reverse circulation.

The heat pump system is also composed of four main parts: compressor, condenser, throttling device and evaporator. On the basis of the steam compression refrigeration system, the heat pump system adds a four-way reversing valve to switch the refrigerant circulation direction, so that the refrigerant can reverse circulation during heating to achieve heating effect.

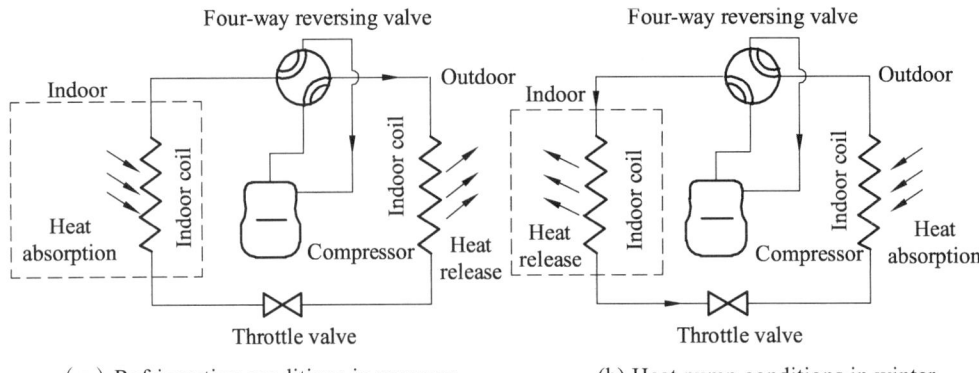

(a) Refrigeration conditions in summer　　(b) Heat pump conditions in winter

Figure 5-1-4　Principle of heat pump

As shown in Figure 5-1-4, (a) shows the refrigeration condition in summer. The compressor compresses the refrigerant into high-temperature and high-pressure steam, which is sent to the outdoor condenser through the four-way reversing valve. Through the external environmental medium, the outdoor condenser releases the refrigerant heat energy into the external environment. After that, the normal-temperature and high-pressure refrigerant liquid changes into low-temperature and low-pressure refrigerant liquid through the throttling action of the throttle valve, and then flows through the evaporator in the room, absorbs the heat of the indoor air, thus cooling the indoor air.

(b) shows the heat pump condition in winter, the compressor compresses the refrigerant into high-temperature and high-pressure steam, and changes the refrigerant flow direction through the four-way reversing valve, so that the refrigerant first enters the indoor evaporator. At this time, the indoor evaporator is used as a condenser to release heat to the indoor air, and then the refrigerant passes through the throttle valve (pressure reduction and temperature reduction), the outdoor condenser (at this time, it is used as an evaporator to absorb heat), the four-way reversing valve, and again the compressor, and then enter the next cycle.

In the heat pump system, due to the need to absorb heat from the cold outside, the boiling point temperature of the refrigerant under the specific pressure is very low. The surface of the heat exchanger (condenser during refrigeration) used as the evaporator outdoors may be frosted, thus blocking the air path and affecting the heat exchange. Therefore, appropriate defrosting measures should be taken in the system. In general cold environment, heat pump heating has certain energy-saving advantages over electric heating pipe heating. However, affected by the boiling point temperature of the refrigerant under the specific pressure, the effect of heat pump heating will be greatly reduced in the extremely cold regions.

5. Routine Maintenance of Electric Heater

After the vehicle leaves the factory, check the electric heater regularly to keep the surface of the electric heater dry and clean. The electric heater is generally used under the ambient temperature of $-40\ °C\ —+40\ °C$ and the relative humidity of air $\leqslant 90\%$. Before use in winter every year, the electric heating plate shall be tested on the premise that it is dry, clean, well insulated and firmly connected. It can be used normally only after meeting the requirements of electrical standards and the performance requirements of the electric heating plate.

1) Precautions during use

(1) Do not put your hand into the cover to touch the electric heating plate and other accessories to prevent scalding or electric shock.

(2) Do not step on the electric heater at will to avoid damaging the electric heater cover.

(3) Do not put water or sundries into the electric heater cover to prevent electric shock or damage to the equipment.

(4) The surface of the electric heater shall not be covered with anything to prevent fire.

(5) When the electric heater is stopped, the main power supply of each part of the electric heater device shall be cut off.

2) Treatment measures in case of failure

(1) In case of breakdown or flashover of the electric heating plate, turn off the power supply and check and replace it.

(2) If the insulation value of the hot plate falls below the specified value, check and replace it.

(3) If the electric heating plate does not generate heat after being electrified, the heat is too small or too large, and it does not meet the requirements, check and replace it.

Task 2 Ventilation System

【Task Objective】

(1) Master the structure and function of ventilator, air duct and air outlet in the ventilation system.

(2) Understand the principle and characteristics of induced ventilation.

【Knowledge Reserve】

1. Overview

When we take the high-speed rail, we can feel the wind from the top of the car, the seat near the window, and even under the legs. The cool wind in summer and the hot wind in winter are sent out. This is because there are evenly distributed air outlets on the top and both sides of the car. The treated air is transmitted through the air duct through the car and enters the car from the air outlet, as shown in Figure 5-2-1. The evenly distributed air supply in the space can ensure the ride comfort. There is no side air vent on the passenger trains of ordinary speed, only the top air vent. Therefore, the ride comfort is greatly reduced compared with high-speed railway.

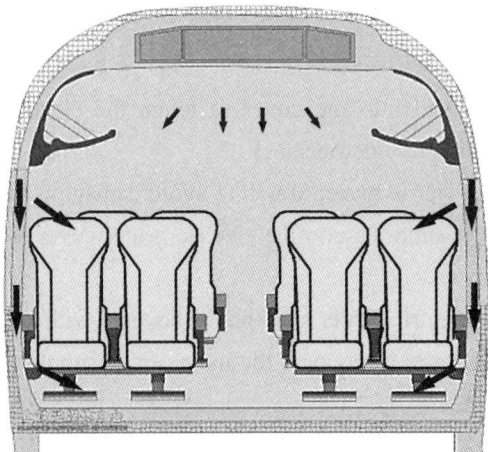

Figure 5-2-1 EMU ventilation system

Whether it is refrigeration or heating, if there is no air flowing from the evaporator or preheater to force cold air or hot air to be carried everywhere in the car, the air conditioning device of the passenger car cannot achieve the air conditioning function. In addition, the fresh air needed in the car also needs to be "pumped" into the car. Air conditioning is a technology that sends the treated air into the vehicle in a certain way to control the temperature, humidity, cleanliness and airflow speed of the air in the vehicle within an appropriate range. Therefore, the ventilation system for conveying fresh air, cold air or hot air is an indispensable part of the air conditioning system.

According to different working modes, the ventilation system can generally be divided into the following three categories:

(1) Natural ventilation system: It depends on the pressure difference formed in the natural environment to deliver air, such as natural ventilator.

(2) Forced ventilation system: It uses special fans and air ducts to deliver air, such as the air conditioning system of passenger cars.

(3) Induced ventilation system: The inducer is used to make the secondary air circulate locally in the room without centralized treatment and main air duct transmission, so the air duct size is small and the equipment is compact.

The ventilation system is composed of centrifugal fan, dust filter, supply air duct, exhaust device, return air duct, etc. Its functions are: air filtration, air transmission, and air distribution. The centrifugal fan sucks the fresh air outside the vehicle into the vehicle and mixes it with the recirculated air inside the vehicle. After the dust and other impurities in the air are filtered by the dust filter, it is sent into the passenger compartment. At the same time, the exhaust fan will exhaust the excess dirty air outside the vehicle. Due to the demand for fresh air in the vehicle, the ventilation system is the only system in the passenger car air conditioning system that operates year-round regardless of season, so its quality status directly affects the comfort of passengers and the economy of the air conditioning device.

Under the action of the ventilation unit, the outdoor fresh air is sucked into the vehicle through the fresh air inlet, filtered by the dust filter and mixed with the return air, and then sent into the air treatment room, cooled by the evaporator or preheated by the electric preheater, and then sent into the main air duct, and then evenly sent into the room through each air supply outlet. A part of the indoor air is sucked in by the ventilator through the return air inlet and return air duct and reused as recirculated air; The other part is discharged from the outside of the vehicle through the exhaust outlet and exhaust fan.

2. Ventilation Unit

The ventilation unit is the power unit of the ventilation system, which is composed of centrifugal fan and motor. It inhales the outdoor fresh air and indoor return air, pressurizes the filtered mixed air, and sends it into the passenger compartment through the main air duct. The ventilation unit is usually composed of a double-speed motor with two-way shaft extension and two centrifugal fans.

The ventilator motor of the domestic unitary air conditioning unit is a three-phase AC motor, which can achieve double speed through pole change. In recent years, double-winding motors have been used to realize two-speed operation. Most fans are multi-blade, low-noise, centrifugal fans. The structure of centrifugal fan is shown in Figure 5-2-2.

Generally, the ventilator is set at high speed in summer and low speed in winter; In addition, different rotational speeds can be adopted according to the number of passengers in the vehicle. When the temperature and the humidity are high in summer and there are few passengers in the vehicle, the ventilator can be placed at low speed to reduce the amount of fresh air in the vehicle, so as to achieve the purpose of dehumidification. According to the installation position of the ventilator, it can be divided into:

1. Suction structure

If the ventilator is installed behind the air treatment equipment (evaporator, preheater), the mixed air is first treated by the treatment equipment, and then inhaled and pressurized by the ventilator before being sent into the main air duct, it is called suction structue.

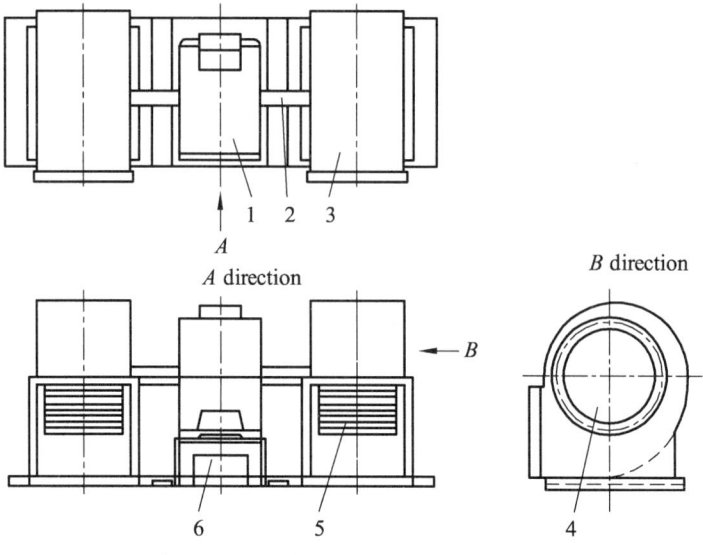

1—Two-speed motor; 2—Bidirectional motor shaft; 3—Centrifugal fan;
4—Fan volute; 5—Impeller; 6—Base.

Figure 5-2-2 Centrifugal fan

2. Press-out structure

If the fan is installed in front of the air treatment equipment, the mixed air is first sucked by the fan and then pressed to the treatment equipment, and then enters the main air duct after treatment, it is called press-out structure.

The unitary air conditioning unit usually adopts the suction structure.

3. Air duct and regulating plate

In the air supply system, the treated fresh air can be delivered to all parts of the vehicle through the air duct. In the exhaust system, the dirty air in the vehicle can be delivered to the outside of the vehicle through the air duct. This kind of pipe for conveying air can be made of various materials, and can also have many different structures and section forms. In the passenger car air conditioning device, the air duct shall meet the requirements of comfort, economy, lightweight and cost as much as possible according to the space conditions. Common materials include galvanized iron plate, aluminum alloy plate, glass fiber reinforced plastic and plywood.

1) Main air duct

The main air duct is used to mix the fresh air and return air and deliver them to all parts of the vehicle. The section of the main air duct is generally rectangular. Because rectangular air duct is easy to process, convenient for passenger compartment decoration and installation, it is widely used on passenger cars. When air is transmitted in a long main air duct, the flow rate will gradually decay. If the air flow rate in the air duct is to be kept constant, the variable cross-section air duct can be used, that is, the cross-sectional area of the air duct is getting smaller and smaller. However, the variable-section air duct has a complex structure and is difficult to manufacture. Usually, the equal-section air duct is used, and the adjustment plate is installed, which can also achieve the effect of uniform air supply at each air supply outlet, but manual adjustment is required.

The joint of air duct made of metal sheet generally adopts the form of "bite". The connection between the two sections of air ducts generally adopts flange plates, and fillers are added between the flange plates to prevent gas leakage. Most of the wooden air ducts are made of plywood, and the top is combined with the roof inside the roof to form a closed space. Before making the air duct, the wood shall be subject to anti-corrosion treatment, and after making the air duct, it shall be painted with fireproof paint. The air duct joint shall be pasted with fine cloth or thick oil paper with good quality. A layer of 3.5 mm thick polyurethane foam plastic is pasted inside the air duct, which can effectively absorb the noise of the ventilator and air flow noise, and reduce the heat exchange in the transmission process.

2) Adjusting plate

The function of the regulating plate is to regulate the air flow through the air duct, and its structure depends on the cross-section shape of the air duct. The simplest and widely used regulator is the shutter type. The commonly used round and rectangular adjusting plates can be used to adjust the air volume by changing the angle of the adjusting plate by turning the handle. The opening of the adjusting plate on the passenger car is adjusted manually.

3) Return air duct

The return air duct is used to extract indoor recirculated air, and its section shape depends on the location and space size in the vehicle. Most of the return air outlets on the passenger car are located at the lower part of the end wall of the first position, and are led to the upper part of the flat roof plate of the first position by the return air duct to facilitate the suction of the ventilator. If it is a private passenger car, the lower part of the private door is equipped with a return air inlet, and the corridor is used as the return air duct. The doors at both ends of the corridor are closed. There is a return air outlet on the flat-top plate of the corridor near the first end, and then the return air duct will lead the recirculated air into the ventilator.

4) Exhaust duct

The exhaust duct is used to exhaust the dirty air in the vehicle, so one end of it is connected to the exhaust outlet, and the other end is connected to the exhaust fan or natural ventilator. The air outlet of passenger car is generally set on the roof at the opposite end of the air outlet. There are also passenger cars without special exhaust outlets. At this time, the excess air in the passenger car will be discharged from the door gap or the defecator in toilet by relying on the indoor positive pressure.

4. Tuyere

1) Fresh air outlet

The fresh air inlet is generally arranged at the upper part of the door with the ventilator end, and also at the upper part of the vehicle end and the upper part of the roof. The fresh air inlet is equipped with louvers and grids to prevent sundries, rain and snow from entering the vehicle. Most of the fresh air outlets are also equipped with adjustment mechanisms to adjust the intake of fresh air as required. At the same time, it is also convenient to close the fresh air outlet when the ventilator stops running. The new air outlet with the adjusting mechanism can pull the adjusting handle down, and then the valve (shutter) will be opened by the lever action of the adjusting rod. The new air outlet is in the open state, and the spring plate is stuck in the groove of the adjusting rod, which plays the role of fixing the valve opening.

2) Air supply outlet

The air supply outlet is used to distribute air. The air supply outlet is generally equipped with a diffuser, which can not only make the air supply uniform, achieve reasonable indoor air distribution and uniform temperature, but also adjust the size of the air supply volume according to the specific indoor requirements.

For the ventilation system with centralized air supply, the air supply outlets are generally uniformly arranged along the roof or side wall, as shown in Figure 5-2-3. The commonly used air supply outlets are disc type diffusers and straight plate type diffusers. The air volume regulating mechanism is installed in the air duct. The return air outlet and exhaust air outlet are generally set on the partition wall, the outer surface is equipped with grille to increase the beauty, and the inner part is equipped with wire mesh to prevent sundries from entering the air duct.

Figure 5-2-3 **Air supply outlet evenly distributed along the main air duct**

5. Air Filter

The air always contains various kinds of dust and impurities in varying degrees. Excessive dust entering the vehicle will not only affect the comfort and health of passengers, but also affect the normal operation of air handling equipment, because the accumulation of dust on the evaporator surface will reduce its heat transfer effect. Therefore, the ventilation system is equipped with air filter. The filter shall be installed in front of the air handling room, which can be installed horizontally or vertically.

The working principle of air filtration is to make the dusty air pass through the gap with a diameter smaller than the dust particle or through the large but sufficiently long and tortuous hole to leave the dust. In addition, when dust particles pass through the filter, they will be left behind due to diffusion, friction, electrostatic force or adhesion force generated when the material surface is wet. The filtering effect of the filter depends on the thickness and density of the air passage of the material used and the wind speed passing through the filter. Nylon fiber material is durable, acid-resistant and alkali-resistant, easy to use and long service life. It can be washed with clean water after being stained. It is the material commonly used for air filter of passenger car air conditioning system now.

Only by keeping the air filter clean and effective can the cleaning cycle of the evaporator be extended, because it is always easier to maintain the air filter than the evaporator. Therefore, the filter screen must not be missing. If it is lost or damaged, it must be replaced in time, otherwise the evaporator will soon be blocked by dirt and seriously affect the cooling effect.

6. Natural Ventilator and Exhaust Fan

The natural ventilator is installed on the upper part of the vehicle body. It uses the ventilator to form a back pressure vacuum in the air flow outside the vehicle and the difference in air volume density due to the difference in temperature between the upper and lower parts of the vehicle to drain the air inside the vehicle out so as to complete the ventilation function.

As shown in Figure 5-2-4, the exhaust fans are all axial flow fans, which are installed on the top of the car in the washroom, toilet, etc., and directly extract the exhaust gas from the car.

7. Induced Ventilation

In the centralized air conditioning system, the section size of the air duct is large, which not only occupies a large indoor space, but also often brings difficulties to the construction and installation. Therefore, for some places where the space is tight and the interior decoration has certain requirements, such as vehicles, ships, underground works, etc., induced ventilation is often used to reduce the cross-sectional size of the air duct and simplify its system structure.

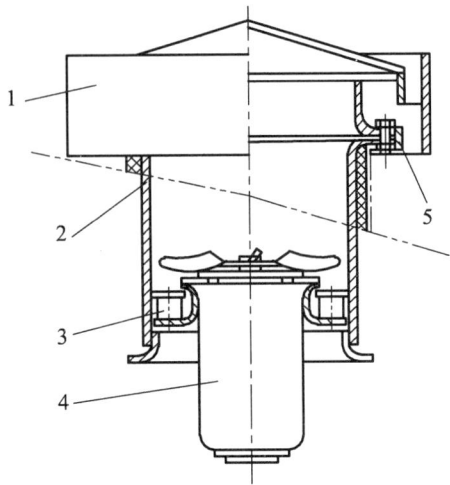

1—Exhaust cap; 2—Connecting barrel; 3—Pillar shock absorber;
4—Exhaust fan and motor; 5—Sealing gasket.

Figure 5-2-4　Exhaust fan

1) Principle of induced ventilation

As shown in Figure 5-2-5, when the induction ventilation system is working, the fresh air and part of the return air form primary air after being processed by the treatment box, and then are sent into the static chamber of the induction device in the vehicle by the ventilator. In the static chamber, the dynamic pressure of the primary air is changed to static pressure, and under the static pressure, the primary air is evenly distributed to each nozzle to reduce the air flow noise. After that, the primary air is sent out by the nozzle to induce the secondary air, which is mixed in the mixing chamber and finally sent into the vehicle through the air outlet.

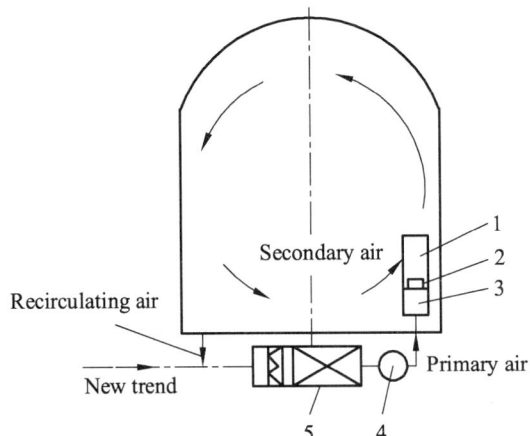

1—Mixing box; 2—Nozzle; 3—Static pressure chamber; 4—Ventilator;
5—Centralized air treatment box.

Figure 5-2-5　The induction air conditioning system

Induced ventilation is to use the inducer to make the secondary air circulate locally in the room without centralized treatment and main air duct transmission. The main air duct is only used for conveying primary air. If the primary air is all fresh air, the return air of the system can be canceled, so the section of the main air duct and the centralized air treatment equipment can be reduced accordingly.

2) Characteristics of induced ventilation

(1) Saving the interior space of the car.

The wind speed in the main air duct of induced ventilation can reach 15—25 m/s, while the wind speed in the general air duct is only 5—7.5 m/s, so the corresponding air duct section is smaller. Take the trunk hard sleeper as an example, the sectional area of the general large air duct is 0.29 m^2, while the sectional area of the induced air duct is 0.0154 m^2, and is only 1/19 of the large air duct, which would be greatly beneficial to the layout of the air duct. Compact equipment and small air duct size are the most obvious advantages of induced ventilation, which can save space for the interior of the car.

(2) Locally adjustable air supply volume.

For the inducer with a certain structure, when the primary air volume is fixed, the secondary air volume of the inducer is related to the size of the return air inlet area. Therefore, by adjusting the opening of the movable shutter at the return air inlet, the total supply air volume of the inducer can be adjusted, thus achieving the effect of regulating the indoor air flow disturbance. Passengers can adjust the opening of the return air inlet as required without affecting the stability of the whole system. For example, when the room temperature is high, the return air shutter can be opened to increase the air supply volume (and also reduce the temperature difference of the supply air) and speed up the air flow in the passenger living area to increase the comfort of passengers.

(3) Adjustable air volume day and night.

For sleeper cars, when driving at night, in order to reduce the noise and air volume, the air inlet valve of the primary air can be adjusted, or the speed of the ventilator can be reduced, so that the primary air volume will be reduced, and the total air supply will also be reduced, so as to meet the environmental conditions required for passengers to sleep.

(4) Easier to meet the humidity requirements.

The temperature of the primary air after dehumidification and cooling by the air refrigerant is not limited by the temperature difference of the supply air, because the primary air is not directly sent into the room, but mixed with the indoor return air through the inducer and then sent out. The more secondary air is induced, the higher the temperature of the mixed air supply will be. Therefore, the primary air can be processed to obtain a larger enthalpy difference and humidity difference. In this way, the dehumidification and heat removal capacity of the unit air supply can be greater, which can make the passenger car with a larger humidity load and a large seating capacity obtain satisfactory humidity requirements. Of course, in order to achieve this goal, the air refrigerant should also be improved accordingly. Therefore, the air refrigerant used for induced ventilation has the characteristics of large number of tube rows, low evaporation temperature and low frontal wind speed of the cooler.

(5) No crosstalk at adjacent air supply outlets.

The static chamber of the inducer is also a muffler with a wide attenuation rate, which has a certain silencing effect. It overcomes the crosstalk problem of adjacent rooms passing through the air supply outlet when using the common air supply outlet.

(6) The system requiring muffler.

The inducer will produce large noise due to the high wind speed of the nozzle, so the necessary noise elimination measures should be considered on the inducer. In addition, although the air volume of the primary air treatment system for induced ventilation is small, the resistance is large, so the speed of the fan equipped is generally high, so the noise of the fan is also high. If necessary, a muffler is required.

(7) Longer operation period of the refrigerator.

Because the secondary air volume of induced ventilation is small, when the outdoor temperature is appropriate, the outside fresh air can not be fully used to ventilate and cool the passenger compartment in the vehicle. Therefore, the operation time of the refrigerator is longer than that of the general air-conditioning system in the whole year.

Task 3 Structure and Maintenance of Ventilation System of 25T Passenger Car

【Task Objective】

(1) Master the structure and function of ventilation system of 25T hard sleeper and soft sleeper.

(2) Be able to repair the ventilator in the passenger car ventilation system.

【Knowledge Reserve】

1. Ventilation System Structure of 25T Semi-cushioned Berth Sleeping Car

1) Air supply system

The air conditioning unit of the 25T semi-cushioned berth sleeping car is a unitary unit, which is installed on the top of the car end. The air supply of the air conditioner is sent to the passenger compartment through the air supply duct from the air conditioning unit and through the carriage, and the air supply hood installed on the flat roof of the luggage compartment is sent to the passenger compartment, as shown in Figure 5-3-1. One air volume regulating mechanism and four groups of wind direction regulating mechanisms are installed in the deflector plate of each compartment. Among them, the air volume regulating mechanism has been adjusted to the proper working position by the commissioning personnel during the factory commissioning. Generally speaking, during the normal operation of the vehicle, passengers are not required to adjust themselves. When it is really necessary to adjust, the stewards need to use the railway special key to adjust according to the operation instructions on it. After the adjustment, the adjustment handle needs to be locked. For the wind direction adjustment mechanism, passengers can manually adjust the blade angle and change the outflow direction as required.

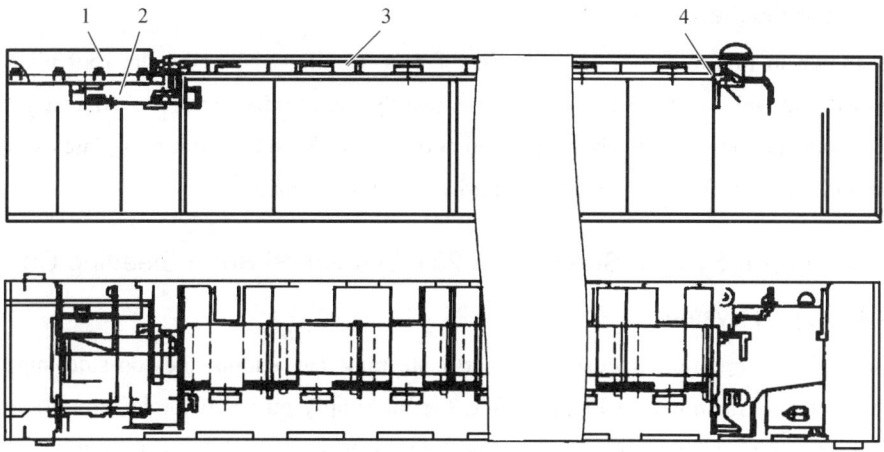

1—Air conditioning unit; 2—Air supply duct; 3—Return air duct; 4—Waste exhaust duct.

Figure 5-3-1 Schematic diagram of air supply and return of air conditioning system of 25T semi-cushioned berth sleeping car

2) Return air system

The 25T semi-cushioned berth sleeping car adopts implicit return air, as shown in Figure 5-3-1. The cavity at the top of the large corridor at the side of the carriage, the back of the luggage deck and the cavity between the two side walls are closed to form a return air and waste exhaust air cavity. After passing through the compartment, the air supply flow in each compartment flows from the open door to the large corridor, enters the return air cavity through the return air orifice plate set at the curtain slide of the large corridor, and finally converges into the return air channel set at the top of the flat top plate of the small corridor at the one end, and then return to the unit through the air return port at the lower part of the unit.

The return air duct at the lower part of the air conditioning unit is equipped with a pull-type return air filter screen, which needs to be cleaned regularly according to the requirements of the operating instructions. When cleaning, first open the inspection door on the flat-top plate of the pass-through table at the first position, draw out the return air filter screen, and then insert the filter screen along the slide after cleaning, and then insert the plug plate to prevent the filter screen from sliding out and falling off when the vehicle is running.

A filter screen is set in front of the evaporator of the air conditioning unit to filter the return air in the passenger compartment and the fresh air from the outside again. The filter screen in front of the evaporator also needs to be cleaned regularly. During cleaning, open the inspection door near the end sliding door of the flat top plate of the small corridor of position-1 and the inspection door on the flat top plate of the end-1pass-through table, first extract the return air filter screen, then remove the filter screen in front of the evaporator, and then install and lock it in sequence after cleaning.

3) Waste discharge device

As shown in Figure 5-3-1, an axial flow fan is installed above the flat roof plate of the small corridor at end-2 of the vehicle, which is mainly used to discharge the exhaust gas inside the vehicle outside the vehicle. The inspection door is installed on the flat roof plate of the small corridor, and the axial flow fan can be repaired after being opened.

2. Ventilation System Structure of 25T Cushioned Berth Sleeping Car

1) Air supply system

The 25T air-conditioned cushioned berth sleeping car adopts the top-side supply and down-return type. As shown in Figure 5-3-2, the air supply outlet of the air conditioner is of concealed structure, and each air supply outlet is equipped with an electric air volume regulating mechanism. The air supply decorative plate is installed under the air volume adjustment mechanism, and the air supply is made by using the strip gap formed between the decorative plate and the flat top plate. The air supply flow is the strip gap flat top plate attached jet. The indoor circulating air is discharged from the passenger compartment through the return air grille set on the partition wall of the compartment, thus forming the air flow organization form of up supply and down return. This air distribution form can make the indoor air distribution more uniform and enhance the indoor comfort. The air volume regulating mechanism is equipped with regulating valves to control the size of the air supply volume by adjusting the net area of the air supply, so as to meet the requirements of regulating the air temperature in the compartment.

When it is necessary to repair the electric air volume regulating mechanism, please open the locking mechanism of the air supply trim panel and open the trim panel downward. After opening the trim panel. After the operation is completed, the lock nut must be fastened to avoid abnormal noise due to the gap between the adjusting plates during the vehicle operation. The

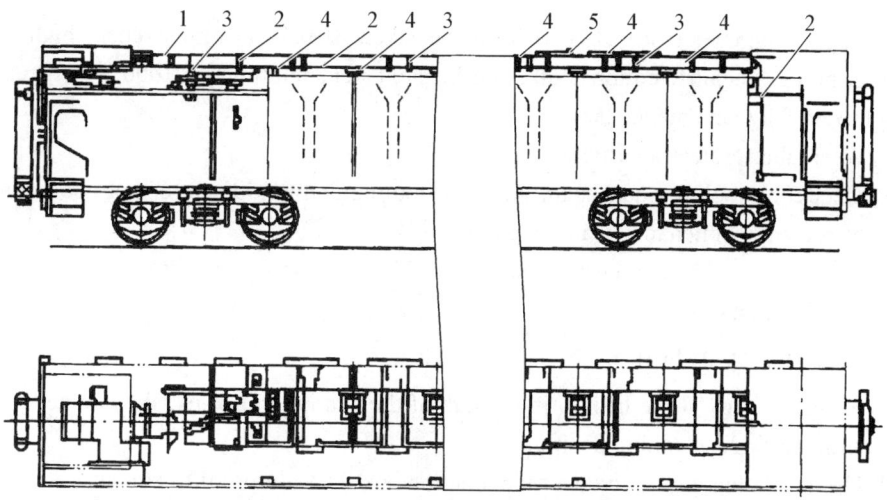

1—Air supply hose; 2—Adjustable air supply outlet of small room; 3—Air supply duct composition; 4—Air volume regulating device; 5—Air supply grille.

Figure 5-3-2　Air supply schematic diagram of the 25T air conditioning system of a cushioned berth sleeping car

regulating control of the electric air volume regulating mechanism is set under the window of each compartment, and the manual knob on the panel can make stepless adjustment of the regulating valve. Each compartment is provided with an independent air volume adjustment device. Passengers can adjust the air volume through the adjustment knob on the wall according to their own adaptation to the temperature of the compartment.

2) Return air system

The circulating air in the cushioned berth sleeping car enters the large corridor through the return air grille set on the partition wall of the compartment, and the concealed return air outlet is set behind the window trim panel. The circulating air in the vehicle enters the closed return air duct from the return air inlet and is sucked into the air conditioning unit by the unit ventilator. The cleaning method of the return air filter screen and evaporator filter screen in the return air duct is similar to that of the 25T semi-cushioned berth sleeping car, which will not be repeated here.

3) Waste discharge device

Similar to the 25T semi-cushioned berth sleeping car, an axial flow fan is installed above the flat roof plate of the small corridor at end-2 of the vehicle, which is mainly used to exhaust the exhaust gas inside the vehicle. An inspection door is installed on the flat roof plate of the small corridor at position-2, which can be opened for maintenance of the axial flow fan.

3. Fan Maintenance

1) Operation preparation

(1) Preparation of tools and materials: screwdriver, wire pliers, electric tools, torque

wrench, copper hammer (rod), 8/10/14/17 mm socket, 8/10/14/17 mm wrench, high-pressure washer, grinding machine, cotton cloth, brush, paint pen, multimeter, 1000 V megger, sling, bearing loader, fan maintenance table.

(2) Wear labor protection articles.

(3) Check the tooling equipment, all tools, tooling and equipment are in good condition, and the instrument maintenance is not expired.

(4) Clean the workbench, ensure that the workbench is free of sundries and dirt, and keep the workbench clean.

2) Cleaning operation

(1) Hang the hook at the lifting ring mouth of the ventilator, and use the overhead crane to lift the ventilator to the cleaning position.

(2) Use insulating gloves to cover the junction box for waterproof treatment.

(3) Use a high-pressure water gun to clean the fan surface and internal air duct.

(4) Lift the cleaned ventilator to the maintenance position for drying and wipe it with cotton cloth.

3) Insulation test

(1) Use a multimeter to measure the three-phase winding without short circuit and open circuit, and the three-phase resistance is balanced. Use a 1000 V megger to measure the insulation resistance of the winding to the shell, which is not less than 5 MΩ. The insulation between two different windings of the fan's multi-winding motor shall not be less than 5 MΩ.

(2) If the insulation resistance value does not meet the requirements, update the motor of the same model.

4) Decomposition

(1) After drying, transport the fan to be serviced to the disassembly station of the fan maintenance line, and use an electric wrench to remove the fixing bolts of the fan duct installation, as shown in Figure 5-3-3.

(2) Use a wrench to remove the impeller fixing bolts, as shown in Figure 5-3-4.

(3) Transport the fan to the fan disassembly table, and use the fan disassembly table to remove the impellers on both sides of the fan, as shown in Figure 5-3-5.

(4) Use a wrench to remove the fixing bolts of the covers at both ends of the fan motor and take out the rotor, as shown in Figure 5-3-6.

(5) Remove the bearings on the rotor with the bearing loader, as shown in Figure 5-3-7.

5) Maintenance

(1) Visually check whether the fan frame, protective cover, impeller and end cover are rusted, damaged or deformed. The rusted part shall be derusted and polished with a grinder and painted with anti-rust paint and primary paint. The deformed part shall be corrected, the damaged part shall be renewed, and the end cover shall be renewed if it is defective.

Figure 5-3-3   The fan stack

Figure 5-3-4   The fan

Figure 5-3-5   The fan disassembly table

Figure 5-3-6 The fan rotor

Fig. 5-3-7 The bearing loader

(2) Visually inspect the rotor shaft and rotor. Replace the rotor shaft with new ones if it is scratched, bent or deformed.

(3) Visually check the stator winding to see if it is free of boring and burning, and replace it with a new one if it is found to be defective.

(4) Visually check the outgoing line and terminal of stator winding, ensure that the protective layer is in good condition, replace it in case of aging, burning and damage, and renew all sealing strips.

(5) Replace with new bearings of original specifications and models.

(6) Visually check that the nameplate of the fan is complete, clear and installed firmly.

6) Assembly

(1) Use the bearing disassembler to install the new bearing, and avoid squeezing the bearing outer ring when assembling the new bearing.

(2) Use a white paint pen to mark the left and right on the rotor, as shown in Figure 5-3-8.

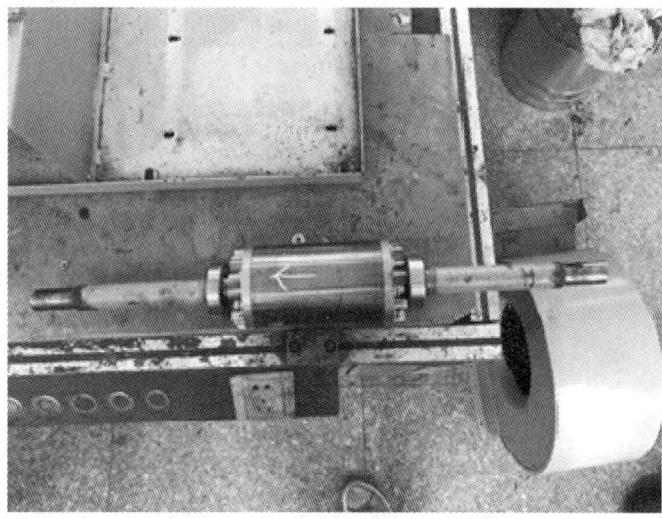

Figure 5-3-8 Arrows on fan rotor

(3) Assemble the rotor, stator and end cover, and tap the end cover with a copper hammer (bar) to make it close.

(4) Assemble the motor and the frame, fasten the connecting bolts between the motor and the frame with electric tools, and apply anti-loosening marks.

(5) Align and install the impeller center hole with the rotating shaft, lock the screw with locking glue and appropriate torque, tighten the shaft end bolt with a wrench, and apply anti-loosening marks. Gently rotate the impeller by hand and observe whether there is friction or jamming at each part.

7) Paint mark

(1) All accessories shall be sprayed with primary color paint, and the paint layer shall be uniform without falling.

(2) After passing the test, according to the positive rotation direction of the fan, a red arrow shall be sprayed on the center directly above one side of the protective cover with a word leak, and the arrow direction shall be consistent with the positive rotation direction of the fan.

8) Finishing after operation

(1) Fill in the maintenance marks and relevant records in *One Vehicle One File*.

(2) Cut off the power supply, count the tools, confirm that they are in good condition and wipe them clean, put them into the tool box, do a good job of equipment maintenance, and leave

the post after confirming that the switch is closed, there is no debris around, and there is no fire source before leaving the post.

【Task Training】

(1) What is the function of the air conditioning and ventilation system of passenger cars? Is the ventilation system only used in summer or winter?

(2) How to ensure safety when using electric heater?

(3) Briefly describe the principle of induced ventilation.

(4) Briefly describe the main components and working process of the ventilation system of 25T passenger car.

(5) Briefly describe the maintenance process and precautions of the ventilator.

Project 6

Electrical Control System of 25T Passenger Car Air Conditioner

【Chinese Railway Culture】

The History of Railway Development in China 6: The Ties between Chinese and Lao people

The China-Laos Railway (the China—Laos Kunming—Wanzhou Railway) starts from Kunming, Yunnan Province, China in the north and ends in Vientiane, the capital of Laos in the south. It is the first international railway invested and constructed by China after the proposal of jointly building the "the Belt and Road" initiative. The whole line adopts Chinese standards, uses Chinese equipment and is directly connected to the Chinese railway network. The China—Laos railway with a total length of more than 1000 kilometers is not only a bridge for the interconnection between China and Laos, but also a link for people of the two countries.

Figure 6-1　The China—Laos Railway

On May 21, 2010, the construction of Kunming—Yuxi, the first section of China—Laos Railway was started; On December 2, 2015, the foundation stone laying ceremony was held for the Mohan—Wanxiang section of the China—Laos Railway; On April 19, 2016, the construction of Yuxi—Mohan section of China—Laos Railway was started; On December 25, 2016, the China—Laos Railway held the commencement ceremony of the whole line; On December 3, 2021, the whole China—Laos Railway opened to traffic.

The construction volume of the China—Laos Railway is huge and the landform is complex. The Yuxi—Mohan section needs to cross the Mopan Mountain, Ailao Mountain, Wuliang Mountain, and the Yuanjiang River, the Amu River, the Babian River, and the Lancang River. The bridge tunnel ratio is as high as 87%. The geology along the line is prone to collapse and block fall, soft rock deformation, mud and water inrush and other problems. Most of the Mohan—Wanxiang section of the China—Laos Railway is located in the tropical area. There is a lot of rainfall in rainy season, so it is difficult to form foundation pits, and is difficult for large machinery and equipment to enter the site. The line adopts the construction technology of bridge pile foundation in rainy season, which solves the problems of bridge pile foundation construction in tropical areas in rainy season, and ensures the follow-up construction of bridge bearing platform and pier body.

The China—Laos Railway helps Laos develop, benefit local people, and serve regional connectivity. From Vientiane, Laos to Luang Prabang, an important tourist city in the north, more and more tourists choose to travel by train, and the tourism economy along the line is developing rapidly. The flow of people, logistics, capital and information accelerated, and various industries expanded and upgraded. China—Laos Railway channel brings large logistics, large logistics drives large trade, and large trade activates large industries. China's "the Belt and Road" initiative is perfectly aligned with Laos' strategy of changing from a "land locked country" to a "land linked country". China—Laos Railway is also an international railway that fully uses Chinese standards, marking an important step forward in "soft connectivity" between China and countries along the Belt and Road Initiative, and will consolidate the foundation of Lancang—Mekong cooperation and the construction of a China-ASEAN community of shared future. The opening and operation of the China—Laos railway is a tangible achievement of the joint construction of the Belt and Road Initiative, a model for China to share development opportunities with the world in a more open attitude, and a milestone in promoting the building of a community of common destiny between China and Laos and promoting the connectivity of countries in the region.

【 Project Description 】

Through the study of this project, students can master the wiring connection, function and operation principle of the electrical control system of 25T passenger car air conditioner, and can use the knowledge learned to ensure the daily use and regular maintenance of the electrical control system of 25T passenger car air conditioner.

This project mainly analyzes the air conditioning electrical control system of 25T semi-cushioned berth sleeping car. For the complete circuit diagram of 25T semi-cushioned berth sleeping car, please refer to Attached Figure 1.

【 Project Objectives 】

1. Knowledge objectives

(1) Understand the composition of the integrated electrical control cabinet.
(2) Master the control process of the main circuit of the air conditioner.
(3) Master the control process of AC/DC conversion and I/II conversion of air conditioning.
(4) Master the control process of air conditioning test mode and automatic mode.
(5) Understand the wiring principle of collection and acquisition of air conditioning operation information.
(6) Master the process of obtaining air conditioning fault information, as well as fault diagnosis and handling.

2. Capability objectives

(1) Be able to use the learned circuit principle knowledge for fault diagnosis.
(2) Be able to learn the maintenance items of the air conditioning electrical control cabinet and circuit independently.
(3) Be able to complete the daily maintenance of the air conditioner electrical system.

3. Quality objectives

(1) Cultivate a meticulous and serious work attitude.
(2) Cultivate awareness and ability of safe use of electricity.
(3) Cultivate teamwork spirit.

 Main Circuit and Power Supply Line Conversion Control of Air Conditioner

【 Task Objective 】

(1) Understand the composition of the integrated electrical control cabinet.

(2) Master the control process of the main circuit of the air conditioner.

(3) Master the control process of AC/DC conversion and I/II conversion of air conditioning.

【 Knowledge Reserve 】

1. TKDT Electrical Integrated Control Cabinet

The 25T air-conditioned passenger car adopts the TKDT type passenger car electrical integrated control cabinet, which is compatible with AC 380 V and DC 600 V power supply, referred to as the compatible control cabinet, as shown in Figure 6-1-1. It is a compatible integrated control cabinet integrating power conversion control, air conditioning unit control, lighting control and other functions. The control core of the control cabinet adopts a programmable controller PLC, which realizes human-computer interaction through a touch screen, receives various instructions and automatically executes corresponding operating steps, and promptly diagnoses, indicates, and protects various faults occurring in the operation of the electrical system.

Figure 6-1-1　TKDT type integrated electrical control cabinet

LON network cables in 39 communication core connectors at both ends of each carriage are led to the PLC in the integrated electrical control cabinet for collection. Axle temperature, anti-skid, smoke and fire alarm, door, and power box under the vehicle transmit the status information to the PLC through the gateway and query on the touch screen. The integrated control cabinet has the functions of detection, control, fault diagnosis and protection, information prompt, and networked communication, achieving comprehensive control of the power supply and control system, and enabling vehicle to vehicle communication.

The compatible control cabinet is mainly composed of PLC host unit, touch screen, contactor, time relay, thermal relay, air switch, etc.

1) PLC host unit

PLC is the core control component of the compatible control cabinet, which is responsible for controlling the entire electrical system, monitoring and analyzing the parameters in the operation process of the electrical system in real time, automatically alarming and processing the faults, realizing human-machine dialogue through the touch screen, responding to the commands and parameters entered by the touch screen, and displaying the fault information and operation records through the touch screen. Its main configuration is:

(1) 0 ~ 10 V analog input point 17 points.

(2) PT100 temperature input point 1 point.

(3) DC 24 V, 8 mA switching value input point 24 points.

(4) The switch value output point of the relay is 24 points.

(5) Maximum switching capacity of output end: AC 250 V, 2 A and DC 24 V, 2 A.

(6) Minimum switching capacity of output end: DC 5 V, 10 mA.

Figure 6-1-2　Omron CPM Series PLC

2) Touch screen display

The touch screen adopts a full Chinese LCD with backlight screen, with character type and image type display, and is communicated through the communication interface and the peripheral interface of the PLC. The main function is to set the field parameters, manually control the operating conditions of the air conditioner, display the operating conditions and parameters, display the operating status of each functional unit in real time, report the faults in real time, and query the operating records and fault records of each functional unit. LCD specification: 320 points × 240 points; Effective display area: 122 mm × 92 mm.

 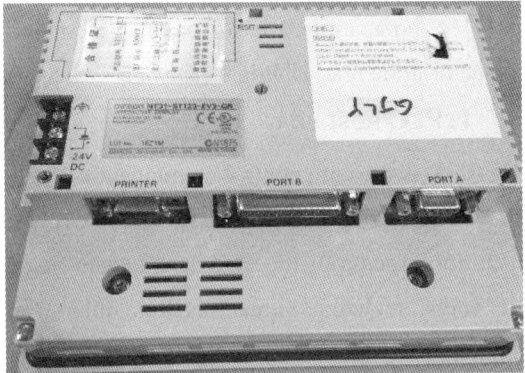

Figure 6-1-3　Omron NT31 series touch screen

3) AC and DC power specifications

The 25T passenger car can be powered by AC 380 V and DC 600 V compatible power supplies. AC 380 V power supply is set at the factory, and DC 600 V power supply wiring is reserved. To operate under DC 600 V power supply mode, 3.5kW single-phase inverter and 2 × 35 kV·A inverter shall be additionally installed. Dual power supply of circuit I and II is adopted, and circuit I or II power supply can be selected as required. In principle, the load of circuit I and circuit II shall be balanced during marshalling, for example, the power of vehicles 1, 3 and 5 shall be supplied by circuit I, and the power of vehicles 2, 4 and 6 shall be supplied by circuit II.

(1) AC 380 V power supply.

The main circuit is powered by one circuit of the dual power supply of circuit I and II of 50Hz three-phase AC 380 V power bus to supply power for AC loads such as charger, air conditioner, lighting, heat tracing, etc.

(2) DC 600 V power supply.

The main circuit is powered by one circuit of the dual power supply of circuit I and II of three-phase DC 600 V power bus to supply power to the inverter and charger, and the inverter outputs AC power to supply power to the AC load.

(3) DC 110 V power supply.

The DC 110 V bus and the vehicle battery supply power to single-phase inverter, lighting, anti-skid device and other DC loads.

(4) DC control power supply.

① Convert DC 110 V power supply into DC 24 V power supply to supply power to PLC, touch screen, gateway, safety electricity recorder, etc.

② Convert DC 110 V power supply to DC 12 V power supply to supply power to the sensor; The sensor output voltage range is: DC 0 ~ 5 V and 0 ~ 10 V.

③ Convert the DC 110 V power supply to the DC 48 V power supply to supply power to the tail lamp and other loads. The rated output current is 6A.

2. Main Circuit of the Air Conditioner

The main power supply of the 25T passenger car air conditioning system is composed of the control circuits of the fan, the condensing fan, the compressor and the electric heater. The electric heater consists of a preheater and an auxiliary heater in the passenger compartment.

1) Main circuit of ventilator

Each air conditioning unit is equipped with a ventilator. The main power circuit of the ventilator is composed of two channels of weak wind and strong wind. Two contactors are used to control the double-winding ventilator to achieve different wind speed control. The advantages of double-winding fan are high reliability and low failure rate. When the air conditioning system is running, it is necessary to close the main air switch Q11, as shown in Figure 6-1-4.

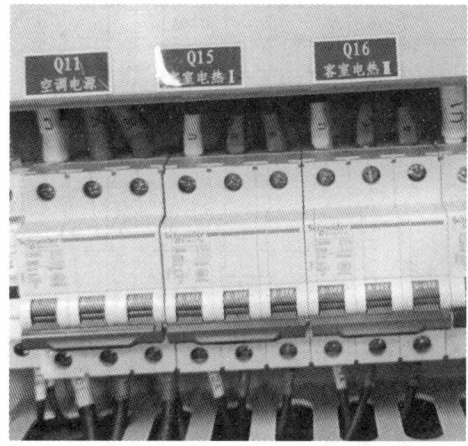

Figure 6-1-4 Air switch Q11 of air conditioning power supply

(1) Main circuit of weak wind.

As shown in Figure 6-1-5, when the wind speed of the fan is weak, the electrical path is: three-phase AC 380 V power supply → main air switch Q11 → normally open contact of contactor KM11 (as shown in Figure 6-1-6) → thermal relay FR11 (as shown in Figure 6-1-6) → fan M11 winding 1. At this time, the contactor KM11 coil is powered on, its normally open contact is closed, and the ventilator M11 operates at low speed after being powered on.

(2) Main circuit of strong wind.

As shown in Figure 6-1-5, when the fan wind speed is strong, the electrical path is: three-phase AC 380 V power supply → main air switch Q11 → contactor KM12 normally open contact → thermal relay FR12 → fan M11 winding 2. At this time, the contactor KM12 coil is powered on, its normally open contact is closed, and the ventilator M11 runs at high speed after being powered on.

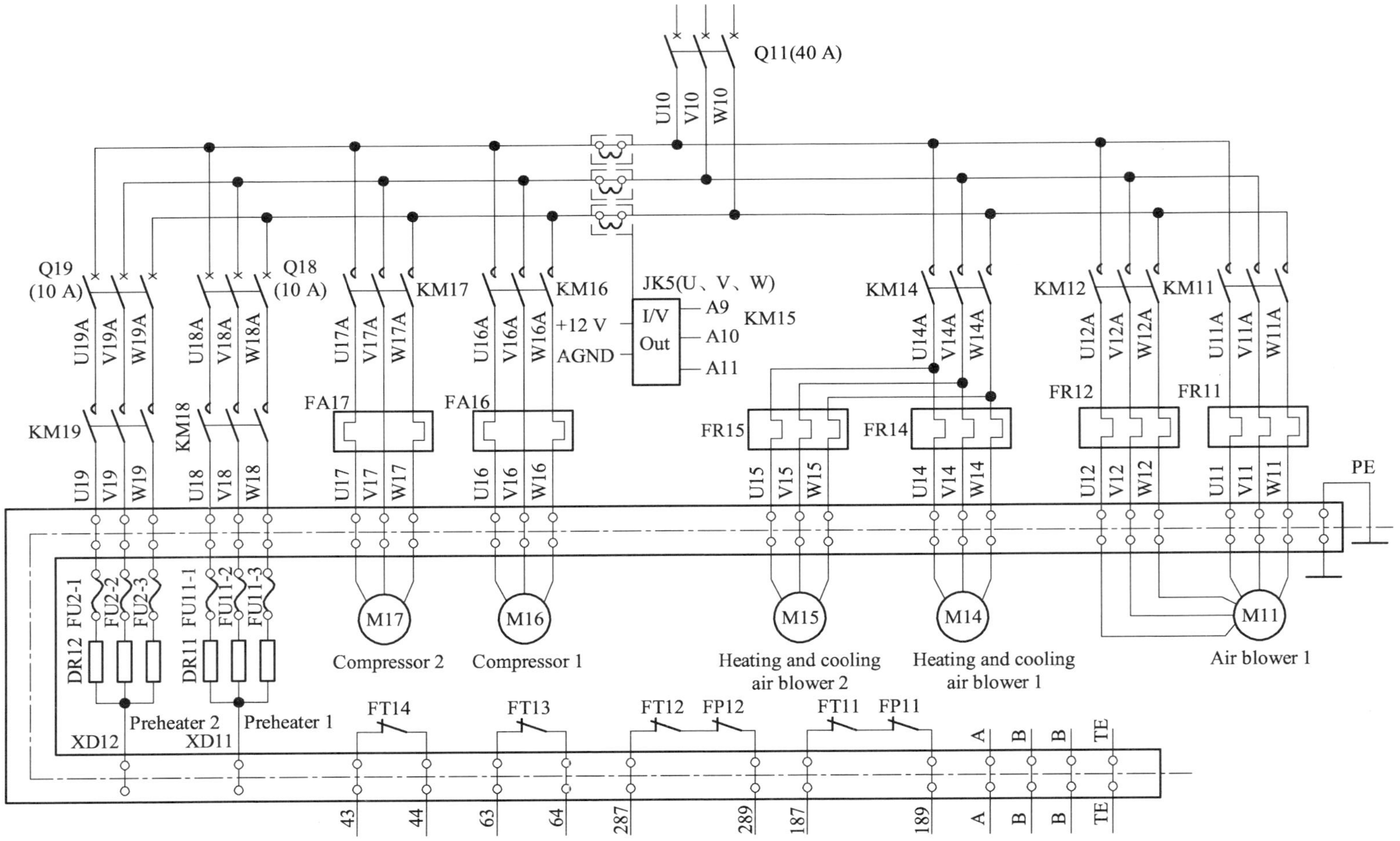

Figure 6-1-5 Main circuit of air conditioner

Figure 6-1-6　KM and FR

The normally open contacts of KM11 and KM12 are interlocked on the weak wind and strong wind control circuits to ensure that the weak wind and strong wind will not be powered on at the same time. The thermal relays FR11 and FR12 play an overload protection role on the ventilator.

2) Main circuit of condenser fan

Two condenser fans provide flowing air to cool the refrigerant. Before starting the refrigeration compressor, the condensing fan must be started first.

As shown in Figure 6-1-5, the electrical path of the main circuit of the condensing fan is: three-phase AC 380 V power supply → main air switch Q11 → normally open contact of the contactor KM14 → thermal relays FR14 and FR15 → condensing fan 1 M14 and condensing fan 2 M15. At this time, the contactor KM14 coil is powered on, its normally open contact is closed, and the condenser fans M14 and M15 are powered on for operation. The thermal relays FR14 and FR15 play an overload protection role for the two condenser fans respectively.

3) Main circuit of refrigeration compressor

Refrigeration can be divided into semi-cooling and full-cooling according to different operating conditions. The refrigeration compressor only operates one of which is called semi-cooling working condition, and the two compressors operate at the same time is called full-cooling working condition.

(1) Semi-cooling working condition.

As shown in Figure 6-1-5, under semi-cooling working condition, the electrical path of the main circuit of the compressor is: three-phase AC 380 V power supply → main air switch Q11 → contactor KM16 normally open contact → FA16 → compressor 1.

Or: three-phase AC 380 V power supply → main air switch Q11 → contactor KM17 normally open contact → FA17 → compressor 2.

At this time, only one coil of contactor KM16 and KM17 is powered on, only one normally open contact is closed, and only one of the two compressors is powered on for operation.

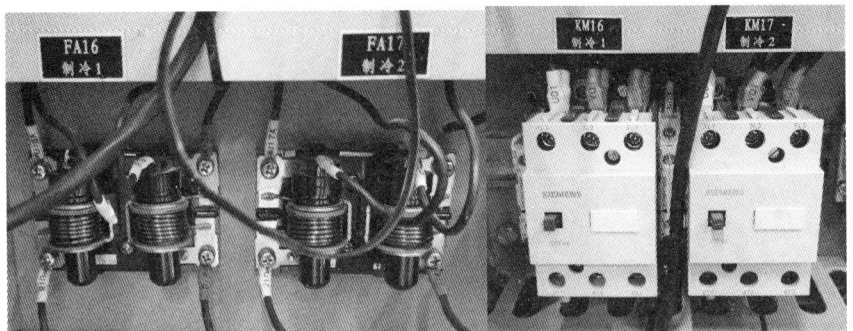

Figure 6-1-7   FA and KM

(2) Full-cooling working condition.

As shown in Figure 6-1-5, the electrical path of the main circuit of the compressor is: three-phase AC 380 V power supply → main air switch Q11 → contactors KM16 and KM17 normally open contacts → FA16 and FA17 → compressor 1 and compressor 2.

At this time, contactor KM16 and KM17 coils are powered on, their normally open contacts are closed, and both compressors are powered on for operation.

4) Main circuit of preheater

The air conditioning preheater is installed near the evaporator to provide heat for air conditioning heating. During heating, only one preheater is operated, which is called semi-heating condition, and two preheaters are operated at the same time, which is called full-hcating condition.

(1) Semi-heating condition of preheater.

As shown in Figure 6-1-5, the electrical path of the main circuit is: three-phase AC 380 V power supply → main air switch Q11 → air switch Q18 → contactor KM18 normally open contact → fuse FU1 → preheater 1 when the preheater is half warm.

Or: three-phase AC 380V power supply → main air switch Q11 → air switch Q19 → normally open contact of contactor KM19 → fuse FU2 → preheater 2.

At this time, only one coil of contactor KM18 and KM19 is powered on, only one normally open contact is closed, and only one preheater 1 and 2 is powered on for operation. The fuse tubes FU1 and FU2 play the role of overload fuse protection for the two preheaters respectively.

(2) Full-heating condition of preheater.

As shown in Figure 6-1-5, when the preheater is of full-heating, the electrical path of the main circuit of the preheater is: three-phase AC 380 V power supply → main air switch Q11 → air switches Q18 and Q19 → contactors KM18 and KM19 normally open contacts → fuse tubes FU1 and FU2 → preheater 1 and preheater 2.

At this time, the coils of contactor KM18 and KM19 are powered on, their normally open contacts are closed, and both sets of preheaters are powered on for operation.

5) Main circuit of auxiliary heater in passenger compartment

When the auxiliary heater works in the passenger compartment, it is also divided into semi-heating and full-heating. Only one set is operated, which is called semi-heating condition, and two sets are operated simultaneously, which is called full-heating condition.

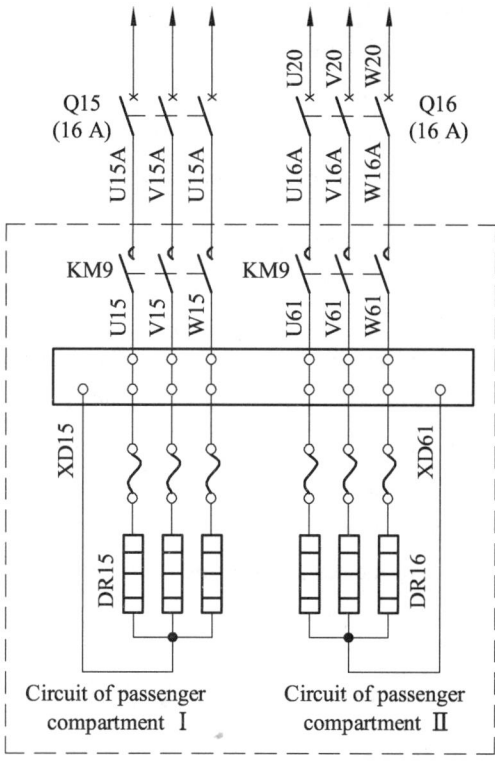

Figure 6-1-8　Main circuit of auxiliary heater

(1) Semi-heating condition of auxiliary heater.

As shown in Figure 6-1-8, the electrical path of the main circuit of the auxiliary heater is: three-phase AC 380 V power supply → air switch Q15 → contactor KM8 normally open contact → fuse FU → auxiliary heater I.

Or: three-phase AC 380 V power supply → air switch Q16 → contactor KM9 normally open contact → fuse FU → auxiliary heater II.

At this time, only one coil of contactor KM8 and KM9 is powered on, only one normally open contact is closed, and only one auxiliary heater is powered on for operation.

(2) Full-heating condition of auxiliary heater.

As shown in Figure 6-1-8, the electrical path of the main circuit of the auxiliary heater is: three-phase AC 380 V power supply → air switches Q15 and Q16 → contactors KM8 and KM9 normally open contacts → fuse FU → auxiliary heater I and II.

At this time, the coils of contactor KM8 and KM9 are powered on, their normally open contacts are closed, and the two sets of auxiliary heaters are powered on for operation.

3. AC/DC Conversion and Circuit I / II Conversion

The air conditioning system of 25T passenger car can be powered by AC 380 V and DC 600 V compatible power supply. It adopts two-way power supply of circuit I and II. It can select circuit I (circuit II) power supply manually or automatically as required. In principle, the load of circuit I and circuit II shall be balanced during marshalling, for example, circuit I power supply for vehicles 1, 3, 5... and circuit II power supply for vehicles 2, 4, 6. The selection of AC and DC power supply and circuit I or II power supply is realized by manually operating the transfer switch.

1) Transfer switch

(1) SA1 AC/DC transfer switch.

SA1 change-over switch is an AC/DC power supply selector switch, and SA1 is a three-gear change-over switch with a total of 3 pairs of contacts. The middle gear is the stop gear. At this time, contacts 1 and 2, contacts 3 and 4, contacts 5 and 6 are all disconnected; Turning 45 degrees counterclockwise from the stop gear is the DC gear. At this time, contact 1 and contact 2 are open, and contacts 3, 4, and 5, 6 are closed; Turning 45° clockwise from the stop gear is the AC gear. At this time, contacts 1 and 2 are closed, while contacts 3 and 4 and contacts 5 and 6 are open.

SA1	DC	Stop	AC
	45°	0°	45°
1-2			●
3-4	●		
5-6	●		

Figure 6-1-9　SA1 AC/DC transfer switch

(2) SA2 circuit I and circuit II transfer switch.

The SA2 transfer switch is the power supply selector switch of circuit I and circuit II, and the SA2 is a five-speed transfer switch with a total of 9 pairs of contacts. The middle gear is the stop gear, at which time all contacts are open; Turning 45° counterclockwise from the stop gear is the automatic gear. At this time, the first four pairs of contacts are open and the last five pairs of contacts are closed; Turning 45° clockwise from the stop gear is the circuit I gear. At this time, contacts 1 and 2, 5 and 6 are closed, and other contacts are open; Turning 90° clockwise from the stop gear is also the stop gear. At this time, all contacts are disconnected. This gear is in the middle of the circuit I and circuit II to ensure the smooth switching of circuit I and circuit II; Turning 135 degrees clockwise from the stop gear is the circuit II gear. At this time, contacts 3, 4, 7 and 8 are closed, and other contacts are open.

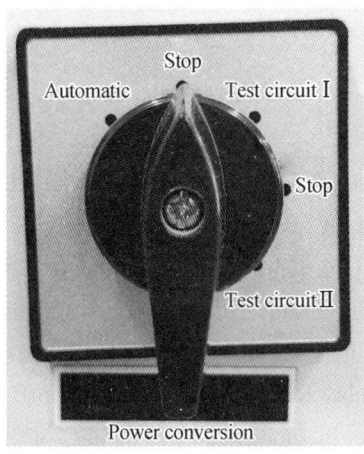

SA2	Automatic	Stop	I	Stop	II
	45°	0°	45°	90°	135°
1-2			●		
3-4					●
5-6			●		
7-8					●
9-10	●				
11-12	●				
13-14	●				
15-16	●				
17-18	●				

Power conversion（电源转换） Automatic（自动） Stop（停止）
Test circuit I（实验 I 路） Test circuit II（实验II路）

Figure 6-1-10 SA2 transfer switch

2) AC/DC and I/II switching control circuit

The 24 V control power supply (+113) is led from the PLC unit. Through the combined conversion of the transfer switch SA1 and SA2, AC/DC switching and circuit I/II switching can be realized. For the circuit diagram, please refer to Attached Figure 1.

(1) DC circuit I control.

When SA1 is switched to DC gear and SA2 is switched to circuit I gear, the electrical path is: 24 V power supply+113 → SA1 contact 3 → SA1 contact 4 → contactor KM1 normally closed contact → air switch Q1 → contactor KM2 normally closed contact → air switch Q2, and then divided into two paths, one path is through leakage protector → relay KA29 coil, the other path is through SA2 contact 5 → SA2 contact 6 → contactor KM4 normally closed contact → contactor KM3 coil and relay KA30 coil, so that the DC 600 V I main circuit is connected. At this time, the two normally closed contacts of contactor KM3 in the figure are disconnected to ensure that the AC path is disconnected, the contactor KM4 and relay KA40 coil are powered off, and the DC 600 V circuit II is disconnected, that is, the DC 600 V circuit I and circuit II form an interlocking relationship. At the same time, the normally open contact of the relay KA29 is closed, and the 24 V power supply flows from the SA2 contact 6 to the right interface 31 pin (566) of the PLC, allowing the PLC control unit to receive a signal that the DC 600 V I-circuit is operating normally.

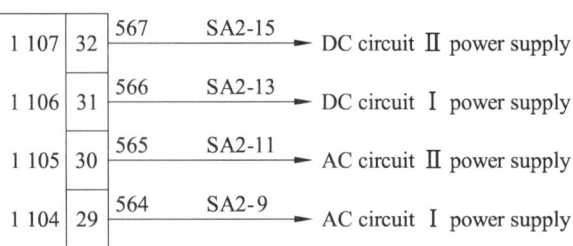

Figure 6-1-11　PLC interface for AC/DC and I/II control

(2) DC circuit II control.

When SA1 is turned to the DC gear and SA2 is turned to the circuit II gear, the electrical path is: 24 V power supply follows the flow direction of DC circuit I to the other circuit to SA2 contact 7 → SA2 contact 8 → contactor KM3 normally closed contact → contactor KM4 coil and relay KA40 coil, so that the DC 600 V circuit II main circuit is connected. At this time, the two normally closed contacts of contactor KM4 in the figure are disconnected to ensure that the AC path is disconnected, and the contactor KM3 and relay KA30 coil are powered off, that is, the DC 600 V circuit I is disconnected. At the same time, the normally open contact of the relay KA29 is closed, and the 24 V power supply flows from the SA2 contact 8 to the 32 pin (567) of the right interface of the PLC, so that the PLC control unit receives the signal of the normal operation of the DC 600 V circuit II.

(3) AC circuit I control.

SA1 is switched to AC gear and SA2 is switched to I gear. At this time, the electrical path is: 24 V power supply → SA1 contact 1 → SA1 contact 2 → air switch Q3 → contactor KM3 normally closed contact → contactor KM4 normally closed contact → air switch Q4, and then it is divided into two paths, one path is through relay KA19 coil, the other path is through SA2 contact 1 → SA2 contact 2 → contactor KM2 normally closed contact → relay KA10 coil. At this time, the 24V power supply+100 makes the main circuit of AC 380 V circuit I through the normally open contact of relay KA10 → contactor KM1 coil. At this time, the two normally closed contacts of contactor KM1 in the figure are disconnected to ensure that the DC path is disconnected, the relay KA20 and contactor KM2 coils are powered off, that is, the AC 380 V circuit II is disconnected, and the AC 380 V circuit I and circuit II form an interlocking relationship. At the same time, the normally open contact of the relay KA19 is closed, and the 24 V power supply flows from the SA2 contact 2 to the 29 pin (564) of the right interface of the PLC, so that the PLC control unit receives the signal of the normal operation of the AC 380 V circuit I.

(4) AC circuit II control.

SA1 is set to AC gear and SA2 is set to circuit II gear. At this time, the electrical path is: 24 V power supply goes another path according to the flow direction of AC circuit I to SA2 contact 3 → SA2 contact 4 → contactor KM1 normally closed contact → relay KA20 coil. At this time, the 24 V power supply+100 connects the main circuit of AC 380 V circuit II through the normally open contact of relay KA20 → contactor KM2 coil. At this time, the two normally closed contacts of contactor KM2 in the figure are disconnected to ensure that the DC path is disconnected, and the relay KA10 and contactor KM1 coils are powered off, that is, the AC 380 V circuit I is disconnected. At the same time, the normally open contact of the relay KA19 is closed, and the 24 V power supply flows from the SA2 contact 4 to the right interface 30 pin (565) of the PLC, so that the PLC control unit receives the signal of the normal operation of the AC 380 V circuit II.

Task 2 Test Mode and Automatic Mode Control of Air Conditioning

【Task Objective】

(1) Master the switching method of air conditioning mode.
(2) Master the control process under the air conditioning test mode.
(3) Master the control process under the automatic mode of air conditioning.

【Knowledge Reserve】

1. Air Conditioning Operation Mode of 25T Passenger Car

1) Change-over switch of air conditioning operation mode

SA3 change-over switch is the air conditioning operation mode selection switch, and SA3 is the four-gear change-over switch, with a total of 6 pairs of contacts. The middle gear is the stop gear. At this time, the six pairs of contacts are open; Turning 45° counterclockwise from the stop gear is the heating test gear. At this time, contacts 7, 8, 11 and 12 are closed, and other contacts are open. Turning 45° clockwise from the stop gear to the automatic gear, at this time, contacts 3, 4, 5 and 6 are closed, and other contacts are open; Turning 90° clockwise from the stop gear to test the cold gear, at this time, contacts 1, 2, 9 and 10 are closed, and other contacts are open. When running in the test position, PLC can only detect the air conditioning unit, and cannot perform protection action.

2) Operation mode control circuit of air conditioning

2. Test Mode of 25T Passenger Car Air Conditioning

1) Heating test gear

As shown in Figures 6-2-2 and 6-2-3.

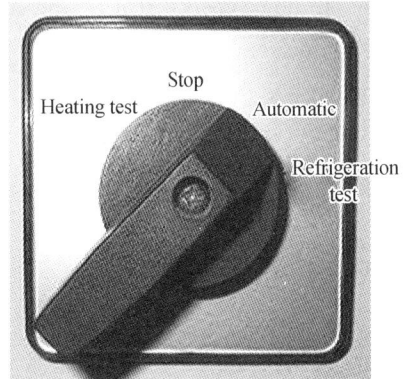

SA3	Heating test	Stop	Automatic	Refrigeration text
	45°	0°	45°	90°
1-2				●
3-4			●	
5-6			●	
7-8	●			
9-10				●
11-12	●			

Heating test（试验暖） Stop（停止） Automatic（自动） Refrigeration test（实验冷）

Figure 6-2-1 Air conditioning operation mode switch

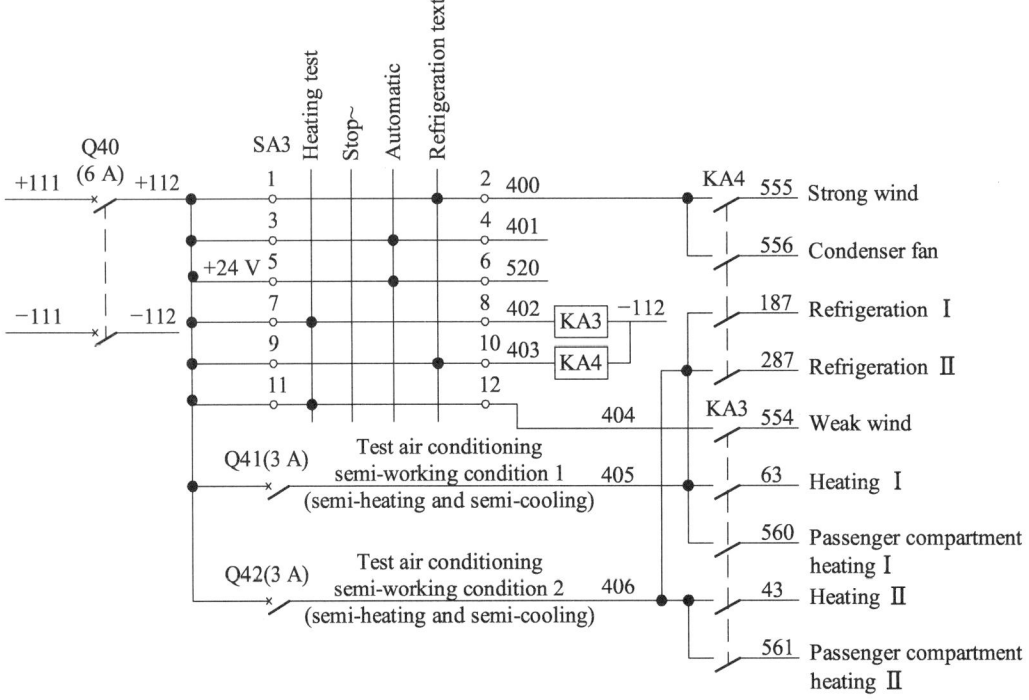

Figure 6-2-2 Air conditioning operation mode control circuit

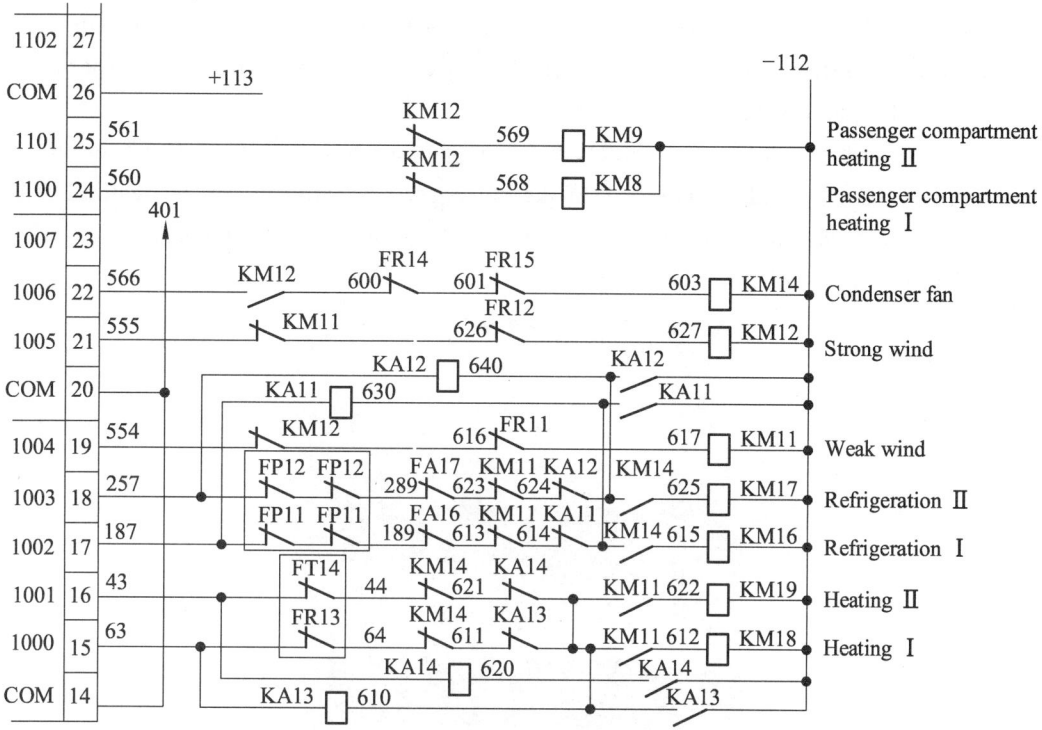

Figure 6-2-3　PLC air conditioning control circuit

When SA3 is turned to the test heating gear, the electrical path is: 24 V power supply+111 → air switch Q40 → SA3 contact 7 → SA3 contact 8 → relay KA3 (see Figure 6-2-4) coil, and the five normally open contacts of relay KA3 are closed.

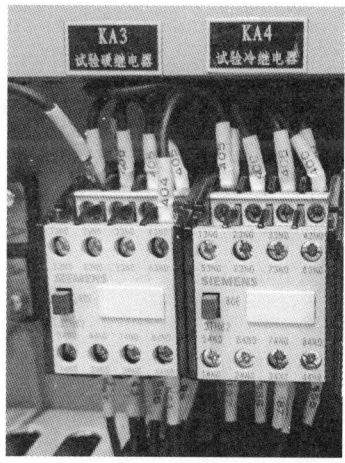

Figure 6-2-4　Test cooling and heating relay

(1) Weak air path of fan.

24V power supply → SA3 contact 11 → SA3 contact 12 → relay KA3 normally open contact → PLC right interface 19 pin (554) → contactor KM12 normally closed contact →

thermal relay FR11 normally closed contact → contactor KM11 coil, at this time, the contactor KM11 normally open contact in the main circuit is closed, and the fan operates at low speed.

(2) Weak wind heating path.

① If the air switch Q41 (see Figure 6-2-5) is closed, the semi-heating condition of the preheater 1 and the auxiliary heater 1 in the passenger compartment can be realized. The electrical path is: 24 V power supply → air switch Q41 → two normally open contacts of relay KA3 → PLC right interface 15, 24 (63, 560).

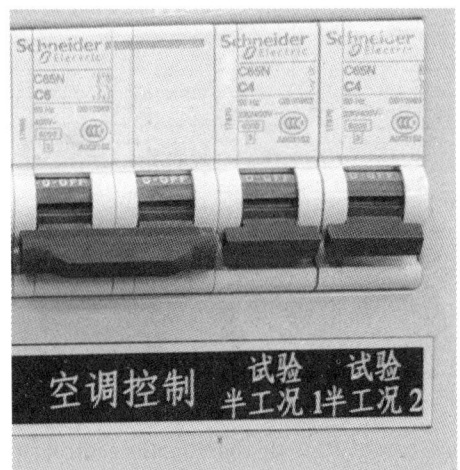

Figure 6-2-5 Air switch Q41 and Q42

Preheater 1 path: PLC interface 15 outputs 24 V power → FT13 normally closed contact → contactor KM14 normally closed contact → relay KA13 normally closed contact → contactor KM11 normally open contact → contactor KM18 coil, at this time, contactor KM18 normally open contact in the main circuit is closed, and preheater 1 operates.

Passenger compartment auxiliary heater 1 path: PLC interface 24 outputs 24 V power → contactor KM12 normally closed contact → contactor KM8 coil, at this time, the contactor KM8 normally open contact in the main circuit is closed, and passenger compartment auxiliary heater 1 operates.

② If the air switch Q42 (see Figure 6-2-5) is closed, the semi-heating working condition of the preheater 2 and the auxiliary heater 2 in the passenger compartment can be achieved. Then the electrical path is: 24 V power supply → air switch Q42 → two normally open contacts of relay KA3 → PLC right interface 16, 25 (43, 561).

Preheater 2 path: PLC interface 16 outputs 24 V power → FT14 normally closed contact → contactor KM14 normally closed contact → relay KA14 normally closed contact → contactor KM11 normally open contact → contactor KM19 coil, at this time, contactor KM19 normally open contact in the main circuit is closed, and preheater 2 operates.

Passenger compartment auxiliary heater 2 path: PLC interface 25 outputs 24 V power →

contactor KM12 normally closed contact → contactor KM9 coil, at this time, contactor KM9 normally open contact in the main circuit is closed, and passenger compartment auxiliary heater 2 operates.

③ If both air switches Q41 and Q42 are closed, a full-heating working condition in which preheaters 1 and 2 and auxiliary heaters 1 and 2 in the passenger compartment are powered on can be achieved.

2) Cooling test gear

As shown in Figures 6-2-2 and 6-2-3.

When SA3 is turned to the test cooling gear, the electrical path is: 24 V power supply+111 → air switch Q40 → SA3 contact 9 → SA3 contact 10 → relay KA4 coil, and the four normally open contacts of relay KA4 are closed.

(1) Strong wind path of ventilator.

24 V power supply → SA3 contact 1 → SA3 contact 2 → relay KA4 normally open contact → PLC right interface 21 pin (555) → contactor KM11 normally closed contact → thermal relay FR12 normally closed contact → contactor KM12 coil, at this time, the contactor KM12 normally open contact in the main circuit is closed, and the ventilator operates at high speed. The interlock of strong and weak wind paths is realized by the normally closed contacts of contactors KM11 and KM12 in series in the control circuit of the other side.

(2) Condenser fan path.

24 V power supply → SA3 contact 1 → SA3 contact 2 → relay KA4 normally open contact → PLC right interface 22 pin (556) → contactor KM12 normally open contact → thermal relay FR14 normally closed contact → thermal relay FR15 normally closed contact → contactor KM14 coil, at this time, the contactor KM14 normally open contact in the main circuit is closed, and the two condensing fans are powered on for operation.

(3) Refrigeration path.

① If the air switch Q41 is closed, the semi-cooling working condition of compressor 1 can be realized. The electrical path is: 24 V power supply → air switch Q41 → relay KA4 normally open contact → PLC right interface 17 pin (187) → FT11 normally closed contact → FP11 normally closed contact → FA16 normally closed contact → contactor KM11 normally closed contact → relay KA11 normally closed contact → contactor KM14 normally open contact → contactor KM16 coil. At this time, the normally open contact of contactor KM16 in the main circuit is closed, and the refrigeration compressor 1 runs.

② If the air switch Q42 is closed, the semi-cooling working condition of compressor 2 can be realized. The electrical path is: 24 V power supply → air switch Q42 → relay KA4 normally open contact → PLC right interface 18 pin (287) → FT12 normally closed contact → FP12 normally closed contact → FA17 normally closed contact → contactor KM11 normally closed contact → relay KA12 normally closed contact → contactor KM14 normally open contact → contactor KM17 coil. At this time, the normally open contact of contactor KM17 in the main circuit is closed, and the refrigeration compressor 2 runs.

③ If the air switches Q41 and Q42 are closed, the full-cooling working condition of both refrigeration compressors can be realized.

When operating under cooling or heating test conditions, in order to prevent the compressor or heater from starting at the same time, resulting in excessive instantaneous load, the air switch Q41 and Q42 cannot be closed at the same time. Generally, the air switch Q41 is closed first, and then the air switch Q42 is closed after a proper delay.

3. Automatic Mode Control of 25T Passenger Car Air Conditioner

1) Automatic operation mode of air conditioner

As shown in Figures 6-2-2 and 6-2-3.

When the air conditioner is in normal operation, the change-over switch SA3 is set to the automatic gear, and the electrical path is: 24 V power supply+111 → air switch Q40 → SA3 contacts 3 and 5 → SA3 contacts 4 and 6 → PLC right interface 14, 20 and left interface 00 pins (401 and 520). 24 V power is introduced from the 00 pin to make the PLC air conditioning part run. It will automatically enter the cooling or heating condition according to the program according to the sensor input signal. 24 V power is introduced from pins 14 and 20 to provide DC power for PLC output.

After the power supply starts, the PLC controls the air conditioning unit to automatically enter the "automatic" operation. The PLC compares the detected value of the temperature sensor in the compartment with the preset "cooling" and "heating" temperature values, and then carries out the "automatic" operation of the air conditioning unit. The air conditioning unit has six working conditions: "strong wind", "weak wind", "strong wind half cold", "strong wind full cold", "weak wind half warm", and "weak wind full warm". In the "heating" condition, the auxiliary heater in the passenger compartment is linked with the preheater.

The operation modes such as "strong wind", "weak wind", "strong wind half cold", "strong wind half cold", "strong wind half warm", "weak wind half warm", and "weak wind full warm" can be forcibly selected according to the menu and prompt displayed on the touch screen. At this time, the air conditioner is not under automatic control. Press the "full automatic" touch switch to return to the automatic control state.

2) Automatic operation control process of air conditioner

When the air conditioner is in normal operation, it works under automatic conditions.

(1) Automatic refrigeration process of air conditioner.

Refrigeration setting value: upper limit 26 °C, lower limit 24 °C, return difference 1.5 °C.

When the temperature rises to the set value plus the return difference, the refrigeration will start. In the range of return difference, the compressor will not be cooled, that is, the compressor will not start, which can prevent the compressor from starting frequently to prolong its life. As shown in Figure 6-2-6:

① When the room temperature is below 22.5 °C, the fan operates in weak wind mode and the two compressors are in shutdown state.

② When the room temperature rises to 22.5 °C, the ventilator operates in strong wind mode, and the two compressors are in shutdown state.

③ When the room temperature rises to the return difference of (24+1.5) °C at the lower limit of the set temperature, that is, 25.5 °C, one compressor will be started and the fan will operate in strong wind mode.

④ When the room temperature continues to rise to a return difference of the set temperature limit of (26+1.5) °C, or 27.5 °C, both compressors are started and the ventilator operates in strong wind mode.

⑤ When the room temperature drops to 26 °C above the set temperature limit, only one compressor will operate and the ventilator will operate in strong wind mode.

⑥ When the room temperature drops to the lower limit of the set temperature of 24 °C, both compressors stop running, and the ventilator operates in strong wind mode.

⑦ When the room temperature continues to drop to 21 °C, both compressors will stop running and the fan will operate in weak wind mode.

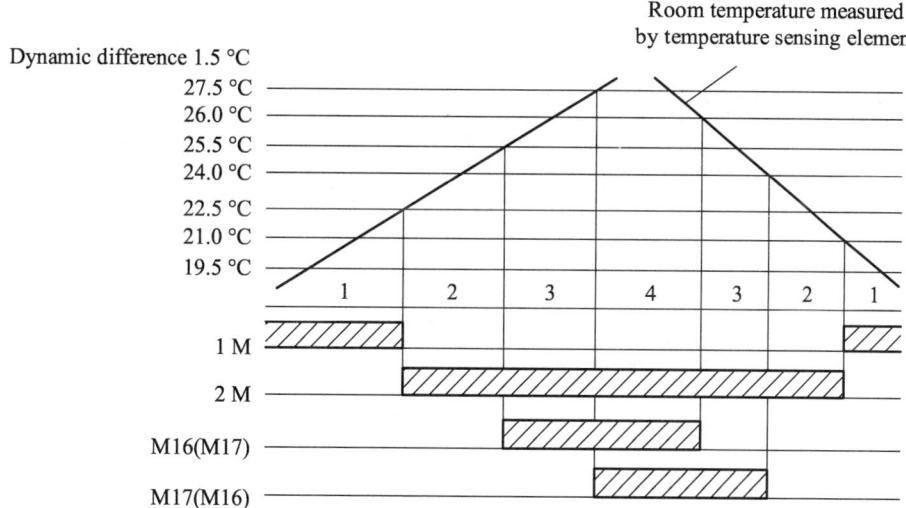

1—Weak ventilation; 2—Strong ventilation; 3-Semi-heating, weak ventilation;
4—Full-heating, weak ventilation.

Figure 6-2-6　Automatic refrigeration process

(2) Automatic heating process of air conditioner.

Heating setting value: upper limit 18 °C, lower limit 16 °C, return difference 1.5 °C. As shown in Figure 6-2-7:

① When the room temperature is above 21 °C, the fan operates in strong wind mode, and the two preheaters are in shutdown state.

② When the room temperature drops to 21 °C, the fan operates in weak air mode, and the two preheaters are in shutdown state.

③ When the room temperature drops to 18 °C of the upper limit of the set temperature, start a set of preheater, and the fan operates in the weak air mode.

④ When the room temperature continues to fall to the lower limit of the set temperature of 16, both sets of preheaters will start and the fan will operate in the weak air mode.

⑤ When the room temperature rises to (16+1.5)°C of the lower limit of the set temperature, that is, 17.5 °C, the preheater only operates one set, and the fan operates in the weak air mode.

⑥ When the room temperature rises to a return difference of (18+1.5)°C above the set temperature limit, that is, 19.5 °C, the preheater stops operating and the fan operates in a weak wind mode.

⑦ When the room temperature continues to rise to 22.5 °C, the preheater stops running and the fan operates in strong wind mode.

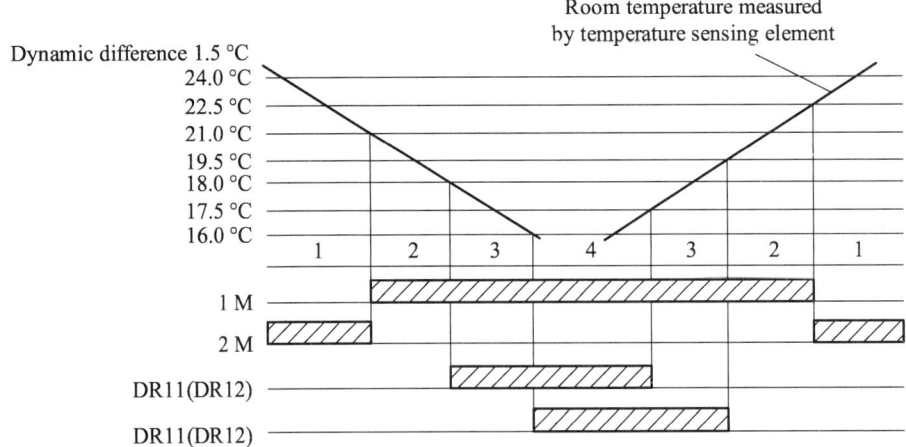

1—Strong ventilation; 2—Weak ventilation; 3—Semi-heating, weak ventilation; 4—Full-heating, weak ventilation.

Figure 6-2-7 **Automatic heating process**

Task 3 Operation and Fault Information Acquisition of Air Conditioner

【Task Objective】

(1) Understand the wiring principles for collecting and obtaining air conditioning operation information.

(2) Master the process of obtaining air conditioning fault information and fault judgment.

(3) Be able to handle faults.

【Knowledge Reserve】

1. Operation Information Acquisition of Air Conditioner

1) Temperature information collection

As shown in Figure 6-3-1, A, B and B of temperature sensor pt100 are connected to pins 5, 6 and 7 of the left interface of the PLC. The resistance of the temperature sensor corresponds to the temperature to a certain extent. The PLC can obtain the current temperature value through measurement and conversion, which provides the basis for the automatic working condition, and displays it through the display touch screen.

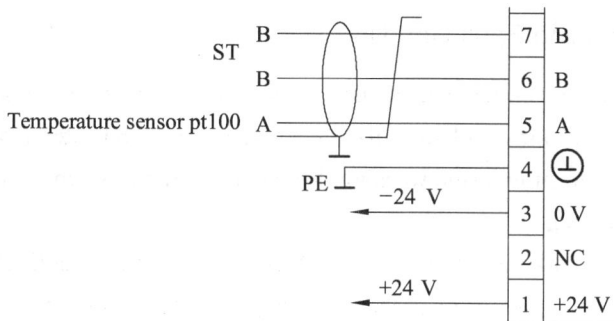

Figure 6-3-1　PLC and pt100 circuit connection diagram

2) Air conditioning operation

As shown in Figure 6-3-2, the operation of refrigeration compressor 1 and 2 will send signals to the 4 and 5 pins of the right interface of PLC through KM16 and KM17 normally open contacts respectively, so that the PLC control unit can obtain the real-time operation of refrigeration compressor 1 and 2, and display the corresponding status information on the display touch screen.

The operation of heating preheater I and II will send signals to the 2 and 3 pins of the right interface of PLC through the KM18 and KM19 moving and closing contacts respectively, so that the PLC control unit can obtain the real-time operation of preheater 1 and preheater 2, and display the corresponding status information on the display touch screen.

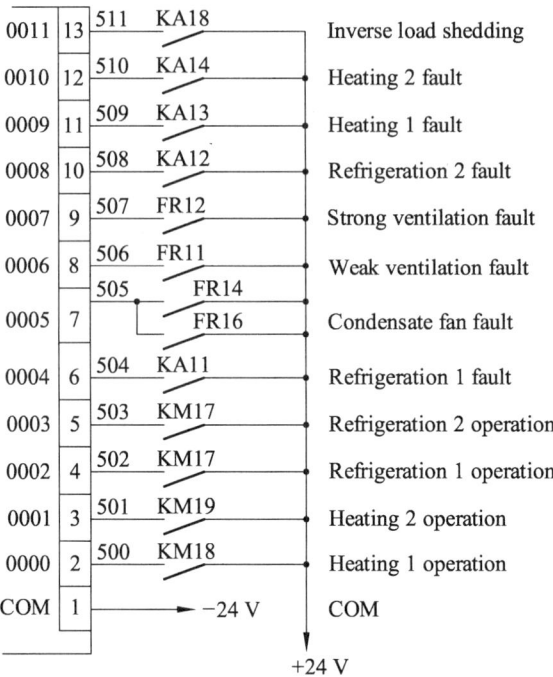

Figure 6-3-2   PLC interface circuit of air conditioning operation information

2. Air Conditioning Fault Handling

(1) When the strong ventilator fails, the corresponding condenser fan and compressor stop working; When the weak air ventilator fails, the corresponding preheater and auxiliary heater in the passenger compartment will stop working. When the condensing fan fails, the corresponding compressor stops working.

(2) Under the working conditions of "strong wind semi-cooling" or "weak wind semi-heating", if the compressor or preheater fails during operation, the faulty compressor or preheater will stop operation and automatically switch to another group of compressor or preheater to start; Under the working conditions of "strong wind full cooling" and "weak wind full heating", in case of failure, the compressor or preheater with failure will stop operation, and the compressor or preheater without failure will continue to operate.

(3) When the air conditioning unit has a fault, press the "stop air conditioning" button on the display touch screen to stop the air conditioning operation. After the fault is eliminated, press the "start air conditioning" button again. The PLC can restart the air conditioning unit after passing the detection.

3. Fault Information of Air Conditioning

When fault information is detected in the control circuits for ventilation, condensation, refrigeration, or heating, they transmit the information to the PLC interface through the normally open contacts of the relevant thermal relays and fault relays, and the PLC control unit can obtain the fault information.

As shown in Figure 6-2-3 and 6-3-2.

FR11 and FR12 are ventilator thermal relays, FR14 and FR15 are condenser fan thermal relays, KA11 and KA12 are refrigeration fault relays, and KA13 and KA14 are heating fault relays.

1) Ventilation failure

(1) In case of strong wind fault.

If the thermal relay FR12 is overheated, the normally open contact connected with the 9# pin of the PLC interface is closed, and the PLC control unit obtains the strong wind fault information.

(2) In case of weak wind fault.

If the thermal relay FR11 is overheated, the normally open contact connected with the 8# pin of the PLC interface is closed, and the PLC control unit obtains the weak wind fault information.

2) Condensate fan fault

If the thermal relay FR14 or FR15 overheats, the normally open contact FR14 or FR15 connected to 7# pin of the PLC interface closes, and the PLC control unit can obtain fault information about the condenser fan.

3) Refrigeration fault

(1) When refrigeration 1 fails.

If FA16 is triggered, its normally closed contact opens, the fault relay KA11 coil is powered on, the KM16 coil is powered off, the refrigeration compressor 1 stops, and the KA11 normally open contact closes, sending a signal to the 6# pin of the PLC interface.

(2) When refrigeration 2 fails.

If FA17 is triggered, its normally closed contact is open, the fault relay KA12 coil is powered on, the KM17 coil is powered off, the refrigeration compressor 2 stops, the KA12 normally open contact is closed, and the signal is sent to the 10# pin of the PLC interface.

4. Heating Fault

1) When preheater 1 fails

If FT13 is triggered, the FT13 normally closed switch is disconnected, the fault relay

KA13 coil is powered on, the KM18 coil is powered off, the electric preheater 1 stops, the KA13 normally open contact is closed, and the signal is sent to 11# pin of the PLC interface.

2) When preheater 2 fails

If FT14 is triggered, the FT14 normally closed switch is disconnected, the fault relay KA14 coil is powered on, the KM19 coil is powered off, the electric preheater 2 stops, the KA14 normally open contact is closed, and the signal is sent to 12# pin of the PLC interface.

When the above fault occurs, the corresponding load stops, the PLC will receive the corresponding fault signal, and the display touch screen will display the relevant information.

【Task Training】

(1) What are the main components of the compatible control cabinet?

(2) What are the main parts of the air conditioning circuit? Please describe the control process of the main circuit of the fan and the main circuit of the compressor.

(3) Briefly describe the AC/DC switching process.

(4) Briefly describe the switching process of DC circuit I and II.

(5) Briefly describe the automatic refrigeration process and automatic heating process of air conditioning.

(6) How does the control system identify air conditioning faults? What faults can be identified?

References

[1] Zhai Shishu, Ma Bingling. Passenger Car Air Conditioning Device [M] Beijing: China Railway Publishing House Co., Ltd, 2021.

[2] Lu Yujun. Passenger Car Air Conditioning Device [M] Beijing: China Railway Publishing House, 2007.

[3] Wang Xiuyan, Zhang Xiaodong. Fundamentals of Thermal Engineering [M] Beijing: China Electric Power Press, 2013.

[4] Zhang Baoxia. Refrigeration and Air Conditioning of Railway Vehicles [M] Beijing: China Railway Publishing House, 2005.

[5] Shi lei, Shi Gaoshan. Maintenance and Repair of Auxiliary Equipment for High-speed Railway Multiple Units (Version 2) [M] Chengdu: Southwest Jiaotong University Press, 2022.

[6] Locomotive and Rolling Stock Department of China Railway Group Co., Ltd. Operation and Maintenance of Railway Passenger Cars [M] Beijing: China Railway Publishing House Co.,Ltd, 2022.

[7] Transportation Department of China Railway Group Co., Ltd. Introduction to Railway[M]. Beijing: China Railway Publishing House Co.,Ltd, 2022.

项目一　热力学基础

【中国铁路文化】

中国铁路发展史 1　中国第一条自建铁路

京张铁路是中国首条不使用外国资金及人员，由中国人自行设计、自行建造并投入营运的铁路。京张铁路为詹天佑主持修建并负责的铁路，1905 年 9 月开工修建，于 1909 年建成，全长约 200 公里。它连接北京丰台区，经八达岭、居庸关、沙城、宣化等地至河北张家口。

图 1-0-1　京张铁路施工现场

在 1905 年，詹天佑主持修建中国铁路的建议，即京张铁路，经 4 年时间被众人接受，从此拉开了建造中国铁路的序幕。1905 年 9 月 4 日，铁路正式开工修建，12 月 12 日开始铺轨。京张铁路"中隔高山峻岭，石工最多，又有 7 000 余尺桥梁，路险工艰为他处所未有"，特别是"居庸关、八达岭，层峦叠嶂，石峭弯多，遍考各省已修之路，以此为最难，即泰西诸书，亦视此等工程至为艰巨"。"由南口至八达岭，高低相距一百八十丈，每四十尺即须垫高一尺。"中国自办京张铁路的消息传出之后，外国人讽刺说建造这条铁路的中国工程师恐怕还未出世。

詹天佑亲率工程队勘测定线，由于清政府拨款有限，时间紧迫，詹天佑从勘测过的三条路线中选定由西直门经沙河、南口、居庸关、八达岭、怀来、鸡鸣驿、宣化至张家口。当年修建京张铁路最困难的一段是南口至八达岭一带的，不仅地势险峻，而且坡度很大。就在铺轨的第一天，一列工程车的一个车钩链子折断，造成脱轨事故。这一下成了中国人不能自修铁路的证据，各种诽谤中伤纷至沓来。詹天佑想到一个办法：将美国人詹尼发明的自动挂钩加在每节车厢，使之结合成一个牢固整体，确保爬坡时的安全。他还运用"折反线"原理，修筑"之"字形路线降低爬坡度，并利用两头拉车交叉行进。

打通居庸关、五桂头、石佛寺、八达岭四条隧道，其中最长的八达岭隧道1 092米。当时只能靠工人的双手，采用南北两头同时向隧道中间点凿进的同时，采用竖井方法挖掘，中部开凿两个直井，分别可以向相反方向进行开凿，增加工作面，依靠人力建成了这条中国筑路历史上的第一座越岭铁路隧道。

京张铁路从1905年9月4日正式开工，到1909年10月2日在南口举行通车典礼，仅用了4年的时间，京张铁路的建设期比预定计划提前了两年。按当初预算，京张线施工以及购置机车、车辆的费用为白银729万两，实际仅用了约700万两。

京张铁路是中国人自行设计和施工的第一条铁路干线，是中国人民和中国工程技术界的光荣，也是中国近代史上中国人民反帝斗争的一个胜利。由中国人自己修建京张铁路，虽然是当时特殊历史背景下的一个心酸胜利，但詹天佑和京张铁路，以及蕴涵其中的民族精神却成为中国人永远的骄傲。

【项目描述】

热力学主要是从能量转化的观点来研究物质的热性质，它提示了能量从一种形式转换为另一种形式时遵从的宏观规律。空调和制冷设备的工作过程就是热能和机械能的转换过程，热能和机械能之间的相互转换是通过工质在热力设备中的循环状态变化过程来实现的，热力学第一定律、第二定律是热能和机械能转换必须遵循的基本规律。

【项目目标】

1. 知识目标

（1）掌握气体的基本参数定义。

（2）理解理想气体状态方程的内容和表达式。

（3）掌握热力学第一、第二定律。

（4）掌握热量传递的三种方式。

2. 能力目标

能够运用热力学基础知识去理解、分析制冷过程。

3. 素养目标

（1）培养推理、逻辑和抽象思维能力。

（2）培养团队合作能力。

任务一　气体基本参数及理想气体状态方程

【任务目标】

（1）掌握气体基本参数的定义。
（2）理解理想气体状态方程，并能对实际问题进行计算。

【知识储备】

一、热力系统简介

实现能量转化的媒介物质称为工质。例如，在火电厂蒸汽动力装置中，把热能转变为机械能的媒介物质水和水蒸气就是工质；又例如，在制冷装置中，制冷剂从冷库或其他空间中吸热，通过压缩机压缩升压升温后，在冷凝器中向外部环境放热，把机械能转变成热能的媒介物质制冷剂也是工质。

对工质的要求是：① 膨胀性；② 流动性；③ 热容量；④ 稳定性、安全性；⑤ 环保；⑥ 价廉，易大量获取。不同的工质实现能量转换的特性是不同的，有的相差甚远。

当人们研究各种不同形式能量相互转化与传递时，为了分析方便，往往把有相互联系的部分或全体分隔开来作为研究的对象。这种被人为地分隔开来作为热力学研究的对象称为热力学系统，简称热力系或系统。系统以外的部分称为外界，作为外界的最常见的例子就是与系统能量转化或传递有密切关系的自然环境。系统与外界之间的分界面称为边界，热力学系统通过边界与外界间发生各种能量与物质的相互作用。

根据分析对象的不同，常见的热力学系统有以下两种分类方法。

（一）按照系统与外界有无物质交换来分

1．闭口系统

与外界无物质交换的热力学系统称为闭口系统，又称为封闭系统。由于闭口系统内工质的质量固定不变，因此又称为控制质量系统。该系统与外界的能量交换只有容积变化功与热量两种形式，如图 1-1-1 所示，外界对活塞做容积变化功，活塞从位置 1 移动到位置 2，如果系统边界与外界可进行热量交换，则系统从外界吸收热量。

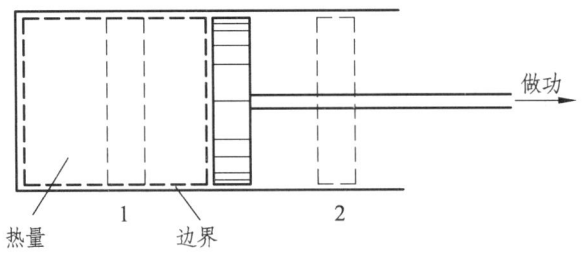

图 1-1-1　闭口系统示意图

2. 开口系统

与外界有物质交换的热力学系统称为开口系统，通常开口系统有一个相对固定的空间，故又称为控制容积系统。这类热力学系统的主要特点是在所分析的系统内工质是流动的，如图 1-1-2 所示。工程上绝大多数设备和装置都是开口系统。

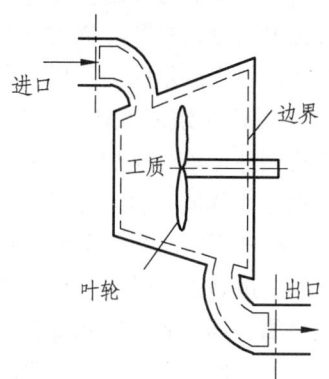

图 1-1-2　开口系统示意图

（二）按照系统与外界在边界上是否存在能量交换来分

1. 孤立系统

这类热力学系统在分界面上与外界既不存在能量交换，也不存在物质交换。

2. 绝热系统

这类热力学系统在分界面上与外界不存在热量交换，但可以有功量和物质交换。

3. 非孤立系统

这类系统的特点是在分界面上，系统与外界存在能量或物质交换。

孤立系统和绝热系统是热力学中的特殊情况，实际的热力学系统多处于非孤立系统状态，但由于这两种特殊的热力学系统在热力学研究中有重要的作用，所以，常常把实际热力学系统理想化，将其转化为孤立系统或绝热系统来分析，这样能使问题简化，便于更好地掌握问题的本质特征。

二、气体状态参数

热力学系统在某一瞬间所呈现的宏观物理状态称为系统的状态。用来描述系统所处状态的一些宏观物理量则称为状态参数。工程热力学上常采用的状态参数有：温度（T）、压力（p）、比容（v）、热量（Q）、比焓（h）和比熵（s）等。其中温度、压力和比容三个参数最为常见，它们可以借助于仪表直接或间接测量，因此常称之为基本状态参数。

(一) 温 度

温度是用来表示物体冷热程度的物理参数。人们感觉越热，就说温度越高；感觉越冷，就说温度越低。但是这样以人的主观感觉来表征温度是不科学的，因为这不但不利于定量地表示物体的温度，有时还会导致一些错误的结论。例如，冬天当用手分别摸室外放在一起的木头和铁块时，会感到铁块比木头冷，如果按照上面的说法，应该就是铁块的温度比木头的温度低。但事实上，只要用仪器去测量就会发现，它们的温度是一样的。

气体分子运动论认为：气体的温度是组成气体的大量分子热运动平均移动动能的度量。气体温度越高，表明分子不规则热运动越剧烈，分子平均动能越大。

温度也是判断工质与外界或两个物体间是否有热量传递的依据。热量总是从温度高的一方传向温度低的一方。若将冷热程度不同的两个系统相互接触，它们之间会发生热量传递。在不受外界影响的条件下，经过足够长的时间，它们将达到共同的冷热程度，而不再进行热量交换，这种情况称为热平衡，即两者温度相等。

为了进行温度测量，需要有温度的数值表示方法，即需要建立温度的标尺或温标。任何一种温度计都是根据某一温标制成的，国际上常用的温标有三种。

1. 摄氏温标

在日常生活中说体温是 37 ℃，气温是 20 ℃，使用的就是摄氏温标，即摄氏温度，用符号 t 表示，计量单位为摄氏度，以符号℃表示。

1742 年，瑞典天文学家摄尔修斯（A. Celsius，1701—1744）制定了百分刻度法。他把水的冰点和沸点之间分为 100 个温度间隔，为避免测冰点以下的低温时出现负值，他把水的沸点规定为零点，而把冰点定为 100 ℃。后来接受他同事的建议才把这种标值倒过来，这就是现在所用的摄氏温标。

2. 热力学温标

建立在热力学第二定律基础上的热力学温标则是一种与测温物质的性质无关的温标。用这种温标确定的温度称为热力学温度，也称为绝对温度，以符号 T 表示，计量单位为开尔文，或简称开，以符号 K 表示。

1954 年以后，国际上规定选用纯水的三相点（纯水的固、液、气三相平衡共存的状态点）作为标准温度点，并规定这个状态下温度的数值是 273.15K。1960 年国际计量大会通过决议，规定摄氏温度由热力学温度移动零点来获得，即绝对温度与摄氏温度间的换算关系为：

$$t = T - 273.15 \;(\text{℃}) \tag{1-1}$$

3. 华氏温标

华氏温标是欧美一些国家常用的一种温标。把纯水的冰点温度定为 32 °F，把标准大气压下水的沸点温度定为 212 °F，中间分为 180 等分，每一等份代表 1 华氏度，这就是华氏温标。用符号 t_F 表示，单位为°F。

华氏温度与摄氏温度的换算关系是：

$$t = \frac{5}{9}(t_F - 32) \quad (\text{°C}) \tag{1-2}$$

在工质的状态参数中，温度通常指的是工质的绝对温度。

（二）压　力

压力是指沿垂直方向作用在单位面积上的作用力，在物理学中又称为压强，以符号 p 表示，即

$$p = \frac{F}{A} \tag{1-3}$$

式中　F——垂直作用力（N）；

　　　A——面积（m²）。

对于容器内的气体工质来说，压力是大量气体分子做不规则运动时对器壁频繁碰击的宏观统计结果，即气体的压力是大量分子与容器壁面碰撞作用力的统计平均值。如图 1-1-3 所示，将外部空气压入水壶内加压后，可将壶内的水雾化喷出。

图 1-1-3　压力水壶喷水

在国际单位制中，压力的单位为 Pa（帕），即 $1\,\text{Pa} = 1\,\text{N/m}^2$。工程上，因单位 Pa 太小，通常采用 kPa（千帕）和 MPa（兆帕）作为压力的单位，它们之间的关系为：

$$1\,\text{MPa} = 10^3\,\text{kPa} = 10^6\,\text{Pa}$$

也曾使用 bar（巴）和 atm（标准大气压）作为压力单位，atm 是 atmosphere 的简写，指标准大气压。但随着国际标准化推动，这两个压力单位已被取消使用，它们与国际标准压力单位之间的关系为

$$1\,\text{bar} = 0.1\,\text{MPa}$$

$$1\,\text{atm} = 1.013 \times 10^5\,\text{Pa}$$

我们的生活环境是处在大气层内的，也就是说我们的周围是有大气压力的。地球表面单位面积上所受到的大气的压力称为大气压力或大气压，以符号 p_b 表示。地球上不同位置的大气压力时不同的，把温度为 0 ℃、纬度 45° 海平面上的气压称为标准大气压。通常情况下，可简单认为大气压力与海拔是成反比的。

空气等工质对容器壁面的实际压力称为绝对压力，以符号 p 表示。容器内压力的读取通常采用压力表来完成。工程上所采用的压力表都是在特定的环境中（比如在大气中）测量的。常见的有 U 形管压力计（见图 1-1-4）和膜盒压力表等，所测出的压力值都是在大气压力 p_b 条件下的相对值，并不是系统内气体的绝对压力。这里分两种情况：

第一种情况，如图 1-1-4（a）所示，此时容器内绝对压力 p 高于大气压力 p_b，压力计指示的读数称为表压力，用 p_e 表示，即：

$$p = p_b + p_e \tag{1-4}$$

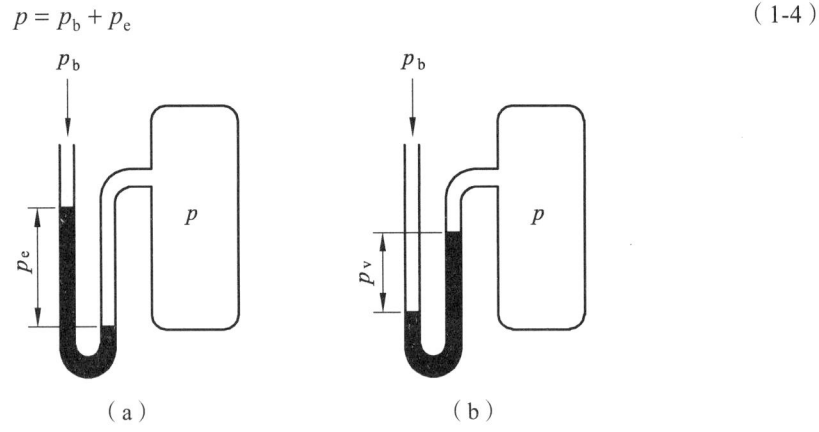

图 1-1-4　U 形压力计示意图

第二种情况，如图 1-1-4（b）所示，此时容器内绝对压力 p 低于大气压力 p_b，压力计指示的读数称为真空度，用 p_v 表示，即：

$$p = p_b - p_v \tag{1-5}$$

由此可见：当绝对压力大于大气压力时，表压力为正；当绝对压力小于表压力时，表压力为负，称为出现真空。如图 1-1-5 所示，指针处在表盘右侧区域为正压；指针处在表盘左侧区域为负压；指针指向 0 时，说明绝对压力等于大气压力。当指针处在表盘左侧区域时，绝对压力越低，真空度越高；反之，绝对相压力越接近大气压力，则真空度就越低。

大气压力随测量的时间、地点不同而不同，可用大气压力计测定。工程计算中，如被测工质的压力相对于大气压力要高很多，可将大气压力视为常数，通常近似地取为 0.1 MPa。如被测工质的压力较低，则须按当地大气压力的具体数值计算。因此，即使绝对压力不变，由于大气压力变化，表压力和真空度也会变化。只有绝对压力才能真正反映工质的热力状态，才是状态参数。工质的基本状态参数之一的压力指的就是工质或系统的"绝对压力"。

图 1-1-5　膜盒压力表

例 1-1　锅炉汽锅内的蒸汽的表压力 p_e 是 3.1 MPa，汽轮机凝汽器内维持 94 643 Pa 的真空压力。如果当时当地的实际大气压力 p_b 为 101 974 Pa，求汽锅和凝汽器内的绝对压力。如果大气压力变动到 97 975 Pa，汽锅和凝汽器的压力表的读数又各为多少？

解：（1）依题意可知，当时当地的大气压力为：

$$p_b = 101\ 974\ \text{Pa}$$

汽锅内的绝对压力为：

$$p_{汽} = p_b + p_e = (101\,974 + 3.1 \times 10^6)\ \text{Pa} = 3.202 \times 10^6\ \text{Pa} = 3.202\ \text{MPa}$$

凝汽器内的真空度为：

$$p_v = 94\ 643\ \text{Pa}$$

凝汽器内的绝对压力为：

$$p_{凝} = p_b - p_v = (101\ 974 - 94\ 643)\ \text{Pa} = 7\ 331\ \text{Pa}$$

（2）当大气压力为 97 975 Pa 时

$$p_b = 97\ 975\ \text{Pa}$$

汽锅内的压力计的读数为：

$$p_e = p_{汽} - p_b = (3.1 \times 10^6 - 97\ 975)\ \text{Pa} = 3.104 \times 10^6\ \text{Pa} = 3.104\ \text{MPa}$$

凝汽器内的压力计的读数为：

$$p_v = p_b - p_{凝} = (97\ 975 - 7\ 331)\ \text{Pa} = 90\ 644\ \text{Pa}$$

（三）比容与密度

比容（又称比体积）是指单位质量工质所占有的容积（体积），用符号 v 表示，在国际单位制中单位是 m^3/kg。如果质量为 m（kg）的工质占有的容积为 V（m^3），则该工质的比容为：

$$v = \frac{V}{m} \tag{1-6}$$

单位容积工质的质量称为密度,用符号 ρ 表示,单位是 kg/m³。很明显,工质的密度 ρ 与比容 v 互为倒数,即

$$\rho = \frac{m}{V} = \frac{1}{V} \tag{1-7}$$

比容和密度都是描述工质在某一状态下分子聚集疏密程度的物理量,都可以作为工质的状态参数。

(四)功与热量

在制冷设备中工质与外界之间的能量传递是通过做功和热传递的形式实现的,因此功和热量就是能量传递的度量,是重要的物理量。

1. 功

功是系统与外界交换能量的一种方式。力学中把物体间通过力的作用而传递的能量称为功,并定义功等于力 F 和物体在力所作用方向上位移 x 的乘积,即

$$W = Fx$$

若物体在力 F 作用下沿着力的方向 x 产生了微小的位移 dx,则该力所做的功为:

$$\delta W = Fdx$$

如果物体在力 F 作用下沿力的方向从 x_1 位移到 x_2,则力 F 所做的功为:

$$W = \int_{x_1}^{x_2} Fdx$$

在国际单位制中,功的单位为 J(焦耳)或 kJ(千焦),单位功的单位为 J/kg 或 kJ/kg。热量转换为机械能的过程是通过工质的体积膨胀实现的。工质在体积膨胀时所做的功称为膨胀功,它是热力学的一种基本功。

如图 1-1-6 所示,假定气缸中盛有质量为 m 的工质,其压力为 p,活塞面积为 A,则工质作用在活塞上的力为 pA。假设活塞在工质压力的作用下向右移动了一个微小距离 dx,由于在此过程中工质体积膨胀很小,其压力近乎不变,如果这个过程是平衡过程,则工质对活塞所做的功为

$$\delta W = pAdx = pdV \tag{1-8}$$

如果活塞从位置 1 移动到位置 2,且过程是平衡过程,则工质所做的膨胀功为:

$$W = \int_1^2 pdV \tag{1-9}$$

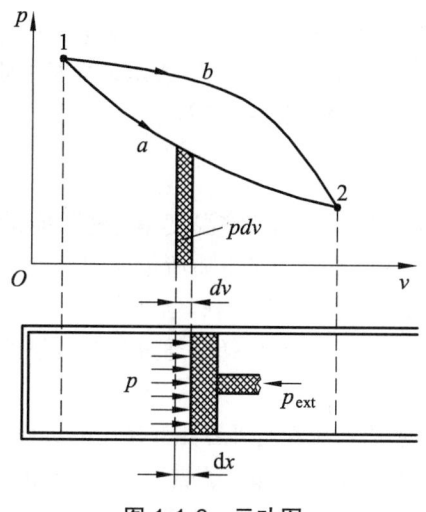

图 1-1-6 示功图

单位质量工质所做的膨胀功称为单位膨胀功，用 w 表示。由式（1-8）、式（1-9）可得

$$\Delta w = p\mathrm{d}v \tag{1-10}$$

$$w = \int_1^2 p\mathrm{d}v = \int_{v_1}^{v_2} p\mathrm{d}v \tag{1-11}$$

式中　p——工质的绝对压力（Pa）；

　　　v_1——工质的初态比容（m³/kg）；

　　　v_2——工质的终态比容（m³/kg）。

对于质量为 m（kg）的工质所做的总功为：

$$W = mw = \int_{v_1}^{v_2} p\mathrm{d}V \tag{1-12}$$

式中　p——工质的绝对压力（Pa）；

　　　V_1——工质的初态体积（m³）；

　　　V_2——工质的终态体积（m³）。

上述推导都是假设热力过程是可逆的，所得到的公式也是计算可逆过程膨胀功的公式。具体计算时，除了工质的初态、终态以外，还必须知道工质在状态变化过程中压力和比容之间的变化规律。如图 1-1-6 所示，从位置 1 到位置 2 走曲线 a 和走曲线 b 的膨胀功是不同的，可见膨胀功的大小不仅取决于工质的初态、终态，而且和过程有关，所以功是过程量而不是状态量。

一个可逆过程可以用压力 p 为纵坐标，比容 v 为横坐标的 p-v 图上的一条曲线来表示，如图 1-1-6 中的曲线 a 所示。根据微积分原理，积分 $\int_1^2 p\mathrm{d}v$ 的数值，即单位膨胀功 $w_{1\text{-}2}$ 的大小可以用过程曲线下面的面积来表示，因此 p-v 图也叫示功图。

虽然膨胀功是从膨胀过程推导出来的，但对于压缩过程同样适用。由式（1-11）、式

（1-12）可知，当工质膨胀时，$dv>0$，$w>0$，膨胀功是正功，表示工质对外界做功；当工质被压缩时，$dv<0$，$w<0$，压缩功是负功，表示外界对工质做功；当工质的容积不变（定容过程）时，则$dv=0$，$w=0$容积功等于零。

2. 热量

在热力学中，热力系统与外界之间依靠温度差传递的能量称为热量，用 Q 表示，单位与功的单位相同，为 J 或 W。单位质量工质所传递的热量，用 q 表示，单位为 J/kg 或 kJ/kg。当温度不同的系统与外界相互接触时，温度高的一方总是把一部分热量传递给温度低的一方。从微观上讲，这种能量的传递是通过相互接触处的分子碰撞或以热辐射的形式完成的。

热量和功量一样，都是热力系统在与外界相互作用的过程中所传递的能量。热量和热能是两个不同的概念。热能是指工质内部分子热运动所具有的能量，它储存于工质内部；而热量是系统与外界传递的那部分热能，它和功量一样，都是能量传递的量度，只在能量传递过程中才有意义。

热量决定于始、终状态及状态变化过程，是过程函数，不是状态参数。在给定状态下，能说系统具有多少热能，而不能说系统具有多少热量或多少功量。

工程热力学规定：工质从外界吸热时，热量为正；工质向外界放热时，热量为负。

（五）焓与熵

1. 焓

焓是一个复合的热力状态参数，是表征系统中所有的总能量，用 H 表示。它是内能与压力位能之和。当工质在一定状态（压力 P、容积 V、温度 T）时，焓的数值，代表工质所具有的总能量。

对于开放系统（即与外界既有能量交换又有物质交换的热力学系统），当工质流进（或流出）系统时，不仅把工质所具有的内能带入（或带出）系统，而且还把它所获得的推动功也带入（或带出系统），就是说对于开放系统，当工质流进（或流出）系统时，它的内能和推动功总是同时出现。例如，对空气进行加热和冷却时，常需要确定空气吸收或放出多少热量。为计算方便，把工质的内能和推动功之和定义为焓。1 kg 工质的焓，称比焓，有时也简称焓，用符号 h 表示，单位为 J/kg 或 kJ/kg。

焓只是个与状态有关而与过程无关的状态参数。在计算中焓通常查表求得。在空气调节和制冷循环中，只计算出工质变化前后的焓差值的大小、正负，而与焓的绝对值无关。

2. 熵

熵是表征工质状态变化时，与外界热交换程度的一个导出的热力状态参数。也就是热量和功量状态变化过程中系统和外界传递的能量，两者具有某些共同特征，在做功过程中，压差是做功的动力，状态参数比容（v）的变化是衡量是否做功的尺度。同样在传热过程中，温差是传热的动力，也有一个参数，它的变化是衡量是否传热的尺度，这个参数定义为熵，用符号 S 表示，单位是 J/(kg·K)。制冷剂被加热时熵增大，反之，从制冷剂中散发热量时，熵就减少，只要制冷剂不吸热也不放热，熵值就不变。

（六）比热

物体温度升高（或降低）1 K（或 1 ℃）所需吸收（或放出）的热量，称为热容量，简称为热容。一定量的物质在吸收或放出热量时，其温度变化的大小取决于工质的性质、数量和所经历的过程。

单位质量温度升高（或降低）1 K（或 1 ℃）所需吸收（或放出）的热量称为该物质的比热（质量比热），用 c 表示，单位为 J/(kg·K)或 kJ/(kg·K)。

三、平衡过程和可逆过程

（一）平衡过程

系统由一个状态到达另一个状态的变化过程称为热力过程，简称过程。状态改变意味着系统原平衡状态被破坏。实际热工设备中进行的热力过程，都是由于系统内部各处的温度、压力和比容的不平衡而引起的，所以热力过程所经历的中间状态是不平衡的。

为了便于对实际热力过程进行分析和研究，假设热力过程中系统所经历的每一个状态都无限地接近平衡状态，这种过程称为准平衡过程，又称为准静态过程。在状态参数坐标图上可以用连续的实线表示。而非平衡过程由于它所经历的不平衡状态没有确定的状态参数，因而不能表示在状态参数坐标图上。

（二）可逆过程

如果系统由始态变化到终态完成了某一热力过程之后，再由终态沿着原来的路径逆行返回到始态时，参与该变化的系统和外界也随之返回到原来的状态，而不留下任何变化，则这一过程称为可逆过程。实现可逆过程从理论上讲，是在没有摩擦的前提下，使系统与外界保持力平衡（没有压力差）时，所作的机械运动过程；使系统与外界保持热平衡（没有温差）时，所进行的传热过程。但是没有温差、压力差就没有传热和机械运动，所以可逆过程可以理解为在无限小的温差下进行的传热过程和在无限小的压力差下进行的机械运动。事实上，一切实际存在的热力过程都是不可逆过程，即可逆过程是不可能实现的。但可逆过程中没有能量损耗，在理论上是热变功最有效的过程。因此，它是实际过程努力接近的方向。

可逆过程是一个理想过程，是一切热力设备工作过程力求接近的目标。可逆过程的概念为热力学分析问题提供了很大的方便。利用这一概念可以将复杂的实际热力过程近似简化为一个可逆过程加以研究，然后再加以修正，所以研究可逆过程在理论上具有十分重要的意义。

四、理想气体状态方程式

在研究气体的性质时,人们最容易发现的是气体状态参量的变化。例如,皮球、充过气的轮胎,若把它们放在夏天的阳光下晒,皮球、轮胎内气体的压强、体积、温度都会变化;压瘪了的乒乓球浸泡到热水中,球里的空气温度升高,使得体积增大,球往往会鼓起来;把氧气装入钢罐中,氧气的压强、体积、温度,这三个参量也会变化。自然界和工程中所遇到的类似现象,大多数都是气体的压强、体积和温度这三个量同时发生变化的情况,只有两个量变化,另一个量不变化的情况也是有的。对于一定质量的气体,如果这三个量都不改变,我们就说气体处于一定的状态。如果这三个量或任意两个量同时变化,我们就说气体的状态改变了。那么在气体状态改变时这三个量的变化是任意的还是相互关联遵循一定的规律呢?

(一) 理想气体

在工质的热力性质中,压力、比容、温度之间的关系具有特别重要的意义。对于实际气体,这种关系一般比较复杂。但是,通过大量实验发现,当密度比较小,也就是比容比较大的时候,处于平衡状态的气态物质的基本状态参数之间将近似地保持一种简单的关系。为此,人们提出了理想气体的模型:气体分子之间的平均距离相当大,分子体积与气体的总容积相比可忽略不计;分子之间无作用力;分子之间的相互碰撞以及分子与容器壁的碰撞都是弹性碰撞。

理想气体是经过科学抽象的假想气体,尽管自然界中并不存在,但引进理想气体的概念仍有很大的实用价值。实验证明,当气体的压力不太高,温度不太低时,气体分子间的作用力及分子本身的体积皆可忽略,气体的性质就接近理想气体,气体可以作为理想气体处理。

例如,在常温下,只要压力不超过 5 MPa,工程上常用的 O_2、N_2、H_2、CO 等气体以及主要由这些气体组成的气体混合物,都可以作为理想气体处理,不会产生很大误差。另外,大气或燃气中所含的少量水蒸气,由于其分压力很低,比容很大,也可作为理想气体处理。

(二) 理想气体状态方程

通过大量实验发现,理想气体在平衡状态下,气体的温度、压力、比容三者之间存在着一定的函数关系,这就是物理学中的波义耳-马略特定律、盖-吕萨克定律和查理定律所表达的内容。这三条定律可以综合表达为

$$pv = R_g T \qquad (1\text{-}13)$$

式(1-13)称为理想气体状态方程式,1834 年由克拉伯龙首先导出,因此也称为克拉伯龙方程式。对于质量为 m(kg)的理想气体,状态方程式的形式为

$$pV = mR_g T \qquad (1\text{-}14)$$

式中 p——气体的绝对压力（Pa）；
v——气体的比容（m³/kg）；
V——质量为 m 的气体的容积（m³）；
T——气体的热力学温度（K）；
R_g——气体常数[J/（kgK）]。

R_g 称为气体常数，它与气体的状态无关，但与气体的种类有关，对于同一种气体，气体常数是一定的。

在国际单位制中，物质的量以 mol（摩尔）为单位。1 mol 物质的质量称为摩尔质量，用 M 表示，单位为 kg/mol。1 mol 物质的质量的数值与气体的相对分子质量相同。例如，氧、氮和空气的摩尔质量分别为 32.00×10^{-3} kg/mol，28.2×10^{-3} kg/mol 和 28.96×10^{-3} kg/mol。1 mol 物质的体积称为摩尔体积，用 V_m 表示，$V_m = Mv$。

对于理想气体，由式（1-13）可得

$$pV_m = MR_g T$$

令 $R = MR_g$，则得

$$pV_m = RT \qquad (1\text{-}15)$$

根据阿伏伽德罗定律，在相同的温度和压力下，所有气体的摩尔体积 V_m 都相等。由式（1-8）可知，所有气体的 R 都相等，并且其数值与气体所处的具体状态无关。R 称为摩尔气体常数，其值可由气体在任意一状态下的参数确定，如在标准状态（$p_0 = 101\,325$ Pa，$T_0 = 273.15$ K）下，1 mol 任何气体所占的体积皆为 22.41 410 m³ 代入式（1-15）可得

$$R = \frac{p_0 V_{m0}}{T_0} = \frac{101\,325 \times 22.41\,410}{273.15 \times 1\,000} = 8.314 [\text{J}/(\text{kg} \cdot \text{K}]$$

有了摩尔气体常数，只要知道气体的摩尔质量（或相对分子质量），任何一种气体的气体常数 R_g 为

$$R_g = \frac{R}{M} \qquad (1\text{-}16)$$

利用摩尔气体常数，质量为 m（kg）的理想气体的状态方程式（1-14）还可以写成

$$pV = nRT \qquad (1\text{-}17)$$

式中，$n = m/M$，n 称为物质的量。

需要注意的是：当理想气体状态方程运用于实际气体时会有所偏差，因为理想气体的基本假设在实际气体中并不成立。如实验测定 1 mol 乙炔在 20 ℃、101 kPa 时，体积为 24.1 dm³，而同样在 20 ℃ 时，在 842 kPa 下，体积为 0.114 dm³，它们相差很多，这是因为它不是理想气体。

一般来说，沸点低的气体在较高的温度和较低的压力时，更接近理想气体，如氧气的沸点为 – 183 °C、氢气沸点为 – 253 °C，它们在常温常压下摩尔体积与理想值仅相差 0.1% 左右，而二氧化硫的沸点为 – 10 °C，在常温常压下摩尔体积与理想值的相差达到了 2.4%。应用一定量处于平衡态的气体，其状态由 P、V 和 T 衡量，表达这几个量之间的关系的方程称之为气体的状态方程，不同的气体有不同的状态方程。但真实气体的方程通常十分复杂，而理想气体的状态方程具有非常简单的形式。

虽然完全理想的气体并不可能存在，但许多实际气体，特别是那些不容易液化、凝华的气体（如氦气、氢气、氧气、氮气等，由于氦气不但体积小、互相之间作用力小、也是所有气体中最难液化的，因此它是所有气体中最接近理想气体的气体。）在常温常压下的性质已经十分接近于理想气体。

各种气体符合理想气体状态方程的温度和压力范围不一样。有如下规律：

（1）越难液化的气体，即沸点越低的气体（如 H_2、He、Ar 等）符合理想气体状态方程的温度和压力范围越宽，即可在比较低的温度和比较高的压力下应用理想气体状态方程。

（2）易液化的气体，即沸点较高的气体（如 CO_2、NH_3、SO_2 等）符合理想气体状态方程的温度和压力范围就较窄，甚至在较高的温度和很低的压力下也与理想行为有明显的偏差。

此外，有时只需要粗略估算一些数据，使用这个方程会使计算变得方便很多。

例 1-2　长期放在室内的一个氧气瓶，容量为 25 L，压力表指示的瓶内氧气的表压力为 5 bar，室温为 20 °C，大气压力为 1×10^5 Pa，试求瓶内所存氧气的质量。

解：据题意可知，瓶内氧气的热力学参数分别为

$$p = (5+1) \text{ bar} = 6 \text{ bar} = 6\,10^5 \text{ Pa}$$
$$T = (20 + 273) \text{ K} = 293 \text{ K}$$
$$V = 25 \text{ L} = 0.025 \text{ m}^3$$

氧的摩尔质量 $M = 32.00 \times 10^3$ kg/mol

例 1-3　某容积为 4 m³ 的容器内充有 $p = 9.81 \times 10^4$ Pa，$t = 20$ °C 的空气，抽气后容器的真空度 $p_V = 93\,310$ Pa，当时当地的大气压力 $p_b = 98\,055.48$ Pa。若抽气前后温度保持不变，试求：

（1）抽气后容器内空气的绝对压力为多少？

（2）抽气后容器内空气的质量为多少？

（3）抽走多少千克空气？

解：以 1 和 2 分别表示抽气前后的状态。

（1）抽气后容器内的空气的绝对压力

$$p_2 = p_b - p_V = (98\,055.48 - 93\,310) \text{ Pa} = 4\,745.48 \text{ Pa}$$

（2）依题意，抽气后容器内的热力学参数为

$$p_2 = 4,745.48 \text{ Pa}$$
$$T_2 = (20+273) \text{ K} = 293 \text{ K}$$
$$V_2 = 4 \text{ m}^3$$

空气的摩尔质量 $M = 28.96 \times 10^{-3} \text{ kg/mol}$

空气的气体常数 $R_g = \dfrac{R}{M} = \dfrac{8.314}{28.96 \times 10^{-3}} = 287 \text{ J/(kg·K)}$

抽气后容器内空气的质量为

$$m_2 = \frac{p_2 V}{R_g T} = \frac{4,745.48 \times 4}{287 \times 293} = 0.226 \text{ kg}$$

（3）抽气前容器内的空气质量为

$$m_1 = \frac{p_1 V}{R_g T} = \frac{9.81 \times 10^4 \times 4}{287 \times 293} = 4.67 \text{ kg}$$

所抽走的空气质量为

$$\Delta m = m_1 - m_2 = 4.67 - 0.226 = 4.44 \text{ kg}$$

任务二　热力学定律及其在制冷中的应用

【任务目标】

掌握热力学第一、第二定律。

【知识储备】

一、热力系统的储存能

储存在热力系统的能量称为热力系统的储存能。工程热力学所涉及的热力系统的储存能主要有两类：一类是取决于系统本身状态的内能；另一类是与系统的宏观运动速度有关的宏观动能和与系统在重力场中所处位置有关的宏观势能。

（一）内能

组成物质的微观粒子所具有的能量称为物质的内能。当不涉及化学变化和原子核反应时，内能是分子的热运动动能和分子之间由于相互作用力而具有的位能之和，即所谓的热能。由物理学可知，气体分子动能的大小主要取决于气体的温度，位能的大小主要与气体的比容有关。

在工程热力学中，一定质量的工质的内能用 U 表示，单位是 J 或 kJ；单位质量（即

1 kg）工质的内能称为比内能，用 M 表示，单位是 J/kg 或 kJ/kg。

气体工质的比内能只取决于工质的热力学温度和比容，即取决于工质的热力状态，是状态参数，于是可表示为

$$u = f(T, v)$$

因为物质的运动是永恒的，不可能有这样一种状态：工质内部的一切运动都停止，内能为零，所以内能的大小是相对的。在工程热力学的计算中，经常遇到的是工质从一个状态变化到另一个状态，需要计算的是内能的变化量，而不是内能的绝对值。因此，计算内能的基准状态可以认为地选定，例如，取 0 K 或 0 ℃ 时气体的内能为零。

（二）宏观动能和宏观势能

除了内能之外，热力系统还由于其宏观运动速度具有宏观动能和由于其在重力场中所处的位置具有宏观位能，分别用 E_k、E_p 表示，单位为 J 或 kJ。

如果质量为 m 的系统的运动速度为 c_f，则系统的宏观动能为

$$E_k = \frac{1}{2} m c_f^2$$

如果质量为 m 的系统的质量中心在系统外部参考坐标系中的高度为 z，则系统的宏观势能为

$$E_p = mgz$$

二、热力学过程

在环境的作用下，系统从一个平衡状态变化到另一个平衡状态的过程称为热力学过程。在实际过程中，系统所经历的一系列状态一般都是不平衡状态，如果所经历的状态都无限接近于平衡状态，并且没有摩擦，则为可逆过程。可逆过程是实际过程所能趋近的极限。

通常热力学过程有以下几类：

（1）等温过程：系统的始态和终态的温度与环境温度相同，且环境温度不变的过程。在变化过程中系统温度不一定恒定。

（2）等压过程：系统的始态和终态的压力与环境压力相等，且环境压力为一恒定值的过程。在变化过程中系统的压力不一定恒定。

（3）等容过程：系统的始态和终态体积相等的过程，即 $\Delta V = 0$。

（4）绝热过程：系统与环境之间用绝热壁隔开，此时系统中所进行的过程称为绝热过程。

（5）循环过程：系统经一系列变化后又回到原来状态的过程。

三、热力学定律

热力学定律是描述物理学中热学规律的定律，主要包括热力学第一定律、热力学第二定律、热力学第三定律和热力学第零定律、。其中热力学第一定律即能量守恒定律；热力学第二定律有多种表述，也叫熵增加原理。热力学定律是热力学的基础。

（一）热力学第一定律

热力学第一定律是能量守恒定律，也叫能量不灭原理。自然界的一切物质都具有能量，能量有不同形式，能量不可能被创造也不可能被消灭，而只能在一定条件下从一种形式转变为另一种形式，而在转变过程中总能量是守恒的。热力学第一定律的实质就是热力过程中的能量守恒和转换定律，它建立了热力过程中的能量平衡关系，是热力学宏观分析方法的主要依据之一。

热力学第一定律可表述为：在热能与其他形式能的相互转换过程中，能的总量始终保持不变。

根据热力学第一定律，要想得到机械能就必须花费热能或其他能量，那种幻想创造一种不花费能量就可以产生动力的机器的企图是徒劳的。因此，热力学第一定律也可以表述为：不花费能量就可以产生功的第一类永动机是不可能制造成功的。

热力学第一定律是能量守恒定律在热能和机械能转换中的具体应用。它指出了热能和机械能相互转换时的总量不变，是热力学宏观分析问题的主要依据。具体可表述为：热和功可以相互转换，为获得一定量的功，必须消耗一定量的热；反之，消耗一定量的功，必产生一定量的热。

热力学第一定律适用于一切热力系统和热力过程，不论是开口系统还是闭口系统，热力学第一定律均可表达为

$$进入系统的能量 - 离开系统的能量 = 系统储存能量的变化 \quad (1-18)$$

（二）热力学第二定律

热力学第一定律阐述了热能和机械能以及其他形式的能量在传递和转换过程中数量上的守恒关系。但经验告诉我们，不是所有满足热力学第一定律的热力过程都能实现，热力过程的发生是有方向、条件和限度的。热力学第二定律揭示了这一规律。

1. 自发过程的方向性

所谓自发过程就是不需要任何外界作用而自发进行的过程。例如热量由高温物体向低温物体传递，就是一个自发过程，反之则不能自发进行。

机械能通过摩擦转变为热能的过程也是一个自发过程。例如，行驶中的汽车刹车时，汽车的动能通过摩擦全部变成热能，造成地面和轮胎升温，最后散逸于大气环境。反之，如果将同等数量的热加给轮胎和地面，却不能使汽车行驶。这说明，机械能可以自发地转

变为热能，而热能却不能自发地转变为机械能。

实践证明，不仅热量传递、热能与机械能的相互转换具有方向性，自然界的一切自发过程都具有方向性。例如，水自动地由高处向低处流动，气体自动地由高压区向低压区膨胀，电流自动地由高电势流向低电势，不同气体的混合过程，燃烧过程，等等，都是只能自发地向一个方向进行。如果要想使自发过程逆向进行，就必须付出某种代价，或者说给外界留下某种变化。这就是说，自发过程是不可逆的。

2. 热力学第二定律的表述

热力学第二定律揭示了自然界中一切热过程进行的方向、条件和限度。自然界中热过程的种类很多，因此热力学第二定律的表述方式也很多。由于各种表述所揭示的是一个共同的客观规律，因而它们彼此是等效的，下面介绍两种具有代表性的表述。

克劳修斯表述：不可能将热从低温物体传至高温物体而不引起其他变化。

这是从热量传递的角度表述的热力学第二定律，由克劳修斯于1850年提出的。他指明了热量只能自发地从高温物体传向低温物体，反之的非自发过程并非不能实现，而是必须花费一定的代价。例如压缩式制冷装置就是以花费机械能为代价，即以机械能变为热能这一自发过程作为实现热从低温物体转移至高温物体所必需的补偿代价。

开尔文-普朗克表述：不可能从单一热源取热，并使之完全转变为功而不产生其他影响。

这是从热功转换的角度表述的热力学第二定律，于1851年由开尔文提出，1897年普朗克也发表了内容相同的表述，后来，称之为开尔文-普朗克表述。"不产生其他影响"是这一表述不可缺少的部分。例如，理想气体定温膨胀过程进行的结果，就是从单一热源取热并将其全部变成了功。但与此同时，气体的压力降低，容积增大，即气体的状态发生了变化，或者说"产生了其他影响"。因此，并非热不能完全变为功，而是必须有其他影响为代价才能实现。

通常人们把假想的从单一热源取热并使之完全变为功的热机称为第二类永动机。它虽然不违反热力学第一定律，转换过程能量是守恒的，但违反了热力学第二定律。如果这种热机可以制造成功，就可以利用大气、海洋等作为单一热源，将大气、海洋中取之不尽的热能转变为功，维持它永远转动，这显然是不可能的。因此，热力学第二定律又可表述为：第二类永动机是不可能制造成功的。

热力学第二定律的以上两种表述，各自从不同的角度反映了热过程的方向性，实质上是统一的、等效的。

四、热力学定律在制冷中的应用

人工制冷是借助于专门的制冷设备，消耗一定的外界能量，迫使热量从温度较低的被冷却物体，传递给温度较高的环境介质，得到人们所需要的各种低温环境。人工制冷的方法很多，大致可分为物理方法和化学方法两类，而绝大多数的人工制冷方法属于物理方法。

在普通制冷技术领域内，应用最广泛的物理方法有相变制冷、蒸汽压缩式制冷、吸收式制冷等。

在这些制冷方法中，不仅有能量的转移，也包括热-功转换的过程。热力学第一定律是能量守恒定律指出：自然界中的一切物质都具有能量，能量能够从一种形式转换为另一种形式，从一个物体转移到另一个物体，而在转换和转移的过程中能量的总量不变。热力学第一定律指出了能量转换和转移在数量上的关系。热力学第二定律提示了能量转换的条件。热力学第二定律指出：机械功可以全部变为热，但热不能无条件的全部转换为机械功，即不可能从单热源取热，使之完全变为功而不引起其他的变化。由此可知，利用一个热源无法完成循环过程。第二定律同时指出：不可能把热从低温物体传到高温物体而不引起其他变化。因此，要使热量从低温物体传到高温物体，必须要有一个补偿过程。人工制冷的过程就是在外界的补偿下，将低温物体的热量向高温物体传送的过程。

除此之外，我们还利用热力学第零定律实现了温度的测量，在无法直接获取被测物体温度的前提下，我们使用第三个物体，通过热平衡来对被测物体的温度进行间接反映。

任务三　热量传递的方式

【任务目标】

掌握热量传递的三种方式。

【知识储备】

热能总是自发地从高温物体传向低温物体，或者从同一物体的高温部分传向低温部分，物体间的这种热量交换，简称为热量传递，简称传热。

传热的应用可归结为两大类：一类是设法增强传热，实现热能的有效传递，如室内暖气散热片的传热（如图1-3-1所示）；另一类是设法削弱传热，减少热量的传递，避免散热损失，如供暖管道在室外的部分外层用隔热材料保温（如图1-3-2所示）。

图1-3-1　家用暖气片

图1-3-2　供暖管道

根据传热过程的不同，热能传递有导热、热对流和热辐射三种方式。

如图 1-3-3 所示，在用灶火做饭时，热量从火传到锅，再传到人的手，这个过程是导热的传热方式；火通过锅加热水的过程是热对流的传热方式；人在火旁边能直接感受到火释放的热量，这个过程就是热辐射的传热方式。

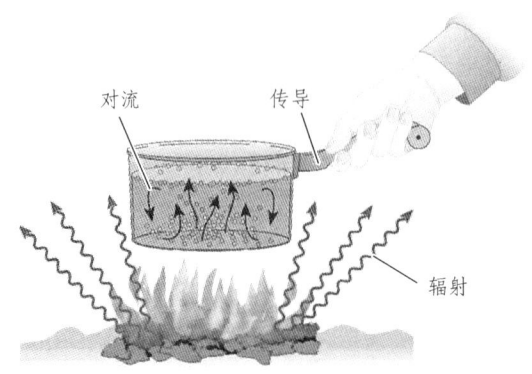

图 1-3-3　热量传递的三种方式

一、导热

导热又称为热传导，是指物体在不发生位移的情况下，借助物质分子、原子和电子的扩散、碰撞和晶格的振动，使热能从同一物体中温度较高的部分传递到温度较低的部分，或者从相接触的物体中，温度较高的物体传递给温度较低的物体的过程。导热可以发生在固体中，在静止的液体或气体层中也会发生导热。

导热率，又称导热系数，表示物质传导热量的能力大小。导热系数越大，导热性能越好。导热系数与物质的成分、结构、状态、温度、压力等有关。通常情况下，物质的分子间距与导热系数成反比，因此固体物质的导热系数最大，液体次之，气体最小。

如发热量大的芯片一般需要加装散热片，而在散热片和芯片之间通常需要加装导热泡棉，如图 1-3-4 所示。导热泡棉具有较大的导热系数，且可以和两者充分接触，因此能保证芯片和散热片之间良好的导热效果。

图 1-3-4　芯片的导热泡棉和散热片

二、热对流

热对流是流体各部分发生相对位移引起的热传递现象。在进行热对流的同时,热量的传递还可以依赖流体本身的导热。流体流过固体表面时发生的热量传递现象,通常称为对流换热过程。根据流体产生流动原因,又有强制对流和自然对流之分。由水泵、风机或其他原因造成的压差,使流体强制流过换热面所造成的换热称为强制对流换热或受迫对流换热。

如图 1-3-5 所示,家用空调制冷时,是室内机将室内空气的热量带走,使室内温度维持在一定范围内,给人们提供舒适的环境。室内空气由室内机风机引流,强制流过蒸发器,与蒸发器通过热对流的方式传递热量,蒸发器通过导热的方式使蒸发器各部分热量传递均匀,制冷剂在蒸发器内与蒸发器通过热对流的方式将热量带走。因此,通常情况下,空调制冷是强制对流换热过程。

图 1-3-5 空调室内机

由于流体内部各部分温度不均,造成密度差所引发的运动过程中的换热称为自然对流换热。以暖气片散热为例,由于暖气片温度高于室内空气,紧靠暖气片表面的空气首先被加热,从而温度升高,密度下降,并向高处浮动。附近温度较低、密度较大的空气随着流动过来,填补上升空气留下的位置,从而引发了流体的运动。上升的空气在流动中如与暖气片表面接触将被进一步加热,如此周而复始地完成了热量交换。可见,换热激发了流体的自由运动,自由运动又使换热过程继续进行。

因为强制对流换热时流体速度较高,换热过程较自然对流换热强烈得多。所以空调制冷通常几分钟就能有效果,而暖气片加热通常需要几个小时才能有效果。

对流换热还包括液体在固体表面的沸腾换热,以及蒸气在固体表面的凝结换热。如制冷装置中,制冷剂在蒸发器和冷凝器中的换热过程就属于对流换热。

三、热辐射

热辐射是通过物体向空间发射电磁波形式的辐射能实现的热传递现象。通过辐射传递能量的时候不需要相互接触,也不需要借助中间介质,即使在高度真空的情况下也可以进行,光也是电磁波,太阳就是通过热辐射将热能传递到地球的。

图 1-3-6 冬天人们利用太阳取暖

自然界中的物体,都在对外辐射能量,同时也在不断地吸收周围物体辐射来的能量。吸收和辐射的综合结果实现了热量的传递,这就是辐射换热过程。

以上三种热量传递方式,可通过增大固态物质导热系数、提高流体流动速度、增大换热面积等措施来提升热量传递的效率。

【任务训练】

(1) 常用的温标有哪几种?它们之间有何关系?

(2) 表压力与绝对压力是否相等?若工质压力不变,测量其压力的压力表读数能否发生变化?

(3) 气体状态参数中的比容的定义是?

(4) 热力学第一定律的实质是什么?

(5) 热力学第二定律有哪两种具有代表性的表述?各是如何表述的?

(6) 热量传递都有哪些方式?

项目二　湿空气

【中国铁路文化】

中国铁路发展史 2　中国第一条电气化铁路

宝成铁路位于陕西省、甘肃省和四川省境内，自宝鸡站向南，跨过渭河，经过 27 千米的展线群爬升 680 米通过秦岭隧道，到秦岭站后沿嘉陵江而下，经过甘肃省后穿过大巴山区，到广元站继续向西南，过剑门山进入四川盆地，经过绵阳、德阳两市到达成都站。全长 668.198 km，宝鸡至阳平关段受地形限制为单线铁路，阳平关至成都段为复线铁路，是中国第一条电气化铁路。1952 年 7 月动工修建，1956 年 7 月建成通车，1958 年 1 月 1 日正式运营。1958 年 6 月开始进行电气化改造，1975 年在中国全国铁路中首先实现电气化。

十多万筑路大军挺进秦岭山脉，秣兵厉马，艰苦鏖战，与石壁千仞、飞瀑高悬、深壑万丈的自然环境展开决战，以"立下愚公移山志，敢教日月换新天"的豪情壮志，不怕牺牲、克服困难，逢山开道、遇水架桥，改写了千里蜀道不与秦塞通人烟的历史。

图 2-0-1　宝成铁路举办建成通车典礼

1956 年 7 月 13 日上午 10 时，宝成铁路在甘肃省徽县黄沙河举行了接轨仪式。像塔一样的三棱形的接轨标志上的红幕被揭去以后，扎彩的火车头响起一声长鸣，吐出一缕白烟，拉着彩车徐徐由南向北开过了接轨点，坐在车厢里的当地两百多名人民代表，都在车窗口，向夹道鼓掌欢呼的人们含笑挥手而去。当施工进入紧张阶段的时候，曾经动用了中国新建铁路一半左右的劳动力和五分之四的机械筑路力量。这条铁路的修建工程，共用了四年多的时间，接轨时间比设计文件规定的日期提前了 13 个月以上。

1961 年，宝成铁路完成电气化改造一期工程，宝鸡至凤州段。1975 年 7 月全线完成电气化改造，成为中国第一条电气化铁路。自此以后，中国电气化铁路从这里走向全国。

作为首条穿越秦巴山区的铁路，在当时的技术条件下，工程难度难以想象，尤其是秦北区段四站，山陡崖深，著名的"观音山展线"设计和用炸药在悬崖上炸出来的小站，展现出宝成铁路建设者不畏困难、战胜困难的巨大精神力量以及非凡的智慧和勇气。宝成铁路点燃了全国电气化铁路的燎原之火，孕育了遍及全国的电气化铁路网，推动着中国电气化铁路从这里走向全国。

【项目描述】

在空调的应用中，无论是各类生产车间、服务器房等工业场合；还是办公室、商场、家居环境等民用场合，要处理的对象都是空气。湿空气是干空气和水蒸气的混合物，空气中的水蒸气对空气造成的影响是无法忽略的，空气调节的任务之一就是对其水蒸气含量进行调节。因而，需要对湿空气的物理性质有所了解。本项目主要讨论以下四个问题：①湿空气的组成；②湿空气的状态参数；③焓湿图的绘制；④焓湿图在实际中的应用。

【项目目标】

1. 知识目标

（1）掌握湿空气状态参数的含义。
（2）掌握湿空气焓湿图组成及在不同场合的应用。

2. 能力目标

（1）能够在现场环境中正确应用湿空气状态参数。
（2）能够根据不同场合正确使用湿空气焓湿图进行分析。

3. 素养目标

（1）培养逻辑思维能力。
（2）培养团队合作能力。

任务一　湿空气的状态参数

【任务目标】

掌握湿空气状态参数的含义。

【知识储备】

一、湿空气的组成

在空调工程中,我们把空气看作是由干空气和水蒸气两部分组成的混合物。通常情况下,大气中干空气的组成比例基本上是不变的,虽然在某些局部范围内,可能因为某些因素(如人的呼吸作用使氧气减少,二氧化碳的含量增加等)使空气的组成比例有所改变,但这种改变对干空气的热工特性影响很小。这样,在研究空气的物理性质时,可以把干空气作为一个整体来看待,以便分析讨论。

表 2-1-1　空气的主要组成成分

主要组成成分	分子量	质量分数/%
氮气	28.016	78.084
氧气	32.000	20.946
氩气	39.944	0.934
二氧化碳	44.010	0.033

相对来说,湿空气中的水蒸气的含量很少,它来源于地球上的海洋、江河、湖泊表面水分的蒸发,各种生物的代谢,以及生产过程中的水分蒸发。在湿空气中,水蒸气的占比不是固定的,常常随着海拔、经纬度、季节、气候、周边环境等各种条件的变化而变化。虽然湿空气中水蒸气的含量少,但它的变化对人们的影响却很大。如在南方地区,空气比较潮湿,湿衣服就不容易干,而且人们会感到周围环境总是湿湿的,很不舒服。而在北方的兰州、北京等地区,由于空气干燥,在同样的温度下,体感就比较舒适。空气中水蒸气的多少,除了对人们的日常生活有影响外,对工业生产也十分重要。如在纺织车间,相对湿度小时,纱线变粗变脆,容易产生飞花和断头。可是空气太潮湿也不行,纱线会粘结,不好加工。

因此,从空气调节的角度来说,空气的潮湿程度是我们十分关心的问题,这也是把水蒸气专门划分出来的主要原因。

二、湿空气的状态参数

湿空气的物理性质是由它的组成成分和所处的状态决定的,湿空气的状态通常可以用压力、温度、相对湿度、含湿量及焓等参数来度量和描述,这些参数称为湿空气的状态参数。

在热力学中,常温常压下的干空气可视为理想气体。所谓理想气体,就是假设气体分子是一些有弹性的、不占有空间的质点,分子相互之间没有作用力。因为空调工程中所涉及的压力和温度都可以看作属于这个范畴,所以空调工程中的干空气也可看作是理想气体。此外，湿空气中的水蒸气由于含量很少，而且处于过热状态，压力小，比体积大，也可近似看作理想气体。这样，水蒸气状态参数之间的关系也可用理想气体状态方程来表示。

（一）压力

1. 大气压力

气体的压力（即压强）是指单位面积上所受到的气体的作用力，在国际单位制（SI）里，压力的单位是 Pa（帕），$1\ \text{Pa} = 1\ \text{N/m}^2$。地球表面单位面积上所受到的大气的压力称为大气压力或大气压。大气的压力随海拔高度不同而变化。同时，在同一地区的不同季节，大气压力也有一些变化。图 2-1-1 是大气压力与海拔高度的关系。同一个海拔高度处，在不同的季节和不同的天气状况下，大气压力也有变化。通常把在 0 ℃ 下、北纬 45° 处海平面上作用的大气压力作为一个标准大气压（atm），其数值为 $1\ \text{atm} = 101\ 325\ \text{Pa}$。

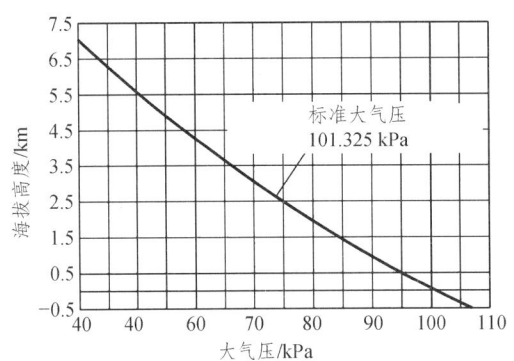

图 2-1-1　大气压力与海拔高度的关系

在空调系统中，空气的压力常用压力表来测定。压力表指示的压力是所测量空气的绝对压力与当地大气压力的差值，称为工作压力（或表压力），工作压力与绝对压力的关系为：

（空气的）绝对压力 = 当地大气压 + 工作压力（表压力）

如果没有特别指出，空气的压力都是指绝对压力。由于大气压力不是定值，因此，在设计和运行中应当考虑由于当地大气压的不同所引起的误差修正。工作压力并不代表空气压力的真正大小，只有绝对压力才是空气的一个基本状态参数。

2. 水蒸气分压力与饱和水蒸气分压力

湿空气中水蒸气的分压力，是指湿空气中的水蒸气单独占有湿空气的体积并具有与湿空气相同温度时所具有的压力。水蒸气分压力的大小，反映了湿空气中水蒸气含量的多少。水蒸气含量越多，其分压力也越大；在一定温度条件下，一定量的空气中能够容纳水蒸气的数量是有限度的。湿空气的温度越高，它允许的最大水蒸气含量也越大。当空气中水蒸气的含量超过最大允许值时，多余的水蒸气会以水珠形式析出，这就是结露现象，此时水蒸气达到饱和状态，所对应的湿空气称为饱和湿空气。由此可知，未饱和空气中，水蒸气含量没有达到最大允许值，它还具有吸收水蒸气的能力。我们周围的大气通常都是未饱和空气。

（二）含湿量及相对湿度

含湿量可以确切地表示空气中实际含有的水蒸气量的多少。空调中常用含湿量的变化来表示空气被加湿或减湿的程度。在湿空气中与 1 kg 干空气并存的水蒸气的质量称为含湿量，用符号 d 表示。

从含湿量的概念可知，其大小只表明了空气中水蒸气含量的多少，而不能表明空气的潮湿程度。怎样才能判断空气的潮湿程度呢？当大气压力不变，温度不变，空气的水蒸气分压力增加时，含湿量也随之增大，空气的潮湿程度增大。所以，湿空气中的水蒸气分压力，与同温度下饱和水蒸气分压力的接近程度就反映了空气的潮湿程度。空气的水蒸气分压力与同温度下饱和空气的水蒸气分压力之比称为相对湿度，用符号 φ 表示，值通常以百分比的形式。

（三）比焓

比焓是用来计算在定压条件下，对湿空气加热或冷却时吸收或放出的热量。湿空气的比焓不是温度的单值函数，而取决于温度和含湿量两个因素。温度升高，焓值可以增加，也可以减少，还要取决于含湿量的变化情况。因此，当温度升高时，若含湿量有所下降，则综合后的结果有可能是湿空气的焓不一定会增加。

（四）干、湿球温度和露点温度

根据空气温度形成的过程和用途不同，可将空气的温度分为干球温度、湿球温度和露点温度。

1. 干球温度

干球温度是指暴露于空气中而又不受太阳直接照射的干球温度表上所读取的数值，用 t 表示。它是温度计在普通空气中所测出的温度，即我们一般天气预报里常说的气温。干球温度计温度是温度计自由的暴露在空气中所测量的温度，同时它应避免辐射和湿气的干扰。

2. 湿球温度

湿球温度也称热力学湿球温度，湿球温度是标定空气相对湿度的一种手段。湿球温度计头部被尾端浸入水中的湿纱布包裹。当空气流过湿球温度计的端部时，湿纱布上的水分蒸发而吸收汽化热，使湿球温度计的温度下降。湿空气和湿纱布之间的温差加大，湿空气向湿纱布传入热量。当汽化带走的热量和传入的热量达到平衡时，湿球温度计上的读数就是湿空气的湿球温度 t_w。周围空气的饱和差愈大，湿球温度表上发生的蒸发愈强，而其湿度也就愈低。根据干、湿球温度的差值，可以确定空气的相对湿度。

干湿球温度计含有两支普通温度计，如图 2-1-2 所示。其中一支温度计的测温包直接和湿空气接触，其测得温度称为干球温度；另一支的温度计的测温包则用保持浸润的湿纱布包着，测得温度称湿球温度。空气的相对湿度愈小，湿球温度比干球温度就低得愈多。如果空气是饱和的，则由于空气不能接纳更多的蒸汽，故纱布上水不会蒸发，这时湿球温度和干球温度是相同的。因此干湿球温度的差值与相对湿度存在一定的函数关系，如图 2-1-3 所示。

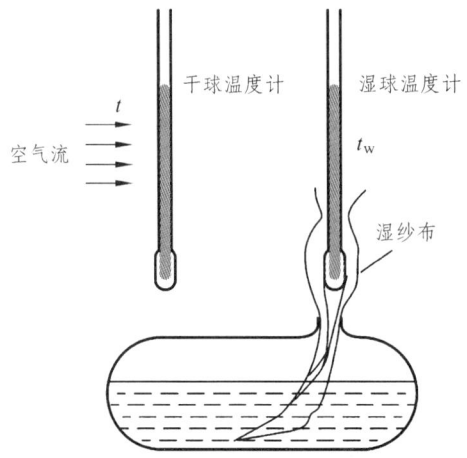

图 2-1-2　干湿球温度计

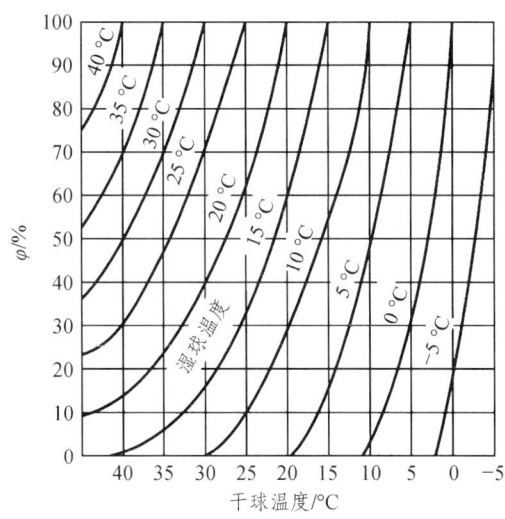

图 2-1-3　干湿球温度与相对湿度关系

3. 露点温度

露点温度指空气在水汽含量和气压都不改变的条件下，冷却到饱和时的温度，用 t_L 表示。形象地说，就是空气中的水蒸气变为露珠时候的温度叫露点温度。当空气中水汽已达到饱和时，气温与露点温度相同；当水汽未达到饱和时，气温一定高于露点温度。所以露点与气温的差值可以表示空气中的水蒸气距离饱和的程度。露点温度对应的含湿量是饱和含湿量，当 $\varphi=100\%$ 时，这时等温线和 100% 相对湿度线的交点就是露点温度。

露点温度在冬天的玻璃窗上或夏季的自来水管上常常可以看到有凝结水或露水存在，这一现象可以用露点温度形成来解释。在空调工程中的除湿过程，通常也是利用结露规律进行的。

根据对露点温度和湿球温度的讨论，干球温度、湿球温度和露点温度的关系如下：

（1）对于未饱和空气：

$$露点温度 < 湿球温度 < 干球温度$$

（2）对于饱和空气：

$$露点温度 = 湿球温度 = 干球温度$$

任务二　湿空气的焓湿图认知及应用

【任务目标】

（1）了解湿空气焓湿图的组成及作用。
（2）掌握湿空气焓湿图在不同场合的应用。

【知识储备】

一、焓湿图的组成

在工程计算中，用公式计算和用查表方法来确定空气状态和参数是比较烦琐的，而且对空气的状态变化过程的分析也缺乏直观的感性认识。因此，为了便于工程应用，通常把一定大气压力下各种参数之间的相互关系做成线算图来进行计算。根据所取坐标系的不同，线算图有多种，国内常用的是焓湿图，简称 $h\text{-}d$ 图。

以比焓 h 为纵坐标，以含湿量 d 为横坐标，表示大气压力 B 一定时，湿空气各个参数之间的关系。它包含等焓线、等温线、等相对湿度线、水蒸气分压力线、热湿比线等。

$h\text{-}d$ 图是取两个独立参数 h 和 d 作坐标轴，另一个独立状态参数 B 取为定值。为了使各种参数在坐标图上反映得清晰明了，两坐标轴之间的夹角取 135°，如图 2-2-1 所示，图中 d 为横坐标，h 为纵坐标，与 h 轴平行的各条线是等焓线，与 d 轴平行的直线是等焓湿量线。此外，图上还作出了以下几条线。

（一）等温线

等温线是根据公式 $h = (1.01+1.84d)t + 2\,500d$ 绘制的。当 $t =$ 常数时，等温线是一直线方程。其中 $1.01t$ 是截距，$(2\,500 + 1.84t)$ 是斜率。当温度取某一定值时，根据过两点可作一条直线的原理，即可在 $h\text{-}d$ 图上作出该条等温线。

下面简要说明等温线的绘制过程。

（1）绘制 $t = 0\ ℃$ 的等温线　当 $t = 0\ ℃$ 时，任取 $d_1 = 0$ 和 $d_2 = d_x$，则可计算出 $h_1 = 0$ 和 $h_2 = 2\,500d$，由（0，0）和（$2\,500d_x$，d_x）在 $h\text{-}d$ 图上可定出两个状态点 O 和 A，则 OA 直线就是 $t = 0\ ℃$ 的等温线。

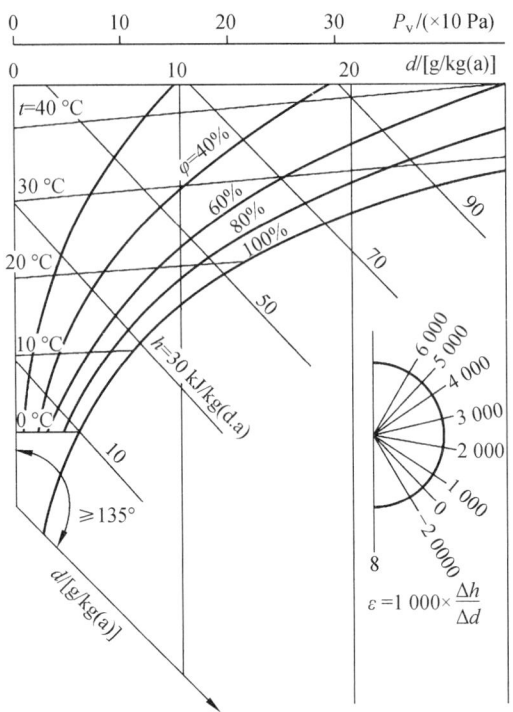

图 2-2-1 湿空气的焓湿图

（2）绘制 $t=10$ ℃ 的等温线 当 $t=0$ ℃ 时，取 $d_1=0$，可计算出 $h_1=10.1$，取 $d_2=d_x$，$h=(1.01+1.84d)t+2\,500d_x$，因为（10.1，0）在纵轴上，即可由点 O 向上截取 OB 段（截距等于 10.1）得到 B 点，又根据（$10.1+2\,518.4d_x$，d_x）可在 h-d 图上定出状态点 C，则 BC 直线就是 $t=10$ ℃ 的等温线。

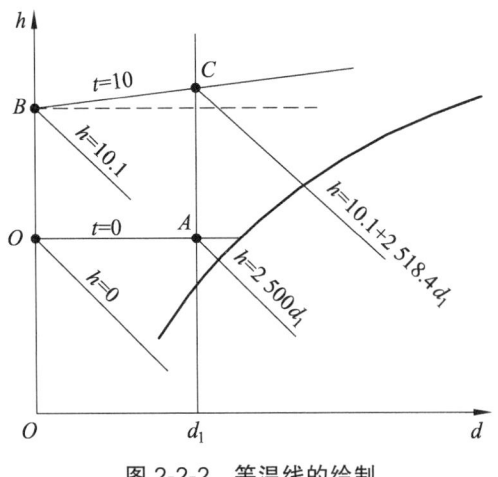

图 2-2-2 等温线的绘制

当 t 取 1 ℃，2 ℃，3 ℃，……一系列的常数时，用上面同样的方法可绘出一簇不同的等温线。因为等温线的斜率（$2\,500+1.84t$）随着 t 值的不同有微小变化，所以各条等温线是不平行的。但由于 $1.84t$ 的数值比 2 500 小得多，t 值变化对等温线斜率的影响很小，因此，各条等温线可近似看作是平行的。

（二）等相对湿度线

含湿量是大气压力 B、相对湿度 φ 和饱和水蒸气分压力 $p_{v,b}$ 的函数，即 $D = F(B, \varphi, p_{v,b})$。由于大气压力 B 在作图时已取为定值，在本式中作为一常数。饱和水蒸气分压力 $p_{v,b}$ 是温度的单值函数，可根据空气温度 t 从水蒸气性质表中查取。所以，实际上有：$d = f(\varphi, t)$。

这样当 φ 取一系列的常数时，即可根据 d 与 t 的关系在 h-d 图上绘出等相对温度线。

如当 $\varphi = 90\%$ 时，有 $d = 6.22 \times 0.9 p_{v,b}/(b - 0.9 p_{v,b})$。任取温度 t，查取 $p_{v,b}$，然后由上式计算出含湿量 d。当 t 取不同的值 t_i（$i = 1, 2, \cdots, n$）时，可从水蒸气性质表中查取 $p_{v,bi}$，计算出相应的 d_i。由于每一对（t_i, d_i）可在 h-d 图上定出一个状态点，把 n 个状态点连接起来，就得出了 $\varphi = 90\%$ 的等相对湿度线。当 φ 取不同的值重复上面的过程时，就可作出不同的等相对湿度线。如图 2-2-3 所示，其中，$\varphi = 100\%$ 的是饱和湿度线，其下方是过饱和区，上方是湿空气区。在湿空气区中的水蒸气处于过热状态。

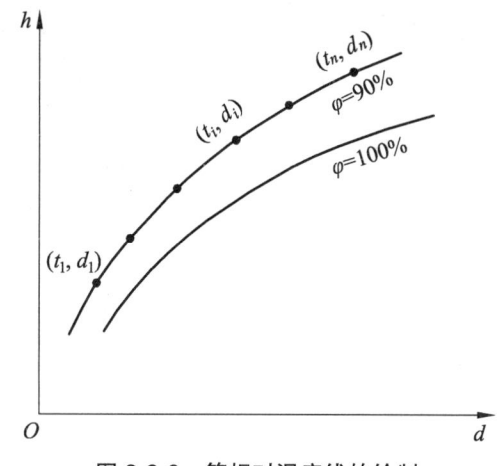

图 2-2-3　等相对湿度线的绘制

（三）水蒸气分压力线

由含湿量的计算式 $d = 622 p_v/(B - p_v)$ 可知：当大气压力 B 等于常数时，$p_v = f(d)$，即水蒸气的分压力 p_v 和含湿量 d 是一一对应的，有一个 d 就可确定出一个 p_v。所以，在 d 轴的上方设了一条水平线，标出了与 d 所对应的 p_v 值。

（四）热湿比线

为了说明空气状态变化的方向和特征，常用空气状态变化前后的焓差和含湿量差的比值来表征，这个比值称为热湿比 ε，即

$$\varepsilon = (h_B - h_A)/(d_B - d_A) = \Delta h / \Delta d$$

从热湿比的定义式可知，ε 实际上是直线 AB 的斜率。因为直线的斜率与起始位置无关，两条斜率相同的直线必然平行。因此，在 h-d 图的右下方作出了一簇射线（ε 线），供在图上分析空气状态变化过程时使用。

需要注意的是，以上 h-d 图的绘制是在大气压力 B 等于某个定值的情况下得出的。如果大气压力不同，所求出的参数也不同。如温度 t 和相对湿度 φ 相同的两种湿空气，如果所处的大气压力 B 不同，则该两种湿空气所具有的含湿量 d 是不同的。如图 2-2-4 所示，由含湿量 d 的计算式可知：含湿量 d 随着大气压力 B 的增加而减少，反之亦然。因此，如果大气压力 B 有变化，等相对湿度线必将会产生相应的变化，如图 2-2-5 所示。所以，在实际应用中，应采用符合当地大气压力的 h-d 图。

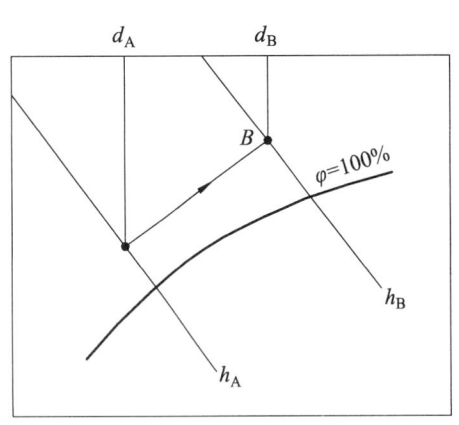

图 2-2-4　热湿比与状态变化过程线的关系

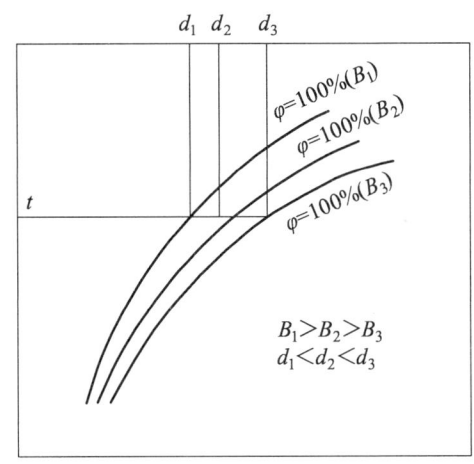

图 2-2-5　大气压对相对湿度的影响

二、焓湿图的应用

湿空气的独立参数共有 t、d、φ、h 和 t_s 五个。当大气压力 B 一定时，可以根据其中任意两个决定空气状态，再从 h-d 图上查得 t_d、p_v、$p_{v,b}$ 及 d_b 等参数。

空气调节过程有升温有降温，有加湿有减湿，这些空气调节过程和焓湿图有哪些关系？利用 h-d 图能表示空气状态的变化过程，各种变化过程的方向和特征可用热湿比 ε 表示。

图 2-2-6 绘制了空气状态变化的几种典型过程。空气调节中常用的 6 种典型空气状态变化过程：从 A 到 B 为等湿加热过程，从 A 到 C 为等湿冷却过程，从 A 到 D 为等焓减湿过程，从 A 到 E 为等焓加湿过程，从 A 到 F 为等温加湿过程，从 A 到 G 为减湿冷却过程。

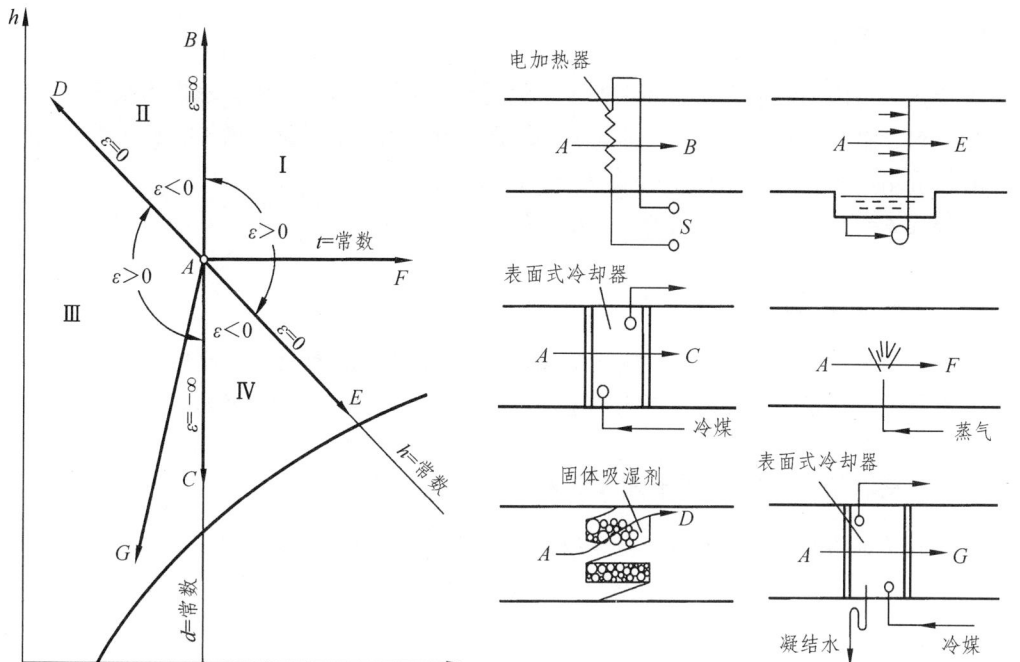

图 2-2-6　几种典型的空气状态变化过程

（一）等湿（或干式）加热过程

如果采用表面式空气加热器，如电加热器来加热空气时，当空气通过加热器时获得了热量，提高了温度，但含湿量没有变化。A 点到 B 点为是等湿增焓升温过程，即 $h_B > h_A$，$d_B = d_A$，因此

湿热比 $\varepsilon = (h_C - h_A)/(d_C - d_A) = (h_C - h_A)/0 = +\infty$

（二）等湿（或干式）冷却过程

采用表面式冷却器处理空气，且其表面温度比空气露点温度高，则空气将在含湿量不变的情况下冷却，其比焓值必然减少。A 点到 C 点为等湿减焓降温过程，即 $h_C < h_A$，$d_C = d_A$，因此

湿热比 $\varepsilon = (h_C - h_A)/(d_C - d_A) = (h_C - h_A)/0 = -\infty$

（三）等焓减湿过程

用固体吸湿剂，如硅胶来处理空气时，水蒸气被吸附，空气的含湿量降低，空气失去潜热而得到水蒸气凝结时放出的汽化热，使温度升高，略微减少了凝结水带走的液体热。A 点到 D 点可近似看作等焓减湿升温过程，即 $h_D = h_A$，$d_D < d_A$，因此

湿热比 $\varepsilon = (h_D - h_A)/(d_D - d_A) = 0/(d_D - d_A) = 0$

（四）等焓加湿过程

在绝热环境内用喷水室喷循环水处理空气时，水吸收空气的热量而蒸发为水蒸气，空气失掉显热，温度降低，水蒸气到空气中，使含湿量增加，潜热量也增加。A 点到 E 点可近似看作等焓加湿过程，即 $h_E = h_A$，$d_E > d_A$，因此

湿热比 $\varepsilon = (h_E - h_A)/(d_E - d_A) = 0/(d_E - d_A) = 0$

（五）等温加湿过程

通过向空气中喷水蒸气，使空气比焓和含湿量都增加。这种情况下比焓的增加值为加入的水蒸气的全热量。A 点到 F 点为等温加湿过程，湿热比 ε 值为一常数。

（六）减湿冷却（或冷却干燥）过程

如果用表面冷却器处理空气，当冷却器表面温度低于空气的露点温度时，空气中的水蒸气将凝结为水，A 点到 G 点为减湿冷却过程，或冷却干燥过程，即 $h_G < h_A$，$d_G < d_A$，因此

湿热比 $\varepsilon = (h_G - h_A)/(d_G/d_A) > 0$

【任务训练】

（1）湿空气中的水蒸气分压力和饱和水蒸气分压力有什么不同？
（2）相对湿度和含湿量有什么区别和联系？
（3）热湿比的物理意义是什么？
（4）已知某一状态湿空气的温度为 30 ℃，相对湿度为 50%，当地大气压力为 101 325 Pa，试求该状态湿空气的密度、含湿量、水蒸气分压力和露点温度。

项目三　制冷原理

【中国铁路文化】

中国铁路发展史 3　"成昆精神"熠熠生辉

1. 成昆铁路

1970 年 7 月 1 日建成通车的成昆铁路（Chengdu—Kunming Railway），简称成昆线，北起四川成都，南至云南昆明，全长近 1100 千米，开创了 18 项中国铁路之最，13 项世界铁路之最，被联合国称为"象征二十世纪人类征服自然的三大奇迹之一"。

图 3-1　成昆铁路

成昆铁路是中国境内一条连接四川省与云南省的国铁 I 级客货共线铁路；线路呈南北走向，为中国西南地区的干线铁路之一，也是中国三横五纵干线铁路网的一纵。成昆线北起川西平原成都，跨过岷江、青衣江；经峨眉，沿大渡河、横贯大小凉山；十跨牛日河、抵达西昌；八跨安宁河、过金沙江；三十余次迂回穿越龙川江峡谷，穿过横断山脉，南至滇池湖滨昆明。在当时，成昆铁路是一项难度极大的工程，沿线地带被外国专家们称作"铁路禁区"，长期被认为是不可能修筑铁路的地方。成昆铁路全线贯穿地势险峻、地形多样、地质复杂的山川河谷，途经崎岖陡峭、奇峰耸立、深涧密布、沟壑纵横及水流奔腾湍急的山岭重丘，线路所经区域有"露天地质博物馆"之称。

2. "成昆精神"的形成

1964 年，受紧张的国际形势影响，中国开始开展三线建设，毛主席强调："要搞第三线基地，大家都赞成，要搞快一些；攀枝花酒泉两个基地一定要落实；如果材料不够，其它铁路不修，集中修一条成昆路"。1966 年，成昆铁路进入建设高潮，施工人员达到 35.97 万余人。

成昆铁路是一条用血肉之躯筑造的建筑工程，施工期间中国军政部统计数据的铁道兵牺牲人数就达2 100多人，沿线留下1 000多座丰碑，烈士陵园20余处。在成昆铁路建设中，建设者们留下了热爱祖国、不怕吃苦、甘于奉献、敢于牺牲的"成昆精神"。

3. "成昆精神"代代相传

成昆铁路是"英雄路"，也是"幸福路"，是幸福四川、幸福中国的真实写照。成昆铁路北接宝成铁路、成渝铁路，南连贵昆铁路，是我国铁路网中的重要干线，对于改善西南地区的交通状况、密切西南边疆与全国各地的联系、加强民族之间的团结、促进西南地区的经济发展，都具有十分重要的意义。这条路带动沿线地区经济发展，成为彝族山寨连接外界的"扶贫路"、"求学路"、"希望路"，以及沿线地区发展的运输"生命线"，不言而喻，成昆铁路是一条"幸福路"。

成昆铁路纵贯五十年，从"英雄路"奔向"幸福路"，让我们更加体会到，成昆铁路不仅是一条铁路，更是一种精神。不怕吃苦、甘于奉献、敢于牺牲的"成昆精神"，让"成昆精神"代代相传。

【项目描述】

用一定的方法使某物体或空间的温度低于周围环境介质的温度，并且使其维持在某一范围内，这个过程称为制冷。空调和冰箱就是典型的制冷装置。夏天，客车车厢外的温度比较高，为了维持车厢内的温度低于外部环境，就必须把进入车内的余热（人体散热、太阳辐射热、设备发热等）不断地"搬运"到外部环境中去。

制冷装置起到转移热量的作用，而且是把热量从低温环境向高温环境进行转移。根据热力学第二定律，要将热量从低温物体转移到高温物体，这是一个非自发的过程，必须要对系统进行能量补偿。能量补偿方法通常有两种：对工质做功或加热。因此根据补偿方法的不同有蒸气压缩式制冷、吸收式制冷等方法。由于蒸气压缩式制冷机结构紧凑，运行安全可靠，制冷温度和制冷量范围大，又便于实现自动控制和调节，目前在铁路冷藏运输和空气调节中应用最广泛。

本项目主要学习蒸气压缩式制冷原理、蒸气压缩式制冷循环、其他制冷方法、常用制冷剂和润滑油的性质及特点。

【项目目标】

1. 知识目标

（1）掌握蒸气压缩式制冷原理和制冷四大件的作用。

（2）了解其他制冷方法的原理、常用制冷剂和润滑油的性质及特点。

2. 能力目标

（1）能够分析蒸气压缩式制冷循环的工作过程。

（2）能够根据现场需要选择合适的制冷剂。

3. 素养目标

（1）增强安全生产及规范作业的意识。
（2）养成科学保养设备的良好习惯。
（3）养成团队合作和好习惯。

任务一　蒸气压缩式制冷原理

【任务目标】

（1）掌握蒸气压缩式制冷的工作原理、制冷剂在制冷过程中的变化过程。
（2）掌握制冷系统四大件的作用。

【知识储备】

一、汽化与冷凝

众所周知，由液态转变为蒸气的过程称为汽化，汽化是液体分子脱离液面的现象，根据剧烈程度，汽化可分为蒸发和沸腾。在水表面进行的汽化过程称为蒸发；在水表面和内部同时进行的强烈的汽化过程称为沸腾。无论是蒸发还是沸腾，都是吸热过程，吸收的热量称为汽化潜热。

蒸发在任何温度下都可进行。蒸发的快慢主要取决于温度，同时还与蒸发面积、液面上的蒸气密度有关。温度越高、蒸发面积越大、液面上蒸气密度越小，蒸发速度愈快；反之，则愈慢。对不同液体，蒸发速度是不同的。

在一定的压力条件下，只有当液体的温度达到一定的值时，才会发生沸腾，且在整个沸腾过程中温度始终保持不变。沸腾时的温度叫沸点。液体的沸点与所受的压力是一一对应的，通常把某一压力下的沸点叫作这一压力下的饱和温度，而对应的压力叫饱和压力。同一物质的饱和压力和温度呈正比例关系，即饱和压力高，饱和温度就高；反之，饱和温度就低。而不同物质即使在同一压力下饱和温度也不同，且有的相差很大。如水在一个标准大气压力下，饱和温度为 100 ℃，汽化潜热为 2 258 kJ/kg；而在两个标准大气压下饱和温度是 120 ℃，汽化潜热为 2 202.2 kJ/kg。而 R12 在一个标准大气压下的饱和温度是 −29.8 ℃，汽化潜热为 165.3 kJ/kg；在两个标准大气压下的饱和温度是 −12 ℃，汽化潜热为 157.3 kJ/kg。在制冷工程中，制冷剂液体在蒸发器中进行的汽化过程实际上是沸腾过程，且把沸点（即饱和温度）叫蒸发温度，相应的压力（饱和压力）叫蒸发压力。

物质由气态转变为液态的过程，称为冷凝（也称液化）。冷凝是汽化的相反过程。在一定压力下，只有当蒸气周围的温度低于其对应的冷凝温度时，蒸气才能向周围放出热量，冷凝成液体。在冷凝过程中放出的热量，称为冷凝潜热（也称液化潜热），冷凝潜热与汽化潜热在数值上相等；冷凝过程中温度同样保持不变。同一物质的冷凝温度与冷凝压力也是一一对应的，与蒸发温度与蒸发压力的对应关系一样。如在两个标准大气压力下，R12气体的冷凝温度与R12液体的蒸发温度都是 -12 ℃，若使两个标准大气压力下的这种蒸气冷凝，只要周围有低于其冷凝温度 -12 ℃ 的介质，则蒸气就会放出热量冷凝成液体。如用温度为 35 ℃ 的环境空气作为R12蒸气的冷却介质，则R12蒸气的冷凝温度一定得在 35 ℃ 以上，而相应的冷凝压力就一定得在 0.9 MPa 以上。

二、蒸气压缩式制冷机的工作原理

蒸汽压缩式制冷系统是由压缩机、冷凝器、节流装置、蒸发器等四个主要部分组成，用管道进行连接，形成一个完全封闭的系统。制冷剂在这个封闭的制冷系统中以流体状态循环，通过相变，连续不断地从蒸发器中吸取热量，并在冷凝器中放出热量，从而实现制冷的目的。

制冷剂在一个封闭的系统中只消耗压缩机的压缩功就能反复地实现制冷剂由液体变成蒸气，再由蒸气变成液体的相态变化，并通过这种相变将低温处的热量转移到高温处，这就是蒸气压缩式制冷机的工作原理。

（一）制冷系统主要部件（四大件）的作用

1. 制冷压缩机

制冷压缩机是制冷循环的动力设备，它通常由电机拖动，除了可以及时抽出流过蒸发器的制冷剂，维持低温低压外，还可以通过压缩制冷剂提高其压力和温度，创造将制冷剂的热量向外界环境介质转移的条件，即将低温低压制冷剂蒸气压缩至高温高压状态，以便能用常温的空气或水作冷却介质来冷凝制冷剂蒸气。

2. 冷凝器

冷凝器是一个热交换设备，其作用是利用空气或水等冷却介质，将来自制冷压缩机的高温高压制冷剂蒸气的热量带走，使高温高压制冷剂蒸气冷却、冷凝成高压常温的制冷剂液体。冷凝器散发热量的多少，与冷凝器的面积成正比，与制冷剂蒸气温度和冷却介质温度之间的温度差成正比。因此，要满足散热需求，就需要足够的冷凝器面积，和一定的换热温差。

3. 节流元件

高压常温的制冷剂液体不能直接送入低温低压的蒸发器。根据饱和压力与饱和温度一一对应原理，可通过降低制冷剂液体的压力，从而实现降低制冷剂的温度。将高压常温的制冷剂液体通过降压装置（节流元件），即可得到低温低压的制冷剂，再送入蒸发器吸热汽化。蒸气压缩式制冷系统中常用的节流元件有膨胀阀和毛细管。

4. 蒸发器

蒸发器也是一个热交换设备。节流后的低温低压制冷剂液体在蒸发器内吸热蒸发（沸腾）变为蒸气，吸收被冷却介质的热量，使被冷却介质温度下降，达到制冷的目的。蒸发器吸收热量的多少与蒸发器的面积成正比，与制冷剂的蒸发温度和被冷却介质温度之间的温度差成正比。当然，也与蒸发器内液体制冷剂的多少有关。所以，蒸发器要吸收一定的热量，就需要与之相匹配的蒸发器面积，也需要一定的换热温差，还需要供给蒸发器适量的制冷剂。

（二）制冷剂在制冷系统（四大件）中的循环过程

制冷剂在四大件中的工作过程如下：

如图 3-1-1 所示，低温低压的制冷剂液体在蒸发器中吸收被冷却介质的热量 Q_0 后而汽化成低温低压的蒸气，然后被压缩机吸入；压缩机消耗一定的机械功 W_0（一般用电能驱动电机来实现）将低温低压的制冷剂蒸气压缩成高温高压的制冷剂蒸气，并排入冷凝器；高温高压的制冷剂蒸气在冷凝器内被环境介质（空气或水）冷却，制冷剂蒸气放出热量 Q_K 后被冷凝成液体；高温高压的制冷剂液体经过节流装置（膨胀阀或毛细管）节流降压，同时温度也降低，低温低压的制冷剂进入蒸发器；在蒸发器中，低温低压的制冷剂液体又吸收被冷却介质的热量 Q_0，蒸发成低温低压制冷剂蒸气，再次被压缩机吸入，如此周而复始地循环。

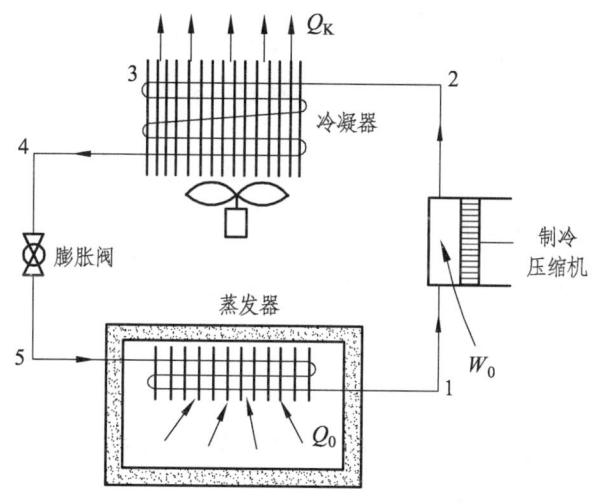

图 3-1-1　蒸气压缩式制冷工作原理

这样，制冷剂在封闭的制冷系统中经压缩、冷凝、节流和蒸发等四个热力过程，才能完成一次循环。在循环中，压缩机要消耗一定的功，才能将低温物体放出的热量转移到高温的环境介质中去，以达到制冷的目的。只要压缩机正常运行，制冷剂在四大件中的循环就不断，即可达到持续的制冷效果。

任务二　其他制冷方法

【任务目标】

（1）理解吸收式制冷循环过程。
（2）了解干冰、液氨及半导体制冷方法的原理及应用。

【知识储备】

制冷的工作过程是利用制冷机从被冷却介质中获得热量，并将其转移到高温环境介质中去。根据热力学第二定律，这个过程必须对其进行能量补偿才能实现。能量补偿的方法有两种：一种是做功；另一种是热传递。蒸汽压缩式制冷是采用做功的方式，当然，除了蒸汽压缩式制冷之外，还有一些其他的制冷方法。

一、吸收式制冷

吸收式制冷是用热能作动力的制冷方法，它也是利用制冷剂汽化吸热来实现制冷的。吸收式制冷和蒸气压缩式制冷一样，都是利用液体在汽化时吸收汽化潜热这一物理性质来实现制冷的，所不同的是蒸气压缩式制冷机是靠消耗压缩机的机械能为动力，而吸收式制冷机是以热能为动力的制冷机。吸收式制冷机在利用余热、废热作为热源的场合使用将获得较好的经济性。

（一）吸收式制冷机原理

吸收式制冷机中所用的工质是由两种沸点不同的物质组成的混合溶液。低沸点的物质是制冷剂，高沸点的物质是吸收剂，称为工质对。如氨-水吸收式制冷机中，氨为制冷剂，水为吸收剂，制冷温度范围为 $1 \sim -45\ ℃$，可为一些工艺生产过程提供冷源。吸收式制冷机中有两个循环（制冷剂循环和溶液循环）。吸收式制冷循环是由发生器、吸收器、冷凝器、蒸发器、溶液泵以及节流器等组成。

如图 3-2-1 所示，在吸收器中，由发生器来的稀溶液吸收蒸发器来的制冷剂蒸气，而成为浓溶液，吸收过程释放出的热量用冷却水带走。由吸收器出来的浓溶液经溶液泵提高压力，并输送到发生器中。在发生器中，利用外热源对浓溶液加热，其中低沸点的制冷剂蒸气被蒸发出来，而浓溶液成为稀溶液。溶液经吸收器→发生器→吸收器的循环，实现了将低压制冷剂蒸气转变为高压制冷剂蒸气。

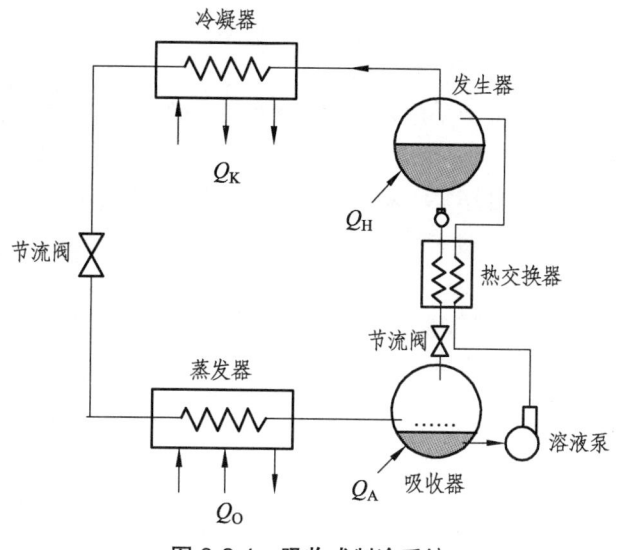

图 3-2-1 吸收式制冷系统

(二)常用的吸收式制冷循环工质对

常用的吸收式制冷循环工质对,随制冷剂的不同主要分为以下两类。

1. 以氨为制冷剂的工质对

主要有氨水(NH_3-H_2O)、乙胺-水($C_2H_5NH_2$-H_2O)、甲胺-水(CH_3NH_3-H_2O)以及硫氰酸钠-氨(NaSCN-NH_3)等。用甲胺、乙胺能减轻氨固有的毒性和爆炸性,而乙胺还因其蒸气压比较低,用于热泵很有好处。硫氰酸钠用于太阳能吸收式制冷循环中性能好,造价低。

2. 以甲醇和乙醇作为制冷剂的工质对

主要有甲醇-溴化锂(CH_3OH-LiBr)、甲醇-溴化锌(CH_3OH-$ZnBr_2$)、甲醇-溴化锂-溴化锌(CH_3OH-LiBr-$ZnBr_2$)、乙醇-溴化锂-溴化锌(C_2H_5OH-LiBr-$ZnBr_2$)等。甲醇有较大的汽化热,可制取0℃以下的低温,而对金属材料不起腐蚀作用,是一种比较理想的制冷剂。用乙醇作制冷剂,其性能比甲醇差一些,但其最大的优点是发生器加热温度较低,因而用于太阳能吸收式制冷机中比较合适。

在实际中使用的通常是氨-水溶液与溴化锂-水溶液两种。

二、冰盐混合物制冷

冰的融化温度为0 ℃,如单纯利用冰融化时要吸热这一物理特性来制冷,只能得到0 ℃以上的温度,为了得到较低的温度,可以利用冰和盐的混合物来制冷。所用的盐通常是食盐,即氯化钠(NaCl)。将盐与冰混合,当冰盐混合物融化时,要同时发生两种吸热反应:一种是冰融化时要吸收熔化热;另一种是盐溶解于水时,要吸收熔解热。这两种吸热反应的综合使得冰盐混合物的融化温度远低于0 ℃。在一定的范围内，所加的盐越多，混合物的融化温度越低，但熔化热也减小。

冰盐混合物在铁路上广泛地采用来作为冷藏车的冷源。装有冰盐混合物的冷藏车冰箱设置在车顶部。冰盐混合物融化时吸收的热量来自车内的货物，货物因失去热量而获得低温。车内温度是通过空气的自然循环来降低的。用冰盐混合物来冷却货物的冰箱冷藏车较长期以来是我国铁路冷藏运输的主要运输工具。冰盐混合物制冷系统设备简单，使用方便，在正常整备条件下，制冷系统能连续、安全可靠的使用。但是，由于受冰盐混合物最低融化温度的限制，冰箱冷藏车只能制取 – 8 ℃ 以上的车内温度，所以只适合运输中冷却货物。另外，温度不能调节，排出车外的盐水对车辆结构和线路钢轨腐蚀较大也是冰箱冷藏车的主要缺点。

三、干冰制冷

压力在 0.518 MPa 以下时，干冰吸热后产生升华现象，即吸热后，固体状态的干冰不经过液态而直接挥发成气体二氧化碳。由于干冰有很低的升华温度和较大的升华热，所以将干冰升华的吸热过程用于冷藏车制冷，不但可以取得较低的车内温度，而且能获得较大的制冷量。冷藏车用干冰制冷有接触式和非接触式两种形式。接触式干冰制冷，是升华后的 CO_2 气体直接与货物接触。当车内空气中 CO_2 含量超过 10% 时，对人体有害，使用场合需保证空气流通；采用非接触式干冰制冷时，干冰相变所产生的 CO_2 气体由密闭的干冰箱直接排出车外。

干冰特别适用于对制冷效果和视觉效果要求都比较高的场合，如高端酒店，如图 3-2-2 所示。采用干冰制冷的冷藏车可以获得 – 20 ℃，甚至更低的温度。但干冰制冷用的干冰成本太高，干冰的储运损耗又大，限制了干冰制冷在冷藏车中的采用。

图 3-2-2 干冰制冷的食物

四、液氨制冷

液氨在一个大气压力下的蒸发温度为 –33.5 ℃。液氨是惰性物质，无色、无味、无腐蚀性，不可燃等特性，可迅速冷冻和运输食品。

液氨制冷用于铁路冷藏运输有两种方法。一种是用液氨将易腐货物进行预冷，预冷的最低温度可达 –80 ~ –100 ℃，预冷可以装货时在车上进行，也可以在冷库内完成。运输过程的冷源是用货物和车辆的蓄冷量，所能运输的距离取决于预冷时的初温、货物允许的终温、外气条件、车体的隔热性能和气密性，这种冷藏车实际上是无专门冷源的隔热车。另一种方法是将盛有液氨的容器设置在车内，利用液氨连续或周期性的蒸发来抵消由车外传入的热量和车内货物的生理发热量。液氨可以由车顶部带孔的分配管向车内直接喷射，称为接触式；也可以通过空气冷却器来冷却车内货物，此时，氨气和货物不接触，称为非接触式。采用接触式的液氨冷却系统时，能够为新鲜果菜创造一个缺氧的低温运输条件，因此可以减少果菜的呼吸发热量。

液氨制冷设备简单，工作可靠，缺点是液氨成本高。

五、半导体制冷

半导体制冷是借助半导体元件的温差电效应，利用电能直接来制冷的方法，所以又称为温差电制冷或热电制冷。半导体制冷是通过半导体电热元件来实现的，最基本的半导体热电元件是由 N 型和 P 型半导体元件串联组成的温差电偶，如图 3-2-3 所示。

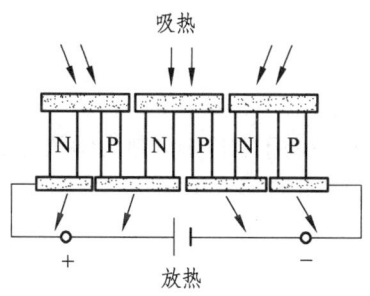

图 3-2-3 半导体制冷原理

根据温差电效应，当直流电流流过半导体热电元件时，除产生焦耳热以外，在半导体元件的一端会产生吸热现象，而另一端产生放热现象。当外加电场使得 N 型半导体中的电子和 P 型半导体中的空穴都接头运动时，为了补充电子和空穴，在接头附近将激发大量的电子、空穴对。这些电子、空穴对的动能和势能取自于晶格的热振动能，所以在接头处就出现吸热现象，该接头称冷端；相反地，当外加电场反向时，使得 N 型半导体中的电子和 P 型半导体中的空穴都朝接头处运动时，这些电子、空穴对将在接头附近复合。电子、空穴对复合前的动能和势能将转变成晶格的热振动能，因此在接头处将释放出热量，该接头称为热端。利用冷端的吸热现象来冷却其周围介质，就可以实现制冷的目的。如电流方向相反，吸热端（冷端）就会变成放热端（热端），而放热端变成吸热端，半导体制冷元件就变成加热元件了。

由于半导体材料性能所限，目前一般一对温差电偶的制冷量是很小的，约几百毫瓦至两瓦。所以实际使用时，常把若干对温差电偶串联或并联起来组成制冷电堆，这样可以获得几瓦至数千瓦的制冷量。

半导体制冷器与一般制冷机不同，它没有机械运动部件，也不用制冷剂。只要用一些半导体制冷元件组合起来，利用直流电源就可以直接制冷，并且调节工作电流能方便地改变制冷量和制冷温度。如变换电流方向，制冷就变成制热，因而半导体空调器就与冷暖风机一样了。半导体制冷器工作时，无磨耗、无振动、无噪声、无制冷剂的泄漏，工作可靠，维护使用方便，寿命长。但目前因受材料性能和制造成本所限，半导体制冷只适合于小型制冷装置，如小型冰箱、小型空调器、仪器仪表的小型冷源等。

任务三　制冷剂与压缩机润滑油

【任务目标】

（1）掌握制冷剂的特性与选型。
（2）掌握压缩机润滑油的特性。

【知识储备】

一、制冷剂

制冷剂是制冷系统中完成制冷循环所必需的工作介质。制冷剂的热力学状态在制冷循环中是不断发生变化的，制冷机借助于制冷剂的热力学状态变化将被冷却系统的热量连续不断地传递给高温热源，以完成制冷循环。

（一）对制冷剂的要求

1. 热力学方面的要求

（1）制冷剂的沸点要低，这样可以获得较低的蒸发温度。

（2）制冷剂的临界温度要高、凝固温度要低，以保证制冷剂在较广的温度范围内安全工作。气体在一定的温度和压力条件下都可以使其液化，但当温度升高超过某一数值时，压力再增加也不能使气体液化，这一温度就叫做临界温度。临界温度高制冷剂在常温条件下能够液化，即可用普通冷却介质使制冷剂冷凝，同时能使制冷剂在远离临界点下节流而减少损失，提高循环的性能。凝固点低，可使制冷系统安全地制取较低的蒸发温度，使制冷剂在工作温度范围内不发生凝固现象。

（3）制冷剂要具有适宜的工作压力。要求蒸发压力接近或高于大气压力，以避免制冷机回气压力出现真空而增大空气渗入制冷系统的机会，提高制冷机的工作效率，减少相应的无效功耗。要求冷凝压力不能过高。冷凝压力低可降低对制冷机器、设备、管道的强度要求，减少压缩机的功耗。

（4）要求制冷剂的汽化潜热大，比容小。这样在一定的工况条件下单位容积制冷量大。当所需要的制冷量一定时，单位容积制冷量大，制冷剂的循环量就可以减少，压缩机和系统的尺寸就可缩小，使之便于安装和更经济。

（5）要求制冷剂的绝热指数小。绝热指数越小，压缩机排气温度越低，对提高压缩机容积效率和改善压缩机润滑越有利。

2. 物理化学方面的要求

（1）制冷剂的黏度和密度尽可能的小。黏度和密度小可以减少制冷剂在制冷系统中流动阻力，有利于制冷剂的循环和降低压缩机的功耗，并且可缩小系统的管径，降低金属的使用量。

（2）制冷剂的导热系数与放热系数尽量大。以提高换热器的传热效率，减少传热面积。

（3）制冷剂有一定的溶水性。制冷剂最好不含水分，但实际上制冷系统中难免渗入极少量的水分。如制冷剂能溶解少量的水分，则在蒸发温度低于 0 ℃ 时，系统就不易产生"冰塞"现象而影响制冷装置的正常运转。

（4）制冷剂的热化学稳定性好，高温下不易分解。制冷剂与油、水混合时对金属材料不应有明显的腐蚀作用。对制冷机的密封材料的膨润作用要尽可能的小。

3. 安全、环境方面的要求

（1）要求制冷剂在工作温度范围内不燃烧、不爆炸，一般场合应避免使用易燃和易爆的制冷剂。

（2）要求制冷剂无毒或低毒，对生物环境影响小。由于某些制冷剂带有一定的毒性和危险性，要求所选择的制冷剂应具有易于检漏的特点，以保证运行的安全。要求万一泄漏的制冷剂与食品接触时，食品不会变色、变味，不会被污染，空调用制冷剂应对人体的健康无害、无刺激性气味。

（3）制冷剂应具有良好的电绝缘性能。在密封式的压缩机系统中，电机线圈与制冷剂、润滑油直接接触，电绝缘性好的制冷剂可保证系统安全运行。

（4）要求制冷剂对地球温室效应影响较小，对大气中臭氧层没有破坏作用。

（二）制冷剂的种类及代号

1. 制冷剂的种类

可作为制冷剂的物质较多，其种类如下：
（1）无机化合物，如水、氨、二氧化碳等。
（2）饱和碳氢化合物的氟、氯、溴衍生物，俗称氟利昂，主要是甲烷和乙烷的衍生物，如 R12、R22、R134a 等。

（3）饱和碳氢化合物，如丙烷、异丁烷等。

（4）不饱和碳氢化合物，如乙烯、丙烯等。

（5）共沸混合制冷剂，如R502等。

（6）非共沸混合制冷剂，如R407c等。

通常按照制冷剂的标准蒸发温度，将其分为三类，即高温、中温和低温制冷剂。所谓标准蒸发温度，是指在标准大气压力下的蒸发温度，也就是通常所说的沸点。

（1）高温（低压）制冷剂。标准蒸发温度$t_s > 0\ ℃$，冷凝压力$p_k \leqslant 0.3\ \text{MPa}$。常用的高温制冷剂有R123等。

（2）中温（中压）制冷剂。$0\ ℃ > t_s > -60\ ℃$，$0.3\ \text{MPa} < p_c < 2.0\ \text{MPa}$。常用的中温制冷剂有氨、R12、R22、R134a、丙烷等。

（3）低温（高压）制冷剂。$t_s \leqslant -60\ ℃$。常用的低温制冷剂有R13、乙烯、R744等。

2. 制冷剂的代号

为书写方便，我国国家标准《制冷剂编号方法和安全性分类》（GB/T 7778—2017）规定了各种通用制冷剂的代号，以代替其化学名称、分子式或商业名称。标准中规定用字母R和它后面的一组数字或字母作为制冷剂的代号。字母R表示制冷剂，后面的数字或字母则根据制冷剂的种类及分子式组成，按一定的规则编写。

1）无机化合物

作为制冷剂的无机化合物有氨、二氧化碳、水等。对于这类制冷剂，其代号"R"后的第一位数为7，7后面的数字为该物质的分子量的整数部分。如氨的分子式为NH_3，分子量的整数部分是17，其代号为R717，二氧化碳和水的代号分别为R744和R718。

2）卤代烃

卤代烃（氟利昂）是饱和碳氢化合物的氟、氯、溴衍生物的总称。目前用作制冷剂的主要是甲烷和乙烷的衍生物。饱和碳氢化合物的分子式为C_mH_{2m+2}。氟利昂的分子通式为$C_mH_nF_xCl_yBr_z$，其原子数m，n，x，y，z之间的关系为：$2m + 2 = n + x + y + z$。

氟利昂的代号用"R×××B×"表示。R后的第一位数字为$(m-1)$，该数字为零时省略不写；第二位数字为$(n+1)$；第三位数字为x；B后面的数字为z，若z为零时，与字母B一起省略。例如二氟二氯甲烷的分子式为CF_2Cl_2，该化合物的$m = 1$，$n = 0$，$x = 2$，$z = 0$，所以在R后的第一位数字$(m-1) = 0$，第二位数字$(n+1) = 1$，第三位数字$x = 2$，B后面的数字$z = 0$，故CF_2Cl_2的代号为R12。一氟一氯甲烷的分子式为CHF_2Cl，其$(m-1) = 0$，$(n+1) = 2$，$x = 2$，$z = 0$，故代号为R22。一溴三氯甲烷分子式为CF_3Br，$(m-1) = 0$，$(n+1) = 1$，$x = 3$，$z = 1$，代号为R13B1。

3）烃类（碳氢化合物）

用来作为制冷剂的碳氢化合物有烷烃类（如甲烷CH_4、乙烷C_2H_6、丙烷C_3H_8）和链烯烃类（如乙烯C_2H_4、丙烯C_3H_6）。

对于甲烷、乙烷、丙烷，代号表示方法与氟利昂相同。如甲烷 CH_4，$m=1$，$n=4$，$x=0$，$z=0$，则 $(m-1)=0$，$(n+1)=5$，$x=0$，$z=0$，代号为 R50；乙烷 C_2H_6，$(m-1)=1$，$(n+1)=7$，$x=0$，$z=0$，代号为 R170。但丁烷不按上述规则写，而写成 R600。此外，对于同分异构体，在代号后加小写的字母"a""b""c"，如异丁烷的代号为 R600a。

对于乙烯、丙烯的表示方法，是在 R 后面先写一个"1"，其余数字按氟利昂的编号规则书写。如乙烯 C_2H_4，$m=2$，$n=4$，$x=0$，$z=0$，则 $(m-1)=1$，$(n+1)=5$，$x=0$，$z=0$，代号为 R1150。丙烯 C_3H_6，$m=3$，$n=6$，$x=0$，$z=0$，则 $(m-1)=2$，$(n+1)=7$，$x=0$，$z=0$，代号为 R1270。

4）混合工质

混合工质是由两种或两种以上的制冷剂按一定的比例相互溶解而成的溶合物，分为共沸混合工质和非共沸混合工质。

共沸混合工质的性质与单纯工质一样，在恒定的压力下蒸发或冷凝时，蒸发温度或冷凝温度保持不变，而且其气相和液相具有相同的组分。共沸制冷剂代号 R 后面的数字按使用的先后顺序编号。例如最早命名的共沸混合制冷剂的代号表示为 R500，以后命名的按先后次序分别用代号 R501、R502、…、R506 表示。

非共沸工质在恒定的压力下蒸发或冷凝时，其蒸发温度或冷凝温度以及气相和液相的组分，均不能保持恒定，由于非共沸工质在组分不同、混合比不同时，会显示不同的热力学性质，可满足各种制冷要求。非共沸制冷混合工质制冷剂的代号 R 后面的数字按使用的先后顺序编号。例如最早命名的非共沸混合制冷剂的代号表示为 R400，以后命名的按先后次序分别用代号 R401、R402、…、R407 表示。

（三）常用制冷剂的性质

目前在蒸气压缩式制冷装置中采用较为广泛的制冷剂有氨、氟利昂以及混合工质。客车空调中常用 R22 和 R407c 这两种制冷剂。

1. 氨（R717）

氨属于无机化合物制冷剂。氨具有良好的热力学性能，其优点是蒸发压力和冷凝压力适中，单位容积制冷量较大。氨在标准大气压力下的沸点为 -33.4 ℃，当制冷温度为 5~30 ℃ 时，蒸发压力总大于大气压力，不会在蒸发器内形成真空。采用水作为冷却介质时，冷凝压力不超过 1.5 MPa。

氨具有较强的溶水性，在系统中不会发生"冰塞"现象。对钢铁不腐蚀，但氨含水时，对铜及铜合金有腐蚀作用（磷青铜除外）。氨是微溶于润滑油的制冷剂，当系统中有较多润滑油时，由于油的密度大于氨液的密度，在系统运行时会沉积在储液器或蒸发器等设备的底部。为了减轻润滑油在换热器表面形成的油垢，应定期对系统中沉积的润滑油进行排放，并尽量避免过多的润滑油进入系统内部。

氨的缺点是毒性较大，有强烈的刺激性气味，且可以燃烧和爆炸。氨一旦泄漏，将污染空气、食品，并刺激人的眼睛和呼吸器官，当氨液触及皮肤时会形成"冻伤"。如果空气中氨的容积含量达到 0.5%～0.6% 时，人在其中停留半小时便能中毒，当空气中氨的容积含量在 16%～25% 时可引起爆炸。因此在客车空调装置中不易使用，它主要用作大型冷藏库的工质，在小型制冷装置中应用较少。

2. 氟利昂

氟利昂是目前应用最广泛的制冷剂之一。它无味、不易燃烧、毒性小。但含氯原子的氟利昂与明火接触能分解出剧毒的光气（$COCl_2$）；渗透性很强，易于泄漏，而且不易发现；传热性差，密度大、黏度大、流动性能差；绝热指数小，压缩终温低；单位容积制冷量小。

大多数氟利昂溶于润滑油而不溶于水。为了避免发生"冰塞"现象，制冷系统中应装设干燥器。氟利昂不含水分时，对金属无腐蚀作用，对天然橡胶和塑料有膨润作用。氟利昂中含水分时，能分解生成氯化氢、氟化氢，不但会腐蚀金属，还可能产生"镀铜现象"。镀铜现象是指当氯化氢接触到铜表面后，在一定的条件下会产生氯化铜，氯化铜与热的铁制表面接触，铜与铁离子相互置换，将铜离子沉淀在铁制表面上。如果发生镀铜现象，将会破坏压缩机吸、排气阀的严密性和改变轴承与轴颈的间隙，不利于压缩机的正常运转。

氟利昂检漏可用肥皂水、卤素灯等。肥皂水适用于系统安装和明显泄漏时的检查。少量泄漏可用卤素灯检查，随着泄漏量的增大，卤素灯火焰的颜色由微绿、淡绿变成深绿直到紫色。微量的泄漏可用电子检漏仪，该仪器的灵敏度较高。

下面介绍几种氟利昂的主要特性。

（1）氟利昂 12（CCl_2F_2）。

R12 广泛应用于中小型制冷装置中，如冰箱、汽车空调机、降湿机、小冷库等。R12 的凝固点为 -155 ℃，在标准大气压力下的沸点为 -29.8 ℃。当采用水或空气作为冷却介质时，冷凝压力不超过 1.2 MPa，所以它适用于空气冷却制冷机系统。

R12 易溶于润滑油，常温下它可与任意比例的矿物性润滑油相互溶解，在冷凝器内不会出现分层现象，也不会在传热表面形成油垢而影响传热。为了避免蒸发器内润滑油的含量过多，引起蒸发温度升高、传热系数降低和制冷量减少，通常采用非满液式蒸发器，使制冷剂液体从蒸发器上面进入，蒸气从下面流出，以便润滑油随 R12 顺利返回压缩机。R12 的溶水性较差，为避免"冰塞"现象，应严格控制系统中制冷剂的含水量不超过 0.0025%，充灌 R12 以前，必须对系统进行严格的干燥处理，并在系统中或充液管上设置干燥器。

由于 R12 对大气臭氧层的破坏严重，是最早被禁用的制冷剂之一。

（2）氟利昂 22（$CHClF_2$）。

R22 主要用于活塞式制冷压缩机，作为空调制冷和低温用。客车空调装置通常也采用 R22 作为制冷剂。R22 在标准大气压力下的沸点为 -40.8 ℃，凝固点为 -160 ℃，常温下的冷凝压力及单位容积制冷量都与氨接近。R22 无色、无味、不燃烧、不爆炸，使用安全可靠。

R22能够部分与润滑油相互溶解。通常在冷凝器中能与制冷剂相互溶解形成溶液，但在蒸发器内，由于温度较低，润滑油只能部分溶解在制冷剂中而出现分层现象，上层主要为润滑油，下层主要为制冷剂。为了使润滑油顺利返回压缩机，在系统的低压部分应设有油分离器。R22的溶水性比R12大，但仍属于微溶于水的制冷剂。所以系统中制冷剂的含水量仍须控制在0.0025%以下，需要在系统中装设干燥器。

R22对大气臭氧层的破坏作用比R12小得多，所以在一些场合，它正作为某些禁用制冷剂的过渡性替代物使用，但最终将被禁用。

（3）R407c。

R407c是由R32制冷剂、R125制冷剂再加上R134a制冷剂按一定的比例混合而成，是一种不破坏臭氧层的环保制冷剂。在标准大气压下，其沸点是 $-43.4 \sim 36.1\ ℃$。即温度由 $-36.1\ ℃$ 滑移到温度 $-43.4\ ℃$。但应用与空调系统时，其蒸气压力比R22高出10%。在空调工况下，其单位体积制冷量和制冷系数比R22低5%；而在低温工况下，其制冷系数虽变化不大，但单位体积制冷量却低了20%。

R407c由于和R22有着极为相近的特性和性能，所以成为R22的长期替代物，使用于各种空调系统和非离心式制冷系统。R407c可用于原R22的系统，不用重新设计系统，只需更换原系统的少量部件，以及将原系统内的矿物冷冻油更换成能与R407c互溶的润滑油，就可直接充注R407c，实现原设备的环保更换。

由于R407c是混合非共沸工质，为了保证其混合成分不发生改变，R407c必须液态充注。如果R407c的系统发生制冷剂泄漏，且系统的性能发生明显的改变，其系统内剩余的R407c不能回收循环使用，必须放空系统内的剩余R407c制冷剂后，重新充注新的R407c制冷剂。

R407c的传热性能较差，直接影响制冷剂的改变。R407c不能与矿物性润滑油互溶，但能溶解于聚酯类合成润滑油，对干燥有较高要求。

（四）关于氟利昂的替代

氟利昂制冷剂的使用推动了制冷技术的迅速发展。由于氟利昂具有许多的优点，所以它发展很快，目前广泛使用的有R11、R12、R13、R22、R113、R114等。

氟利昂是用氟、氯、溴等部分或全部取代饱和碳氢化合物中的氢而生成的新化合物的总称。其中不含氢的氟利昂称作氯氟化碳，写成CFC_S，是有公害物质，属于限制和禁用的物质；含氢的，氟利昂称作氢氯化碳，写成HCFC，是低公害物质，属于过渡性物质；而不含氯的氟利昂称作氢氟化碳，写成HCF，是无公害物质。

地球表面的大气按其高度分为若干层，在高度约25 km处存在一个臭氧层。臭氧层有效地减少了太阳紫外线对地球表面的辐射危害。它形成了地球上生物和人类的防护罩，是一道天然的屏障。CFC_S类物质对大气中臭氧以及地球高空的臭氧层有严重的破坏作用，而且CFC_S在大气中具有几十年至上百年的生存寿命，因此它对臭氧层的破坏作用就具有积累性和持久性。臭氧层的破坏，增加了太阳对地球表面的紫外线辐射强度。弥散在大气中的CFC_S不仅对臭氧层有破坏作用，而且它能稳定吸收太阳热，导致大气温度上升，即加剧温室效应。根据测算，臭氧减少 1%，紫外线辐射量增加 2%。紫外线辐射量的增加，将使人的免疫系统受破坏，人体抵抗力大为降低，皮肤癌等病患增多；加剧地球温室效应，使世界平均气温上升，海平面增高，沙漠化加速；危害地球上的许多生物破坏生态平衡。曾有人提出，臭氧层减少到原来的 1/5，将是地球存亡的临界点。因此减少和禁止 CFC_S 的生产和使用，已成为国际社会的共识。

20 世纪 80 年代以来世界各国，特别是美国、日本和西欧各国等都投入了大量人力和财力，对 CFC_S 的替代物进行开发和研究。关于 CFC_S 的替代和减少 CFC_S 对大气臭氧层破坏的问题，目前已禁止使用 CFC_S 制冷剂，并限制 HCFC 制冷剂或者由其组成的非共沸混合制冷剂的使用。

因 HFC 类物质不包含氯元素，所以对大气臭氧层无破坏作用，温室效应也比较小。目前，广泛使用 HFC（氢氟化碳）类物质作为制冷剂，如 HFC134A（R134a）制冷剂和 HFC407C（R407c）制冷剂。

二、压缩机润滑油

压缩机润滑采用专用冷冻机油。在制冷系统中，冷冻机油和制冷剂是混合在一起的，因此对冷冻机油物理性能和化学性能有特殊的要求，应用中选用合适的冷冻机油的黏度、凝固点、闪点、含水量和含石蜡量及化学稳定性，使它减少对制冷系统工作的影响。在使用 R12 制冷剂的系统中采用 18 号冷冻机油，使用氨和 R22 的系统中采用 25 号冷冻机油。

（一）冷冻机油的特性

1. 黏度

冷冻机油的黏度是用来衡量冷冻机油黏性的大小，黏度与冷冻机油的种类和温度有关，温度上升，黏度下降，黏度还与压缩机所用的制冷剂有关。如 R12 与冷冻机油相互溶解，使冷冻机油浓度变稀，黏度过小，则使轴承不能建立所需的油膜，但黏度也不能过大，黏度过大，不仅在压缩机启动时会产生更多的泡沫，而且会增加阻力使压缩机启动困难。所以，润滑油的黏度要适中。

2. 凝固点与浊点

冷冻机油在温度降低时，随着黏度的增大，流动性就越差。当冷却到一定温度时，便停止流动，这时的温度称为冷冻机油的凝固点。

当温度降到一定数值时，冷冻机油中析出石蜡，冷冻机油中出现絮状物，这时的温度称为冷冻机油的浊点。石蜡的析出，不仅使油变混浊，而且会堵塞制冷管道，零部件的功能受到影响，使制冷系统不能正常工作。

3. 闪点

将冷冻机油进行加热，直到所产生的油蒸气与火焰接触时能产生闪火，这时的温度称为冷冻机油的闪点。选用的冷冻机油的闪点必须比排气温度高 15～30 ℃，以免引起冷冻机油的燃烧和结焦。

4. 击穿电压

对于用在封闭式压缩机的冷冻润滑油要求具有耐电压性。击穿电压是表示冷冻机油和制冷剂电绝缘性能的一个指标。纯净的冷冻机油绝缘性能良好，但当油中有水分、飞尘等杂质时，绝缘性能会降低，冷冻机油的击穿电压一般要求在 25 kV 以上。制冷剂也要求有良好的电绝缘性能。

5. 与制冷剂的溶解性

制冷剂在润滑油中的溶解性可分为完全溶解、微溶解和完全不溶解。

当制冷剂与润滑油完全溶解时，能使机件润滑创造良好的条件，在冷凝器等换热器的换热面上不易形成油膜，传热效果好。但当制冷剂与润滑油互溶时，会使制冷剂的蒸发温度提高，使润滑油的黏度降低，还会使制冷剂沸腾时泡沫增多，蒸发器中的液面不稳定及在运行时使制冷机的耗油量增大，也使系统中的油不易排出。

当制冷剂与润滑油完全不溶时，制冷系统的蒸发温度比较稳定，在制冷设备中制冷剂与润滑油易于分离，并在热交换器换热表面形成油膜而影响换热。

微溶解于油的制冷剂的优缺点介于两者之间。

（二）冷冻机油的变质

冷冻机油的变质通常是因为混入水分、发生氧化反应，以及几种不同牌号的冷冻机油混合使用，产生化学反应、形成沉淀物，影响压缩机的润滑。

一般从外观颜色、气味可以直观地判断冷冻机油的好坏情况。当冷冻机油变质时，颜色变深，将油滴在白色吸墨纸上，若油滴的中央部分没有黑色，说明冷冻机油没有变质，反之说明冷冻机油已经变质。若油中有水分时，油的透明度降低，如果需要准确判断，还需特定设备进行检测。

【任务训练】

（1）简述蒸气压缩机的工作原理和制冷系统的基本构成。
（2）制冷机中为什么要用压缩机来提高蒸气的压力？
（3）简述热泵工作原理。
（4）简述吸收制冷的循环过程。
（5）简述 R22 制冷剂的特性。
（6）对制冷剂有哪些热力学方面的要求？
（7）如何选择合适的制冷剂？
（8）压缩机润滑油的选用需关注哪些特性？

项目四　客车空调制冷系统

【中国铁路文化】

中国铁路发展史 4　中国高铁造福人类

1978年，邓小平同志访问日本，乘坐新干线铁路上的高速列车，高速铁路因此正式进入中国大众的视野。20世纪80年代，中国铁路面临运输能力不足困境，列车行驶速度低于120 km/h，客货混跑矛盾增加，对列车提速的需求相当迫切，但受限于当时经济、科技以及市场环境，中国发展高速铁路需分阶段进行。

1. 中国高速铁路发展历程

20世纪90年代，中国开始高铁技术攻关和试验，并以广深铁路为准高速化改造试点线路。1998年8月28日，广深铁路营运列车最高行驶速度200 km/h，成为中国第一条达到高速指标的铁路。1999年8月16日，秦沈客运专线开工建设，作为中国第一条轮轨高速动车组的试验线路。

2001年3月1日，上海磁浮列车示范运营线开工建设，于2002年12月31日建成，设计速度430 km/h，为中国首条高速轨道系统。2008年8月1日，京津城际铁路开通运营，成为中国第一条设计速度350 km/h级别高速铁路。2009年12月26日，京广高速铁路武广段开通运营，列车最高运营速度350 km/h，首次打破中国铁路春运瓶颈，成为中国正式进入高铁时代的标志。

2017年12月28日，石济高速铁路开通运营，至此，中国铁路"四横四纵"快速通道全部建成通车。2022年8月30日，我国首条跨海高铁——新建福厦铁路全线铺轨贯通。2022年中国铁路营业里程为15.5万 km，其中高铁为4.2万 km，稳居世界第一。

2. 中国动车组发展历程

于2004年开始，中国从日、法、德等国家引进成熟的动车组，代表型号是CRH1、CRH2、CRH3、CRH5，助力2007年的第六次铁路大提速。

2008年2月26日中国启动了拥有自主知识产权的时速350 km/h及以上等级的高速动车组列车的研究。第二代动车组列车被命名为CRH380系列，称为"和谐号"。CRH380A（L）型动车组是由青岛四方公司设计制造的。CRH380B（L）是由长春客车厂和唐山客车厂研制而成的。"和谐号"持续运营速度380 km/h，实际运营速度350 km/h。

2012年中国标准动车组"复兴号"正式步入研发阶段。2015年6月30日，由四方公司和长客公司研发的中国标准动车组诞生，2017年6月25日，中国标准动车组被正式命名为"复兴号"。"复兴号"初期主要有CR400AF和CR400BF，后续又研发了CR300和CR200系列。CR400系列运营速度是350 km/h，CR300系列运营速度是250 km/h，CR200系列运营速度160 km/h。350公里、250公里、160公里不同速度等级、8辆短编、16

辆长编、17辆超长编不同编组形式，动力集中和动力分散不同动力牵引模式，中国标准动车组家族不断壮大，已形成系列化产品。

图 4-1　复兴号动车组

3. 中国高铁造福人类

中老铁路开通运营，是中国标准动车组首次走出国门。针对老挝的具体实际对动车进行适应性设计优化，为老挝人民提供便捷舒适出行方式。中泰铁路是中泰共建"一带一路"的重要项目，这条泰国首条标准轨高速铁路使用的正是中国标准动车组技术。对于这条铁路，许多泰国人士已经开始期待，"从曼谷到呵叻，中泰铁路经停不少地方，通车后会给这些地方带来极大的交通便利，带动当地经济发展。"

凭借具有独立自主知识产权的高铁建设和装备制造技术体系，中国标准动车组不仅开进了高寒、高原地区，实现了跨海过桥不减速，还为世界高铁贡献中国方案，造福全人类。

【项目描述】

客车空调装置制冷系统是由压缩机、蒸发器、冷凝器、自动控制器件及辅助设备等组成，本项目主要学习这些设备的结构、工作原理、检修方法，以及制冷系统的清洁、充放制冷剂、检漏和气密性试验等基本操作方法。通过本项目的学习，使学生能够对客车空调制冷系统进行维护与检修，能够对制冷系统进行清洁、制冷剂的检漏和气密性试验等操作，保障客车空调装置正常运行。

【项目目标】

1. 知识目标

（1）掌握压缩机的结构及工作原理。
（2）掌握蒸发器、冷凝器的结构及工作原理。

（3）掌握自动控制器件及辅助设备的结构及工作原理。
（4）掌握制冷剂的检漏和气密性试验作业。

2. 能力目标

（1）能够进行压缩机、蒸发器、冷凝器的日常维护。
（2）能够深刻理解自动控制器件及辅助设备在制冷系统中的作用。
（3）能进行制冷系统的清洁、制冷剂检漏和气密性试验作业。

3. 素养目标

（1）正确使用、爱护保养设备。
（2）培养规范作业、安全生产的意识。
（3）培养团队精神。

任务一　制冷压缩机

【任务目标】

（1）理解制冷压缩机的类型及结构。
（2）掌握活塞式和涡旋式压缩机的工作原理。
（3）可进行压缩机检修作业。

【知识储备】

制冷压缩机是蒸气压缩式制冷装置的动力部件，它将电能转化为机械能，对制冷剂蒸气进行压缩，它是推动制冷剂在制冷系统中不断循环的动力源泉。在铁路客车空调装置中，压缩机主要采用全封闭活塞式压缩机，也有采用涡旋式压缩机及其他压缩机的。

一、制冷压缩机的类型

（一）按工作原理分类

制冷压缩机按工作原理不同可分为容积型和速度型两大类。

1. 容积型压缩机

容积型压缩机是通过改变工作容积来完成气体的压缩和输送的。容积型压缩机主要有活塞式、涡旋式、螺杆式和滚动转子式（又称旋转式）压缩机。其中活塞式压缩机是通过活塞在气缸内作往复运动来改变工作容积；涡旋式压缩机是通过两涡旋盘相对转动，使形成的月牙形变化来改变工作容积；而螺杆式和旋转式压缩机是通过螺杆或转子在气缸内做旋转运动来改变工作容积。

旋转式压缩机在国内外已普遍用于房间空调器中，几乎取代了活塞式压缩机，日本在铁路客车空调装置中也开始采用旋转式压缩机。旋转式压缩机与活塞式压缩机相比，有结构简单、体积小、重量轻、容积效率高、运行平稳、噪声和振动小、可靠性强等优点。但旋转式压缩机也存在一些不利因素，如主要零件加工精度要求高，电动机绝缘等级高，起动转矩较大等。这些问题随着高科技的发展，已基本解决，因此旋转式压缩机在国内正快速发展。

目前，国内外部分铁路客车的空调装置也有采用封闭式螺杆压缩机及涡旋式压缩机的。本课程主要讨论活塞式压缩机及涡旋式压缩机的工作过程、性能及结构等。

2. 速度型压缩机

速度型压缩机是使气体在高速转动的叶轮中提高速度，而后通过导向器使气体的动能转化为压力能，进而来完成气体的压缩和输送任务。目前常采用的速度型压缩机是离心式压缩机。

（二）按制冷量大小分类

制冷压缩机按标准工况下制冷量的大小分为小型、中型和大型三种类型。

标准工况制冷量小于 58 kW 为小型；标准工况制冷量在 58～580 kW 范围内为中型；标准工况制冷量大于 580 kW 为大型。

活塞式压缩机发展历史悠久，具有丰富的设计、制造和运行的经验，至今在各个领域中依然被广泛采用和得到发展。制冷压缩机的持续进步也反映在其种类的多样化方面，活塞式以外的各类压缩机型，如涡旋式、离心式、螺杆式、滚动转子式和涡旋式等都各具特色。这对于从事制冷工程的技术人员在制冷压缩机类型的选择上提供了更多的可能性。在这种背景下，活塞式压缩机的使用范围必受到影响而出现逐渐缩小的趋势，这种趋势在大冷量范围内表现得更显著。但是，在中小冷量范围内，实用上还是以活塞式压缩机为主。

随着压缩机本身可靠性和耐久性不断得到提高，以及对压缩机紧凑轻量化的追求，制冷压缩机从开启式逐渐向封闭式发展是趋势，如在日本，功率在 15～22 kW 之间的活塞式压缩机中，90%以上实现了半封闭化；对于不能依赖外界维修的船舶、车辆以及边远地区，便于现场维修的开启式压缩机还是有它的优势。对于小型制冷压缩机而言，业内人士一般将开启式活塞压缩机称之为第一代，全封闭活塞压缩机称之为第二代，旋转（滑片）式压缩机称之为第三代，涡旋式压缩机称之为第四代，现正在开发的环形压缩机即为第五代小型制冷压缩机。

二、活塞式压缩机

(一) 活塞式压缩机的工作原理

活塞式制冷压缩机的结构形式有很多种,但其基本组成(见图 4-1-3)通常包含以下几部分:由机体和各种盖板组成的机体组件;由气缸、活塞和吸、排气阀片等构成容积可变的工作空间;由曲轴、连杆等构成的传动机构;由油泵、轴封等构成的润滑和密封设施(小型压缩机没有油泵,封闭式压缩机没有轴封)。

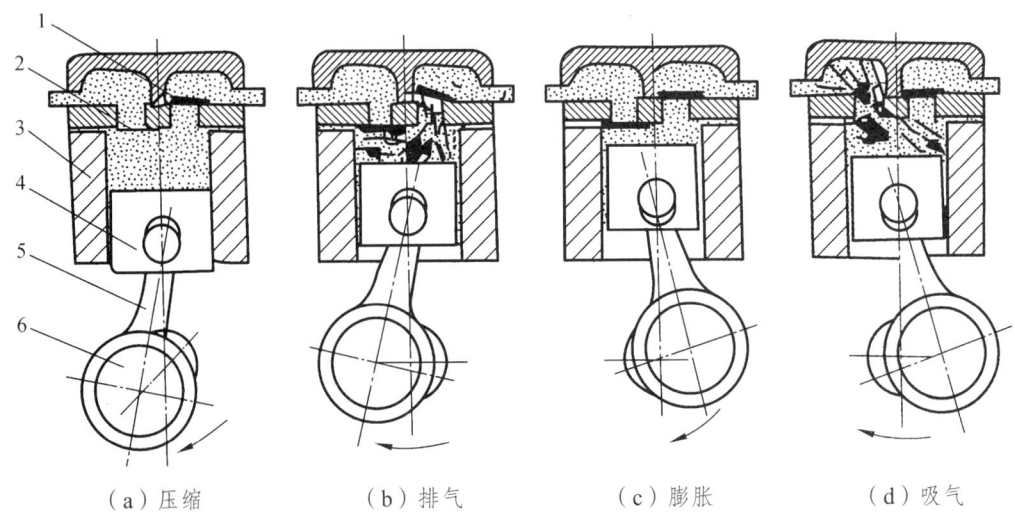

(a) 压缩　　(b) 排气　　(c) 膨胀　　(d) 吸气

1—排气阀片;2—吸气阀片;3—气缸;4—活塞;5—连杆;6—曲轴。

图 4-1-3　活塞式压缩机的基本构成

压缩机的工作是靠电能输入压缩机电机后,电机轴带动压缩机曲轴转动,曲轴通过连杆带动活塞在气缸中作往复运动,同时气缸顶部的吸、排气阀片配合活塞运动开启或关闭,从而使压缩机完成对制冷剂蒸气的压缩。曲轴每旋转一周,活塞就作一次往复运动,压缩机就完成一次工作循环。

(二) 活塞式压缩机的分类

1. 按密封结构分类

从防止制冷剂泄漏所采取的密封结构方式来看,制冷压缩机可分为开启式、半封闭式和全封闭式。

1) 开启式压缩机

开启式压缩机功率的输入是通过伸出机体之外的主轴进行的,压缩机和电动机是分体的,它们通过传动装置(联轴器、传动带或变速箱)相连接。为防止制冷剂蒸气的外泄和外界空气的渗入,必须在主轴伸出部位上采用防止泄漏的轴封装置加以密封。由于轴封装置不可能实现绝对可靠的密封，开启式制冷压缩机的制冷剂的渗出和外界空气的渗入是难以避免的。

2）封闭式压缩机

封闭式压缩机所配用的电动机与压缩机共同组装在一个机体内，并共用一根主轴，且不伸出机体，因而不需设置轴封装置，减少了泄漏的可能性，同时又可降低噪声。使用吸入的低温制冷剂冷却电机，有利于机器的小型轻量化。但由于制冷剂和电动机直接接触，因此要求电机的绝缘材料能耐油和耐制冷剂的腐蚀，且压缩机的油泵能正反转工作。

3）半封闭式压缩机

半封闭式与全封闭式压缩机的区别在于：前者的机体、气缸盖装配后如有必要仍可卸拆，其密封面以法兰连接，靠垫片或垫圈密封；而后者是压缩机和电机全部安装在一个封闭罩壳内，罩壳全部焊死，不能拆卸，这样可大大减轻压缩机的重量。但由于封闭式压缩机不易拆卸，修理不便，因此对机器零部件的加工、装配质量、可靠性和使用寿命要求较高，它们应能保证10年以上使用期限。

2. 按气缸布置形式分类

按气缸布置形式压缩机可分为卧式、直立式和角度式三种类型，如图4-1-4所示。压缩机的气缸布置方式直接影响到外形尺寸和质量大小。

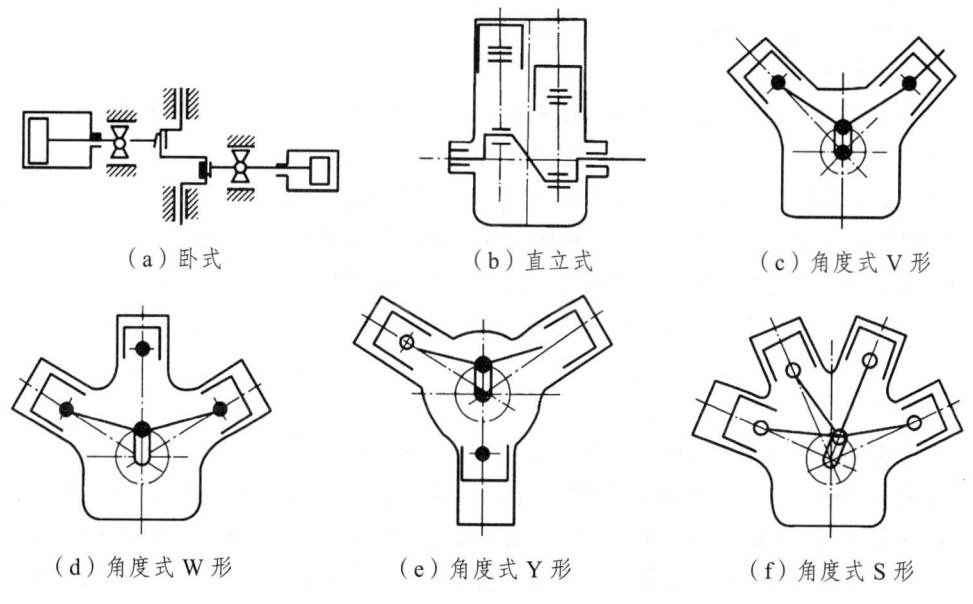

图4-1-4 压缩机气缸布置方式

1）卧式压缩机

卧式压缩机的气缸轴线呈水平布置。这种形式在大型制冷压缩机中较为多见，此外在全封闭制冷压缩机中也有采用。

2）直立式压缩机

直立式压缩机的气缸轴线呈直立布置。考虑到压缩机结构的紧凑性、运转平稳性及振动的大小，以双缸直立式为常见形式。

3）角度式压缩机

角度式压缩机的气缸轴线呈一定的夹角布置，有 V 型、W 型、Y 型和 S 型（扇形）等之分。角度式布置方式能够使压缩机具备结构紧凑，体积和占地面积小、振动小、运转平稳等优点，因此为现代中、小型高速多缸压缩机所广泛采用，是典型的压缩机气缸布置方式。

（三）活塞式压缩机的结构

在单元式客车空调机组的制冷系统中，主机全部采用全封闭式压缩机，主要有日本产的 505FH2-H 型、JH514YZ 型和 JH519YZE 型，还有美国产的 COPELAND 型等。下面以 JH514YZ 型压缩机为例介绍其结构。

JH514YZ 型压缩机是日本三菱电气公司生产的全封闭式压缩机，它被广泛使用在 KLD29 型单元式空调机组中。其主要技术参数为：

气缸直径：44.45 mm；制冷剂：R22；

活塞行程：24 mm；制冷量：12 767 W（空调工况）；

气缸数：3 个；电动机功率：3.75 kW；

转速：2 880 r/min。

JH514YZ 型压缩机的结构如图 4-1-5 所示，它主要由机壳、机体、电动机、曲轴、连杆、活塞、气缸、气阀以及排气消声器等组成。其工作过程如下：

压缩机工作时，温度较低的低压制冷剂蒸气经吸气管进入机壳内，并充满整个机壳，可使电机获得冷却。然后经电机定子内侧机体上的吸气通道进入机体内腔。当活塞由上止点向下运动时，低压制冷剂蒸气经阀板上的吸气孔，顶开吸气阀进入气缸。经过气缸压缩后，高温高压的制冷剂蒸气顶开排气阀排入高压室，再经气缸盖上与排气消声器的连接管排入排气消声器，然后通过排气消声器上的排气管排出压缩机。排气消声器不仅起消声作用，还可使高压气体压力均匀稳定。

压缩机的机壳，由 5 mm 厚的热压或冷压钢板冲压成上、下两部分，装入电机与压缩机组成的机芯后，将上、下机壳焊接成一体，机壳外部只有吸气管、排气管和电源引线。机芯的外观如图 4-1-6 所示，为了减少机器工作时的振动，机芯通过三个减振弹簧支承在机壳上，机壳再通过橡胶减振装置与单元式机组的钢骨架连接。机芯上部是压缩机电机，下部是压缩机机体，机体下部有三个气缸呈卧式星形布置，其中心线成 120°夹角。环形的排气消声器布置在机体外部，下部有三个管分别与三个气缸相连，上部有一个管伸至机壳外。

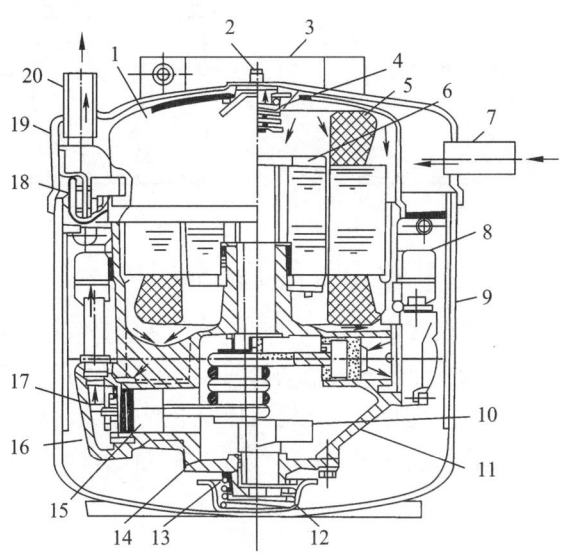

1—电动机壳；2—吊具；3—端子箱；4—上弹簧；5—定子线圈；6—转子；7—吸气管；8—排气消声器；9—下壳体；10—曲轴；11—曲轴箱；12—下弹簧；13—下轴承；14—支承架；15—活塞连杆；16—气缸盖；17—高压室；18—横弹簧；19—上壳体；20—排气管。

图 4-1-5　JH514YZ 压缩机结构

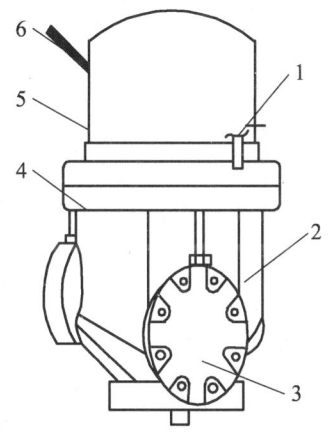

1—排气管；2—机体；3—气缸盖；4—排气消声；5—电机壳；6—电源线

图 4-1-6　机芯外观示意图

压缩机曲轴是一根垂直安装的偏心轴，轴的上端安装电动机转子铁芯，下端偏心销上套有三根整体式连杆。活塞为筒形、平顶结构。为了简化结构，活塞只有一道活塞环，为气环，气环下面开有一道油槽。活塞结构如图 4-1-7 所示。

231

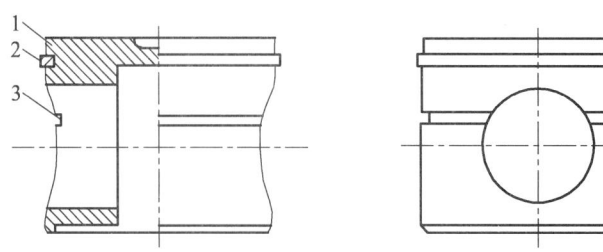

1—活塞体；2—气环；3—油槽。

图 4-1-7 活塞结构图

气阀采用簧片阀。气阀组由阀板、吸排气阀片及排气阀升程限位片组成，并通过中心处的铆钉铆在一起。气阀组总成和阀板的结构如图 4-1-8、图 4-1-9 所示。因簧片阀有较好的弹性，取消了吸、排气弹簧。吸气时，吸气阀片向下弯曲，其升程受到阀片外圆上的四个凸台与气缸壁上相应的凹槽深度所限制；排气时，排气阀片向上弯曲，其升程受到排气阀片升程限位片的限制。

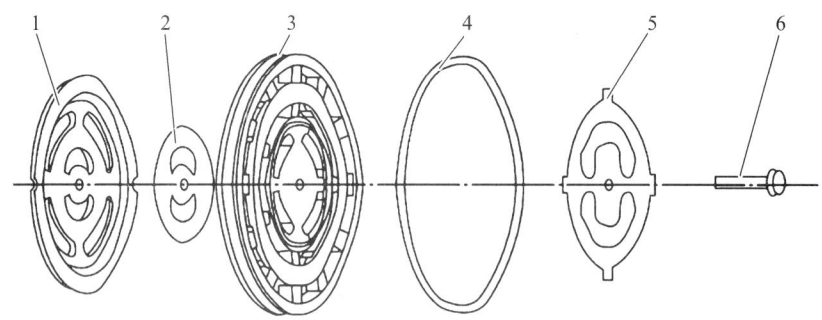

1—排气阀升程限位板；2—排气阀片；3—阀板；4—密封圈；5—吸气阀片；6—铆钉。

图 4-1-8 气阀组总成图

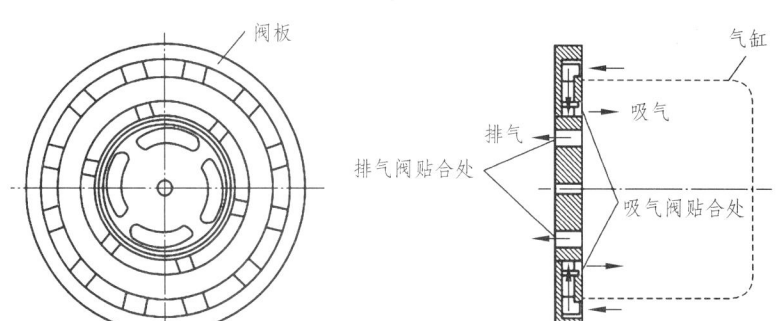

图 4-1-9 阀板结构图

消声器结构如图 4-1-10 所示。它的外部下方有三根进气管，分别与三个气缸相连，上方有一根排气管，管的上部一直伸到机壳外。它的内部分上、下两层；上下层之间只在排气管下部周围缝隙处连通。排气管的下部伸到消声器下层底部。三个气缸中的高压气体首先通过三个进气管进入消声器的下层，再通过排气管排出机壳。这样不但使各气缸排出的高压气体的压力均匀稳定,而且消除了气体高速流动带来的噪声。

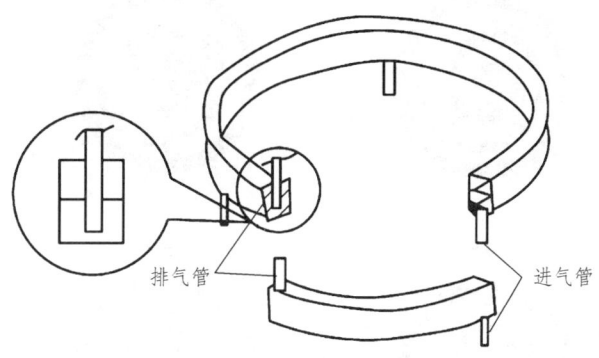

图 4-1-10　排气消声器

JH514YZ 型压缩机利用曲轴上的油孔甩油实现润滑。在曲轴的中心线及偏离中心线 3 mm 处开有两个贯通的纵向油孔,当曲轴高速转动时,润滑油在离心力的作用下,向上沿轴向吸入并流向各运动副。

压缩机的电机有时会因负载过大、压缩机的间断操作过于频繁、气缸和活塞间严重漏泄、系统管路堵塞、冷却效果不好等原因而引起温度过高导致烧损。因此,为了防止电机绕组过热,在电机定子绕组中安装了温度继电器,当温度过高或电流过大时,切断电机电源,强制压缩机停车。

三、涡旋式压缩机

（一）涡旋式压缩机的工作原理

涡旋压缩机是一种容积型压缩机,是由两个涡旋盘相错 180° 对置而成,其中一个是固定涡旋盘,而另一个是旋转涡旋盘,它们在几条直线(在横截面上则是几个点)上接触并形成一系列月牙形容积。旋转涡旋盘由一个偏心距很小的曲柄轴驱动,绕固定涡旋盘平动,两者间的接触线在运转中沿涡旋曲面移动。它们之间的相对位置,靠安装在旋转涡旋盘与固定部件间的十字滑环来保证。

涡旋压缩机的工作过程如图 4-1-11 所示,实心盘为固定涡旋盘,空心盘为旋转涡旋盘。吸气口设在固定涡旋盘的顶部,由于曲柄带动空心盘顺时针转动,将气体吸入,封闭在月牙形容积内。随着旋转涡旋盘和固定涡旋盘的接触线沿涡旋面逐步向中心推进,月牙形容积逐渐缩小使气体受到连续压缩,最后高压气体通过固定涡旋盘上的轴向中心孔排出。图 4-1-11（a）表示吸气完成时的位置,图 4-1-11（b）表示旋转涡旋盘旋转时,依次是吸气过程、压缩过程、排气过程,图 4-1-11（c）、（d）表示吸入过程和压缩过程是连续而同时进行着的。在曲柄轴的每一转中,都形成一个新的吸气容积,所以上述过程不断重复,依次完成。

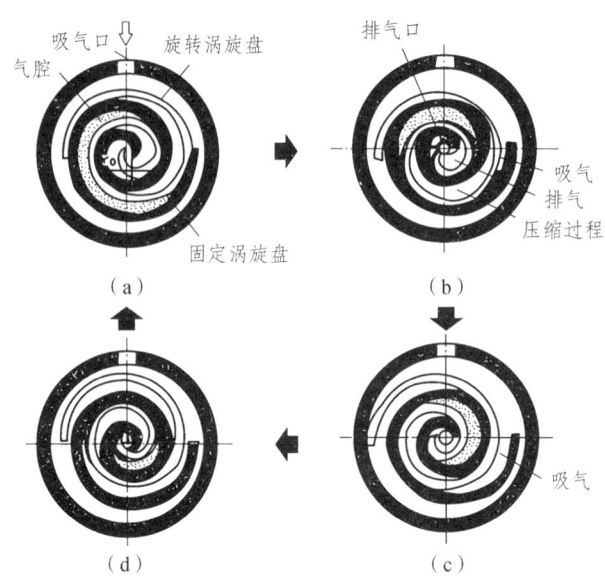

图 4-1-11 涡旋压缩机工作过程

(二) 涡旋式压缩机的结构

图 4-1-12 为 3.75 kW 全封闭涡旋式压缩机剖面图。压缩机主要由固定涡旋盘、旋转涡旋盘、十字滑环、曲轴、支架、机壳等组成。固定涡旋盘 5 和电动机定子安装在机壳内壁

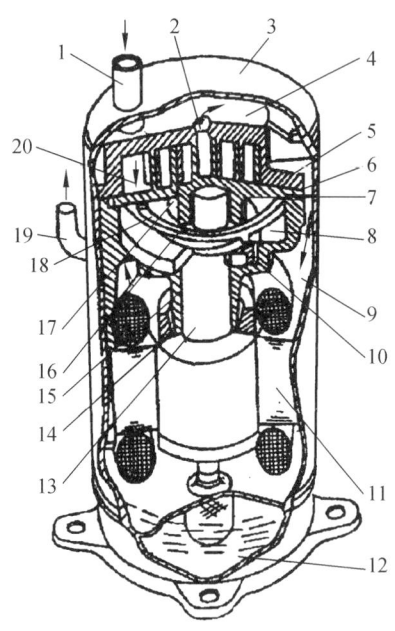

1—吸气管；2—排气口；3—密封外壳；4—排气腔；5—固定涡旋盘；6—排气通道；7—旋转涡旋盘；
8—背压腔；9—电动机腔；10—支架；11—电动机；12—油；13—曲轴；14—轴承；
15—密封；16—轴承；17—背压腔；18—十字滑环；19—排气管；20—吸气腔。

图 4-1-12 全封闭涡旋式压缩机剖面图

上。十字滑环 18 是上、下两面设置互相垂直的两对凸键的圆环，上面凸键装在旋转涡旋盘 7 背面的键槽内，下面的凸键装在支架 10 的键槽内。十字滑环的作用是防止旋转涡旋盘倾斜和自转。在旋转涡旋盘 7 下设有一个背压腔 8，背压腔由旋转涡旋 7 底盘上的小孔引入中压气流自动充气，使气腔压力支撑着旋转涡旋盘，同时在旋转涡旋盘顶部装有可调轴向密封，使得旋转涡旋盘可以轴向移动，这样便可补偿运行中的逐渐磨损，并且也能防止液击或压缩腔中润滑油过多时引起的过载。

在曲柄销轴承处和曲轴通过支架的地方，装有转动密封，以保持背压腔与机壳之间的气密性。轴承的润滑油是利用排气压力和中间压力的压差，由密封壳体的底部经曲轴上的油道来供给的，并最终由背压腔流向压缩腔以润滑涡旋面，然后同压缩气体一起排出，在机壳中将油分离，然后流至底部。再者，在固定涡旋盘外有油流，由这里给涡旋盘运动部位供油。涡旋压缩机停止运转后会逆转，因此在固定涡旋盘上的吸气管内装有止逆阀。

（三）涡旋式压缩机的特点

从结构及工作原理看，涡旋式压缩机具有如下的特点：

1. 效率高

涡旋式压缩机的吸气、压缩、排气过程连续单向进行，因而吸入气体的有害过热小，相邻两室的压差小，气体的泄露量小。没有余隙容积，故不存在引起输气系数下降的膨胀过程，而且容积效率高，通常达到 95% 以上。

2. 振动小、噪声低、转矩小

由于吸气、压缩、排气过程是同时连续进行的，压力上升较慢，因此转矩变化幅度小，振动小，噪声小。涡旋式转矩仅为滚动转子式和往复式的 1/10。

3. 体积轻便、可靠性高

涡旋式压缩机构成压缩室的零件数目与滚动式以及往复式的零件数目之比为 1：3：7，所以涡旋式的体积比往复式小 40%，质量小 15%。又由于没有吸、排气阀，易损零件少，加之有轴向、径向间隙可调的柔性机构，允许带液压缩，一旦压缩腔内压力过高，可使动盘和静盘端面脱离，压力立即得以释放，能避免液击造成破坏，故涡旋式压缩机的运行可靠性高。

4. 输气系数高

机壳内腔为排气室，减少了吸气预热，提高了压缩机的输气系数。

5. 制造工艺复杂

涡线体型线加工精度要求非常高，必须采用专用的精密加工设备，而且密封要求高，密封结构复杂。

四、压缩机检修作业

1. 作业前准备

（1）佩戴劳动保护用品，做好安全防护。

（2）检查工装设备，铁刷、兆欧表等工具、工装及设备状态良好，仪表计量检定不过期。

2. 压缩机壳体外观检查

（1）目视检查压缩机外壳、固定卡子及底座，无锈蚀、变形、裂损，清除压缩机表面及底座污垢，外壳锈蚀处用钢刷除锈后涂刷防锈漆及原色油漆，铭牌齐全、清晰（图4-1-13）。

图 4-1-13　压缩机

（2）目视检查安装固定螺栓、减震垫齐全，防振垫性能良好，老化、破损不良者需更换。使用专用套筒工具对其螺栓进行紧固，防止压缩机固定不良，造成异响振动，紧固完成后涂打防松标记。

（3）目视检查接线盒及盖无变形、破损，打开压缩机接线盒，用毛刷彻底清洁内外污垢。

3. 压缩机插头外观检查

（1）打开压缩机电源插头（图4-1-14），目视、手摸检查插头接线端子及接线柱紧固良好，烧损、裂损作用不良的更换新品。

（2）检查空调机组压缩机电缆插头限位装置是否完好（见图4-1-15）。

图 4-1-14　压缩机电源插头

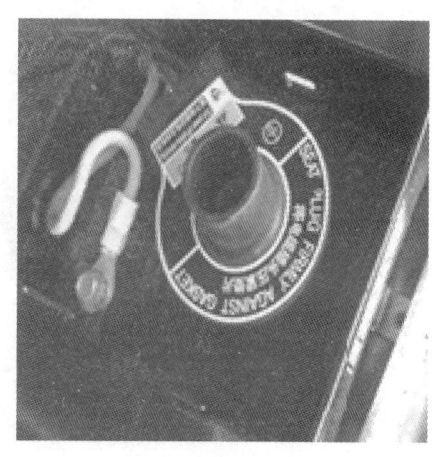

图 4-1-15　电缆插头限位装置

（3）检查空调机组电缆插头三爪保持架是否完好（见图 4-1-16）。

图 4-1-16　电缆插头三爪保持架

4. 压缩机绝缘与密封检查

（1）如图 4-1-17 所示，使用万用表检测 U、V、W 相绕组无断路、短路。使用 500 V 兆欧表检测压缩机各绕组对绝缘阻值，不小于 5 MΩ。当客车空调机组压缩机绝缘小于 5 MΩ 时，对压缩机内部端子进行除锈并烘干，烘干后再次测量，若依然小于 5 MΩ，更换压缩机。若压缩机接线端子出现裂纹时更换压缩机（含配线）。

图 4-1-17　电缆接头

（2）检查高、低压保护装置外观良好，在机组整体试验中无保护动作。测量压缩机绕组对机体绝缘电阻值不小于 5 MΩ。

（3）用万用表检测压缩机热保护开关须无断路。

（4）在接线盒盖内部粘贴检修标签，盖好压缩机接线盒盖。进出线处用防水胶泥进行防护。

（5）接线盒过线孔密封：须使用密封胶和橡胶泥做成条形夹在各散线之间，再在电线外涂密封胶或橡胶泥压紧成圆柱形，须使胶和电线之间没有缝隙，然后把电缆压入孔内，并在盒外侧用胶密封所有空隙，最后把线理顺，确保过线孔与电线之间完全密封。

（6）在接线盒与压缩机外壳中间涂密封胶，保证把缝隙填满，并用毛刷磨平表面。

（7）接线盒盖安装后，必须用密封胶或橡胶泥塞进盖子与盒子缝隙之间，并在外表抹平形成一道密封带。（见图 4-1-18）。

图 4-1-18　接线盒作密封处理

5. 作业后整理

（1）粘贴检修标记，填记一车一档内相关记录。

（2）切断电源，清点工具，确认状态良好并擦拭干净后放入工具箱内，做好设备保养，离岗前确认电闸关闭、周围无杂物、无火源后方可退岗。

任务二　换热器

【任务目标】

（1）理解蒸发器和冷凝器的结构。
（2）掌握影响换热器换热的主要因素。
（3）可进行换热器清洗作业。

【知识储备】

在空调制冷系统中，除了压缩机外，还包括换热器（主要指蒸发器和冷凝器）、节流装置、自动控制器件、辅助设备等。空调制冷时，对室内空气直接进行降温的是蒸发器，室外机吹的热风是经过冷凝器的气流，换热器的散热性能对制冷系统的性能影响非常大。

一、蒸发器

在蒸发器中，一定压力的制冷剂液体在较低温度下蒸发（沸腾）而转变为蒸气，利用制冷剂的汽化潜热，吸收被冷却介质（空气或水）的热量而使被冷却介质的温度降低。因此，蒸发器是制冷系统中产生和输出冷量的设备。蒸发器中制冷剂是由液态变为气态，吸收热量；而冷凝器内制冷剂则是由气态转变为液态，放出热量。

（一）蒸发器的类型

蒸发器按冷却介质的不同分为冷却液体（水、盐水等）的蒸发器和冷却空气的蒸发器两种。

冷却液体的蒸发器有壳管卧式蒸发器（载冷剂在管内流动，制冷剂在管外壳内流动蒸发）、干式蒸发器（制冷剂在蒸发器内全部蒸发）和沉浸式蒸发器（直接将蒸发器浸在载冷剂中）。

冷却空气的蒸发器有冷却排管和直接蒸发式空气冷却器两种。

冷却排管式蒸发器的特点是空气在管外自然对流，制冷剂在管内蒸发，传热系数较小。因此多用于冷库和冷藏箱中。

直接蒸发式空气冷却器也称冷风机。其特点是制冷剂在管内蒸发，管外空气在风机作用下强迫流动,传热系数比冷却排管高。它适用于各种空调机组、冷藏库及低温试验箱中。客车空调系统中,均采用直接蒸发式空气冷却器。

直接蒸发式空气冷却器其结构如图 4-2-1 所示,空气冷却器也是制作成长方体形的蛇形管组,外部有边框以形成空气通道。蛇形管组是将预先冲好孔的铝肋片用套片机套在铜管簇上,肋片根部带有卷边,以保证套装后的肋片间距。然后将套完片的管簇内部充高压水,使基管涨大,保证铝片与基管间接触良好,减小热阻并提高强度。由于蒸发器安装在车内比较干净,故空气冷却器的肋片间距较冷凝器的小。但一些低温制冷设备中,蒸发温度低,蒸发器易结霜,其肋片间距应适当增大。

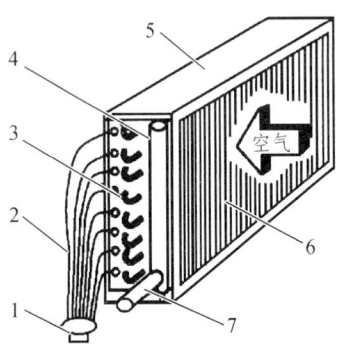

1—分液器;2—毛细管;3—蛇管;4—汇集管;5—边框;6—肋片;7—回气管。

图 4-2-1 直接蒸发式空气冷却器

由于制冷剂分配到各通路是否均匀对蒸发器的冷却效果影响很大,所以在蒸发器的进液处设有分液器,使制冷剂液体通过毛细管均匀分配到各蛇管中,同时节流降压。蒸发后的制冷剂蒸气汇合到汇集管后,经回气管再次被压缩机吸入。

(二)影响蒸发器换热的因素

蒸发器内的传热过程主要包括:制冷剂的沸腾换热,被冷却介质(空气或水)的对流换热以及通过金属层和污垢层的导热。

蒸发器的传热效果受到制冷剂换热系数、传热表面污垢物热阻及被冷却介质换热系数等因素的影响。制冷剂液体在蒸发器中是处于泡状沸腾状态,即沸腾时在传热表面产生许多气泡,这些气泡逐渐增大、脱离表面并在液体中上升。气泡的直径越大,气泡从生成到离开传热壁面的时间就越长,单位时间内产生的气泡就越少,换热系数就越低。

在蒸发器的结构设计中,应从材质、壁厚、肋管形式及结构布置等方面考虑,尽量提高其传热系数。应考虑有利于蒸发器中制冷剂在沸腾过程中产生的蒸气能够尽快从传热面脱离,并从蒸发管道中排出。除了其结构,对蒸发器换热有影响的还有制冷剂和被冷却介质。

1. 制冷剂对换热的影响

(1)制冷剂的蒸发温度。同一种制冷剂其蒸发(沸腾)温度越低,饱和温度下的密度差(蒸气与液体的密度差)越大,液体的表面张力就越大,气泡的直径就越大,换热系数就越小。反之,蒸发温度越高,换热系数越大。

(2)制冷剂的润湿能力。制冷剂润湿能力是指制冷剂与管路内壁充分接触的能力。如果制冷剂对受热表面的润湿能力强,则沸腾时形成的气泡小,能迅速地脱离传热表面,换热系数就大。如果制冷剂不能很好地润湿传热表面,则沸腾时形成的气泡就很大甚至形成气膜,使换热系数明显下降。

(3)制冷剂的物理性质。主要指制冷剂的导热率、密度、黏度等因素。热导率较大的制冷剂,在传热方向的热阻小,其沸腾换热系数就大。密度和黏度较小的制冷剂液体,沸腾时单位时间内产生的气泡多,其对流换热系数就大。

(4)制冷剂中润滑油含量。制冷剂中含有润滑油的浓度对换热系数有一定的影响。实验证明:当制冷剂中含油的浓度在8%~12%时换热系数比无油时还高,但含油量再进一步增加时,换热系数将会降低。

2. 被冷却介质对换热的影响

客车空调的被冷却介质通常就是空气,空气的流速,不管是风冷还是水冷,流速越快,传热系数就越大。但过大会使动力消耗增大,同时客车空调对流入客室内的空气流速及流量都有具体规定,故应综合考虑。

虽然蒸发器通常都在机组内部,不易受外界粉尘和杂物影响,但在运用过程中,如出现表面积水或结霜也同样会影响传热。

二、冷凝器

冷凝器的作用是使从压缩机出来的高温高压的制冷剂蒸气,在其内向外部冷却介质(空气或水)放热,冷却、冷凝成高温高压的饱和(过冷)制冷剂液体。

在冷凝器中,制冷剂的冷却过程可以分作三个阶段:由过热蒸气冷却为饱和蒸气;由饱和蒸气凝结为饱和温度下的液体;如果冷却介质的流量较大或温度较低,饱和液体还可以进一步被冷却成为该压力下的过冷液体。

(一)冷凝器的类型

冷凝器按冷却介质和冷却方式的不同分为三种类型:
(1)水冷式冷凝器:用水作为冷却介质。
(2)空气冷却式冷凝器:用空气作为冷却介质,也称风冷式冷凝器。
(3)蒸发式冷凝器:用少量的水和空气作为冷却介质,主要是靠水蒸发把热量带走。

水冷式和蒸发式冷凝器可以获得较低的冷凝温度,但容易在冷凝器表面结水垢;空气冷却式冷凝器冷凝温度高,尺寸大,能量消耗也较大。但在车辆空调制冷系统中,由于受运用条件的限制,无法采用水冷式或蒸发式冷凝器,只能采用空气冷却式冷凝器。其他小型制冷机上如冰箱、冷藏柜、汽车空调及民用空调器等,受使用环境限制,也都采用风冷式冷凝器。

风冷式冷凝器工作时，制冷剂蒸气在系统管路内冷却、冷凝（过冷），空气在轴流式风机作用下在蛇管外横向流过，从而把热量带走。风冷式冷凝器常做成蛇管式，外套肋片。蛇管一般用直径较小的铜管制成，铜管接头用银焊密封，沿空气流动方向的蛇管排数一般为6-8排，肋片为铝片。为使结构紧凑，将几根蛇管并联在一起，做成长方体形，肋片用套片机套在管簇上，然后向管内充压力水，使管簇涨大与肋片充分接触，保证散热效果。

冷凝器根据制冷剂在其中的流动情况不同有上进下出和横进横出式。上进下出式冷凝器在工作过程中，制冷剂蒸气从上部的分配集管进入每根蛇管中，冷凝后的液体沿蛇管向下流动，汇于集液管中，然后流入储液器。这种结构每根蛇管的流程较长，蛇管后面部分常被液体充满，使得传热效率降低，故也有用横进横出式结构的，这种冷凝器工作过程中制冷剂基本是在一个水平面上流动，可实现散热。图4-2-2为横进横出式冷凝器。

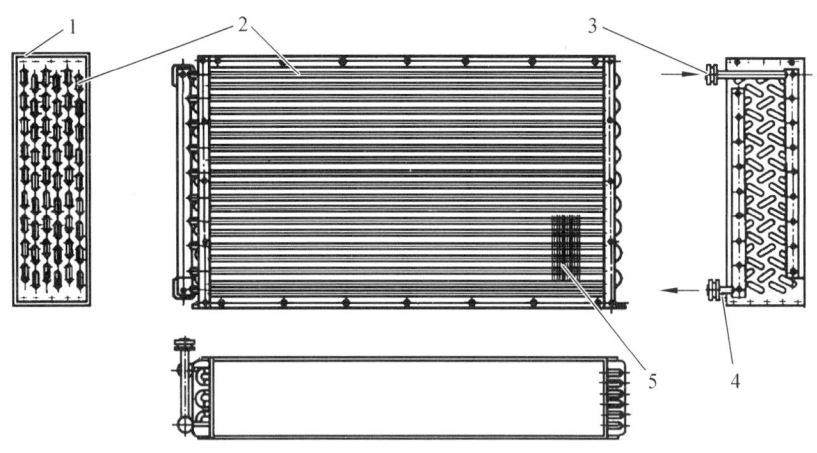

1—外框；2—蛇管；3—进气管；4—出液管；5—肋片。

图 4-2-2 横进横出式冷凝器

客车空调制冷装置为扩大冷凝器的容量，常将冷凝器设计成并联工作的两组。

（二）影响冷凝器换热的因素

制冷剂在冷凝器中流动通过冷却介质（空气或水）向外散热，在该过程中有很多因素会对其散热效果造成影响。

如冷凝器内壁面的粗糙度，冷凝液膜在内壁面上的厚度，不仅与制冷剂液体黏度等因素有关，内壁面粗糙度对其也有很大的影响。当壁面很粗糙或有氧化皮时，液膜流动阻力增大，使液膜增厚，换热系数降低。因此，应保持冷凝器内表面光滑和清洁，以获得较大的凝结换热系数。影响冷凝器换热的，还有以下因素：

1. 制冷剂对换热的影响

（1）制冷剂蒸气的流速和流向。制冷剂在冷凝器中的凝结一般都是膜状凝结，当制冷剂蒸气与低于饱和温度的冷凝器壁面接触时，便凝结成一层液体薄膜，液膜在重力作用下向下流动。液膜是冷凝器中制冷剂侧的热阻，液膜越厚，热阻越大，换热系数越小。当制冷剂蒸气的流动方向与液膜的流动方向一致时，冷凝液体与传热表面（冷凝器的管路）分离较快，换热系数增大，而且随蒸气流速的增加而增加。因此适当增加蒸气的流速，可获得较大的换热系数。

（2）制冷剂蒸气的过热度。制冷系统在工作过程中，进入冷凝器的是温度为 40~50℃ 的过热蒸气，过热蒸气必须先冷却成饱和蒸气后才能凝结。而过热蒸气冷却时的放热系数较小，因此过热度越高，将使整个冷凝过程的换热系数越低。

（3）制冷剂蒸气中是否含有不凝性气体。在制冷系统中，总会有一些不凝性气体存在，如组装、检修时不慎或低压段处有渗漏点进入了空气以及制冷剂、润滑油在高温下分解出的氮气、氢气等，这些不凝性气体在冷凝器中附着在凝结液膜上，由于不凝性气体的分压力很高，因而使制冷剂蒸气的压力减小，其饱和温度也相应降低，制冷剂蒸气的凝结速度减慢。因此应注意防止空气等不凝性气体进入系统，一旦进入要及时排出。

（4）制冷剂中是否含有润滑油。如果制冷剂与润滑油不相溶，随制冷剂蒸气进入冷凝器的润滑油将形成油膜沉积在冷凝器内表面上，降低换热系数。通常制冷剂都能与润滑油互溶，当润滑油浓度小于 6%~7% 时，可不考虑对传热的影响，如超过此限，换热系数也将降低。

2. 冷却介质对换热的影响

（1）冷却介质的流速及流量。换热系数随着冷却介质的流速及流量增加而增大。但是流速太大，会使通过冷凝器的流动阻力增加，从而增加功率消耗。客车空调运用中，综合考虑技术经济指标，一般取空气流速为 2~4 m/s。

（2）冷凝器冷却介质的洁净程度。冷凝器长期使用后，表面会积灰尘或水垢等，这会影响冷凝器的传热效果，因此应定期对冷凝器清扫或清洗。

3. 肋片和肋管对换热的影响

（1）肋片的效率。肋片的材质和面积不同会使其换热能力有所不同，客车空调中都采用铝片作为肋片，并增大传热面积，提升换热效果。

（2）肋管的排列方式。肋管的结构形式、排列方式不同，其换热能力都会有所不同，如管束的散热能力就大于光管的。客车空调的冷凝器均采用多根蛇管并联。

我国现行客车空调中均采用并联的铜蛇管，加铝制肋片的结构，肋管结构对换热影响的变化不大，故在运用中主要考虑空气和制冷剂的影响。

三、换热器清洗作业

（一）工作前准备

（1）准备工具：喷淋壶、铝材清洁剂、高压冲洗机、航空插头护套。

（2）清洁剂不能直接接触皮肤，操作时应带胶皮防护手套、护目镜。

（3）开启排气扇，保持通风良好。

（4）用护套包扎好航空插头，防止配线及线管进水。航空插头严禁落地，防止插针、插孔出现碰伤、脏堵等情况。

（二）清洗作业

图 4-2-3　清洗作业

（1）使用喷淋壶向换热器表面均匀喷洒清洁剂。

（2）静置 15 分钟后，使用高压冲洗机对空调机组蒸发器、冷凝器等部位进行清洗。

（3）冲洗后用 pH 试纸检测冷凝器、蒸发器翅片四角及中心区域残留液的 pH 值，pH 值呈中性确保无酸、碱性溶液残留。

（4）将清洗好的空调机组摆放到组装工位，摆放平稳，配线无挤压。

（5）使用干燥压缩空气将配线及航空插头残留水分去除。

（三）工作后整理

（1）切断电源，清点工具，确认状态良好并擦拭干净后放入工具箱内，做好设备保养，离岗前确认电闸关闭、周围无杂物、无火源后方可退岗。

（2）填记一车一档内相关记录。字迹清晰，记录准确，无遗漏。

任务三　制冷装置的自动控制器件

【任务目标】

（1）掌握膨胀阀和毛细管的结构和原理。

（2）理解温度控制器和压力控制器的结构和原理。

【知识储备】

制冷自动化设备一般通过控制器、传感器、调节结构及执行机构来完成系统的自动控制和保护。节流装置是控制空调制冷系统的供液量和节流降压的元件；温度控制器是控制调节室内温度的元件；压力控制器是压缩机的压力保护元件；电磁阀是控制制冷剂管路通断的自动阀件。

一、节流装置

（一）膨胀阀

膨胀阀是空调制冷系统的节流降压、调节流量的阀件，可自动调节制冷系统中制冷剂的流量。常用的有以下三种：

（1）热力膨胀阀：利用蒸发器出口过热度来控制制冷剂流量。
（2）热电膨胀阀：靠电加热产生的热量驱动阀杆来控制制冷剂流量。
（3）电子膨胀阀：通过电子信号实现制冷剂流量的控制。

1. 热力膨胀阀

热力膨胀阀是一种能自动调节供液量的节流降压机构。它是利用蒸发器出口处制冷剂蒸气的过热度来调节制冷剂流量的。由于膨胀阀具有自动调节制冷剂流量的功能，因此在采用膨胀阀节流的系统中，通常配有储液器。在早期的分体式客车空调装置制冷系统中，就采用了热力膨胀阀作为节流装置。

热力膨胀阀根据其膜片下方所检测压力的不同，可分为内平衡式和外平衡式两种，内平衡式检测的是蒸发器入口的压力，而外平衡式则检测蒸发器出口的压力。

1）内平衡式热力膨胀阀

内平衡式热力膨胀阀的结构如图 4-3-1 所示，它主要由感温包、毛细导管、膜片、顶杆、阀座、阀针及调节机构等组成。膨胀阀安装在蒸发器的进口管上，感温包包扎在蒸发器的出口处。感温包、毛细导管及膜盒（膜片上方空腔）构成的密闭空间称感温系统。在感温系统中充注低沸点液体，该系统感受制冷剂离开蒸发器时的温度，与该温度相对应的感温系统中蒸气的饱和压力经毛细管传至膜片上方，使膜片受一向下的推力 P_1。膜片下方承受两个向上的力：一个是经过阀孔节流后制冷剂的压力 P_0，通过传动杆与阀体间的空隙传递到膜片下方；另一个是阀针下面弹簧的弹力 P_2，通过传动杆作用在膜片下方。膜片在这三个力作用下保持平衡（忽略重力），即

$$P_1 = P_0 + P_2$$

① 当蒸发器的供液量较少时，蒸发器出口处制冷剂蒸气的过热度增大，因而使感温包中蒸气温度升高，压力 P_1 增大。由于 $P_1 > (P_0 + P_2)$，使膜片向下弯曲，并通过传动杆压缩阀针下面的弹簧使阀针下移，阀孔开大，供液量增加。

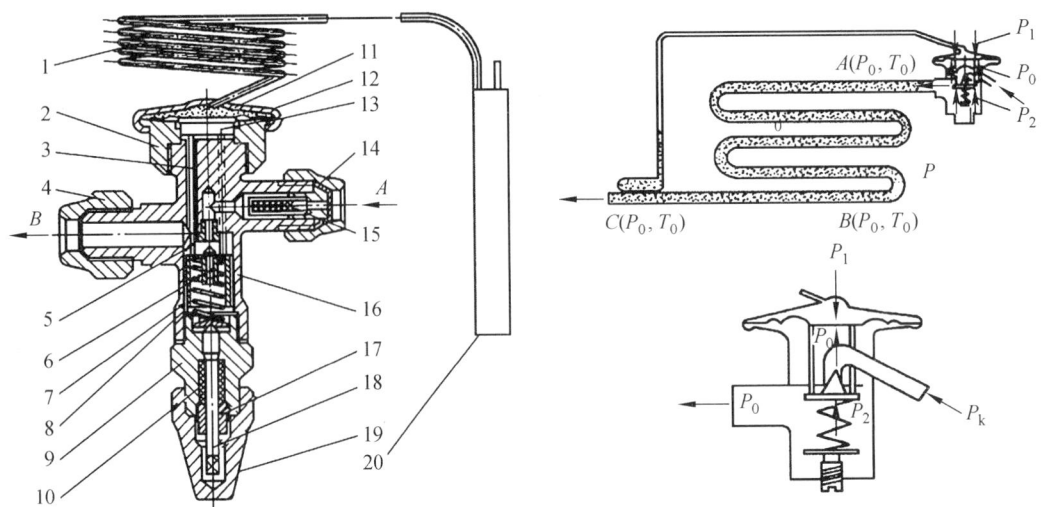

1—毛细管；2—密封室座；3—传动杆；4—出管锁母；5—座孔体；6—阀针；7—阀针座；8—弹簧；9—调节阀；10—密封填料；11—密封盖；12—波纹薄膜；13—传动盘；14—进管锁母；15—滤网；16—阀体；17—填料压母；18—调节杆；19—螺母；20—感温包。

图 4-3-1 内平衡式热力膨胀阀

② 当蒸发器的供液量较多时，蒸发器出口处制冷剂蒸气过热度减小，感温系统中的压力 P_1 降低，$P_1 < (P_0 + P_2)$，阀针上移，将阀孔关小，供液量随之减少。

③ 当蒸发器的供液量比较稳定时，蒸发器出口处制冷剂蒸气过热度稳定，感温系统中的压力 P_1 基本无变化，$P_1 = (P_0 + P_2)$，阀针不动，供液量不变化。

在客车空调制冷系统中，通常采用内平衡式热力膨胀阀。

2）外平衡式热力膨胀阀

外平衡式热力膨胀阀的结构与内平衡式热力膨胀阀基本相同，不同之处是前者的膜片下方不与供入蒸发器的制冷剂相通，而是设有一个空腔，用平衡管与蒸发器出口连通。因此，它的膜片下方不再承受蒸发器进口处制冷剂压力，而是蒸发器出口处制冷剂的压力。外平衡式热力膨胀阀在膜片上下所受的力均来自蒸发器的出口，对制冷剂流量的调节更精确。所以当蒸发器冷却盘管较长，阻力损失较大，特别是低温情况下，应采用外平衡式热力膨胀阀。

3）热力膨胀阀的不足

热力膨胀阀以蒸发器出口处温度为控制信号，通过感温包将此信号转换成感温包内蒸气的压力，进而控制膨胀阀阀针的开度，达到反馈调节的目的。热力膨胀阀在应用中存在一些不足之处：

① 信号的反馈有较大的滞后，因而使制冷装置在启动和负荷突变时，被调参数发生周期性振荡。

② 低的蒸发温度下，过热度增大，蒸发温度不稳定，制冷系统效率下降。

③ 制冷剂流量调节范围小。因为薄膜的变形量有限，从而使阀针开度的变化范围较小。
④ 允许负荷变动小。

为了克服以上的缺点和不足，热电膨胀阀和电子膨胀阀就出现了。

2. 热电膨胀阀

热电膨胀阀是将一只热敏电阻串接在阀加热器的电路中，电路中的电流与热敏电阻阻值有关，而热敏电阻阻值又与热敏电阻所处的制冷剂状态有关。将热敏电阻暴露在制冷剂中，当蒸发器出口为过热蒸气时，由于加热作用，使热敏电阻温度升高，电阻值下降，电路中的电流增大，阀加热器上的电压升高将阀开大，使制冷剂流量增加。制冷剂液滴或湿蒸气接触到热敏电阻时，使之冷却，热敏电阻阻值升高，阀又开始关小。最终结果是将阀稳定在蒸发器出口所选定过热度蒸汽状态所对应的开度上。

为了达到良好的控制性能，热敏电阻可根据所需控制的过热度要求进行更换。热电膨胀阀可以在高精度的范围内控制制冷剂流量，特别适用于热泵装置。

3. 电子膨胀阀

电子膨胀阀是以电子控制器实现制冷系统制冷剂流量的控制，使制冷装置处于最佳运行状态而开发的新型制冷系统控制器件。电子膨胀阀的应用，克服了热力膨胀阀的缺点。电子膨胀阀有电磁式和电动式两种。它具有反应快、适应范围大的特点。

电子膨胀阀的组成如图 4-3-2 所示，由检测、控制和执行三大部分构成。采用电机直接驱动轴，以改变阀的开度。该阀接收由控制器传来的信号进行动作，驱动转子回转，将其以螺旋回转运动转换为轴的直线运动，用其轴端头的针阀调整节流孔开口的大小，来调节制冷剂流量。

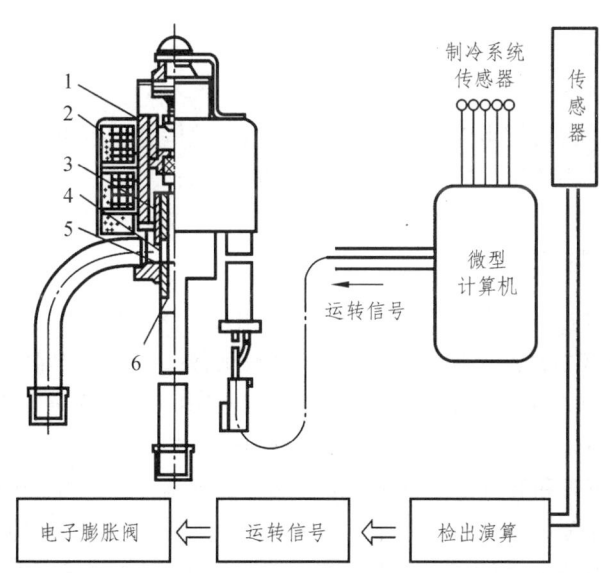

1—电机转子；2—电机定子；3—螺旋部；4—轴；5—针阀；6—节流孔。

图 4-3-2 电子膨胀阀

(二)毛细管

当制冷剂流体沿管内流动时,由于管道摩擦阻力而产生压降,管径越小、管子越长则流动阻力就越大,产生的压降也越大。利用这一性质,在一些封闭式压缩机、小型制冷装置中,采用小内径(0.6~2.0 mm)并有一定长度(0.6~2.5 m)的紫铜管,代替膨胀阀作为节流降压元件,连接在冷凝器与蒸发器之间,作为制冷循环的节流降压元件,这种细长的管路就是毛细管节流装置。

毛细管节流装置的优点是结构简单,价格低廉,无运动部件,不易产生漏泄,不存在节流机构进、出口的问题,而且在压缩机停车后,冷凝器与蒸发器内的压力可较快地自动达到平衡,减轻起动时电动机的负载,很适用于装有全封闭式活塞压缩机的制冷系统。

但毛细管节流主要的缺点是其供液量不能随工况变动而调节。因毛细管的长度和直径是根据一定的工况确定的,如果使毛细管的供液量能随工况的变化而变化,就得使毛细管的直径能随工况的变化而变化,显然,这是不可能的。采用毛细管节流的制冷装置,当蒸发压力下降时,容易引起压缩机的湿冲程;当蒸发压力上升时,容易出现蒸发器供液不足的情况。因此,毛细管节流宜用于蒸发温度变化范围不大、负荷比较稳定的场合,且通常在系统中配有气液分离器,以防止压缩机湿冲程,而不配储液器。

另外采用毛细管节流的制冷装置,对制冷剂充注量十分敏感。所以制冷剂充注量要很准确,否则影响制冷装置的正常工作。毛细管可以用一根也可以多根并联。当用多根并联时要配分液器,且应仔细调整,使这些毛细管的工作情况大致相同(可由结霜情况来判断)。在毛细管前应设过滤器,以防毛细管脏堵。毛细管的供液能力主要取决于毛细管入口处制冷剂的状态(压力和温度)以及毛细管的几何尺寸长度和内径。

二、温度控制器

温度控制器又称温度继电器,是对室温及其波动范围进行控制的电路开关,常用它控制压缩机的开停。常用的温度控制器有机械式和电子式。

(一)机械式温度控制器

WT-1226 型温度控制器在空调制冷系统中使用较广泛,其动作原理如图 4-3-3 所示。

WT-1226 型温控器是两位控制式,即有两个静触头。电源线与静触头 B 和动触头 A 连接。动触头 A 串联在压缩机电机交接触器线圈电路中,动触头 A 与静触头 B 接触,压缩机运转;动触头 A 与静触头 B 断开,压缩机停止运转。

由感温包、毛细管和波纹管室组成温度控制器的感温系统。感温包根据控制温度范围的不同,内充不同工质(如乙醚、丙酮、氟利昂等)。感温包把检测的室温变化,变为波纹管室内气体对波纹管压力的变化(温度与压力成正比)。波纹管压力的变化使杠杆绕支架发生转动。感温包检测的温度下降到整定值时,波纹管的顶力矩小于定值弹簧的拉力矩,杠杆绕刀口支架顺时针转动,动触头 A 与静触头 B 断开,压缩机停车。当感温包检测的

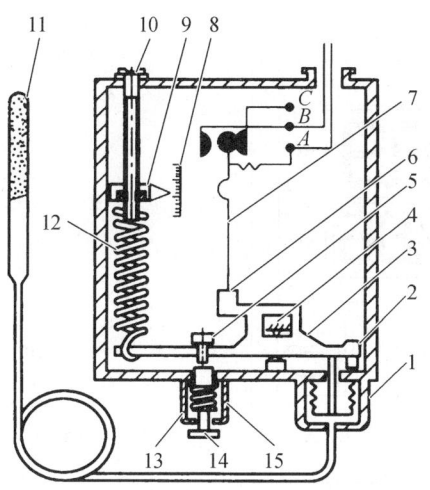

1—波纹管室；2—止动螺钉；3—杠杆；4—支架；5—螺钉；6—拨臂；7—弹簧；8—主标尺；9—指针；10—调节螺杆；11—感温包；12—主弹簧；13—差动弹簧；14—差动旋钮；15—差动器。

图 4-3-3　WT-1226 型温度控制器

温度上升，波纹管推动杠杆克服定值弹簧的拉力矩逆时针转动，转过一定角度后杠杆又要克服差动弹簧的弹力方可继续转动。当温度升到整定值加幅差值时，动触头 A 重新与静触头 B 闭合，压缩机转动。

因此，定值弹簧（主弹簧）的拉力决定所控制温度的下限值即整定值，其数值大小可以通过旋转调节螺杆，改变定值弹簧的拉力来整定。而幅差弹簧（差动弹簧）则决定控制温度上下限的范围即幅差值（也称差动值），幅差值可通过旋转差动旋钮进行整定。

（二）电子式温度控制器

电子式温度控制器，一般是利用热敏电阻等敏感元件感受温度变化，在电路中形成的微弱电信号作为其工作的输入信号，经测量、比较、放大后，控制继电器是否动作，从而控制微动开关的闭合或断开。现阶段的客车空调单元式空调装置中均采用电子式温控器。下面介绍客车空调常用的 E5AZ-R3-38 型电子式温度控制器的使用。

E5AZ-R3-38 型电子式温度控制器正面结构如图 4-3-4 所示。显示装置和常用的按键功能如下：

按菜单键 3 秒以上，可进入初始菜单，设置温度传感器的输入类型，按上调键或下调键设置该值，一般设置为 1。之后通过按模式键，并配合上调键或下调键可依次设置温度单位（°C）、ON/OFF 方式、报警 1-3 的报警功能（0 为无报警，8 为绝对值上限报警）、初始通信保护、低温控制输出控制温度、低温控制回差值、高温控制输出控制温度、高温控制回差值等参数。

按菜单键 1 秒以上，可进入运行菜单，将菜单键和模式键同时按 3 秒以上，可进入保护菜单。将菜单键和模式键同时按 1 秒以上，可再返回运行菜单。

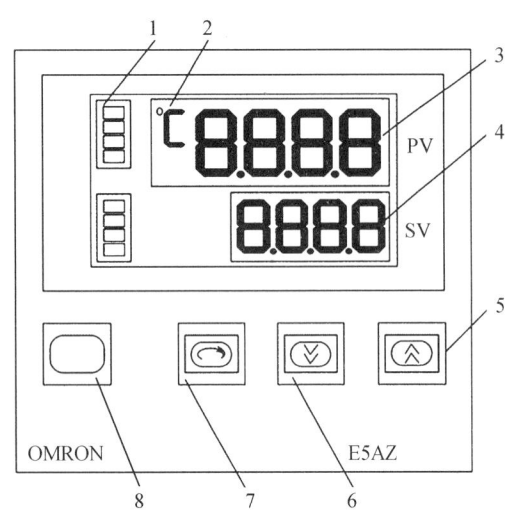 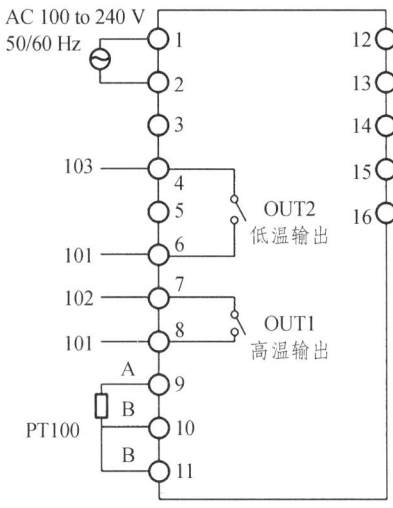

（a）E5AZ-R3-38型电子式温度控制器正面　　（b）温度控制器接线图

1—运行显示；2—温度单位；3—室温显示，显示各设定项目符号；温度控制器工作异常时，显示故障；
4—设定温度1显示，即显示控制输出1所设定的低温控制值；
5—上调键；6—下调键；7—模式键；8—菜单键。

图4-3-4　E5AZ-R3-38型电子式温度控制器

在温度控制器中，低温输出线路中串联了一个低温输出继电器的常开开关，可由温度控制器控制其通断。高温输出线路中串联了一个高温输出继电器的常开开关，可由控制器控制其通断。PT100温度传感器通过A、B、B三条线连接到温度控制器，给温度控制器提供实时的温度数据，由温度控制器决定低温输出继电器和高温输出继电器的通断。

三、压力控制器

压缩机作为空调制冷系统的动力设备，将低压制冷剂蒸气压缩成高压蒸气，推动制冷剂在制冷系统中循环往复。但是，压缩机排气口的压力是否达到要求？是否过高而造成危险？这就需要压力监测与控制装置，即压力控制器。压力控制器的作用是当监测到压缩机吸气或排气压力超出其正常工作范围时，自动切断压缩机工作电源使其停车，以保护压缩机。

压力控制器的形式有多种，结构也略有区别，但动作原理基本相同，都是以波纹管（膜片），接收到高压或低压部分的压力信号后，波纹管（膜片）变形，从而带动传动杆或杠杆机构，使电触点接通或断开，使压缩机工作或停机。

压力控制器包括高压控制器和低压控制器，有组合成一体的，也有各自做成单体的。高压控制器与压缩机的排气腔接通，以监视和控制排气压力。如果压缩排气压力过高，会导致压缩机电机过载运行而受损害，所以，当压缩机排气压力高于正常压力时高压控制器就发生作用，使压缩机停车。

低压控制器与压缩机的吸气腔接通,以监视和控制吸气压力。当压缩机吸气压力过低时,一方面会影响制冷机组的正常工作,甚至不能制冷而浪费电力,另一方面压缩机近于空载运行也会损害电机,故当压缩机吸气压力低于正常值时,低压控制器发生作用,使压缩机停车。

现行铁路客车中较多采用高、低压分开控制的形式,且其控制压力不可调节。下面仅对这两种压力控制器做简单介绍。

1)ACB 型高压控制器

图 4-3-5 为 ACB 型高压控制器,高压管接头与压缩机排气管连接,工作过程中,如果出现排气压力大于规定压力时,膜片被推动,进而推动顶杆将动触头与静触头分开,从而切断压缩机工作电路,使压缩机停止工作,保护压缩机。在压力正常时,动触头在弹性金属片的作用下始终和静触头接触,压缩机正常工作。

2)LCB 型低压控制器

图 4-3-6 为 LCB 型低压控制器示意图,其工作与高压控制器相似,在吸气压力太低时,膜片收缩,动触头在弹性金属片的作用下与静触头脱离,切断压缩机的工作电路,保护压缩机。当压缩机吸气压力正常时,顶杆推动动触头与静触头连接,压缩机正常工作。

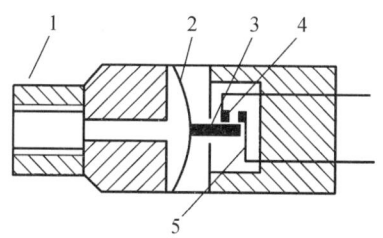

1—高压管接头;2—膜片;3—顶杆;
4—静触头;5—动触头。

图 4-3-5　ACB 型高压控制器

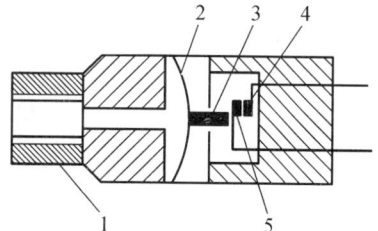

1—低压管接头;2—膜片;3—顶杆;
4—静触头;5—动触头。

图 4-3-6　LCB 型低压控制器

任务四　制冷装置的辅助设备

【任务目标】

(1)掌握气液分离器和分油器的结构与原理。
(2)理解热交换器、干燥过滤器和储液器的结构与原理。

【知识储备】

除了压缩机、换热器和自动控制器件之外,制冷系统还需要一些其他辅助设备来完成油剂分离、气液分离、制冷剂的存储与净化等工作。制冷剂在这些辅助设备中,状态并不变化，它们不是完成制冷循环所必需的设备，所以，在一些小型制冷机中，为简化设备起见，往往将一些辅助设备省去。但是在中大型制冷设备中，为了改善制冷机的工作条件，保证制冷机正常运转和提高运行经济性，这些辅助设备是必不可少的。

一、气液分离器

气液分离器的作用是用来分离蒸发器出口的蒸气中的液体，从而保证压缩机为干压缩。对于毛细管节流的制冷装置由于制冷剂流量不能自动调节，当负荷减小时，蒸发器中制冷剂就有可能不能完全蒸发，如果制冷压缩机吸入了带有液滴的制冷剂蒸气，就有可能产生液击而使阀片、活塞、连杆等损坏。因此为了避免压缩机吸入液体制冷剂，制冷压缩机的回气管上可装设气液分离器，对制冷剂蒸气中的液体分离储存。气液分离器结构如图 4-4-1 所示。

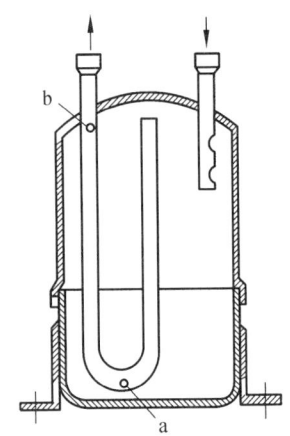

图 4-4-1 气液分离器结构示意

气液分离器的作用原理是：从蒸发器来的制冷剂蒸气由进气管进入分离器后，由于气流突然转向和减速，把液滴分离出来留在容器的底部，而气体则从出气管被压缩机吸入。在 U 形管的底部开有一个小孔 a，能使一定量的冷冻机油随吸入气体一起返回压缩机。b 孔为均压孔，可防止压缩机停机时由于蒸发器侧压力上升，使气液分离器中的液体通过 a 孔流向压缩机。

二、分油器

空调制冷系统中，作为动力设备，压缩机是需要润滑油润滑的。因为它能对各运动副起润滑、散热作用，还能提高活塞与气缸之间的密封性。制冷剂能与润滑油一定程度的相互溶解，R12 能完全溶解，R22 能轻微溶解，所以压缩机的排气中都带有润滑油。另外，压缩机高温部分的润滑油气化成油蒸气，与制冷剂蒸气一起被压缩机排出至冷凝器中，降温后油蒸气又被凝结成液态混于制冷剂中。

除了压缩机,润滑油在制冷系统的其他部件中,非但没有好处还有很多害处。当润滑油被压缩机排气带入制冷系统时,它与制冷剂液体互溶后会使蒸发温度稍有升高,还可能影响传热性能与制冷量。过多的润滑油积存在蒸发器中,会使蒸发器传热面减少;若积存在管路中,还可能阻塞管道。润滑油进入膨胀阀小孔或毛细管中,由于制冷剂节流时,温度突然下降,部分冷冻油积存于小孔处,其黏度升高,甚至可能析出石蜡等而将小孔阻塞。

为改善这种不利状况,可采用润滑油分离器(简称分油器),它能将混在压缩机排气管制冷剂中的大部分润滑油分离出来,并使其自动地回流至压缩机中。制冷剂中还有少量的润滑油,可在制冷剂气流带动下经压缩机吸气管返回压缩机,从而可维持压缩机曲轴箱中的油位,尽量减少润滑油对制冷过程的不良影响。

分油器的工作原理是:分油器安装在压缩机排气口与冷凝器之间,它的基本工作原理是利用液态油滴和制冷剂蒸气的比重不同,使混合气体流经直径较大的油分离器时,突然扩大通过面积,降低其流速,同时改变其流向或利用离心力,使油滴沉降而分离。对于润滑油蒸气,则可采用洗涤或水冷却的方式降低其温度,使之凝结为油滴而分离。有的油分离器中,则采用设置过滤层等方法来增强分离效果。

常用的分油器,用于氨系统的有洗涤式、填料式和离心式三种结构形式。因为氨系统的制冷现在很少利用,故主要介绍用于氟利昂系统的过滤式油分离器。过滤式油分离器的结构如图 4-4-2 所示。

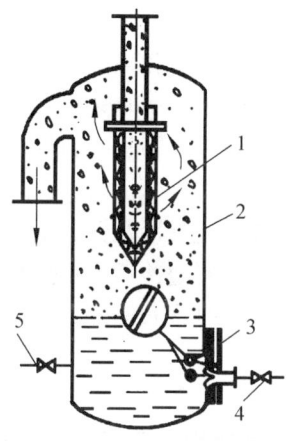

1—滤网;2—壳体;3—浮球阀;4—自动回油阀;5—手动回油阀。

图 4-4-2 过滤式油分离器

其壳体由无缝钢管加上、下封头焊接而成。顶部焊有进气管,在进气管的下方装有钢丝滤网,有的分离器内装有陶瓷环或钢丝绒。带有油雾的高压蒸气经滤网的过滤,一部分油雾与滤网接触,被粘在滤网上,聚积成滴后,下落在分油器底部。另一方面,高压蒸气在排气管内流速很高,一般在 10~25 m/s 之间。当流入分油器后,由于容器的通道面积大十几倍以至几十倍,蒸气流入分油器后流速突然降低,其流速一般不超过 0.8~1 m/s,加上蒸气进出分油器时流向改变，使蒸气容易与容器壁相撞，一部分油雾粘在容器壁上，聚集成滴流至容器底部。同时润滑油比制冷剂蒸气重得多，低流速时，油雾在重力作用下，与蒸气分离，落至容器底部，因此，制冷剂蒸气中的大部分润滑油就被分离出来，积贮在容器中。

当容器底部积贮的润滑油油位足够高将浮球浮起时，连在浮球上的阀针被打开，润滑油在高压作用下，经与压缩机曲轴箱连通的输油管流回曲轴箱，当容器内油位下降，浮球也随之下降，阀针将阀口关闭，回油结束。由此可见，当制冷机在连续的正常工作中，分油器也在连续不断地分油，但分油器放油回曲轴箱是断续进行的。只有当容器内达到一定的油位，阀针才被浮球打开而放油。

三、热交换器

热交换器又称"气-液换热器"，是用于氟利昂制冷系统的一种换热器。从冷凝器来的高温制冷剂液体与从蒸发器来的低温蒸气在其中进行热交换，液体获得过冷，蒸气产生过热。这种回热循环有三个好处：

（1）对于采用R12、R500、R502等制冷剂的系统，通过回热，提高制冷机的制冷系数。

（2）使液体获得过冷，以避免在节流阀前汽化（液体在节流阀前汽化时会影响热力膨胀阀的供液量）。

（3）使蒸气中夹带的液滴（包括油滴中溶解的液体）汽化，防止压缩机发生液击。

热交换器的结构一般采用如图4-4-3所示的套管形式，其外壳由直径较大的无缝钢管两端加封头焊制而成，而内管则为外侧带有肋片的肋管组成。因为制冷剂蒸气对壁面的放热系数比液体小，故气体沿有肋片一侧的外管流动，而液体沿内管逆向流动，以进行热交换。热交换器在制冷系统中的安装位置是在冷凝器、压缩机及蒸发器之间，即自冷凝器来的液体流经热交换器的内管，再一次获得过冷后，受膨胀阀的控制而进入蒸发器。而蒸发器出来的蒸气由回气管引入热交换器，使之过热后，由压缩机吸入。

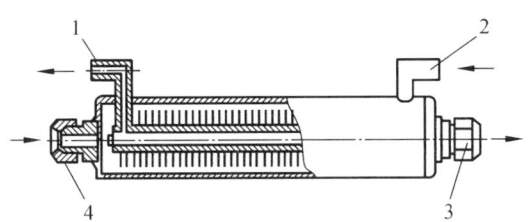

1—出液口；2—进液口；3—出气口；4—进气口。

图4-4-3 套管式回热器

实际使用的还有螺旋管式热交换器，其结构及作用原理与套管式相同，仅中间的肋片管由紫铜管绕制成螺旋形来代替。在客车空调装置中，当管路较长时，也有将输液管和吸气管包扎在一起以代替热交换器使用的。

四、干燥过滤器

在客车空调装置制冷系统进入节流装置前的输液管上,都装有干燥过滤器,它是制冷系统的净化设备。它的作用是消除制冷剂中的水分和杂质(如金属屑末、氧化皮等),以防止水和杂质在膨胀阀(毛细管)、电磁阀处产生冰塞、堵塞以及进入压缩机刮伤气缸和吸排气阀等。另外,也防止了水长期溶解于制冷剂分解而产生盐酸、氢氟酸腐蚀金属及使冷冻机油乳化。

干燥过滤器主要由壳体、滤网、干燥剂、进出液管接头等组成,其结构如图 4-4-4 所示。外壳为无缝钢管,在进口端内装有 2~3 层网孔为 0.1~0.2 mm 的铜丝网,两端有端盖用螺纹与壳体连接,再用锡焊焊接,以防泄漏。端盖外端焊有管接头,以便与系统管路连接。在过滤网与壳体中间装有干燥剂,常用的干燥剂有硅胶、活性氧化铝及分子筛等。有的制冷装置将干燥器和过滤器分别独立安装,如分装式客车空调装置制冷系统。单元式空调机组中采用的干燥过滤器为两端焊接的整体式。

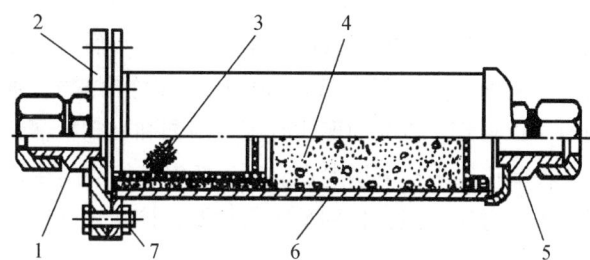

1—进液管接头;2—压盖;3—滤网;4—干燥剂;5—出液管接头;6—壳体;7—连接螺栓。

图 4-4-4 干燥过滤器

五、储液器

储液器亦称贮液器,是用来储存制冷循环中的制冷剂液体,以适应工况变动时制冷剂流量的变化。另外,在检修制冷设备及在制冷系统较长时间不工作时,将系统中制冷剂全部收集在储液器中,以免泄漏而造成损失。

储液器有立式和卧式,但在实际使用中多为卧式,其结构很简单,图 4-4-5 为卧式储

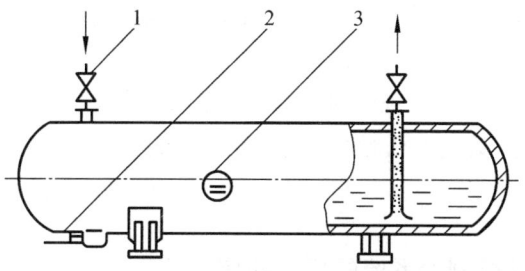

1—进液阀;2—放油排污口;3—视液镜。

图 4-4-5 储液器

液器。储液器的筒体由钢板卷制而成，筒体上设进、出液口，其安装位置应低于冷凝器，容积应大于需储存的制冷剂液体的体积，储存的制冷剂量不允许超过容积的80%。对于负荷变动不大的制冷设备，如单元式空调机组制冷系统，经严格控制充入的制冷剂量，可不用储液器。

任务五　制冷装置的检漏及气密性试验

【任务目标】

（1）掌握制冷装置的检漏及气密性试验方法。
（2）会进行抽真空试验作业。

【知识储备】

制冷设备和管路，经过空运转、空气负荷试车和系统排污后，将各设备和管路连接并封闭成一个制冷系统后，对整个系统进行气密性试验（简称检漏）。通过气密性试验及时发现系统漏泄点并及时予以处理。检漏的形式有压力检漏和真空检漏，并用肥皂水或浸水法、卤素检漏灯和卤素检漏仪等来检测漏泄点。对于新安装好的制冷装置或经过大修的制冷设备，一般都要通过上述方法检漏，特别是压力检漏，检漏合格后，方可进行下一步的工作。

一、压力检漏

压力检漏是将具有一定压力的空气或氮气充入制冷系统，使设备和管道受压，以检查安装后的接头、焊缝、管材和设备是否严密。

压力检漏所用的气源，对于氨制冷机组通常采用压缩空气；对于氟利昂制冷系统一般采用工业氮气。氮气具有价廉、无腐蚀、无水分、不燃不爆等优点，广泛地作为氟利昂制冷系统的试压气源。用钢瓶装的压缩氮气，装满瓶时其压力高达 14 710 kPa，使用时应根据操作规程的要求，在钢瓶出口处加装带压力表的减压阀，以控制试漏时的充气压力。

由于不同的制冷剂在制冷系统中的工作压力不同，检漏时，试漏压力要求不同，应根据系统所使用的制冷剂，确定其试漏时的充气压力。试压的方法应根据不同的压缩机采用不同的方法。

（一）开启式压缩机制冷系统的压力检漏

图 4-5-1 为开启式压缩机制冷系统的压力检漏操作示意图。

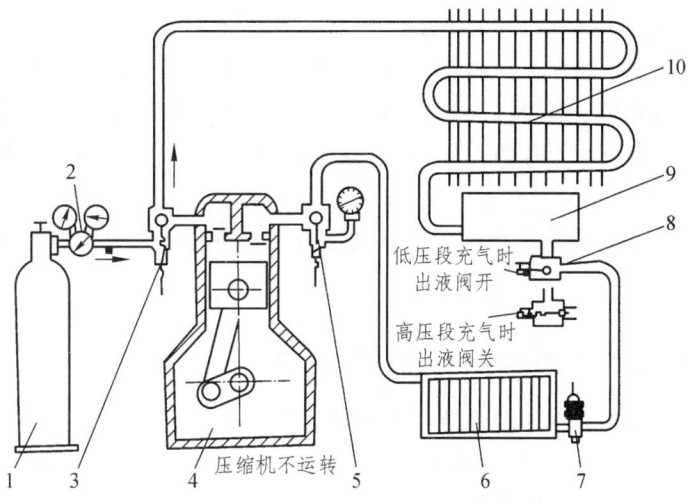

1—氮气瓶；2—减压阀；3—排气截止阀；4—压缩机；5—吸气截止阀；
6—蒸发器；7—膨胀阀；8—出液阀；9—储液器；10—冷凝器。

图 4-5-1　开启式压缩机制冷系统压力检漏

（1）将制冷系统中连通大气的阀门关闭，其他阀门全部打开（如有电磁阀，应通电令其打开）。用铜管或耐压胶管将氮气瓶与压缩机排气截止阀"多用通道"孔锥牙接头接起来，转动阀杆，使"多用通道"与截止阀处于全开状态。

（2）旋开氮气钢瓶上的阀门，此时钢瓶上的高压压力表将指示出钢瓶内氮气的压力值。按顺时针方向慢慢旋动减压阀阀杆，另一只压力表指示出减压后的压力，此压力随减压阀开度的增大而增大，直到压力表指示值达到规定低压侧压力值后，即停止转动减压阀阀杆，等系统内充足氮气后，关掉储液器出液阀。再开大减压阀，使储液器出液阀前的高压侧升到规定值，稍等 10～20 s 就停止充气，关闭减压阀及压缩机排气截止阀上的多用通道保压。但应注意：若排气阀片有严重渗漏，则高压侧压力不能充到规定值。为此，可在吸气截止阀多用通道处装一只量程为 1.6×10^6 Pa 的压力表，检查低压侧压力升高的状况，及时发现排气阀片的渗漏。

（3）拆下排气截止阀上的充气管，将锥形螺塞旋上拧紧。顺时针转动排气截止阀阀杆，将排气截止阀关闭，以防高压侧氮气向低压侧流动。

（4）将肥皂液涂在接头的缝隙与焊缝处。每涂一处，仔细观察有无气泡出现，有气泡出现，则该处有漏泄。查出漏泄点应做好标记，若在接头处发现泄漏，应设法旋紧后再次检漏，待全部检漏完毕后，再进行补漏。

（5）补漏：补漏时应将系统内氮气全部放空，经过补焊、接头更换垫片或重新扩制喇叭口后再次进行充气检漏，直至系统内不漏为止。

（6）保压：为避免微小渗漏处被漏检，当检漏完毕时，不要将系统内氮气放掉，记下压力值并保压，经 24～48 h 后，观察压力有无变化。一般由于环境温度变化而压力下降 1.0×10^4～3.0×10^4 Pa 时，则属正常。压力明显下降，应查明原因或复检。

（7）用分段检查法查找泄漏点：对于辅助阀或设备较多的系统，若检漏过程中发现压力显著下降,但原因不好查,可采用分段检查法,即关闭所有阀门,切断各管路间的相互连通关系。保压过 7~8 h 后,从高压侧压力表查起,逐次旋开各阀门,每打开一个,观察压力表读数。若打开某一阀门后,压力值明显下降,则说明该阀之后的一段管路处很可能有泄漏点,应重点检查。如有必要,可拆下这一段的部件,进行单独充气保压,并浸入水池里检漏。

有时,也可在制冷系统中充注少量氟利昂蒸气,再充入规定压力的氮气,用校漏灯校漏。

(二)单元式空调装置制冷系统的压力检漏

由于单元式空调装置的制冷系统一般都采用全封闭式压缩机和毛细管节流,在制冷系统中没有任何阀门。因此要对系统进行压力检漏可先在压缩机的灌气口接一只修理阀,进行充氮保压试验,并进行泄漏检查。

在充入氮气之前先注入少量的制冷剂,通过修理阀入口注入干燥的氮气,对于 R12 的制冷系统,充注压力为 10^6 Pa;对于 R22 的制冷系统,充注压力为 1.5×10^6 Pa。充注完毕后进行 24 h 保压试验。在试验中,前 6 h 的压力降不应超过 2%,其余 18 h 应能保持压力稳定(环境温度变化造成的影响除外)。

对于其他家用空调制冷机组也可依此办法进行压力检漏。

二、真空检漏

(一)真空检漏目的

真空检漏一般是在压力检漏合格后,将制冷系统内的压力空气或氮气泄压,再进行真空检漏。其目的是:

(1)进一步检查制冷系统在低压状态下的密封性能,特别是在真空状态下的密封性能,防止设备和管路有单向漏气的缺陷,防止外界空气的不断渗入。

(2)通过真空检漏将系统内的空气或氮气抽尽。由于空气或氮气在常温下属于不凝结气体,在系统工作时,它们将在冷凝器中占据一定的容积,减少了冷凝器的传热面积,降低传热效率,使冷凝压力增高,而影响制冷效果。

(3)通过真空检漏排除系统内的水分,使水分在低压下蒸发,达到干燥之目的。

(4)为充注制冷剂做准备。

(二)进行真空检漏的方法

主要有利用单独的真空泵进行真空检漏和用制冷系统本身的压缩机进行真空检漏两种。对于大的制冷系统为了节省真空检漏的时间,也可用压缩机和真空泵交叉进行,即先用制冷系统的压缩机将系统内大量空气抽去,再用真空泵把残余的空气进一步抽出。

1. 利用系统的压缩机抽真空

如图 4-5-2 所示,开启式压缩机制冷系统抽真空的操作步骤如下:

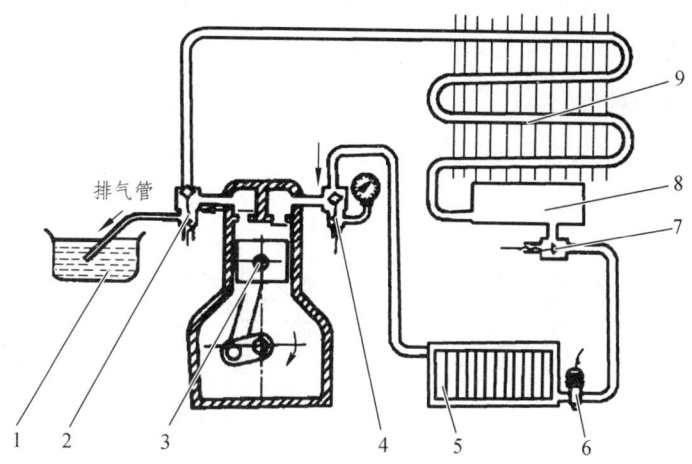

1—油杯;2—排气截止阀;3—压缩机;4—吸气截止阀;5—蒸发器;
6—膨胀阀;7—出液阀;8—储液器;9—冷凝器。

图 4-5-2 开启式压缩机制冷系统抽真空

(1)关闭压缩机的排气截止阀,旋下"多用通道"的螺塞,装上锥牙接头和排气管,少开吸气截止阀,并在吸气截止阀的旁通孔装低压表(真空压力表)。用手转动压缩机的飞轮或按下电源开关起动压缩机,开后即关,借此判断压缩机转向是否正确。判断压缩机排气管是否有气流喷出,若有气流声,可再重复检查一次,若无气流声,应查明原因。

(2)将压力控制器低压接点短接,使之保持常通状态,以免在抽真空过程中,触点动作起保护,而影响机组的抽真空。

(3)起动压缩机抽气,直至排气管听不到喷气声时,将吸气截止阀开大,并将排气管口浸入冷冻机油油杯中,观察管口的冒气情况。

(4)在抽真空过程中,若在 5 min 内无气泡冒出,即可认为系统内的气体已基本抽完,且系统无渗漏。此时,可拆下排气管,用手指按住排气截止阀"多用通道"孔接口,或拆下锥牙接头,旋上螺塞并扳紧,将排气截止阀杆反旋退足(关闭"多用通道"),然后停机。抽气,工作基本结束。

(5)若有连续或间断的气泡冒出,说明系统内有剩余气体未抽净或有渗漏现象,此时可继续运行 1~2 h,通过磨合,排除轴封摩擦面不密合而出现的渗漏。若冒气泡依然出现,可采取分段抽空,检查每一段的密封性。先关闭压缩机的吸气截止阀,若几分钟内不冒气泡,说明渗漏不在压缩机内;将吸气阀重新打开,关闭储液器出液阀,观察冒气泡情况,这样分段检查下去,直到发现渗漏点。对有怀疑部位的接头顶紧程度以及焊缝可能有孔隙处应重点检查,必须将渗漏点找出补好,方可再继续抽真空。

2. 利用真空泵抽真空

对于较大型的压缩机或半封闭式压缩机所构成的制冷系统，一般不宜用自身的压缩机来抽真空，可用真空泵来抽真空。只要将真空泵的吸气口与排气截止阀的"多用通道"孔相接即可。抽真空结束时，应先将排气截止阀"多用通道"孔关闭，然后再停真空泵。

3. 利用真空泵检漏

由全封闭式压缩机所组成的制冷系统必须用真空泵进行检漏。其抽真空的操作如图 4-5-3 所示。

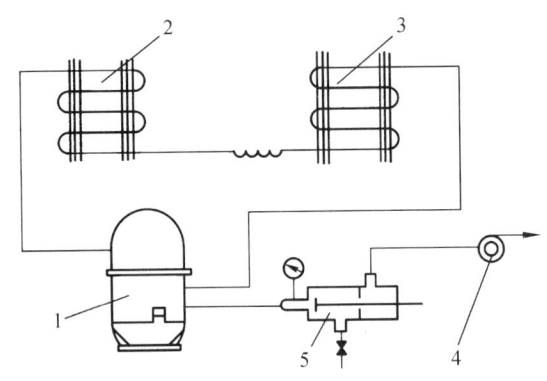

1—压缩机；2—冷凝器；3—蒸发器；4—真空泵；5—修理阀。

图 4-5-3　全封闭制冷系统真空泵安装

（1）将带压力真空表的修理阀 5 分别与真空泵 4，压缩机 1 的灌气管连接起来。

（2）打开修理阀 5，开启真空泵 4，观察压力真空表读书是否向零刻度以下方向移动，若不移动，表明系统有泄漏，应及时处理。

（3）当真空压力表指针达到或接近 -10^5 Pa 时，关闭修理阀 5，然后停止真空泵 4 运转，抽真空完毕。

制冷系统一次抽真空到规定的真空度时，所需时间较长，特别是灌气口在低压侧时，由于毛细管的节流作用，使高压侧真空度难以达到要求。这时，可采用两次抽真空法，即在第一次将系统抽真空后，注入少量制冷剂，使压力真空表恢复到零位，然后再一次抽真空（真空压力表指针指到 -10^5 Pa）。这样可在短时间内得到较高真空度。这是由于第一次抽真空后充入适量 R22 气体，使高压部分空气被 R22 冲淡，剩余气体中的空气比例减少。

（三）真空检漏操作时注意事项

真空度的要求一般是根据厂、段修修程规定执行。对于无明确规定的机组，可将当地当天的大气压力乘上 0.96 系数，即为所要抽的真空度，在此真空度下，稳压 18 h，若真空度稳定不变，即为合格。

（1）在抽真空时，各阀门的阀帽应盖上旋紧，以防阀杆填料渗漏。

（2）真空检漏应尽可能用真空泵来完成，特别是全封闭或半封闭压缩机的制冷系统，必须要用真空泵进行真空检漏。

（3）在用真空泵抽真空的系统管道中，最好设干燥器，以便吸出抽真空时系统内空气中的水分和有害气体，保证泵内油质完好。

对于采用压力润滑的压缩机在抽真空时，应注意它的油压大小，其油压和吸气压力的差值应不低于 26.7 kPa，若系统装有油压继电器，应将其接点暂时保持常通状态，以免再利用系统压缩机进行抽真空时，因油压继电器处在低于控制压差的情况下而动作。

抽真空时，最好把系统周围造成高温环境，有利于系统中的水分全部蒸发，随空气一起排出机外。

三、客车空调系统抽真空试验

（一）工作前准备

将制冷剂回收充注机推入机组流水现台位，准备进行制冷系统抽真空。

（二）制冷系统抽真空

（1）放掉制冷系统保压试验中氮气，将真空泵高压、低压管路同时与压力表连接。

（2）确保蓝色高、低压软管连接到空调制冷系统上，且控制面板上高、低压阀都是打开的。

（3）打开真空泵电源，按 SHIFT/RESET 键，触发显示屏显示出 "PROGRAM VACUUM MINUTES15.00"。15 min 设备所默认的抽真空时间，若要改变时间，就直接按相应的数字键，显示出所要的时间，然后按 ENTER 键。(KLD29 空调机组设定抽真值为 30 min，KLD40 空调机组设定时间为 40 min，按键盘相应的数字键，到所要的时间显示在显示屏上。然后按 ENTER 键)。

（4）按下 VACUUM 键，开始抽真空，此时显示屏上的数值将递减，显示所剩时间。

注：如果显示屏上有 "U-HI" 出现，此时必须进行压力排放（制冷剂回收），使空调系统压力降下来，才能继续进行抽真空。

（5）当设定的时间递减到 0，真空泵会自动停止。显示屏会显示 "CPL" 信息。真空泵高压、低压压力表达到绝对真空 0 MPa，则表示抽真空完成。

（6）系统抽真空至绝对压力 75 kPa 以下时，保持 5 min 后无变化。

注意：真空泵每累计运行 10 h，必须更换真空泵油。

（三）工作后整理

（1）关闭高压、低压阀，拆下连接到空调制冷系统上的红、绿色高、低压软管。

（2）填写《抽真空试验记录》。

（3）准备进行制冷剂充注。

【任务训练】

（1）涡旋式压缩机有何特点？

（2）冷凝器和蒸发器有什么作用？各有哪些类型？影响其换热的因素有哪些？

（3）膨胀阀有哪些类型？热力膨胀阀的作用是什么？说明热力膨胀阀的工作原理。

（4）简述 ACB 型和 LCB 型压力控制器的工作原理。

（5）分油器的作用是什么？简单说明过滤式分油器的工作原理。

（6）试述真空检漏的作用，如何进行真空检漏？

项目五　客车空调采暖及通风系统

【中国铁路文化】

中国铁路发展史 5　中非友谊的结晶

亚吉铁路，全称为埃塞俄比亚至吉布提标准轨距铁路，西起埃塞俄比亚的瑟伯塔站，东至及吉布提的吉布提多拉雷港站，全长752.7千米，设置45座车站，设计速度120千米/小时。亚吉铁路是非洲大陆一条连接埃塞俄比亚和吉布提以货运为主的铁路，是东非地区首条标准轨距电气化铁路，是落实"一带一路"倡议的早期收获，是中非"三网一化"和产能合作的标志性工程，是中国企业在海外建设的第一条全产业链的铁路，被誉为"新时期的坦赞铁路"。

图 5-0-1　亚吉铁路

2012年，亚吉铁路开工建设；2016年10月5日，亚吉铁路埃塞俄比亚段建成通车；2017年1月10日，亚吉铁路吉布提段建成通车；2018年1月1日，亚吉铁路开通商业运营。

亚吉铁路是海外首条集设计标准、投融资、装备材料、施工、监理和运营管理全产业链的铁路项目，是"一带一路"的标志性成果。亚吉铁路是中非历史友谊的延伸和发展，是中国'一带一路'倡议非洲业务板块的良好开端，对东非乃至非洲经济纵深发展发挥重要拉动作用。同时，来自中国等亚洲国家的货物也可通过亚吉铁路运输到埃塞俄比亚等非洲多国。

亚吉铁路不仅是一条运输线，更是一条经济走廊、一条繁荣之路，为世界唯一人口过亿的内陆国家埃塞打通了出海铁路大通道，并有效带动了铁路沿线工业化和城镇化发展，在疫情期间更是彰显了巨大价值。

【项目描述】

通过本项目学习，使学生掌握客车空调采暖及通风系统的设备及其结构、功能及运行原理，同时能运用所学知识保障25T型客车的采暖及通风系统的日常使用及定期检修。

【项目目标】

1. 知识目标

（1）掌握电加热和热泵制热的原理及维护方法。
（2）掌握客车通风系统各部分的结构及作用。
（3）掌握25T客车通风系统的维护方法。

2. 能力目标

（1）能够将学习的客车采暖和通风系统的知识用于检修作业。
（2）能够自主学习25T客车通风系统的维护周期及项目。
（3）能够完成25T客车通风系统日常检修作业。

3. 素养目标

（1）培养学以致用、勤思考、爱创新。
（2）培养灵活使用设备、爱护设备的意识和能力。
（3）培养规范作业、安全生产的意识和能力。
（4）培养团队协作精神。

任务一　电热采暖装置

【任务目标】

（1）掌握电热装置的结构与原理。
（2）掌握热泵的原理，理解热泵与制冷的区别与联系。
（3）掌握电热器的日常维护方法。

【知识储备】

冬季，尤其是北方，车外环境温度比较低，为保证乘客的舒适体感，外界新鲜空气在送入车内之前，必须进行预热。预热，即在空调系统中进行加热。经过预热的空气，从车内各出风口吹进车内。对大多数采用车顶送风的空调客车来说，由于热气上升、凉气下降的特点，车内上下温度相差较大，车内温度很不均匀。同时，车体与外界环境也在进行热量传递，车内的热损失较多。因此，在车内两侧地板面上还设置有其他加热设备来补偿热量损失。所以，客车空调的加热系统一般由两部分组成，一部分是设置在风道内的空气预热器，另一部分是设置在客室内的补偿加热器。

目前国内主流客车采暖都是采用电预热与补偿电加热全电热的形式，如 25G、25Z、25K、25T 型客车。在南方一些地区的客车也有采用热泵采暖的。

一、管状电热元件

空调客车上使用的电热采暖装置，通常采用管状电热元件（如图 5-1-1）。利用电流热效应，电流通过电阻丝而产生热量，流过的空气将热量带走，达到采暖的作用。它具有制热快、温度均匀、结构紧凑、控制方便、不易受外界环境影响等特点。

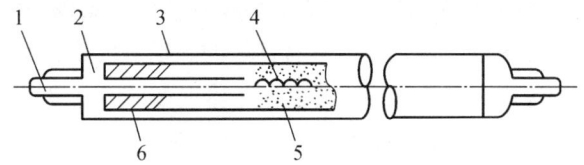

1—连线端子；2—绝缘垫；3—金属套管；4—电热丝；5—绝缘粉末；6—封口材料。

图 5-1-1 管状电热元件结构

如图 5-1-1 所示，在金属管内沿管子的轴线方向放入一根螺旋形的电阻丝，在其空隙部分均匀的填满具有良好导热性和电气绝缘性的结晶氧化镁粉。并用缩管机将管径轧小，以增加氧化镁粉的密度而使导热系数提高。同时还要保证管内螺旋状电阻丝不能因电热元件经受弯曲或碰撞发生偏移而碰及管壁。在电阻丝引出棒出口处浇以硼酸钡的混合物密封，以避免空气中的水分和液体介质潜入氧化镁粉中，引起绝缘不良。由于电阻丝是埋在紧密的导热性较高的氧化物介质中，不与空气接触，其单位负载功率较裸露式电阻丝可大大增加，寿命也相应提高。

二、电预热器

电预热器是当冬季需要取暖时，在客车内部采用电热元件补充车内热量的一种采暖装置。电预热器采用电流热效应，目前客车空调上应用的有管状电热元件和电热板两种电预热器。

电预热器由电热元件和框架组成，在使用时与通风机实现电气联锁（必须同时运行），与制冷机实现电气互锁（不可同时运行）。电热元件一般分成两组，通过空调温度控制器根据室内空气温度自动控制其一组工作、两组工作或停止工作。电预热器的安装位置通常在蒸发器附近，制冷或采暖时共用送风风道。与电预热器相接部分的风道，应采用阻燃保温材料。

为了防止电预热器在通风不良时工作而导致表面温度过高，特设有两级过热保险：

（1）当温度超过 70 ℃时，继电器跳开，切断加热主回路，使电预热器停止工作。当电预热器温度下降到一定值后，继电器可以恢复闭合，继续加热。

（2）当温度超过 139 ℃时，熔断器熔断，切断加热主回路，使电预热器停止工作。此时，加热主回路无法自动恢复，需要人工检查后更换熔断器，电预热器才可恢复加热。

三、电加热器

电加热器是地面加热器的一种，使用时与制冷设备实现电气互锁。工作时通过温度控制器实现自动控制。电加热器主要由电加热器体、电热管或电热板、熔断保护器、接线板、防水盒、耐高温连接导线和罩板组成。

电热器体一般采用钢板制作而成，其中电热板或电热管是核心器件。无散热风扇结构，类似家用的电热板加热器。电热板因具有良好的热辐射性能、使用寿命长、体积小、重量轻、温度分布均匀等优点，客车采暖的电加热器现多采用电热板。电热板通过接线板和连接导线与车上电源相连，因此，接线板和连接导线都采用耐高温材料制作。并采用笼式弹簧端子接线，每个电热板上装一个不可恢复式超温保护器。

电热板主要由发热板、散热翅片组成，结构如图 5-1-2 所示。电热板接线柱部分采用耐温聚四氟乙烯材料密封。

电热器安装采用 M4×30 木螺钉与车体侧墙固定，如图 5-1-3 所示。嵌入式电热器采用 M4×30 木螺钉与车体侧墙固定。

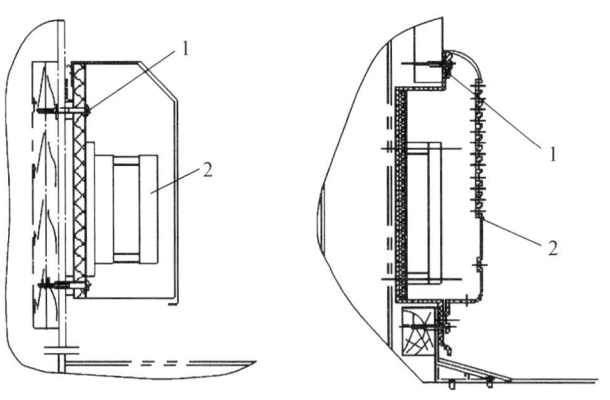

1—散热翅片；2—发热板。

图 5-1-2 电热板结构

1—木螺钉；2—电热器。

图 5-1-3 电热器安装剖面

四、热泵原理

利用制冷机从低温环境中吸热,而在温度较高的环境中放热,比直接利用电能加热所能获得的热量大得多,这种从低温环境中将热量"泵"入室内的装置就称为热泵。热泵是在采用蒸气压缩式制冷的基础上,依然采用做功的方式,让制冷剂在逆循环中实现采暖。

热泵系统也是由压缩机、冷凝器、节流装置、蒸发器等四个主要部分组成,在蒸汽压缩式制冷系统的基础上,热泵系统增加了一个四通换向阀,用于切换制冷剂循环方向,制热时让制冷剂逆向循环,实现采暖。

如图 5-1-4 所示,(a)为夏季制冷工况,压缩机将制冷剂压缩成高温高压的蒸气,经过四通换向阀输送给室外冷凝器,通过外部环境介质,室外的冷凝器将制冷剂热量释放到外部环境中,之后常温高压的制冷剂液体经过节流阀的节流作用,变为低温低压的制冷剂液体,流经置于室内的蒸发器,吸收室内空气的热量,从而冷却室内的空气。

(b)为冬季热泵工况,压缩机将制冷剂压缩成高温高压的蒸气,经过四通换向阀转换制冷剂流向,使制冷剂首先进入室内蒸发器中,此时室内蒸发器被用作冷凝器,对室内空气进行放热,之后制冷剂依次经过节流阀(降压降温)、室外冷凝器(此时被用作蒸发器吸收热量)、四通换向阀,重新进入压缩机,进入下一个循环。

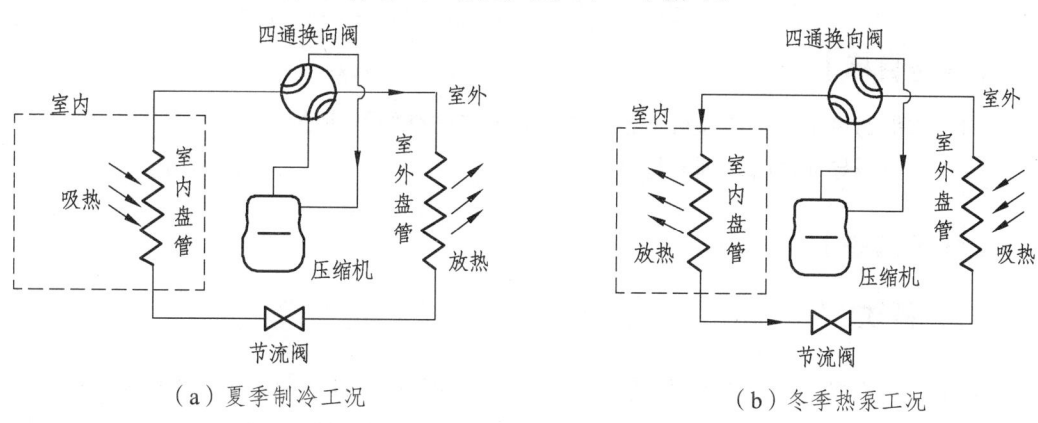

(a)夏季制冷工况　　(b)冬季热泵工况

图 5-1-4　热泵原理

热泵系统中,因为要从寒冷的室外吸热,因此制冷剂在特定压力下的沸点温度非常低,在室外作为蒸发器的换热器(制冷时的冷凝器)有可能表面结霜,以致堵塞空气通路影响换热,所以在系统中应采取适当的融霜措施。在一般的寒冷环境中,热泵制暖比电热管加热制暖有一定的节能优势。但是,受制冷剂特定压力下的沸点温度影响,在异常寒冷的地区,热泵制热的效果会大打折扣。

五、电热器的日常维护

车辆出厂后,应定期检查电热器,使电热板表面保持干燥、清洁。电热器一般在环境温度 $-40 \sim +40$ ℃,空气相对湿度 $\leq 90\%$ 的条件下使用。每年冬天使用前,应在保证电热板干燥、清洁、绝缘良好、接线牢固的前提下先进行试开，符合电气标准要求及电热板性能要求后方可正常使用。

1. 使用过程中的注意事项

（1）不准随意将手伸进罩内触摸电热板等配件，以防烫伤或触电。
（2）不准随意踏上电热器，以防踩坏电热罩。
（3）不许将水或杂物进入电热器罩内，以防触电或损坏设备。
（4）电热器表面禁止覆盖任何物件，以防火灾。
（5）电热器停止使用时，应切断电热器装置各部分总电源。

2. 遇到故障时的处理措施

（1）如电热板发生击穿或闪络现象，应关闭电源，进行检查更换。
（2）如电热板绝缘值下降到规定值以下时，进行检查更换。
（3）如电热板通电后不发热、发热量过小或过大，不符合要求时，进行检查更换。

任务二　通风系统

【任务目标】

（1）掌握通风系统中通风机、各风道、各风口的结构及功能。
（2）理解诱导通风的原理与特点。

【知识储备】

一、概述

我们坐高铁时，可以感受到车厢顶部、靠窗的座椅旁，甚至腿下皆有风送出，夏天时送出的凉风，冬天时送出的是热风。这是因为在车厢顶部和两侧有均匀分布的风口，经过处理的空气通过贯穿车厢的风道传输，并从风口进入车内，如图5-2-1所示。空间内均匀分布的送风，可以保证乘坐的舒适性，普速客车无侧面风口，只有顶部风口，因此在乘坐舒适性上与高铁相比是大打折扣的。

无论是制冷还是制热，如果没有空气从蒸发器或者预热器引流，强制将冷空气或热空气带到车内各处，客车空调装置是无法达到空气调节作用的。而且，车内需要的新鲜空气，也需要设备"泵"入车内。空气调节就是把经过一定处理之后的空气，以一定方式送入车内，使车内空气的温度、湿度、洁净度和气流速度控制在适当范围内的技术。因此，起输送新鲜空气、冷空气或热空气作用的通风系统是空调系统中不可或缺的一部分。

按照工作方式不同，通风系统通常可以分为以下三类：

（1）自然通风系统：依靠自然环境中形成的压差输送空气的，如自然通风器。

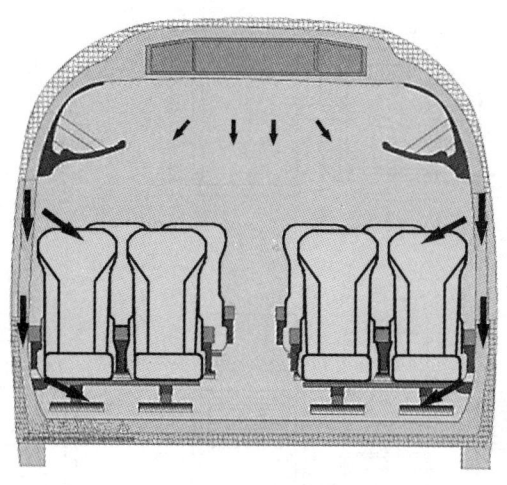

图 5-2-1 动车组通风系统

（2）强迫通风系统：利用专用的通风机和风道输送空气的，如客车空调系统送风。

（3）诱导通风系统：利用诱导器使二次风在室内就地循环，不必集中处理和主风道输送，所以风管尺寸小，设备紧凑。

通风系统由离心式通风机、滤尘装置、送风道、排风装置、回风道等组成，它的作用是：空气过滤、空气输送、空气分配。离心式通风机将车外的新鲜空气吸入车内，并与车内再循环空气混合，经过滤尘装置滤去空气中的粉尘等杂质后，送入客室，同时由排风机将客车内多余的污浊空气排出车外。因车内新鲜空气需求，通风系统是客车空调装置中唯一不分季节而常年运转的系统，因此它的质量状态直接影响到旅客的舒适性和空调装置的经济性。

在通风机组的作用下，室外新鲜空气经新风口吸入车内，经滤尘器过滤并与回风混合后送入空气处理室，经过蒸发器冷却或者由电预热器预热，送入主风道，再由各送风口均匀地送入室内。室内空气的一部分，经回风口、回风道被通风机吸入作为再循环空气重复使用；另一部分则经由排风口和排风扇排出车外。

二、通风机组

通风机组是通风系统的动力装置，由离心式通风机和电动机组成。吸入车外新风和室内回风，并将过滤后的混合空气加压，通过主风道等送入客室。通风机组通常由一台双向伸轴的双速电机和两台离心式风机组成。

国产单元式空调机组的通风机电机为三相交流电机，通过变极获得双速。近几年开始使用双绕组电机来实现双速运行。通风机大多采用多叶片、低噪音、离心式风机。离心风机结构如图 5-2-2 所示。

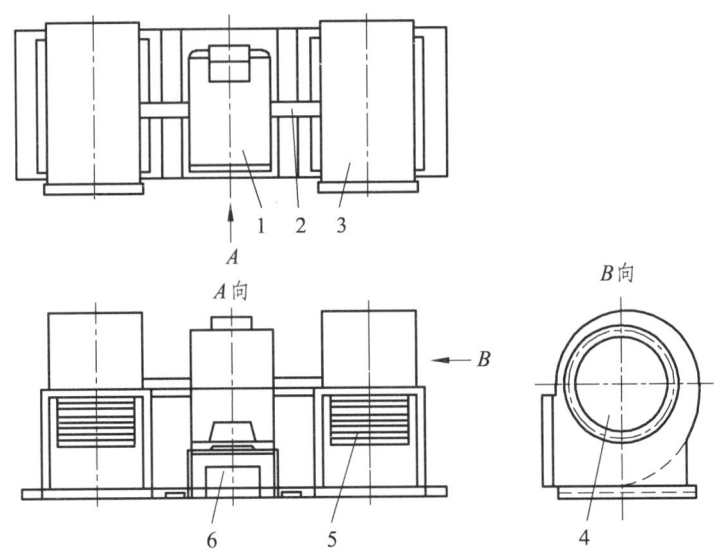

1—双速电动机；2—双向电机轴；3—离心式风机；
4—风机涡壳；5—叶轮；6—机座。

图 5-2-2　离心风机

通常在夏季将通风机置于高速位，冬季则置于低速位；此外，还可根据车内不同的旅客数量采用不同的转速，当夏季高温、高湿且车内旅客较少的情况下，可将通风机置于低速位，减少车内的新风量，以达到减湿的目的。根据通风机安装位置不同，分为：

1. 吸入式结构

如果通风机安装在空气处理设备（蒸发器、预热器）后面，混合空气先经处理设备处理，再经通风机吸入加压后送入主风道，则称为吸入式。

2. 压出式结构

如果风机安装在空气处理设备前面，混合后的空气先经通风机吸入再压向处理设备，经处理后进入主风道，则称为压出式。

单元式空调机组通常采用吸入式结构。

三、风道及调节板

在送风系统里，通过风道，才能把处理好的新鲜空气输送到车内各处。在排风系统里，通过风道，才能把车内各处的污浊空气输送至车外。这种用以输送空气的管道可以由各种不同的材料制成，也可以有很多不同的结构和断面形式。在客车空调装置中，风道应根据所处空间条件，尽量满足舒适性、经济性、轻量化和成本等方面的要求。常用材料有镀锌铁板、铝合金板、玻璃钢和胶合板等。

（一）主风道

主风道的作用是将新风和回风混合处理后输送到车内各处，主风道的截面一般为矩形。由于矩形风道容易加工、便于客室装潢、安装方便，所以在客车上采用较多。空气在较长的主风道中传输，流速会逐步衰减，如果要使风道中空气流速不变，可采用变截面风道，即风道截面面积越来越小。但变截面风道结构复杂，制造困难，通常均采用等截面风道，加装调节板，也可以达到每个送风口能均匀送风的效果，但需手动调节。

用金属薄板制成的风道，其接缝一般采用"咬口"的形式。两节风道之间的连接，一般采用法兰盘，并在法兰盘之间加有填料，以防气体泄漏。木制风道大部分由胶合板制成，顶部与车顶内顶板结合成一封闭空间。木材在制作风道前，需经防腐处理，制成风道后，需涂防火漆。风道接缝处贴以细布或质地优良的厚油纸。在风道内部贴一层 3.5 mm 厚的聚氨酯泡沫塑料，可有效地吸收通风机的噪声及空气流动噪声，并减少传输过程的热量交换。

（二）调节板

调节板的作用就是调节通过风道的空气流量，其结构根据风道截面形状而定。最简单且应用也较广的调节板是百叶窗式。常用的圆形、矩形调节板，使用时只要转动手柄，改变调节板角度，即改变空气通过的截面积，进而达到调节风量的目的。客车上调节板的开度均由人工来进行调节。

（三）回风道

回风道是用来抽取室内再循环空气的，其断面形状根据车内的位置和空间大小而定。客车上的回风口大部分设在一位端墙下部，由回风道引至一位端平顶板上部，以利于通风机吸入。若是包间式客车，则包间门的下部设有回风口，利用走廊作为回风道。走廊两端门是关闭的，在靠近一位端的走廊平顶板上有回风口，再由回风道将再循环空气引入通风机。

（四）排风道

排风道是用来排除车内污浊空气的，所以其一端是连接排风口，而另一端与排风扇相连或与自然通风器连接。客车排风口一般设在与回风口相对的另一端车顶。客车上也有不专设排风口的，这时车内多余空气就依靠室内正压，由门缝隙或厕所的排便器等处排出。

四、风口

（一）新风口

新鲜空气的进风口，即新风口，一般布置在装有通风机端的车门上部，也有设置在车端上部和车顶上部的。新风口上装有百叶窗和网格用以防止杂物和雨、雪进入车内。在多数的新风口上还装有调节机构，以便根据需要调节吸入的新风量。同时，在通风机停止运转时，也便于关闭新风口。带有调节机构的新风口可将调节手把往下拉，则通过调节杆的杠杆作用，将活门（百叶窗）撑开，新风口呈开启状态，弹簧板卡在调节杆的凹槽内，起到固定活门开度的作用。

（二）送风口

送风口是用做分配空气的。送风口处一般都装有散流器，它不但可以使送风均匀，达到室内气流分布合理、温度均匀，而且还可以根据室内具体要求，调节送风量的大小。

集中送风的通风系统，其送风口一般都沿车顶棚或侧壁均匀布置，如图5-2-3所示。常用的送风口形式有圆盘式散流器，直片式散流器，其风量调节机构装在风道中。回风口、排风口一般设置在间壁上，外表面设有格栅以增加美观，内部装有铁丝网以防杂物进入风道。

图 5-2-3　送风口沿主风道均匀分布

五、空气过滤器

空气中总是不同程度的含有各种灰尘和杂质。过多的灰尘进入车内，不仅会影响旅客的舒适和健康，也不利于空气处理设备的正常工作，因为灰尘积聚在蒸发器表面要降低它的传热效果。因此，通风系统中设有空气过滤器。过滤器应装在空气处理室的前面，它可以水平安装，也可以垂直安装。

空气过滤的作用原理是使含尘的空气，通过直径比尘粒还小的空隙或者通过孔径虽大但充分长且又曲折的孔道，将灰尘留下来。此外，尘埃颗粒在通过过滤器时，还会因为扩散作用，摩擦力、静电力或者材料表面湿润时产生的黏附力而使灰尘留下。过滤器的过滤效果取决于所用材料的空气通道的粗细、密实程度和通过过滤器的风速。尼龙纤维型材料耐用，并耐酸、碱、使用方便，寿命长，粘污后用清水冲洗干净即可，是现在客车空调系统空气过滤器普遍采用的材料。

必须保持空气过滤器的清洁有效，才能够延长蒸发器的清洁周期，因为保养空气过滤器总比保养蒸发器要简单得多。所以，过滤网绝不可以没有，丢失、损坏时一定要及时更换新品，否则蒸发器将会很快被污物堵塞，并严重影响制冷效果。

六、自然通风器和排气扇

自然通风器安装在车体的上部，利用通风器处于车外气流中形成背压真空及车内上、下部温度不同而形成空气容重差，引流车内空气排出车外，以完成通风换气作用。

如图 5-2-4 所示，排气扇均采用轴流风机，安装在洗手间、厕所等处的车顶部，直接抽取车内废气排出，也称为废排风扇。

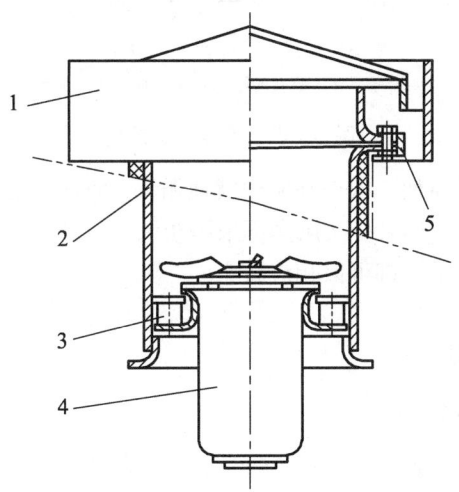

1—排气帽；2—连接筒；3—支柱形减振器；4—排风扇及电动机；5—密封垫。

图 5-2-4　排气扇

七、诱导通风

在集中式的空调系统中，风道的断面尺寸较大，这不仅占去了室内较大的空间位置，而且常给施工安装带来困难。因此，对于一些空间位置比较紧张，而室内装饰又有一定要求的场所，如车辆、舰船、地下工程等，常用诱导通风以减小其风道断面尺寸，简化其系统结构。

（一）诱导通风原理

如图 5-2-5 所示，诱导通风系统工作时，新风和部分回风经处理箱处理后形成一次风，由通风机送入车内诱导器的静压室。在静压室中，一次风的动压变为静压，并在静压作用下，使一次风均匀分配给各个喷嘴，降低气流噪声。之后，由喷嘴送出一次风，诱导二次风，在混合室中二者混合，最后经出风口送入车内。

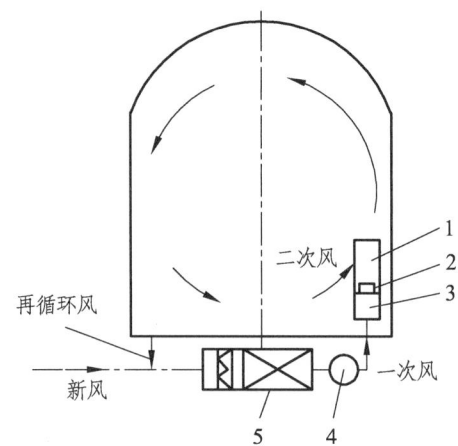

1—混合箱；2—喷嘴；3—静压室；4—通风机；5—集中空气处理箱。

图 5-2-5　诱导空调系统

诱导通风是利用诱导器使二次风在室内就地循环，而不经集中处理和主风道输送。主风道只是用来输送一次风，如果一次风全部采用新风，则可以取消系统的回风，因此主风道的截面和集中空气处理设备都可以相应减小。

（二）诱导通风特点

1. 节省车厢内部空间

诱导通风主风道内的风速可达 15～25 m/s，而一般风道内的风速仅 5～7.5 m/s，因此相应的风道断面就更小了。以干线硬卧车为例，如一般大风道断面积为 0.29 m^2，而诱导风管断面积为 0.0154 m^2，仅是大风道的 1/19，这就大大有利于风道的布置。设备紧凑，风管尺寸小是诱导通风最明显的优点，可为车厢内部节省空间。

2. 送风量局部可调

对于结构一定的诱导器，当一次风量一定时，诱导器的二次风量与回风口面积的大小有关，所以调节回风口活动百叶窗的开启度，就可调节诱导器的总送风量，从而达到调节室内气流扰动的作用。旅客可根据需要，自行调节回风口开启度，而不影响整个系统工作的稳定性，例如室温高时，可开大回风百叶窗，增大送风量（同时也减少了送风温差）和加快旅客生活区域的气流速度，以增加旅客的舒适程度。

3. 日夜风量可调

对卧铺车厢来说，夜间行车时，为减小噪音和风量，则可调节一次风的进风阀门，或降低通风机的转速，使一次风量减小，总送风量也随之减小，以满足旅客睡眠时所需的环境条件。

4. 更易满足湿度要求

经过空气冷却器去湿冷却后的一次风的温度，不受送风温差的限制，因为一次风不是直接送入室内，而是通过诱导器与室内回风混合后再送出。如果诱入的二次风越多，混合后的送风温度就越高，因此一次风可以通过处理得到较大的焓差和湿差，这样一来，单位送风量的除热除湿能力就可以大些，可使湿负荷较大，而且定员多的客车得到满意的湿度要求。当然，要达到此目的，空气冷却器也应作相应的改进，因此用于诱导通风的空气冷却器，具有管排数较多、蒸发温度较低、冷却器的迎面风速较低的特点。

5. 相邻送风口无串音

诱导器的静压室也是一个衰减率很宽的消音器，具有一定的消声作用，它克服了采用普通送风口时，所存在的相邻房间通过送风口的串音问题。

6. 系统需设置消声器

诱导器因喷嘴的风速较大，会产生较大的噪音，所以诱导器上要考虑必要的消声措施。此外，诱导通风一次风处理系统的风量虽小，而阻力却较大，所以配用通风机的转速一般都较高，因而风机噪声也较高，在必要时，需设置消声器。

7. 制冷机运转期较长

因诱导通风的二次风量较小，在室外温度适宜时，也不能充分利用外界新风给车内客室进行通风降温。因而在全年运用中，制冷机的运转时间要比一般空调系统长一些。

任务三　25T 型客车通风系统结构与检修

【任务目标】

（1）掌握 25T 硬卧车和软卧车的通风系统结构及作用。
（2）能够进行客车通风系统中通风机的检修作业。

【知识储备】

一、25T 硬卧车的通风系统结构

（一）送风系统

25T 硬卧车的空调机组是单元式机组，安装在车端顶部。空调送风是通过从空调机组引出并贯穿车厢的送风道，由安装在各包间的行李台平顶板上的送风罩板送入客室内，如图 5-3-1 所示。在每个包间的导流罩板内装有一个风量调节机构和四组风向调节机构。其中，风量调节机构出厂调试时已由调试人员调至适当的工作位置。一般来说，在车辆正常

的运用过程中，不需要乘客来自行调节，确实需要调节时，需由乘务人员用铁路专用钥匙，按照其上的操作指示标识进行调节，调整完毕后，需将调节手柄锁定。对于风向调节机构，乘客可以根据需要手动调整叶片角度，改变出流方向。

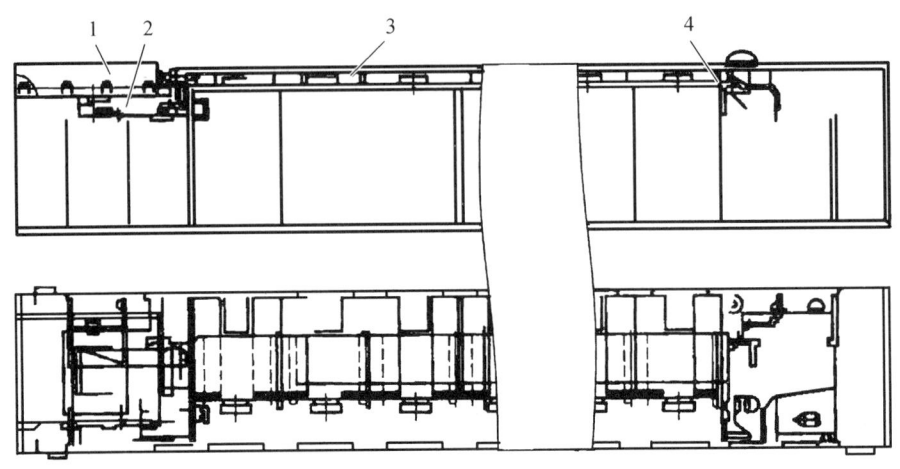

1—空调机组；2—送风道；3—回风道；4—废排风道。

图 5-3-1　25T 硬卧空调系统送风和回风示意

（二）回风系统

25T 硬卧车采用隐式回风，如图 5-3-1 所示，在车厢侧部大走廊顶板上部，行李台背板后侧以及二位侧墙之间的腔体封闭后形成回风及废排风腔，各包间内的送风流经包间后，由敞开门流向大走廊，通过设置在大走廊窗帘滑道处的回风孔板进入回风腔，最后汇集到一位端小走廊平顶板上部设置的回风道内，通过机组下部的回风口回到机组内。

空调机组下部的回风道设有抽拉式回风过滤网，需按照操作说明书的要求定期清洗。清洗时，先打开一位端通过台平顶板上的检查门，将回风过滤网抽出，清洗完毕后，再将过滤网沿滑道插入，并把插板插好，以防过滤网在车辆运行时自行滑出脱落。

在空调机组蒸发器前设有过滤网，用以再次过滤客室内的回风和室外进入的新风。蒸发器前过滤网亦需定期清洗。清洗时，打开一位小走廊平顶板靠近端拉门处检查门，以及一位端通过台平顶板上的检查门，先将回风过滤网抽出，再将蒸发器前过滤网取下，清洗完成后再依次装回，锁闭。

（三）废排装置

如图 5-3-1 所示，车辆二位端小走廊平顶板上方装有一台轴流风机，主要作用是将车内废气排出车外。小走廊平顶板上装有检查门，打开后即可对轴流风机进行检修操作。

二、25T 软卧车的通风系统结构

(一) 送风系统

25T 型空调软卧车包间内采顶部侧送下回风式。如图 5-3-2 所示，空调送风口为隐蔽式结构，各送风口处均设有电动风量调节机构。在风量调节机构下安装送风装饰板，利用装饰板与平顶板之间形成的条缝送风，送风气流为条缝式平顶板贴附射流，室内循环空气通过设在包间顺间壁上的回风格栅排出客室，从而形成了上送下回的气流组织形式。这种气流组织形式可以使室内气流组织更趋均匀，增强室内舒适性，风量调节机构装有调节阀门，通过调节送风净面积来控制送风量大小，以达到调节包间空气温度的要求。

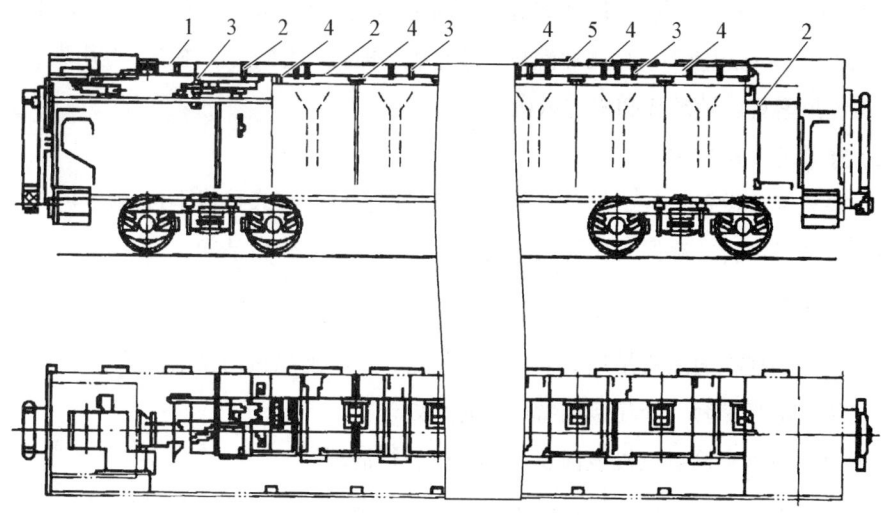

1—送风软道；2—可调小间送风口；3—送风道组成；4—风量调节装置；5—送风格栅。

图 5-3-2　25T 软卧空调系统送风示意图

在需要对电动风量调节机构检修时，请将送风装饰板上锁机构打开，向下打开装饰板。打开装饰板后。操作完成后须将锁固螺母紧固，以免在车辆运行过程中因调节板之间留有缝隙而产生异常响声。电动风量调节机构的调节控制设在每个包间窗下，面板上手动旋钮可以使调节阀门做无级调整。在每个包间提供独立的风量调节装置，旅客可根据自身对客室温度的适应需要，通过设在墙壁上的调节旋钮进行调节。

(二) 回风系统

软卧包间内循环空气由设在包间顺间壁上的回风格栅进入大走廊，隐藏式回风口设在窗饰板后面。车内循环空气由回风口进入密闭的回风道内由机组通风机吸入空调机组内。回风道内的回风过滤网和蒸发器过滤网的清洁方法与 25T 硬卧车类似，此处不再赘述。

（三）废排装置

与25T硬卧车类似，车辆二位端小走廊平顶板上方装有一台轴流风机，主要作用是将车内废气排出车外。二位小走廊平顶板上装有检查门，打开后即可对轴流风机进行检修操作。

三、通风机检修作业

1. 作业准备

（1）工具材料准备：螺丝刀、钢丝钳、电动工具、扭力扳手、铜锤（棒）、8/10/14/17 mm套筒、8/10/14/17 mm扳手、高压冲洗机、砂轮机、棉布、毛刷、油漆笔、万用表、1 000 V级兆欧表、吊索具、轴承装卸机、风机检修台。

（2）穿戴劳动保护用品。

（3）检查工装设备，各工具、工装及设备状态良好，仪表检修不过期。

（4）清洁工作台，确保工作台无杂物、污物，保持工作台洁净。

2. 清洗作业

（1）将吊钩挂在通风机吊环口处吊起，使用天吊将通风机吊至清洗位。

（2）使用绝缘手套，套住接线盒进行防水处理。

（3）使用高压水枪对风机表面及内部风筒进行清理。

（4）将清洗完成后的通风机，吊至检修位进行晾干，并使用棉布进行擦拭。

3. 绝缘测试

（1）使用万用表测量三相绕组无短路、断路现象，三相阻值均衡，用1 000 V兆欧表测量绕组对壳体绝缘电阻值不小于5 MΩ。通风机的多绕组电机测量两种不同绕组间绝缘不小于5 MΩ。

（2）绝缘电阻值不符合要求时，更新同型号电机。

4. 分解

（1）将晾干（烘干）后的待检修风机运至风机检修线的分解工位，使用电动扳手卸开通风机风筒安装固定螺栓，见图5-3-3。

（2）使用扳手卸开叶轮固定螺栓，见图5-3-4。

（3）将风机运送至风机分解台，使用风机分解台将通风机两侧叶轮卸下，见图5-3-5。

（4）用扳手卸开通风机电机两端盖固定螺栓，取出转子，见图5-3-6。

图 5-3-3 通风机风筒

图 5-3-4 通风机

图 5-3-5 通风机分解台

图 5-3-6 通风机转子

（5）用轴承装卸机分别卸下转子上的轴承，见图 5-3-7。

图 5-3-7 轴承装卸机

5．检修

（1）目视检查风机构架、防护罩、叶轮、端盖无锈蚀、破损、变形，锈蚀处用砂轮机除锈打磨并涂刷防锈漆及原色漆，变形者校正，破损者更新，端盖不良者更新。

（2）目视检查转子轴及转子，转子轴出现划痕、弯曲、变形作用不良的更换新品。

（3）目视检查定子绕组，无扫镗、烧损情况，发现不良者更换新品。

（4）目视检查定子绕组引出线及接线端子，防护层良好，老化、烧损、破损时更换新，各密封胶条更新。

（5）更换为原规格型号新品轴承。

（6）目视检查风机铭牌齐全、清晰，安装紧固。

6. 组装

（1）用轴承拆装机安装新轴承，组装新轴承时避免挤压到轴承外圈。

（2）在转子上方用白色油漆笔涂打箭头标明左右，见图5-3-8。

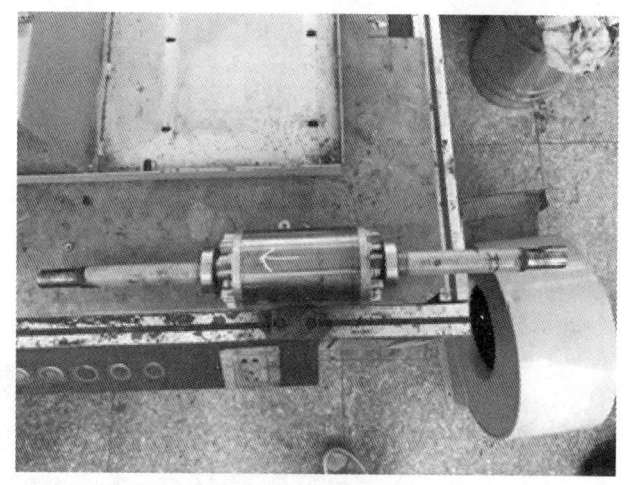

图5-3-8 通风机转子上打箭头

（3）对转子、定子和端盖进行组装，使用铜锤（棒）轻敲端盖使其紧密结合。

（4）将电机与机架进行组装，用电动工具紧固电机与机架各连接螺栓，涂打防松标记。

（5）将叶轮中心孔与转轴对齐安装，使用锁固胶和适当的扭矩将螺钉锁死，用扳手紧固轴端螺栓，涂打防松标记。用手轻轻转动叶轮，观察各部有无摩擦、卡阻现象。

7. 油漆标记

（1）各配件喷涂原色油漆，漆层均匀，不坠流。

（2）试验合格后根据风机正向转动方向，在防护罩一侧正上方中央用字漏喷涂红色箭头，箭头指向与风机正向转动方向一致。

8. 作业后整理

（1）填写检修标记，一车一档内相关记录。

（2）切断电源，清点工具，确认状态良好并擦拭干净后放入工具箱内，做好设备保养，离岗前确认电闸关闭、周围无杂物、无火源后方可退岗。

【任务训练】

（1）客车空调通风系统的作用是什么？通风系统只在夏天或冬天用吗？

（2）使用电加热器时，如何做才能保证安全？

（3）简述诱导通风原理。

（4）简述25T客车通风系统的主要组成及工作过程。

（5）简述通风机检修作业过程及注意事项。

项目六　25T客车空调电气控制系统

【中国铁路文化】

中国铁路发展史6　中老民心的纽带

中老铁路（中老昆万铁路）北起中国云南省昆明市，南至老挝首都万象，是共建"一带一路"倡议提出后，首条以中方为主投资建设、全线采用中国标准、使用中国设备并与中国铁路网直接连接的国际铁路。全长1 000多千米的中老铁路，不仅是中国和老挝互联互通的桥梁，也是民心相通的纽带。

图6-1　中老铁路

2010年5月21日，中老铁路昆玉先建段开工建设；2015年12月2日，中老铁路磨万段举行开工奠基仪式；2016年4月19日，中老铁路玉磨段开工建设；2016年12月25日，中老铁路举行全线开工仪式；2021年12月3日，中老铁路全线通车运营。

中老铁路建设体量庞大、地形地貌复杂，玉磨段需要翻越磨盘山、哀牢山、无量山，需要跨越元江、阿墨江、把边江、澜沧江，桥隧比高达87%，沿线地质较易出现溜塌掉块、软岩变形、突泥涌水等问题。中老铁路磨万段大部分位于热带地区，雨季降水多，基坑难以成型，大型机械设备进场较为困难。线路采用雨季桥梁桩基施工工艺，解决了热带地区雨季桥梁桩基施工难题，确保了桥梁承台和墩身的后续施工。

中老铁路助力老挝发展、造福当地民众、服务地区联通，从老挝万象到北部重要旅游城市琅勃拉邦，越来越多的游客选择乘坐火车出行，沿线旅游经济快速发展。人流、物流、资金流、信息流加速流动，各类产业扩能升级。中老铁路大通道带来大物流，大物流带动大贸易，大贸易激活大产业。"一带一路"建设助力老挝从"陆锁国"变为"陆联国"。中老铁路也是一条完全使用中国标准的国际铁路，标志着中国与"一带一路"沿线国家的"软联通"迈出了重要的一步,并将夯实澜湄合作、中国-东盟命运共同体建设的基础。中老铁路开通运营,是共建"一带一路"实打实的成就,是中国以更开放的姿态与世界分享发展机遇的典范,对推动中老命运共同体建设不断走深走实、促进区域内国家互联互通具有里程碑意义。

【项目描述】

通过本项目学习,使学生掌握25T客车空调电气控制系统的线路连接、功能及运行原理,同时能运用所学知识保障25T型客车空调电气控制系统的日常使用及定期检修。

本项目主要对25T硬卧客车空调电气控制系统进行分析,完整的25T硬卧客车空调电路图请参照附图1。

【项目目标】

1. 知识目标

(1)了解综合电气控制柜的组成。
(2)掌握空调主电路的控制过程。
(3)掌握空调交直流转换和Ⅰ路Ⅱ路转换的控制过程。
(4)掌握空调试验模式和自动模式下的控制过程。
(5)理解空调运行信息的采集与获取接线原理。
(6)掌握空调故障信息获取过程与故障判断、处理。

2. 能力目标

(1)能够将学习的电路原理知识用于故障诊断。
(2)能够自主学习空调电气控制柜和电路的维护项目。
(3)能够完成空调电气系统日常检修作业。

3. 素养目标

(1)培养细致认真的工作态度。
(2)培养安全用电的意识和能力。
(3)培养团队协作精神。

任务一 空调主电路及供电线路转换控制

【任务目标】

(1)了解综合电气控制柜的组成。
(2)掌握空调主电路的控制过程。
(3)掌握空调交直流转换和Ⅰ路Ⅱ路转换的控制过程。

【知识储备】

一、TKDT 型电气综合控制柜

25T 空调客车采用 TKDT 型铁路客车电气综合控制柜，兼容 AC 380 V 和 DC 600 V 供电，简称兼容控制柜，如图 6-1-1 所示。是集电源转换控制、空调机组控制、照明控制等功能于一体的兼容综合控制柜。控制柜的控制核心采用可编程控制器 PLC，PLC 通过触摸屏实现人机互动，接收各种指令并自动执行相应的操作步骤，对电气系统运行中出现的各种故障及时进行诊断、指示并保护。

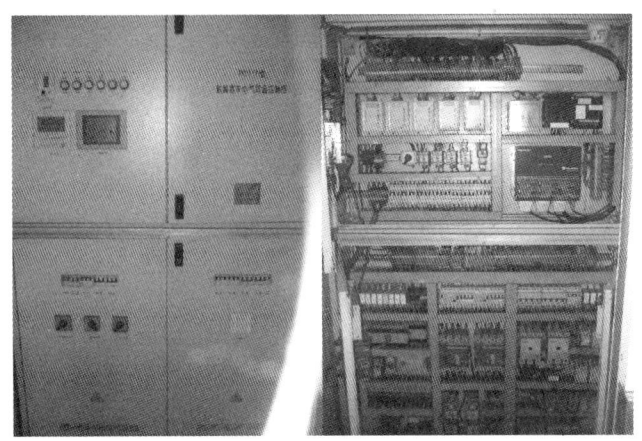

图 6-1-1　TKDT 型电气综合控制柜

每节车厢两端 39 通信芯连接器中的 LON 网络电缆引至电气综合控制柜内的 PLC 汇集，轴温、防滑、烟火报警、车门、车下电源箱通过网关将状态信息传输给 PLC，在触摸屏上查询。综合控制柜具有检测、控制、故障诊断保护、信息提示、联网通信功能，实现供电及控制系统的综合控制，可进行车对车通信。

兼容控制柜主要由 PLC 主机单元、触摸显示屏、接触器、时间继电器、热继电器、空开等组成。

（一）PLC 主机单元

PLC 是兼容控制柜的控制核心部件，负责对整个电气系统进行控制，实时监测电气系统运行过程中的参数并进行分析，对出现的故障自动报警、处理，通过触摸显示屏实现人机对话，响应触摸显示屏输入的命令、参数，将故障信息、运行记录通过触摸显示屏显示等。其主要配置为：

（1）0～10 V 的模拟量输入点 17 点。

（2）PT100 温度输入点 1 点。

（3）直流 24 V，8 mA 的开关量输入点 24 点。

（4）继电器开关量输出点 24 点。

（5）输出端最大开关能力：AC 250 V，2 A 和 DC 24 V，2 A。

（6）输出端最小开关能力：DC 5 V，10 mA。

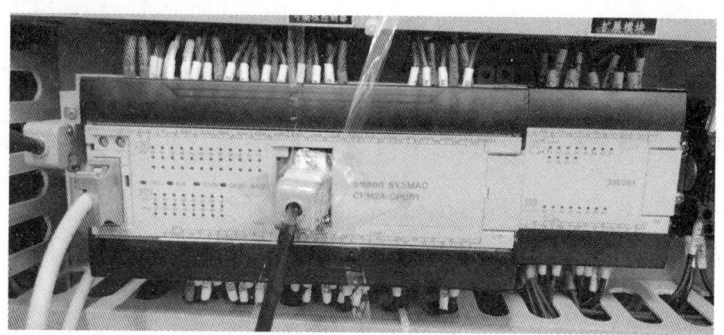

图 6-1-2　欧姆龙 CPM 系列 PLC

（二）触摸显示屏

触摸显示屏采用全中文液晶带背光屏，具有字符类型和图像类型显示，由通信接口和 PLC 的外设接口进行通信。主要功能是现场参数设定，空调运行工况的人为控制，运行工况、参数的显示，实时显示各功能单元的运行状态，实时报告故障，并可查询各功能单元的运行记录及故障记录。液晶显示器规格为：320 点 × 240 点；有效显示面积：122 mm × 92 mm。

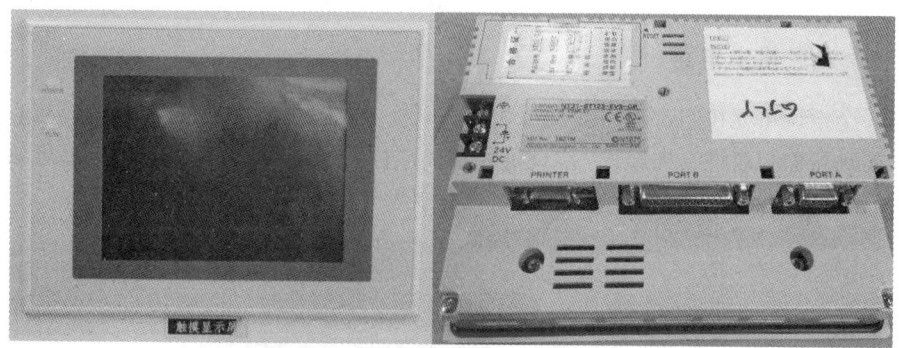

图 6-1-3　欧姆龙 NT31 系列触摸屏

（三）交直流电源规格

25T 客车可以由 AC 380 V 和 DC 600 V 兼容供电。出厂时设置为 AC 380 V 供电，并预留 DC 600 V 供电配线。若要在 DC 600 V 供电方式下运行，需另加装 3.5 kW 单相逆变器和 2 × 35 kV·A 逆变器。采用Ⅰ路、Ⅱ路双路供电，可根据需要选择Ⅰ路或Ⅱ路供电。编组时原则上Ⅰ路、Ⅱ路负载应均衡，例如 1、3、5 等车由Ⅰ路供电，2、4、6 等车由Ⅱ路供电。

1）AC 380 V 供电

主电路由Ⅰ路、Ⅱ路两路 50Hz 三相交流 380V 电源母线中的一路提供电源，给充电机、空调、照明、伴热等交流负载供电。

2）DC 600 V 供电

主电路由Ⅰ路、Ⅱ路两路 DC600V 电源母线中的其中一路提供电源，给逆变器、充电机供电，逆变器输出交流电给交流负载供电。

3）DC 110 V 供电

由直流 110 V 母线及本车蓄电池给单相逆变器、照明、防滑器等直流负载供电。

4）直流控制电源

① 将直流 110 V 电源转换成直流 24 V 电源给 PLC、触摸显示屏、网关、安全用电记录仪等供电。

② 将直流 110 V 电源转换成直流 12 V 电源给传感器供电；传感器输出电压范围为：直流 0～5 V 和 0～10 V。

③ 将直流 110 V 电源转换成直流 48 V 电源向尾灯等负载供电。额定输出电流为 6 A。

二、空调主电路

25T 客车空调系统的主电路由通风机、冷凝风机、压缩机和电热器四部分的控制电路组成。电热器由预热器和客室辅助加热器组成。

（一）通风机主电路

每一个空调单元机组都有一台通风机，通风机主电路由弱风和强风两条通路组成，采用两个接触器控制双绕组通风机，实现不同的风速控制。双绕组通风机的优点是可靠性高，故障率低。空调系统在运行时，需要先闭合主空气开关 Q11，如图 6-1-4 所示。

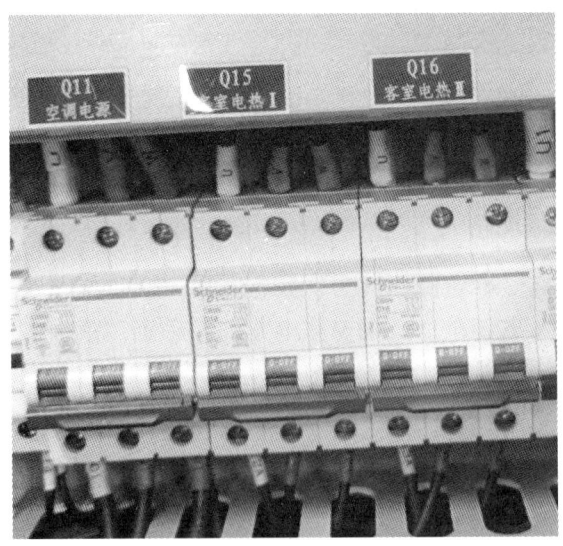

图 6-1-4　空调电源空开 Q11

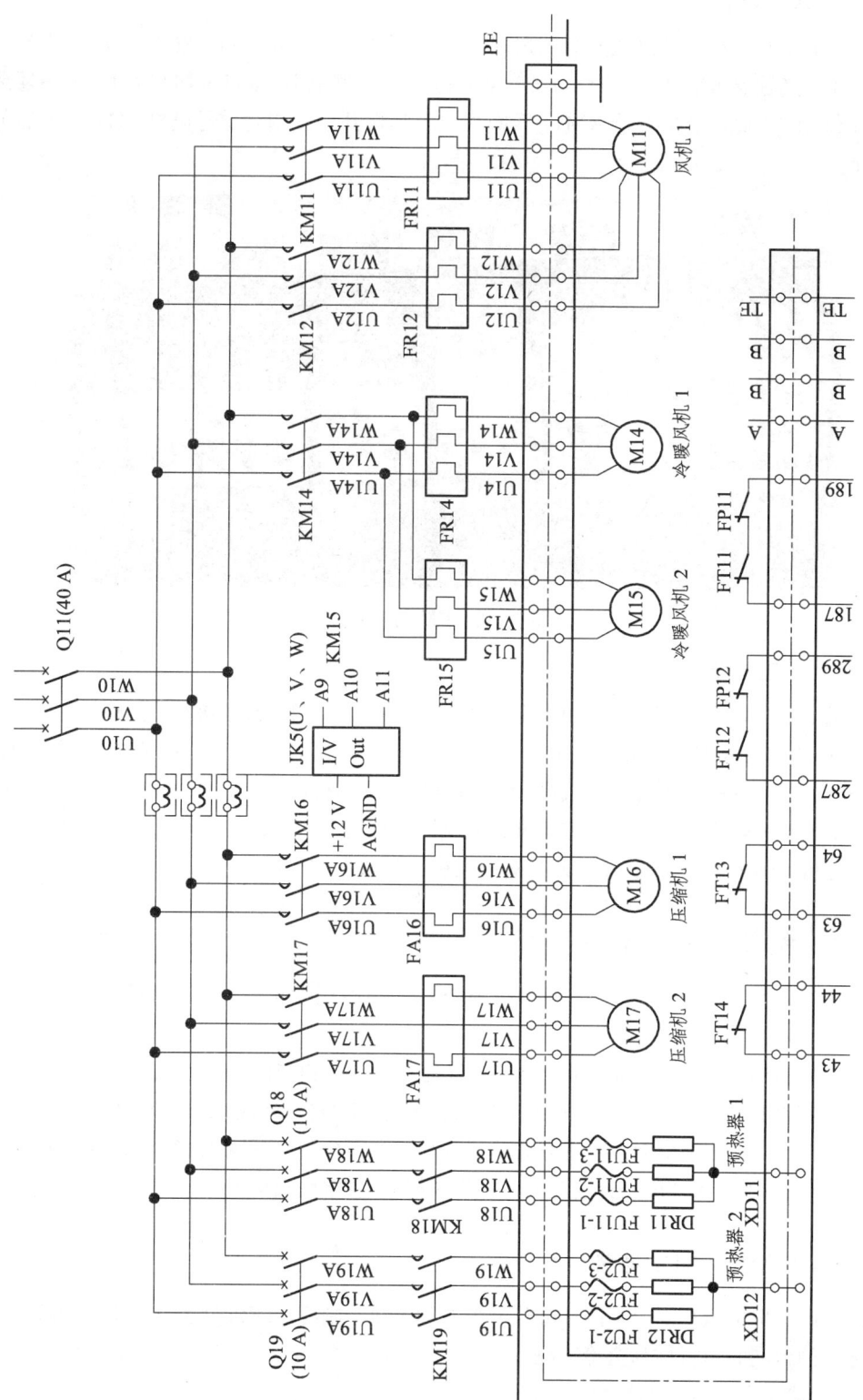

图 6-1-5 空调主电路

1. 弱风主电路

如图 6-1-5 所示,风机风速为弱风时的电气通路为:三相交流 380 V 电源→主空气开关 Q11→接触器 KM11(见图 6-1-6)常开触点→热继电器 FR11(如图 6-1-6)→通风机 M11 绕组 1。此时,接触器 KM11 线圈得电,其常开触点闭合,通风机 M11 得电后低速运行。

图 6-1-6　KM 与 FR

2. 强风主电路

如图 6-1-5 所示,风机风速为强风时的电气通路为:三相交流 380 V 电源→主空气开关 Q11→接触器 KM12 常开触点→热继电器 FR12→通风机 M11 绕组 2。此时,接触器 KM12 线圈得电,其常开触点闭合,通风机 M11 得电后高速运行。

KM11 和 KM12 的常开触点在弱风和强风控制电路上互锁,保证了弱风和强风不会同时得电运行。热继电器 FR11 和 FR12 对通风机起过载保护作用。

(二)冷凝风机主电路

两台冷凝风机提供流动空气为制冷剂降温。制冷压缩机启动前,必须先启动冷凝风机。

如图 6-1-5 所示,冷凝风机主电路的电气通路为:三相交流 380 V 电源→主空气开关 Q11→接触器 KM14 常开触点→热继电器 FR14 和 FR15→冷凝风机 1 M14 和冷凝风机 2 M15。此时,接触器 KM14 线圈得电,其常开触点闭合,冷凝风机 M14 和 M15 得电运行。热继电器 FR14 和 FR15 分别对两台冷凝风机起过载保护作用。

(三)制冷压缩机主电路

制冷时,根据运行工况不同,可分为半冷和全冷。制冷压缩机只运行其中 1 台称为半冷工况,两台同时运行称为全冷工况。

1. 半冷工况

如图 6-1-5 所示，半冷工况时，压缩机主电路的电气通路为：三相交流 380 V 电源→主空气开关 Q11→接触器 KM16 常开触点→FA16→压缩机 1。

或：三相交流 380 V 电源→主空气开关 Q11→接触器 KM17 常开触点→FA17→压缩机 2。

此时，接触器 KM16 和 KM17 只有一个线圈得电，其常开触点只有一个闭合，两台压缩机只有一台得电运行。

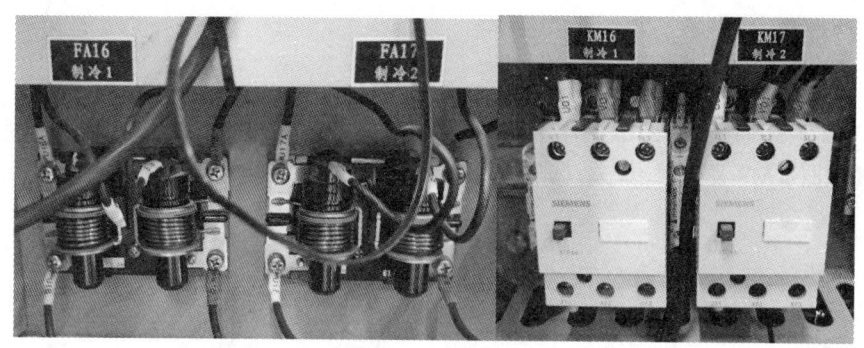

图 6-1-7　FA 与 KM

2. 全冷工况

如图 6-1-5 所示，全冷工况时，压缩机主电路的电气通路为：三相交流 380V 电源→主空气开关 Q11→接触器 KM16 和 KM17 常开触点→FA16 和 FA17→压缩机 1 和压缩机 2。

此时，接触器 KM16 和 KM17 线圈都得电，其常开触点都闭合，两台压缩机都得电运行。

（四）预热器主电路

空调预热器安装在蒸发器附近，为空调制暖提供热量。制热时，预热器只运行其中 1 台称为半暖工况，两台同时运行称为全暖工况。

1. 预热器半暖工况

如图 6-1-5 所示，预热器半暖工况时，主电路的电气通路为：三相交流 380V 电源→主空气开关 Q11→空气开关 Q18→接触器 KM18 常开触点→保险管 FU1→预热器 1。

或：三相交流 380V 电源→主空气开关 Q11→空气开关 Q19→接触器 KM19 常开触点→保险管 FU2→预热器 2。

此时，接触器 KM18 和 KM19 只有一个线圈得电，其常开触点只有一个闭合，预热器 1 和 2 只有一台得电运行。保险管 FU1 和 FU2 分别对两台预热器起过载熔断保护作用。

2. 预热器全暖工况

如图 6-1-5 所示，预热器全暖工况时，预热器主电路的电气通路为：三相交流 380V

电源→主空气开关 Q11→空气开关 Q18 和 Q19→接触器 KM18 和 KM19 常开触点→保险管 FU1 和 FU2→预热器 1 和预热器 2。

此时，接触器 KM18 和 KM19 线圈都得电，其常开触点都闭合，两套预热器都得电运行。

（五）客室辅助加热器主电路

客室辅助加热器制热时，也分为半暖和全暖。只运行其中 1 套称为半暖工况，两套同时运行称为全暖工况。

1. 辅助加热器半暖工况

如图 6-1-8 所示，辅助加热器主电路的电气通路为：三相交流 380V 电源→空气开关 Q15→接触器 KM8 常开触点→保险管 FU→辅助加热器 I。

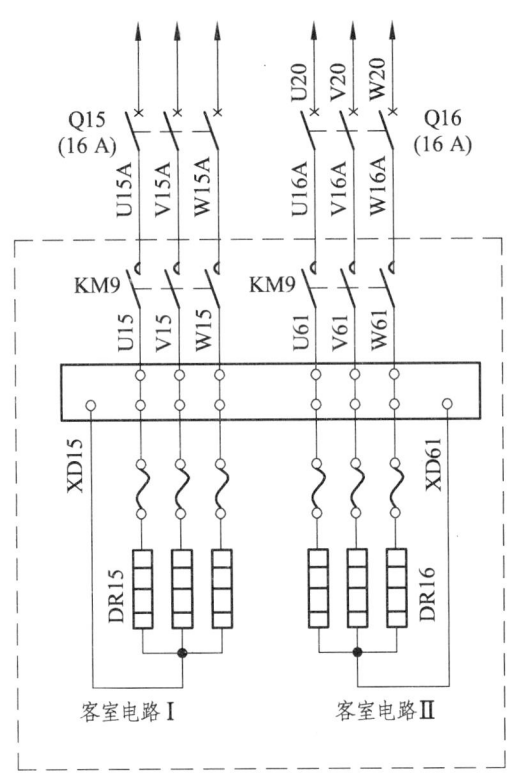

图 6-1-8　辅助加热器主电路

或：三相交流 380 V 电源→空气开关 Q16→接触器 KM9 常开触点→保险管 FU→辅助加热器 II。

此时，接触器 KM8 和 KM9 只有一个线圈得电，其常开触点只有一个闭合，辅助加热器只有一台得电运行。

2. 辅助加热器全暖工况

如图 6-1-8 所示，辅助加热器主电路的电气通路为：三相交流 380 V 电源→空气开关 Q15 和 Q16→接触器 KM8 和 KM9 常开触点→保险管 FU→辅助加热器Ⅰ和Ⅱ。

此时，接触器 KM8 和 KM9 线圈都得电，其常开触点都闭合，两套辅助加热器都得电运行。

三、交直流转换和Ⅰ路Ⅱ路转换

25T 客车空调系统可由 AC 380 V 和 DC 600 V 兼容供电，采用Ⅰ、Ⅱ路双路供电，根据需要可手动或自动选择Ⅰ路（Ⅱ路）供电。编组时原则上Ⅰ路、Ⅱ路负载应均衡，例如 1、3、5…车由Ⅰ路供电，2、4、6…车由Ⅱ路供电。交直流供电的选择和Ⅰ路或Ⅱ路供电的选择是通过手动操作转换开关来实现的。

（一）转换开关

1. SA1 交直流转换开关

SA1 转换开关是交直流供电选择开关，SA1 为三挡转换开关，共 3 对触点。中间挡是停止挡，此时 1、2 触点，3、4 触点和 5、6 触点都是断开状态；从停止挡逆时针旋转 45°是直流挡，此时 1、2 触点断开，3、4 触点和 5、6 触点闭合；从停止挡顺时针旋转 45°是交流挡，此时 1、2 触点闭合，3、4 触点和 5、6 触点断开。

SA1	直流	停止	交流
	45°	0°	45°
1-2			●
3-4	●		
5-6	●		

图 6-1-9　SA1 交直流转换开关

2. SA2 Ⅰ路Ⅱ路转换开关

SA2 转换开关是Ⅰ路和Ⅱ路供电选择开关，SA2 为五挡转换开关，共 9 对触点。中间挡是停止挡，此时所有触点都是断开状态；从停止挡逆时针旋转 45°是自动挡，此时前 4 对触点断开，后 5 对触点闭合；从停止挡顺时针旋转 45°是Ⅰ路挡，此时 1、2 触点和 5、6 触点闭合，其他触点断开；从停止挡顺时针旋转 90 度也是停止挡，此时所有触点都断开，此挡处在Ⅰ路和Ⅱ路的中间，保证Ⅰ路和Ⅱ路顺利切换；从停止挡顺时针旋转 135°是Ⅱ路挡，此时 3、4 触点和 7、8 触点闭合，其他触点断开。

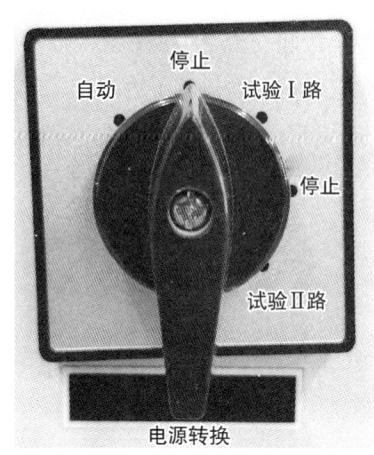

SA2	自动	停止	Ⅰ路	停止	Ⅱ路
	45°	0°	45°	90°	135°
1-2			●		
3-4					●
5-6			●		
7-8					●
9-10	●				
11-12	●				
13-14	●				
15-16	●				
17-18	●				

图 6-1-10 SA2 转换开关

（二）交直流和Ⅰ路Ⅱ路切换控制电路

24V 控制电源（+113）从 PLC 单元引出，通过转换开关 SA1 和 SA2 的组合变换，可实现交直流切换和Ⅰ路Ⅱ路切换，电路图请参照附图 1。

1. 直流Ⅰ路控制

SA1 打到直流挡，SA2 打到Ⅰ路挡，此时电气通路为：24 V 电源 + 113→SA1 触点 3→SA1 触点 4→接触器 KM1 常闭触点→空开 Q1→接触器 KM2 常闭触点→空开 Q2，之后分成两路，一路走漏电保护器→继电器 KA29 线圈，另一路走 SA2 触点 5→SA2 触点 6→接触器 KM4 常闭触点→接触器 KM3 线圈和继电器 KA30 线圈，使 DC 600 V Ⅰ路主电路导通。此时，图中接触器 KM3 两个常闭触点断开，确保交流通路断开，接触器 KM4 和继电器 KA40 线圈断电，DC 600 V Ⅱ路断开，即 DC 600 V 的Ⅰ路与Ⅱ路形成互锁关系。同时继电器 KA29 常开触点闭合，24 V 电源从 SA2 触点 6 流向 PLC 右侧接口 31 引脚（566），使 PLC 控制单元接收到 DC 600 V Ⅰ路正常运行的信号。

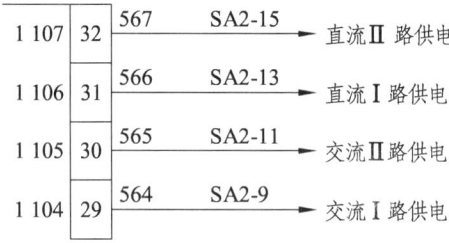

图 6-1-11 交直流、Ⅰ路Ⅱ路控制的 PLC 接口

2. 直流Ⅱ路控制

SA1 打到直流档，SA2 打到Ⅱ路档，此时电气通路为：24 V 电源按照直流Ⅰ路的流向走另一路到 SA2 触点 7→SA2 触点 8→接触器 KM3 常闭触点→接触器 KM4 线圈和继电器 KA40 线圈，使 DC 600 V Ⅱ路主电路导通。此时，图中接触器 KM4 两个常闭触点断开，确保交流通路断开，接触器 KM3 和继电器 KA30 线圈断电，即 DC 600 V Ⅰ路断开。同时继电器 KA29 常开触点闭合，24 V 电源从 SA2 触点 8 流向 PLC 右侧接口 32 引脚(567)，使 PLC 控制单元接收到 DC 600 V Ⅱ路正常运行的信号。

3. 交流Ⅰ路控制

SA1 打到交流档，SA2 打到Ⅰ路挡，此时电气通路为：24 V 电源→SA1 触点 1→SA1 触点 2→空开 Q3→接触器 KM3 常闭触点→接触器 KM4 常闭触点→空开 Q4，之后分成两路，一路走继电器 KA19 线圈，另一路走 SA2 触点 1→SA2 触点 2→接触器 KM2 常闭触点→继电器 KA10 线圈。此时，24 V 电源 +100 通过继电器 KA10 常开触点→接触器 KM1 线圈，使 AC 380 V Ⅰ路主电路导通。此时，图中接触器 KM1 两个常闭触点断开，确保直流通路断开，继电器 KA20 和接触器 KM2 线圈断电，即 AC 380 V Ⅱ路断开，AC 380 V 的Ⅰ路与Ⅱ路形成互锁关系。同时继电器 KA19 常开触点闭合，24 V 电源从 SA2 触点 2 流向 PLC 右侧接口 29 引脚（564），使 PLC 控制单元接收到 AC 380 V Ⅰ路正常运行的信号。

4. 交流Ⅱ路控制

SA1 打到交流挡，SA2 打到Ⅱ路挡，此时电气通路为：24 V 电源按照交流Ⅰ路的流向走另一路到 SA2 触点 3→SA2 触点 4→接触器 KM1 常闭触点→继电器 KA20 线圈。此时，24 V 电源 +100 通过继电器 KA20 常开触点→接触器 KM2 线圈，使 AC 380 V Ⅱ路主电路导通。此时，图中接触器 KM2 两个常闭触点断开，确保直流通路断开，继电器 KA10 和接触器 KM1 线圈断电，即 AC 380 V 路断开。同时继电器 KA19 常开触点闭合，24 V 电源从 SA2 触点 4 流向 PLC 右侧接口 30 引脚(565)，使 PLC 控制单元接收到 AC 380 V Ⅱ路正常运行的信号。

任务二　空调试验模式和自动模式控制

【任务目标】

（1）掌握空调模式的切换方法。
（2）掌握空调试验模式下的控制过程。
（3）掌握空调自动模式下的控制过程。

【知识储备】

一、25T 客车空调运行模式

（一）空调运行模式转换开关

SA3 转换开关是空调运行模式选择开关，SA3 为四挡转换开关，共 6 对触点。中间挡是停止挡，此时 6 对触点都是断开状态；从停止挡逆时针旋转 45° 是试验暖挡，此时 7、8 触点和 11、12 触点闭合，其他触点断开。从停止挡顺时针旋转 45° 是自动挡，此时 3、4 触点和 5、6 触点闭合，其他触点断开；从停止挡顺时针旋转 90° 是试验冷挡，此时 1、2 触点和 9、10 触点闭合，其他触点断开。在试验位运行时，PLC 只能对空调机组进行检测，不能进行保护动作。

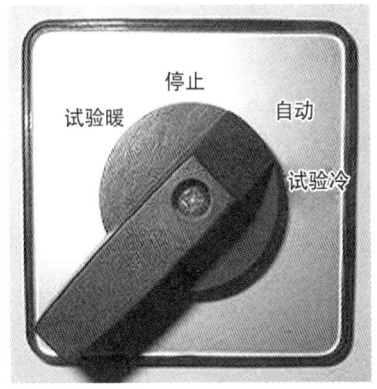

SA3	试验暖	停止	自动	试验冷
	45°	0°	45°	90°
1-2				●
3-4			●	
5-6			●	
7-8	●			
9-10				●
11-12	●			

图 6-2-1　空调运行模式转换开关

（二）空调运行模式控制电路

二、25T 客车空调试验模式

（一）试验暖

如图 6-2-2、6-2-3 所示。

SA3 打到试验暖，电气通路为：24V 电源+111→空开 Q40→SA3 触点 7→SA3 触点 8→继电器 KA3（见图 6-2-4）线圈，继电器 KA3 五个常开触点闭合。

1. 通风机弱风通路

24 V 电源→SA3 触点 11→SA3 触点 12→继电器 KA3 常开触点→PLC 右侧接口 19 引脚（554）→接触器 KM12 常闭触点→热继电器 FR11 常闭触点→接触器 KM11 线圈，此时主电路中接触器 KM11 常开触点闭合，通风机低速运转。

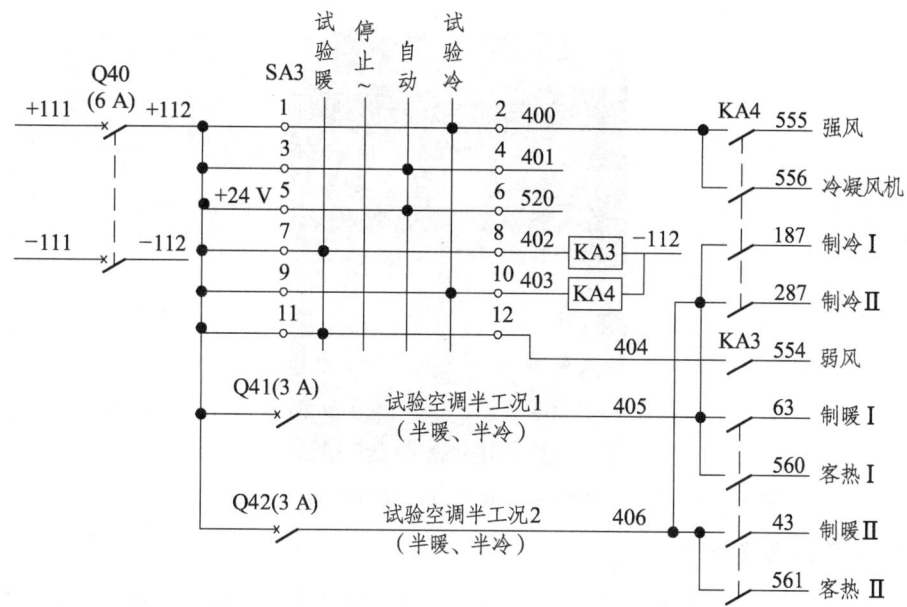

图 6-2-2 空调运行模式控制电路

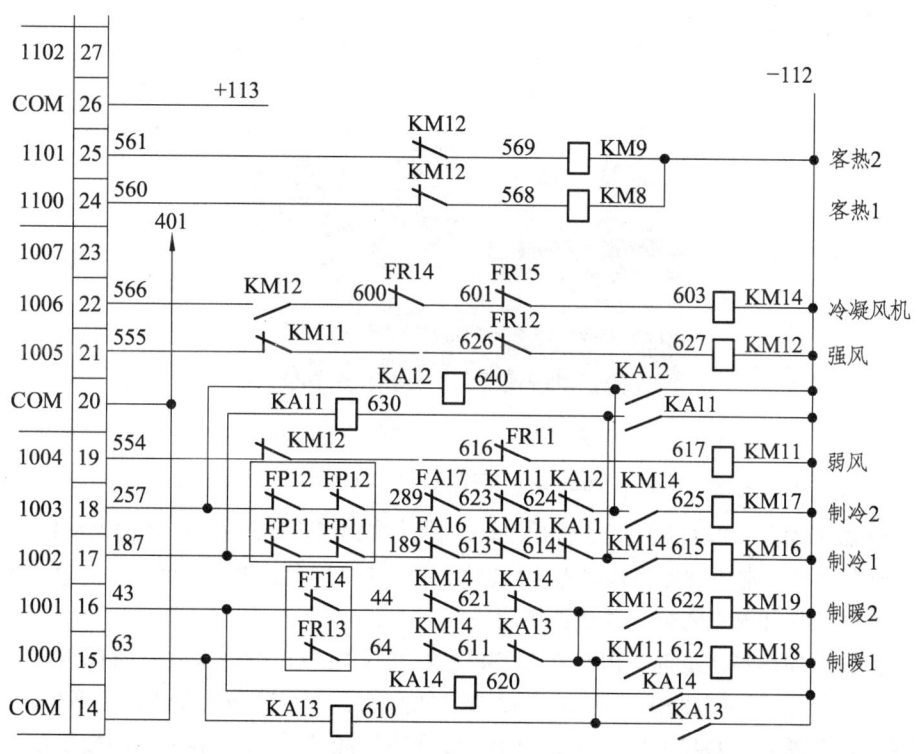

图 6-2-3 PLC 空调控制电路

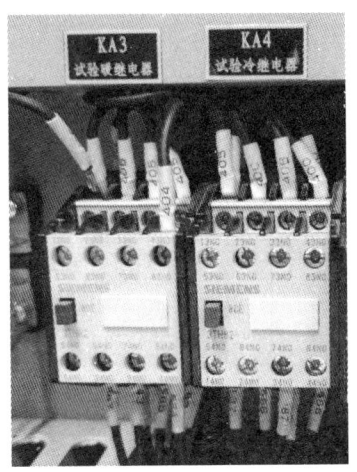

图 6-2-4　试验冷、暖继电器

2. 弱风制暖通路

（1）如果将空开 Q41（见图 6-2-5）闭合，可实现预热器 1 和客室辅助加热器 1 通电的半暖工况。电气通路为：24 V 电源→空开 Q41→继电器 KA3 的两个常开触点→PLC 右侧接口 15、24（63、560）。

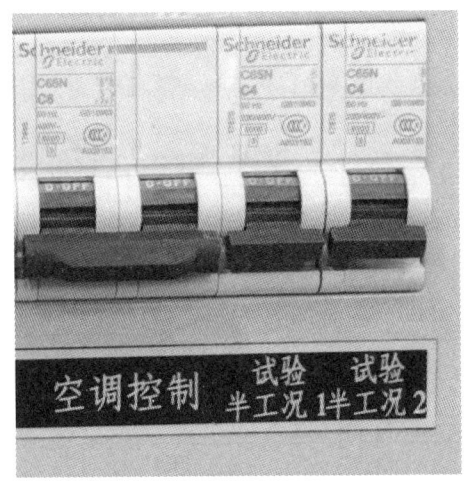

图 6-2-5　空开 Q41 和 Q42

预热器 1 通路：PLC 接口 15 输出 24 V 电→FT13 常闭触点→接触器 KM14 常闭触点→继电器 KA13 常闭触点→接触器 KM11 常开触点→接触器 KM18 线圈，此时主电路中接触器 KM18 常开触点闭合，预热器 1 运行。

客室辅助加热器 1 通路：PLC 接口 24 输出 24 V 电→接触器 KM12 常闭触点→接触器 KM8 线圈，此时主电路中接触器 KM8 常开触点闭合，客室辅助加热器 1 运行。

（2）如果将空开 Q42（见图 6-2-5）闭合，可实现预热器 2 和客室辅助加热器 2 通电的半暖工况。则电气通路为：24V 电源→空开 Q42→继电器 KA3 的两个常开触点→PLC

右侧接口 16、25（43、561）。

预热器 2 通路：PLC 接口 16 输出 24V 电→FT14 常闭触点→接触器 KM14 常闭触点→继电器 KA14 常闭触点→接触器 KM11 常开触点→接触器 KM19 线圈，此时主电路中接触器 KM19 常开触点闭合，预热器 2 运行。

客室辅助加热器 2 通路：PLC 接口 25 输出 24V 电→接触器 KM12 常闭触点→接触器 KM9 线圈，此时主电路中接触器 KM9 常开触点闭合，客室辅助加热器 2 运行。

（3）如果将空开 Q41 和 Q42 都闭合，可实现预热器 1、2 和客室辅助加热器 1、2 都通电运行的全暖工况。

（二）试验冷挡

如图 6-2-2、6-2-3 所示。

SA3 打到试验冷挡，电气通路为：24 V 电源 +111→空开 Q40→SA3 触点 9→SA3 触点 10→继电器 KA4 线圈，继电器 KA4 四个常开触点闭合。

1. 通风机强风通路

24 V 电源→SA3 触点 1→SA3 触点 2→继电器 KA4 常开触点→PLC 右侧接口 21 引脚（555）→接触器 KM11 常闭触点→热继电器 FR12 常闭触点→接触器 KM12 线圈，此时主电路中接触器 KM12 常开触点闭合，通风机高速运转。强风与弱风通路的互锁，是由接触器 KM11 和 KM12 的常闭触点在对方控制电路中串联来实现的。

2. 冷凝风机通路

24 V 电源→SA3 触点 1→SA3 触点 2→继电器 KA4 常开触点→PLC 右侧接口 22 引脚（556）→接触器 KM12 常开触点→热继电器 FR14 常闭触点→热继电器 FR15 常闭触点→接触器 KM14 线圈，此时主电路中接触器 KM14 常开触点闭合，两台冷凝风机得电运行。

3. 制冷通路

（1）如果将空开 Q41 闭合，可实现压缩机 1 通电的半冷工况。电气通路为：24 V 电源→空开 Q41→继电器 KA4 常开触点→PLC 右侧接口 17 引脚（187）→FT11 常闭触点→FP11 常闭触点→FA16 常闭触点→接触器 KM11 常闭触点→继电器 KA11 常闭触点→接触器 KM14 常开触点→接触器 KM16 线圈。此时主电路中接触器 KM16 常开触点闭合，制冷压缩机 1 运行。

（2）如果将空开 Q42 闭合，可实现压缩机 2 通电的半冷工况。电气通路为：24 V 电源→空开 Q42→继电器 KA4 常开触点→PLC 右侧接口 18 引脚（287）→FT12 常闭触点→FP12 常闭触点→FA17 常闭触点→接触器 KM11 常闭触点→继电器 KA12 常闭触点→接触器 KM14 常开触点→接触器 KM17 线圈。此时主电路中接触器 KM17 常开触点闭合，制冷压缩机 2 运行。

（3）如果将空开 Q41 和 Q42 都闭合，可实现两台制冷压缩机都通电运行的全冷工况。在试验冷或试验暖工况下运行时，为防止压缩机或加热器同时启动，造成瞬间负载过大，空开 Q41 和 Q42 不可同时合上，通常先合上空开 Q41，适当延时后再合上空开 Q42。

三、25T 客车空调自动模式控制

（一）空调自动运行模式

如图 6-2-2、6-2-3 所示。

空调在正常运行时，转换开关 SA3 是打到自动的，电气通路为：24 V 电源 + 111→空开 Q40→SA3 触点 3 和 5→SA3 触点 4 和 6→PLC 右侧接口 14、20 和左侧接口 00 引脚（401 和 520）。从 00 引脚引入 24 V 电，使 PLC 空调部分运行，它将根据传感器输入信号，按照程序自动进入制冷或制暖工况。从 14 和 20 引脚引入 24 V 电，为 PLC 的输出提供直流电源。

（1）电源供电开始后，PLC 控制空调机组自动进入"自动"运行，PLC 根据车厢里温度传感器检测值与预先设定的"制冷""制暖"温度值进行比较后，进行空调机组的"自动"运转，空调机组有六种工况"强风""弱风""强风半冷""强风全冷""弱风半暖""弱风全暖"。在"制暖"工况中，客室辅助加热器与预热器联动。

（2）可以根据显示触摸屏上的菜单和提示，强制选择"强风""弱风""强风半冷""强风全冷""弱风半暖""弱风全暖"等运行方式，此时空调不受自动控制，按下"全自动"触摸开关可以返回自动控制状态。

（二）空调自动运行控制过程

空调在正常运行时，是在自动工况下工作的。

1. 空调自动制冷过程

制冷设定值：上限 26 ℃，下限 24 ℃，回差值 1.5°。制冷时，当温度上升到设定值加回差值时才开始制冷，在回差范围内是不制冷的，即压缩机不启动，可防止压缩机频繁启动以延长其寿命。如图 6-2-6 所示：

（1）室温在 22.5° 以下时，通风机以弱风模式运行，两台压缩机处于停机状态。

（2）当室温升至 22.5° 时，通风机以强风模式运行，两台压缩机处于停机状态。

（3）当室温升至设定温度下限（24 + 1.5）℃ 的回差值，即 25.5 ℃ 时，压缩机启动 1 台，通风机以强风模式运行。

（4）当室温继续升至设定温度上限（26 + 1.5）℃ 的回差值，即 27.5 ℃ 时，两台压缩机都启动，通风机以强风模式运行。

（5）室温下降到设定温度上限 26 ℃ 时，压缩机只运行一台，通风机以强风模式运行。

（6）室温下降到设定温度下限 24 ℃ 时，两台压缩机都停止运行，通风机以强风模式运行。

（7）室温继续下降到 21 ℃ 时，两台压缩机都停止运行，通风机以弱风模式运行。

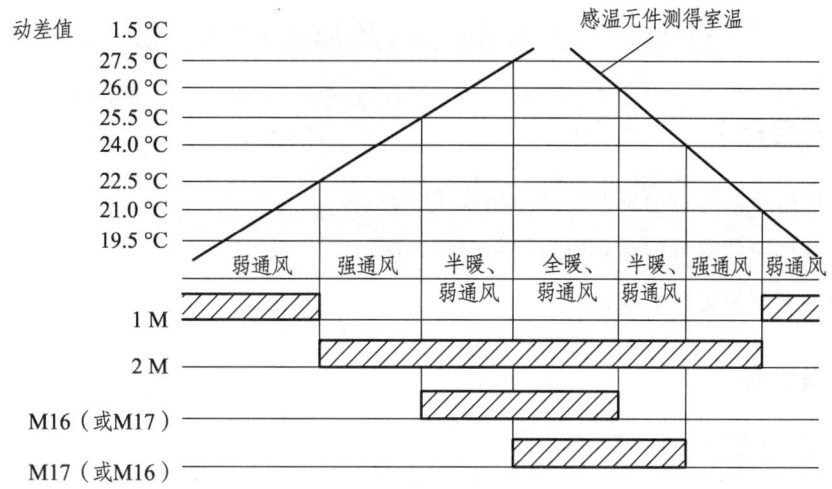

图 6-2-6　自动制冷过程

2. 空调自动制暖过程

制暖设定值：上限 18 ℃，下限 16 ℃，回差值 1.5 ℃。如图 6-2-7 所示：

（1）室温在 21 ℃ 以上时，通风机以强风模式运行，两套预热器处于停机状态。

（2）当室温降至 21 ℃ 时，通风机以弱风模式运行，两套预热器处于停机状态。

（3）当室温降至设定温度上限 18 ℃ 时，启动 1 套预热器，通风机以弱风模式运行。

（4）当室温继续降至设定温度下限 16 时，两套预热器都启动，通风机以弱风模式运行。

（5）室温上升到设定温度下限（16 + 1.5）℃ 的回差值，即 17.5 ℃ 时，预热器只运行一套，通风机以弱风模式运行。

（6）室温上升到设定温度上限（18 + 1.5）℃ 的回差值，即 19.5 ℃ 时，预热器都停止运行，通风机以弱风模式运行。

（7）室温继续上升到 22.5 ℃ 时，预热器都停止运行，通风机以强风模式运行。

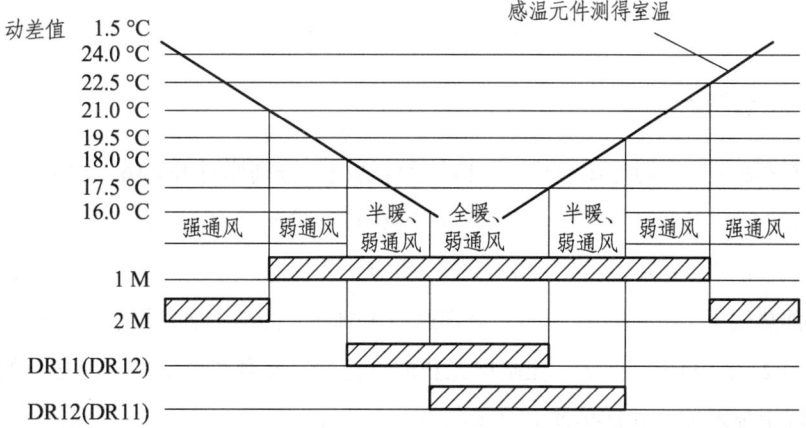

图 6-2-7　自动制暖过程

任务三　空调的运行及故障信息获取

【任务目标】

（1）理解空调运行信息的采集与获取接线原理。
（2）掌握空调故障信息获取过程与故障判断。
（3）能对故障进行处理。

【知识储备】

一、空调运行信息获取

（一）温度信息采集

如图 6-3-1 所示，温度传感器 pt100 的 A、B、B 连接到 PLC 左侧接口的 5、6、7 引脚，温度传感器的电阻与温度成一定的对应关系，PLC 通过测量、换算即可获取当前温度值，为自动工况提供工作依据，并且通过显示触摸屏显示。

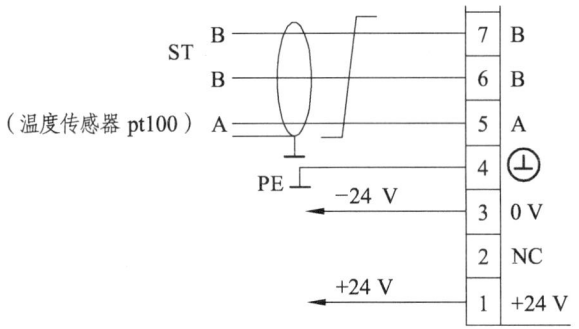

图 6-3-1　PLC 与 pt100 电路连接

（二）空调运行情况

如图 6-3-2 所示，制冷压缩机 1、2 的运行情况，分别通过 KM16、KM17 常开触点，将信号送至 PLC 右侧接口的 4、5 引脚，使 PLC 控制单元获取制冷压缩机 1 和制冷压缩机 2 的实时运行情况，并在显示触摸屏上显示相应状态信息。

制暖预热器 Ⅰ、Ⅱ 的运行情况，分别通过 KM18、KM19 动合触点，将信号送至 PLC 右侧接口的 2、3 引脚，使 PLC 控制单元获取预热器 1 和预热器 2 的实时运行情况，并在显示触摸屏上显示相应状态信息。

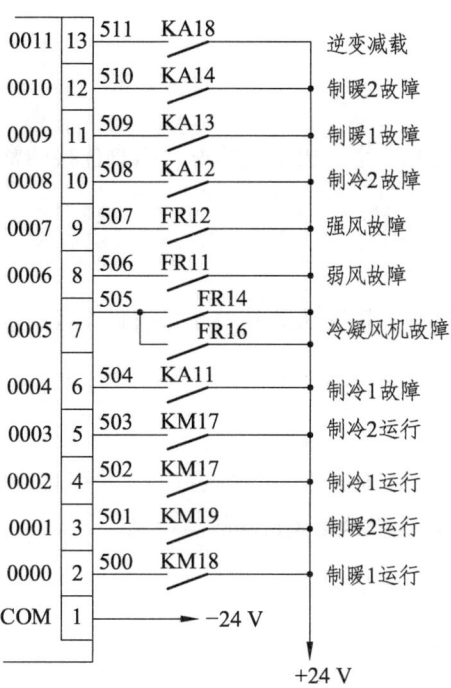

图 6-3-2 空调运行信息的 PLC 接口电路

二、空调故障处置

（1）强风通风机发生故障时，对应的冷凝风机、压缩机停止工作；弱风通风机发生故障时，对应的预热器、客室辅助加热器停止工作。冷凝风机发生故障时，对应的压缩机停止工作。

（2）在"强风半冷"或"弱风半暖"工况下，如果压缩机或预热器运行时发生故障，有故障的压缩机或预热器将停止运行，并自动切换让另一组压缩机或预热器启动；在"强风全冷""弱风全暖"工况下，发生故障时，有故障的压缩机或预热器停止运行，无故障的压缩机或预热器继续运行。

（3）空调机组有故障时，按下显示触摸屏上的"停空调"停止空调运行，故障排除后，再按下"启空调"，PLC 通过检测后可以重新启动空调机组。

三、空调故障信息

在通风、冷凝、制冷或制暖的控制电路中检测到故障信息时，它们将信息通过相关热继电器、故障继电器的常开触点，传到 PLC 接口上，PLC 控制单元即可获取故障信息。

如图 6-2-3、6-3-2 所示，FR11、FR12 为通风机热继电器，FR14、FR15 为冷凝风机热继电器，KA11、KA12 为制冷故障继电器，KA13、KA14 为制暖故障继电器。

1. 通风故障

1）强风故障时

如果热继电器 FR12 过热，其与 PLC 接口 9 号引脚连接的常开触点闭合，PLC 控制单元获得强风故障信息。

2）弱风故障时

如果热继电器 FR11 过热，其与 PLC 接口 8 号引脚连接的常开触点闭合，PLC 控制单元获得弱风故障信息。

2. 冷凝风机故障

如果热继电器 FR14 或 FR15 过热，PLC 接口的 7 号引脚连接的 FR14 或 FR15 常开触点闭合，PLC 控制单元即可获得冷凝风机的故障信息。

3. 制冷故障

1）制冷 1 出现故障时

如 FA16 触发，其常闭触点断开，故障继电器 KA11 线圈得电，KM16 线圈失电，制冷压缩机 1 停止，KA11 常开触点闭合，将信号送至 PLC 接口的 6 号脚。

2）制冷 2 出现故障时

如 FA17 触发，其常闭触点断开，故障继电器 KA12 线圈得电，KM17 线圈失电，制冷压缩机 2 停止，KA12 常开触点闭合，将信号送至 PLC 接口的 10 号脚。

4. 制暖故障

1）预热器 1 出现故障时

如果 FT13 触发，FT13 常闭开关断开，故障继电器 KA13 线圈得电，KM18 线圈失电，电预热器 1 停止，KA13 常开触点闭合，将信号送至 PLC 接口的 11 号引脚。

2）预热器 2 出现故障时

如果 FT14 触发，FT14 常闭开关断开，故障继电器 KA14 线圈得电，KM19 线圈失电，电预热器 2 停止，KA14 常开触点闭合，将信号送至 PLC 接口的 12 号引脚。

当上述故障情况发生时，相应负载停机，PLC 会接收到相应的故障信号，显示触摸屏会显示相关信息。

【任务训练】

（1）兼容控制柜主要由哪些部件组成？

（2）空调主电路主要包括哪些部分？请阐述通风机主电路和压缩机主电路的控制过程。

（3）简述交直流切换过程。

（4）简述直流Ⅰ路Ⅱ路切换过程。

（5）简述空调自动制冷过程和自动制热过程。

（6）控制系统是如何识别空调故障的？有哪些故障可以被识别？

参考文献

[1] 翟士述，麻冰玲. 客车空调装置[M]. 北京：中国铁道出版社有限公司，2021.

[2] 卢毓俊. 客车空调装置[M]. 北京：中国铁道出版社，2007.

[3] 王修彦，张晓东. 热工基础[M]. 北京：中国电力出版社，2013.

[4] 张宝霞. 铁道车辆制冷与空气调节[M]. 北京：中国铁道出版社，2005.

[5] 时蕾，石高山. 高速铁路动车组辅助设备维护与检修[M]. 2版. 成都：西南交通大学出版社，2022.

[6] 中国国家铁路集团有限公司机辆部. 铁路客车运用维修[M]. 北京：中国铁道出版社有限公司，2022.

[7] 中国国家铁路集团有限公司运输部. 铁道概论[M]. 北京：中国铁道出版社有限公司，2022.

Appendix

Attached Figure 1
Electrical Schematic Diagram of Air Conditioner for 25T Semi-cushioned Berth Sleeping Car

Electrical schematic diagram of air conditioner for 25t semi-cushioned berth sleeping car is shown in the attached page.

附 录

附图1 25T型硬卧客车空调电气原理图

25T型硬卧客车空调电气原理图见书末插页。

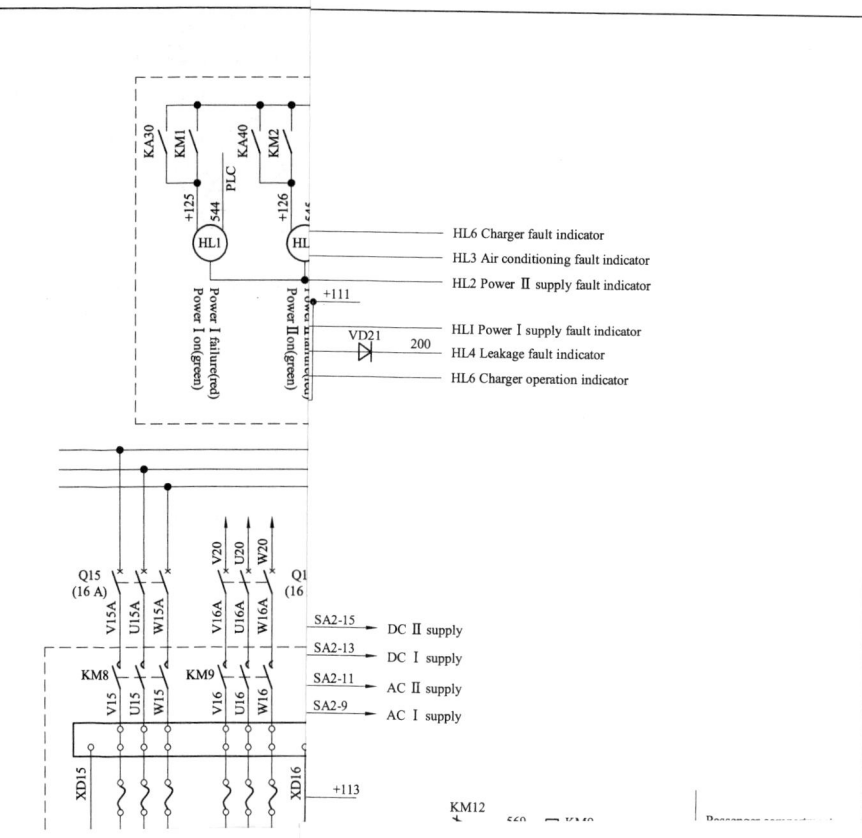